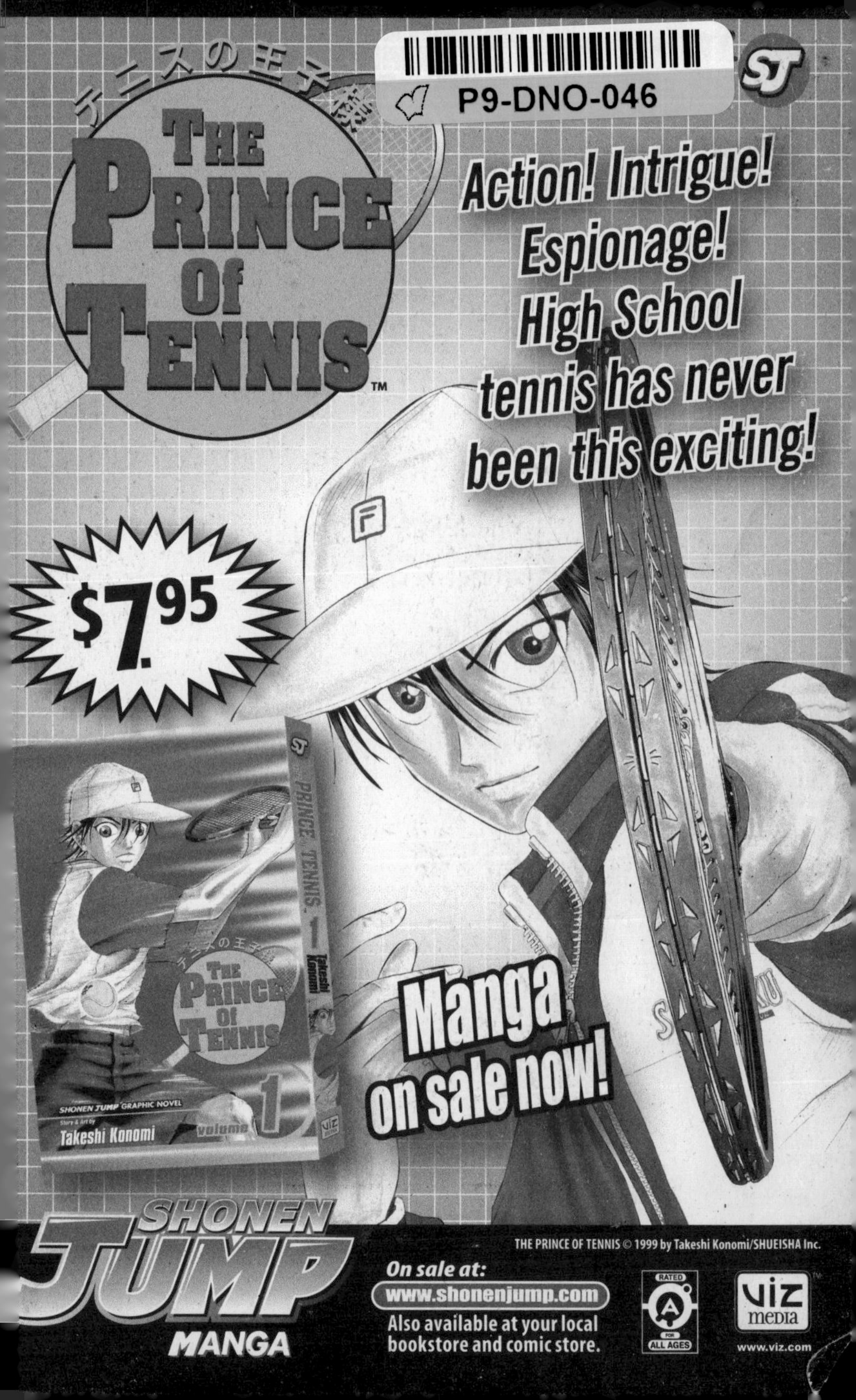
P9-DNO-046
SJ
テニスの王子様
THE PRINCE OF TENNIS™
Action! Intrigue! Espionage! High School tennis has never been this exciting!
$7.95
SJ PRINCE OF TENNIS 1 Takeshi Konomi
THE PRINCE OF TENNIS
SHONEN JUMP GRAPHIC NOVEL
Story & Art by Takeshi Konomi
volume 1
Manga on sale now!
SHONEN JUMP MANGA
THE PRINCE OF TENNIS © 1999 by Takeshi Konomi/SHUEISHA Inc.
On sale at:
www.shonenjump.com
Also available at your local bookstore and comic store.
RATED A FOR ALL AGES
VIZ media
www.viz.com

THE LEGEND OF ZELDA™
— ORACLE OF AGES —

VIZ Kids Edition

STORY & ART BY
AKIRA HIMEKAWA

TM & © 2009 Nintendo.
© 2002 Akira HIMEKAWA/Shogakukan
All rights reserved.
Original Japanese edition
"ZELDA NO DENSETSU - FUSHIGI NO KINOMI JIKU NO SHO"
published by SHOGAKUKAN Inc.

Translation/John Werry, Honyaku Center Inc.
English Adaptation/Stan! Brown
Touch-up Art & Lettering/John Hunt
Cover & Interior Design/Sean Lee
Editor/Mike Montesa

The stories, characters and incidents mentioned in this publication are entirely fictional.

Printed in the U.S.A.

Published by VIZ Media, LLC
P.O. Box 77010
San Francisco, CA 94107

10 9 8 7 6 5
First printing, June 2009
Fifth printing, September 2011

PARENTAL ADVISORY
LEGEND OF ZELDA is rated A and is suitable for readers of all ages.
ratings.viz.com

www.viz.com

www.vizkids.com

ORACLE OF AGES—THE GAME

The Legend of Zelda™: *Oracle of Ages* was created for the Nintendo Game Boy Color. Like the previous game in the series, *The Legend of Zelda*™: *Oracle of Time*, gamers did not have to play the other games in order to enjoy *Oracle of Ages*. Finishing either game provided a password that unlocked different events in the companion game, increasing replay value and interest in the game series.

AKIRA HIMEKAWA

I like ruins. When I stand in front of ancient ruins,
I feel like the breath of all the people who once
lived there come back across space and time. It's a
good, mysterious feeling.

Akira Himekawa is the collaboration of two
women, A. Honda and S. Nagano. Together they
have created nine manga adventures featuring
Link and the popular video game world of *The
Legend of Zelda*™, including *Ocarina of Time*,
Oracle of Seasons and *Four Swords*. Their
most recent work, *Legend of Zelda*™ *: Phantom
Hourglass*, is serialized in *Shogaku Rokunensei*.

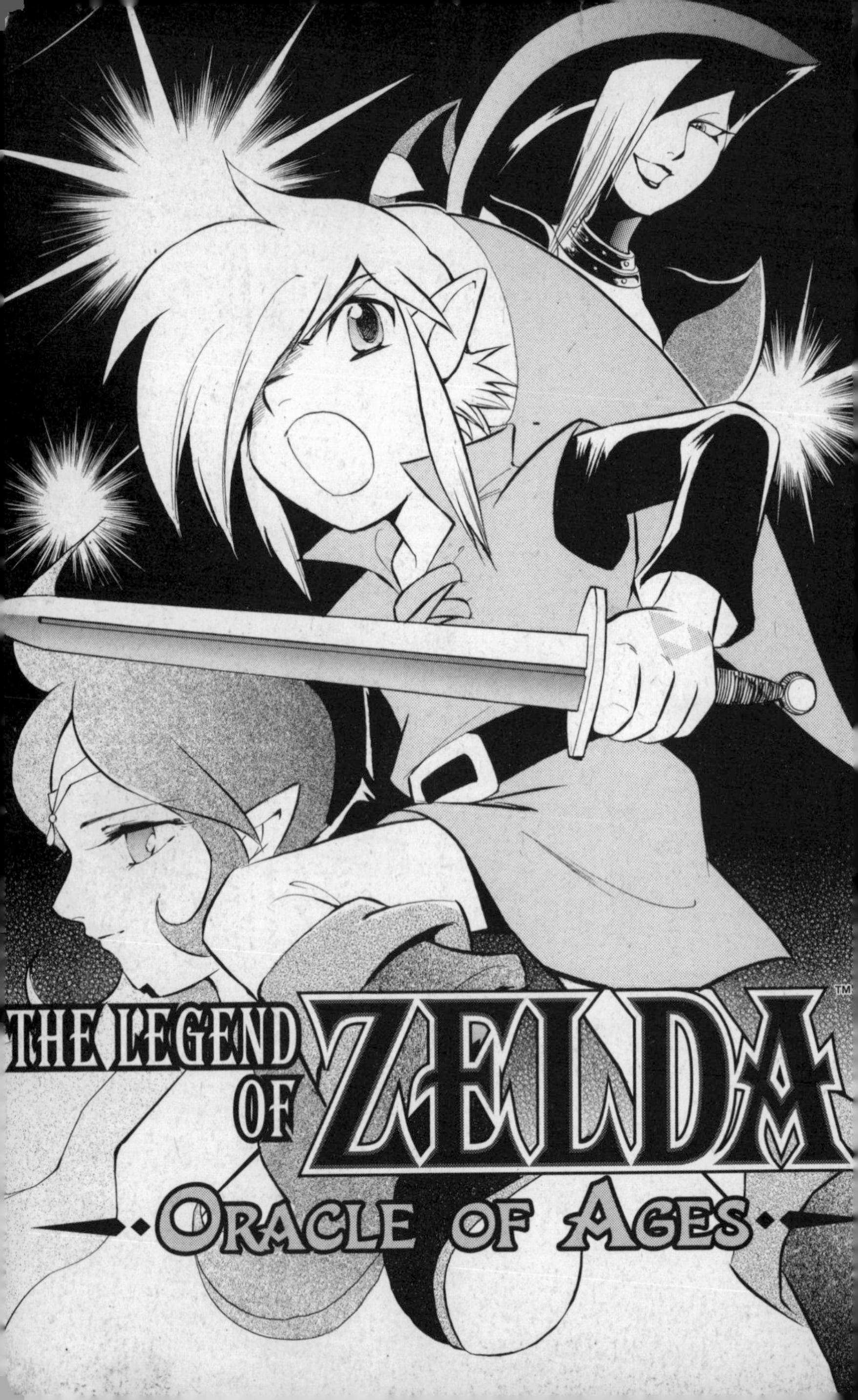
THE LEGEND OF ZELDA™
ORACLE OF AGES

THE LEGEND OF ZELDA™
ORACLE OF AGES

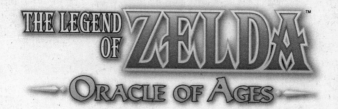

CONTENTS

ORACLE OF AGES

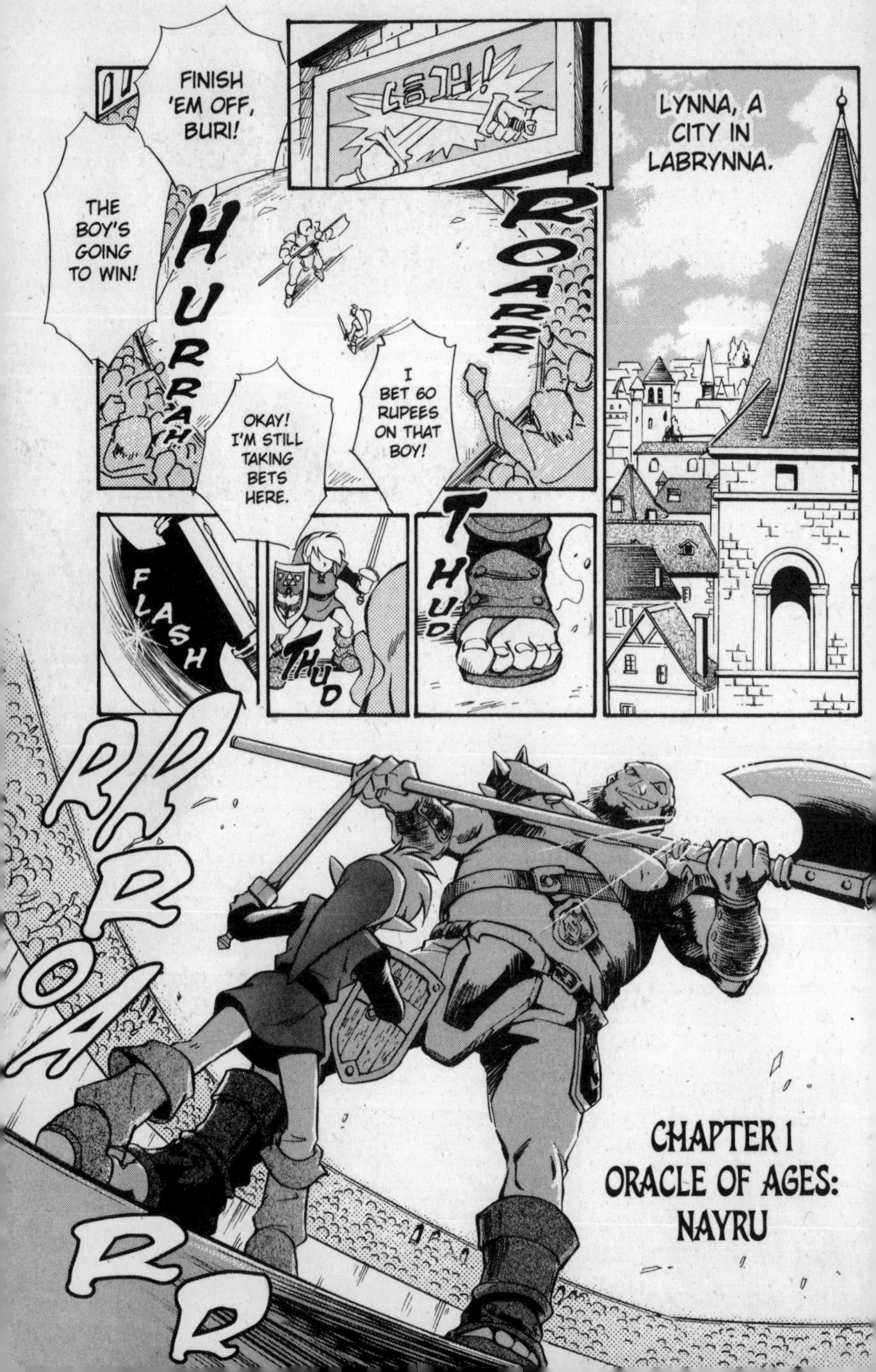

LYNNA, A CITY IN LABRYNNA.
ROARRR
I BET 60 RUPEES ON THAT BOY!
OKAY! I'M STILL TAKING BETS HERE.
HURRAH
FINISH 'EM OFF, BURI!
THE BOY'S GOING TO WIN!
THUD
THUD
FLASH
RRROARR

CHAPTER 1
ORACLE OF AGES: NAYRU

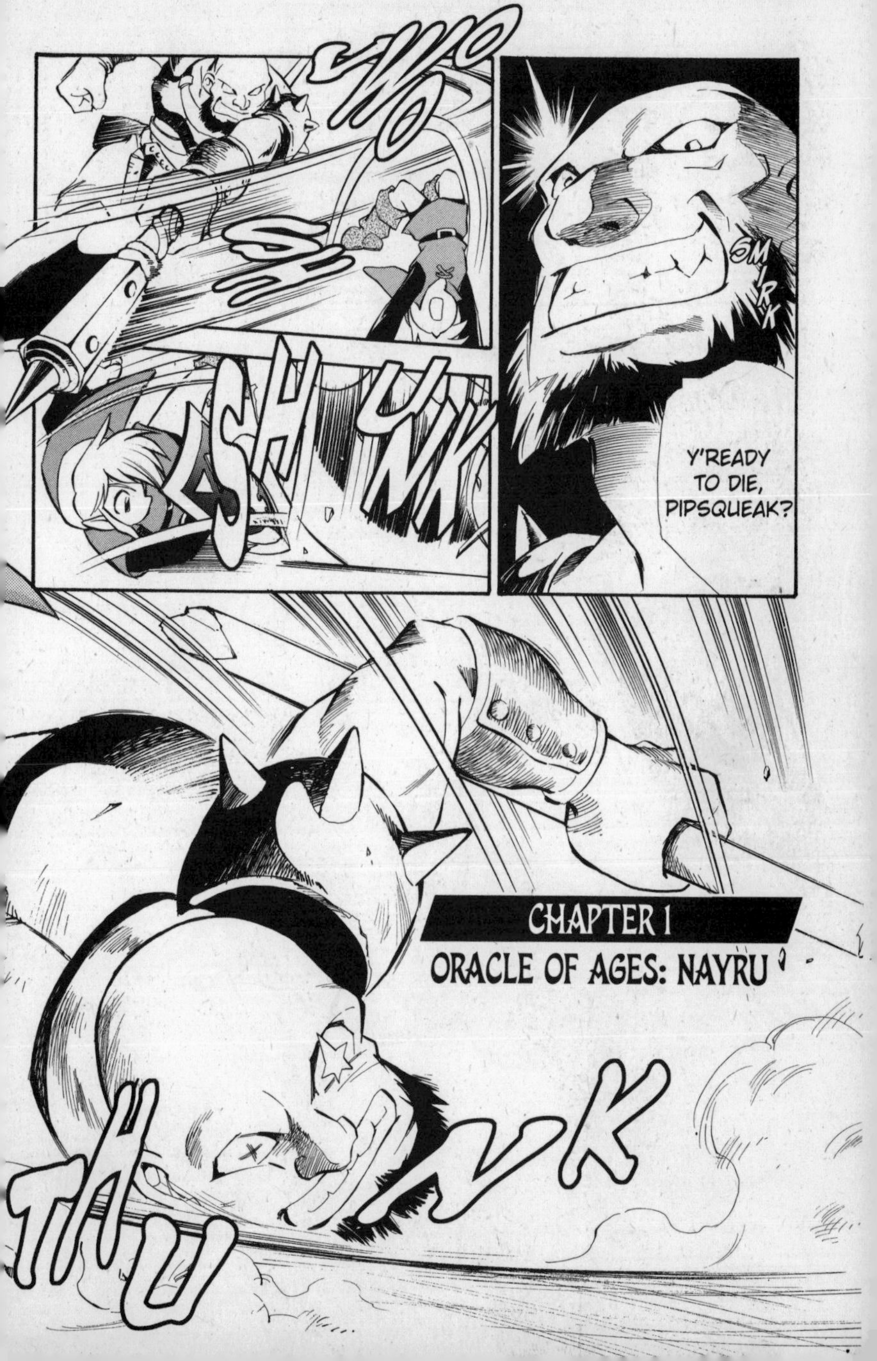
SMIRK
Y'READY TO DIE, PIPSQUEAK?
SHUNK
THUNK

CHAPTER 1

ORACLE OF AGES: NAYRU

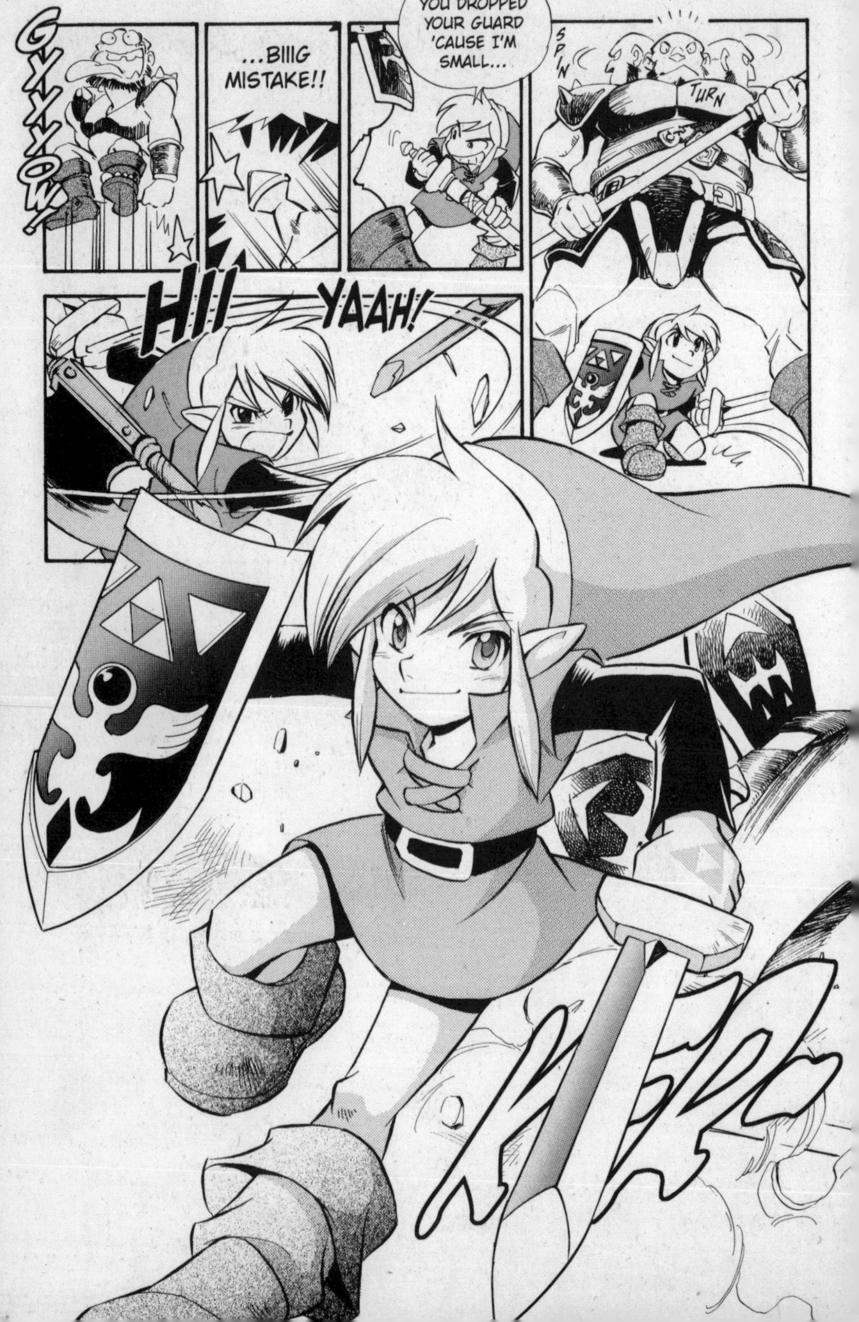
SPIN
TURN
YOU DROPPED YOUR GUARD 'CAUSE I'M SMALL...
...BIIIG MISTAKE!!
GYYYOW!
HII YAAH!

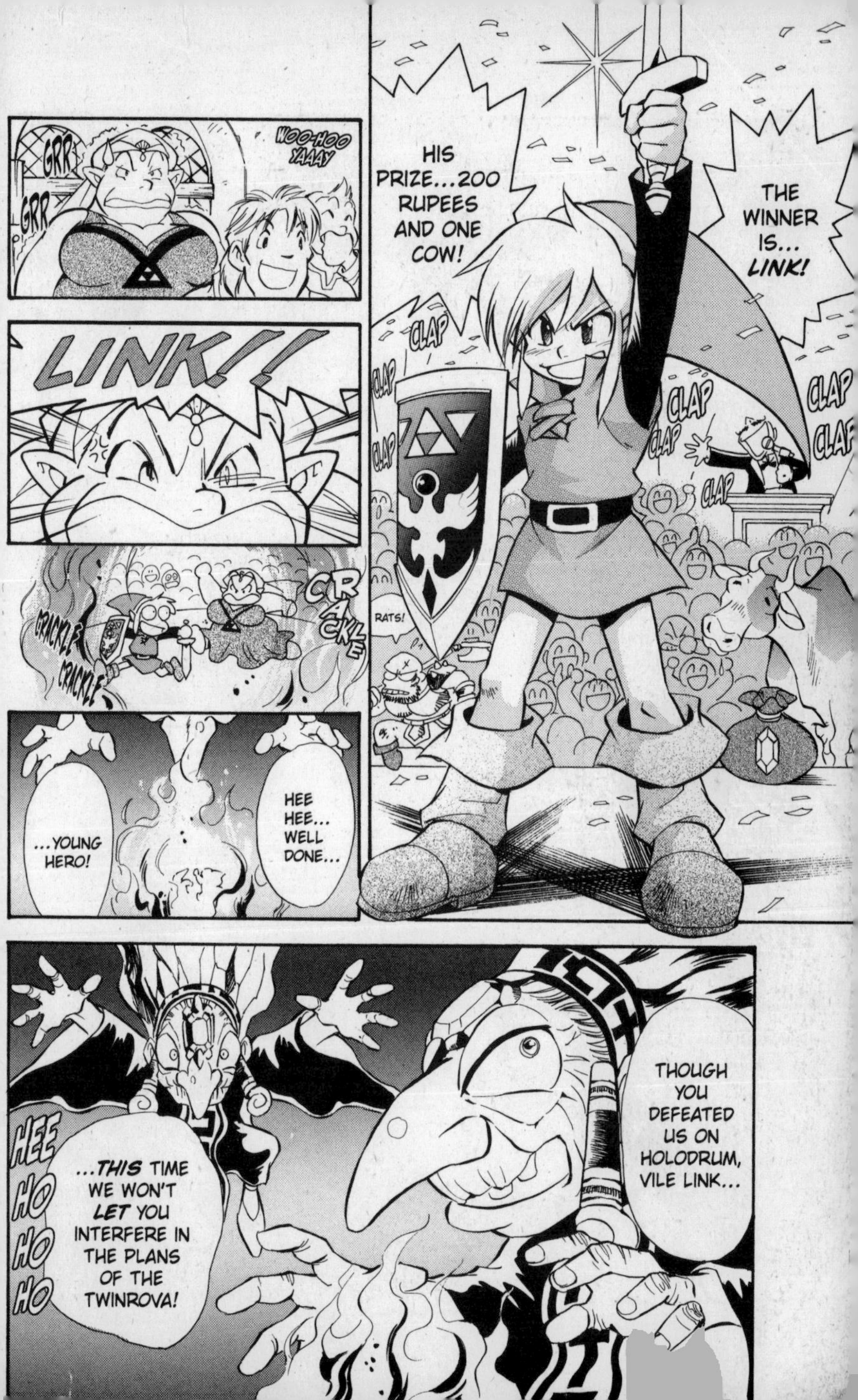
THE WINNER IS... **LINK!**
HIS PRIZE...200 RUPEES AND ONE COW!
CLAP
CLAP
CLAP
CLAP
CLAP
CLAP
CLAP
CLAP
RATS!
GRR
GRR
WOO-HOO YAAAY
LINK!!
CRACKLE
CRACKLE
CRACKLE
HEE HEE... WELL DONE...
...YOUNG HERO!
THOUGH YOU DEFEATED US ON HOLODRUM, VILE LINK...
...*THIS* TIME WE WON'T *LET* YOU INTERFERE IN THE PLANS OF THE TWINROVA!
HEE HO HO HO

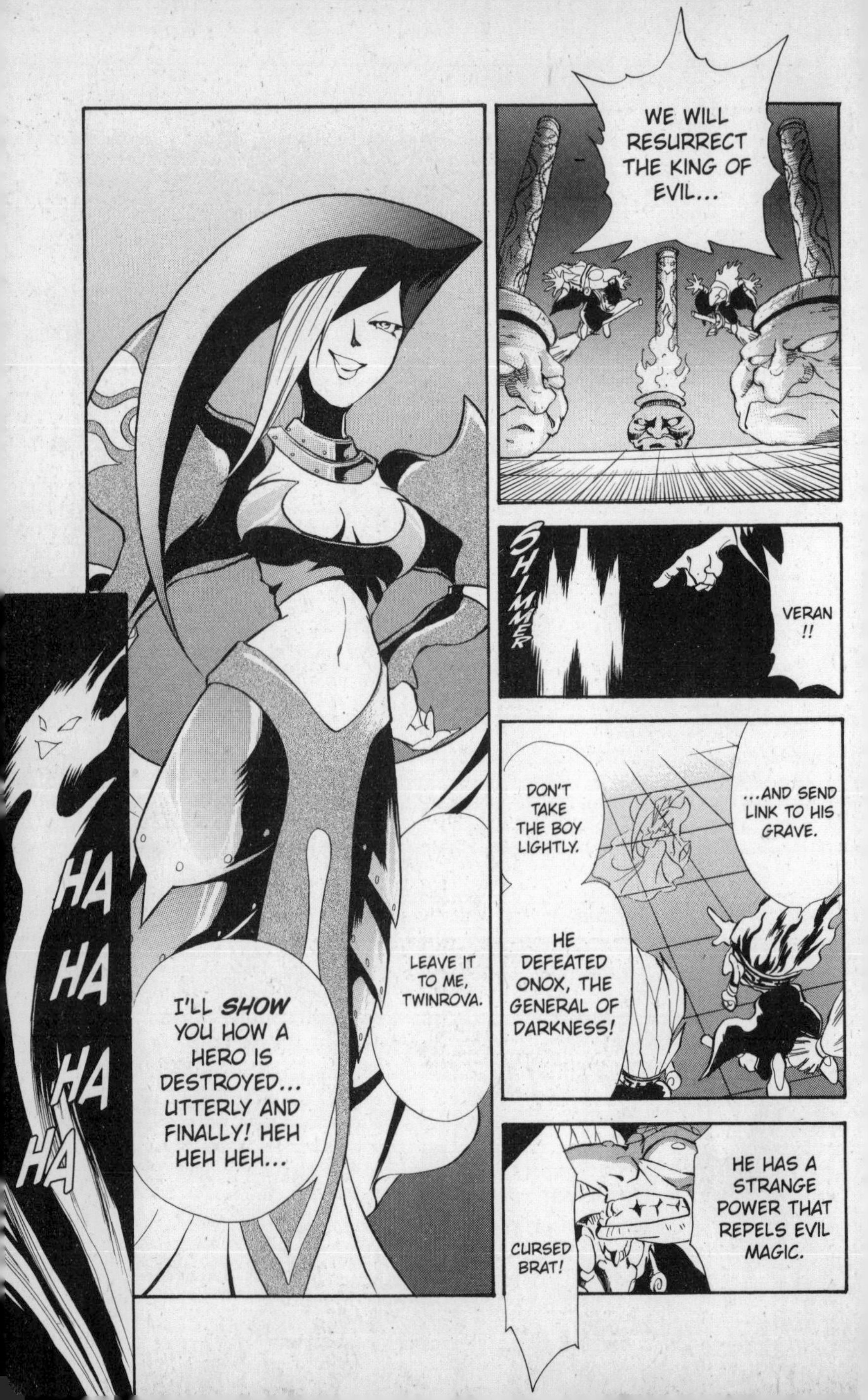
WE WILL RESURRECT THE KING OF EVIL...
SHIMMER
VERAN !!
...AND SEND LINK TO HIS GRAVE.
DON'T TAKE THE BOY LIGHTLY.
HE DEFEATED ONOX, THE GENERAL OF DARKNESS!
HE HAS A STRANGE POWER THAT REPELS EVIL MAGIC.
CURSED BRAT!
LEAVE IT TO ME, TWINROVA.
I'LL **SHOW** YOU HOW A HERO IS DESTROYED... UTTERLY AND FINALLY! HEH HEH HEH...
HA HA HA HA

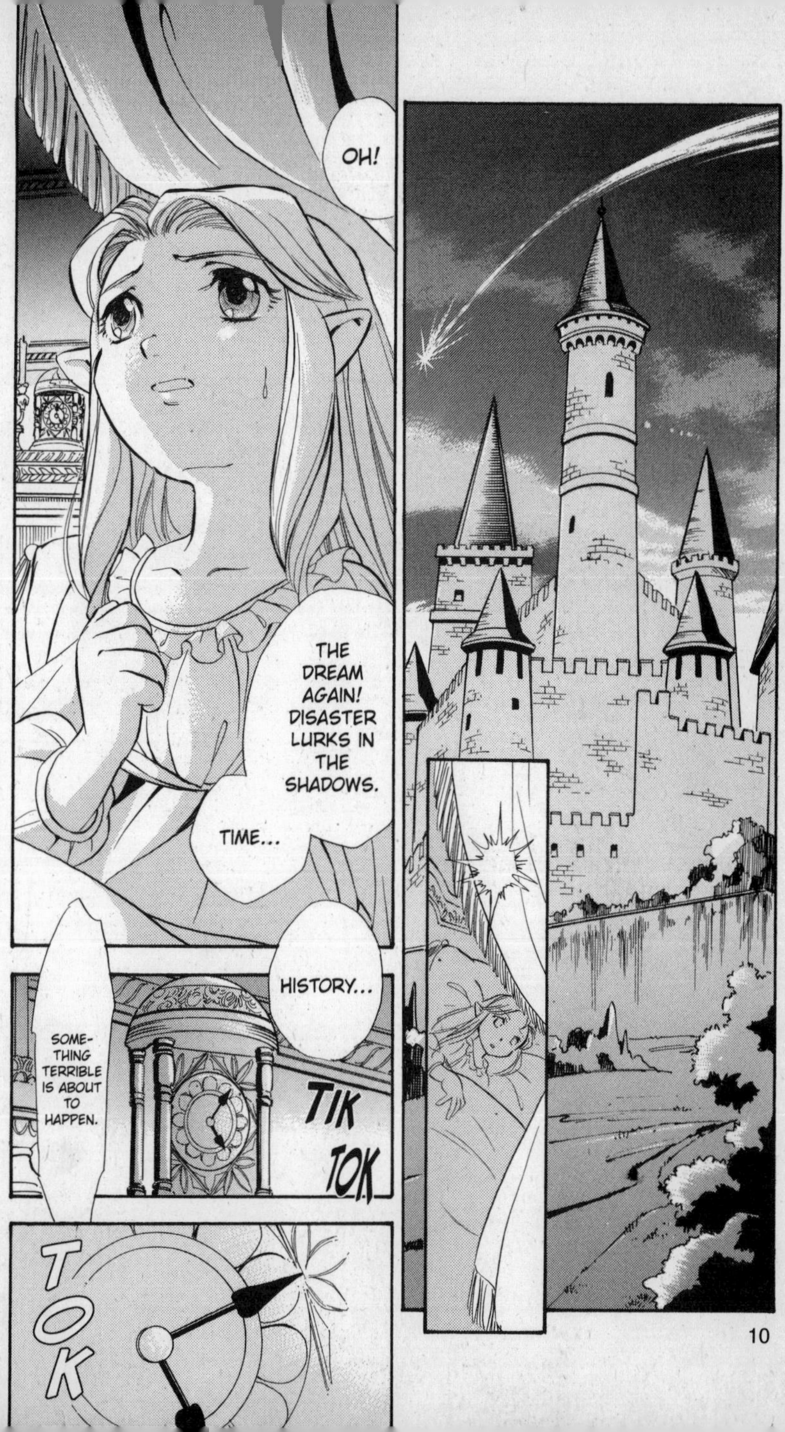
OH!
THE DREAM AGAIN! DISASTER LURKS IN THE SHADOWS.
TIME...
HISTORY...
SOME-THING TERRIBLE IS ABOUT TO HAPPEN.
TIK
TOK.
TOK

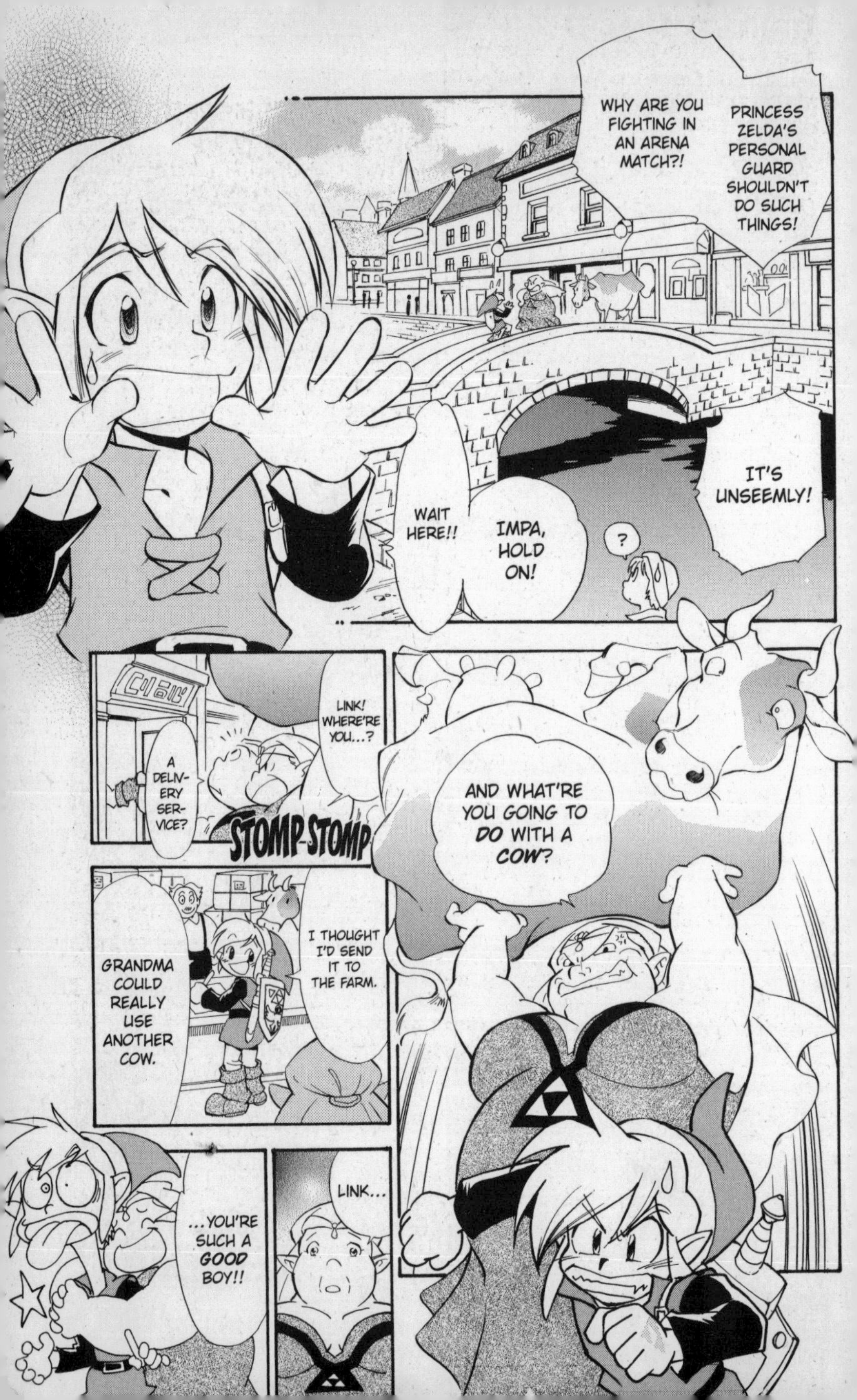
PRINCESS ZELDA'S PERSONAL GUARD SHOULDN'T DO SUCH THINGS!
WHY ARE YOU FIGHTING IN AN ARENA MATCH?!
IT'S UNSEEMLY!
?
IMPA, HOLD ON!
WAIT HERE!!
AND WHAT'RE YOU GOING TO DO WITH A COW?
LINK! WHERE'RE YOU...?
A DELIVERY SERVICE?
STOMP-STOMP
I THOUGHT I'D SEND IT TO THE FARM.
GRANDMA COULD REALLY USE ANOTHER COW.
LINK...
...YOU'RE SUCH A GOOD BOY!!

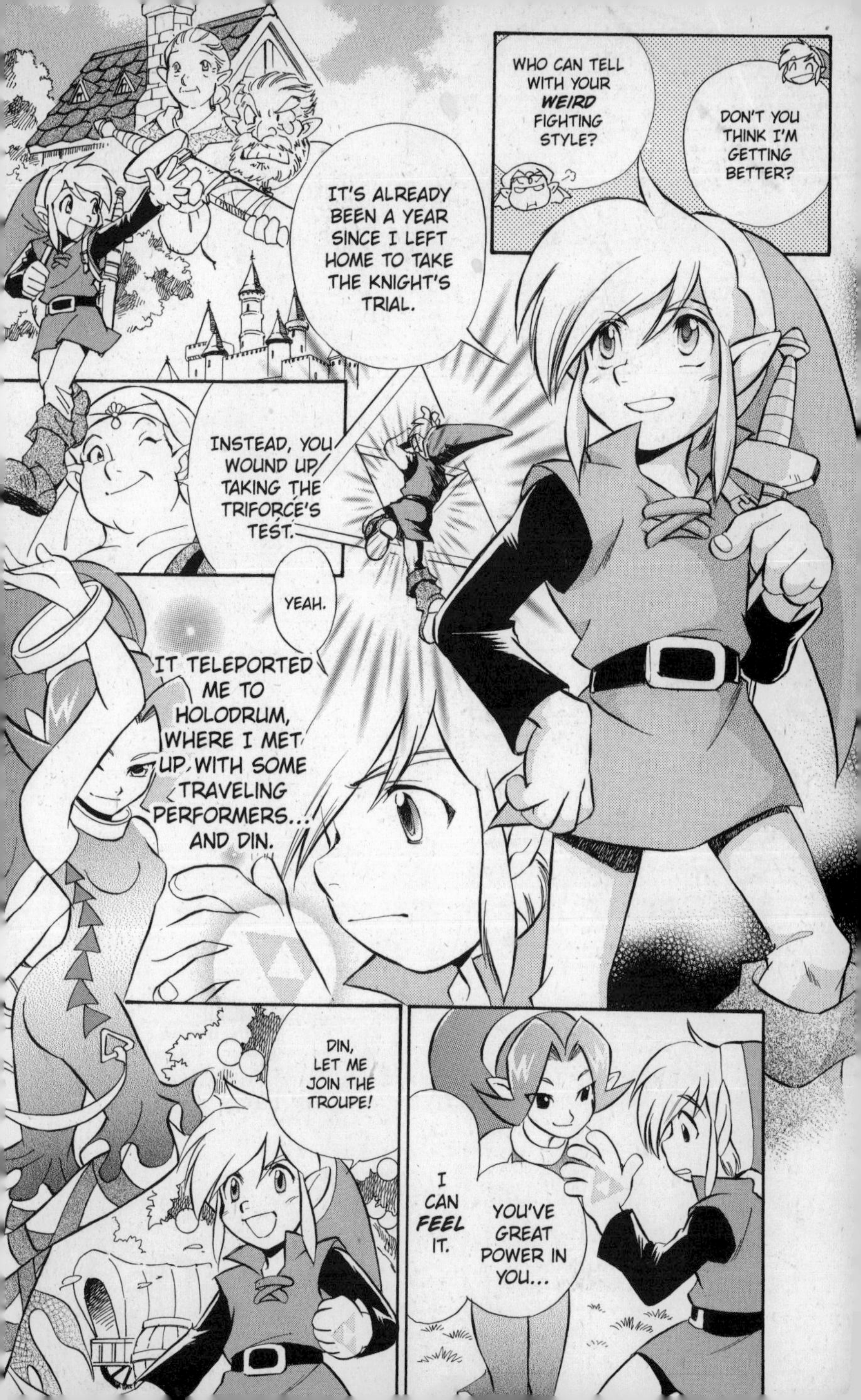
DON'T YOU THINK I'M GETTING BETTER?
WHO CAN TELL WITH YOUR *WEIRD* FIGHTING STYLE?
IT'S ALREADY BEEN A YEAR SINCE I LEFT HOME TO TAKE THE KNIGHT'S TRIAL.
INSTEAD, YOU WOUND UP TAKING THE TRIFORCE'S TEST.
YEAH.
IT TELEPORTED ME TO HOLODRUM, WHERE I MET UP WITH SOME TRAVELING PERFORMERS... AND DIN.
YOU'VE GREAT POWER IN YOU...
I CAN *FEEL* IT.
DIN, LET ME JOIN THE TROUPE!

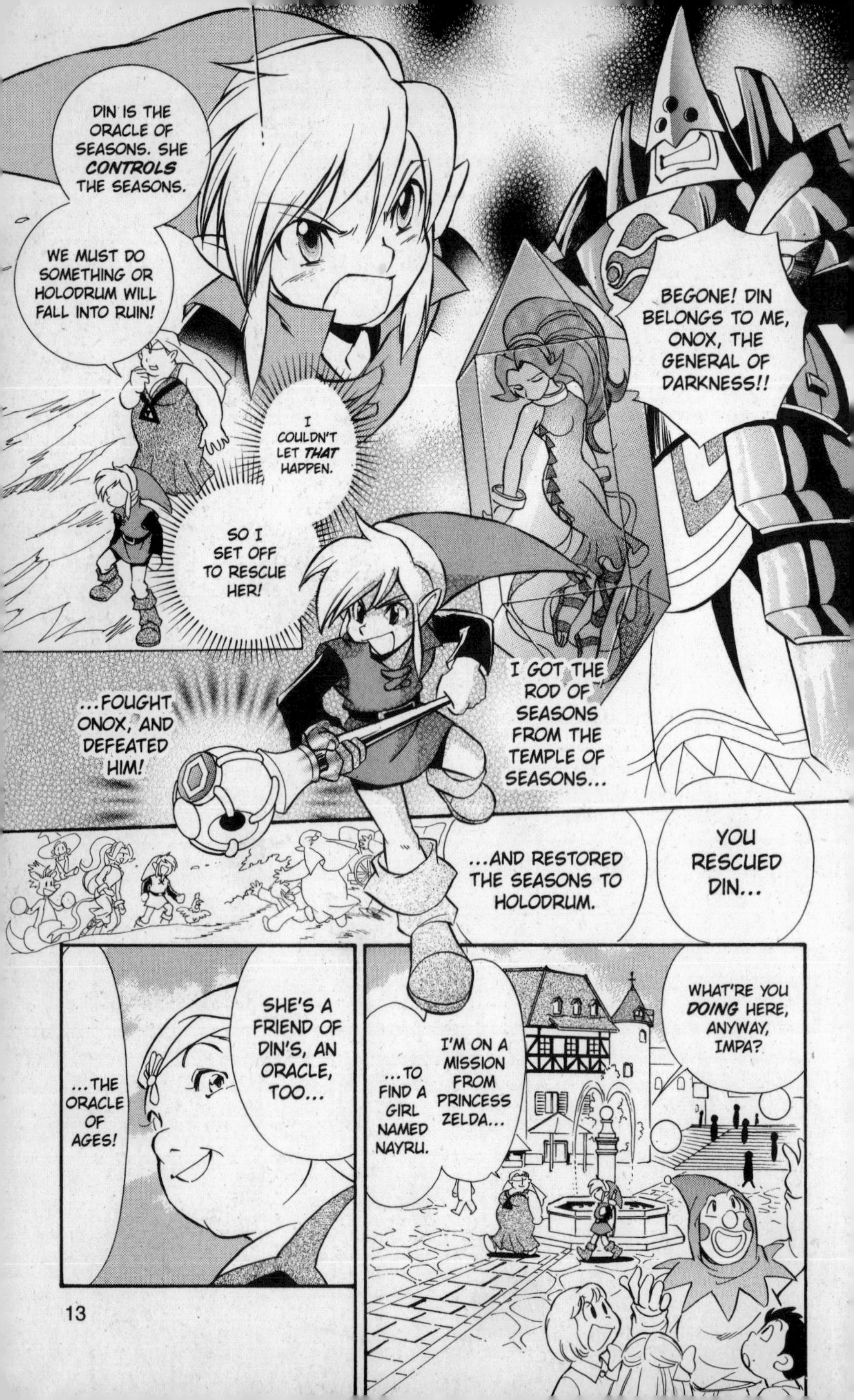

DIN IS THE ORACLE OF SEASONS. SHE *CONTROLS* THE SEASONS.
WE MUST DO SOMETHING OR HOLODRUM WILL FALL INTO RUIN!
BEGONE! DIN BELONGS TO ME, ONOX, THE GENERAL OF DARKNESS!!
I COULDN'T LET *THAT* HAPPEN.
SO I SET OFF TO RESCUE HER!
I GOT THE ROD OF SEASONS FROM THE TEMPLE OF SEASONS...
...FOUGHT ONOX, AND DEFEATED HIM!
YOU RESCUED DIN...
...AND RESTORED THE SEASONS TO HOLODRUM.
WHAT'RE YOU *DOING* HERE, ANYWAY, IMPA?
I'M ON A MISSION FROM PRINCESS ZELDA...
...TO FIND A GIRL NAMED NAYRU.
SHE'S A FRIEND OF DIN'S, AN ORACLE, TOO...
...THE ORACLE OF AGES!

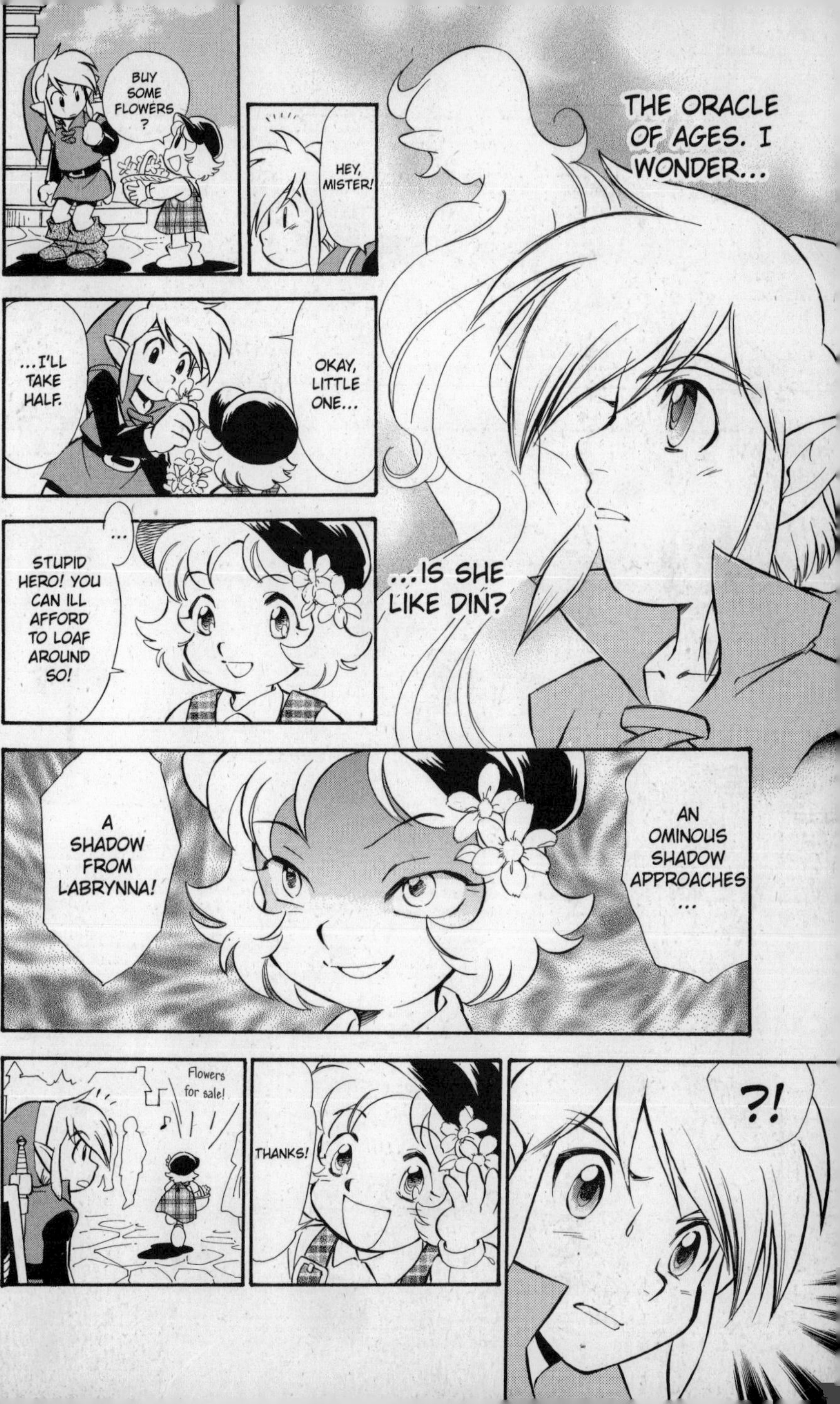
THE ORACLE OF AGES. I WONDER...
...IS SHE LIKE DIN?
HEY, MISTER!
BUY SOME FLOWERS ?
OKAY, LITTLE ONE...
...I'LL TAKE HALF.
...
STUPID HERO! YOU CAN ILL AFFORD TO LOAF AROUND SO!
AN OMINOUS SHADOW APPROACHES ...
A SHADOW FROM LABRYNNA!
?!
THANKS!
Flowers for sale!

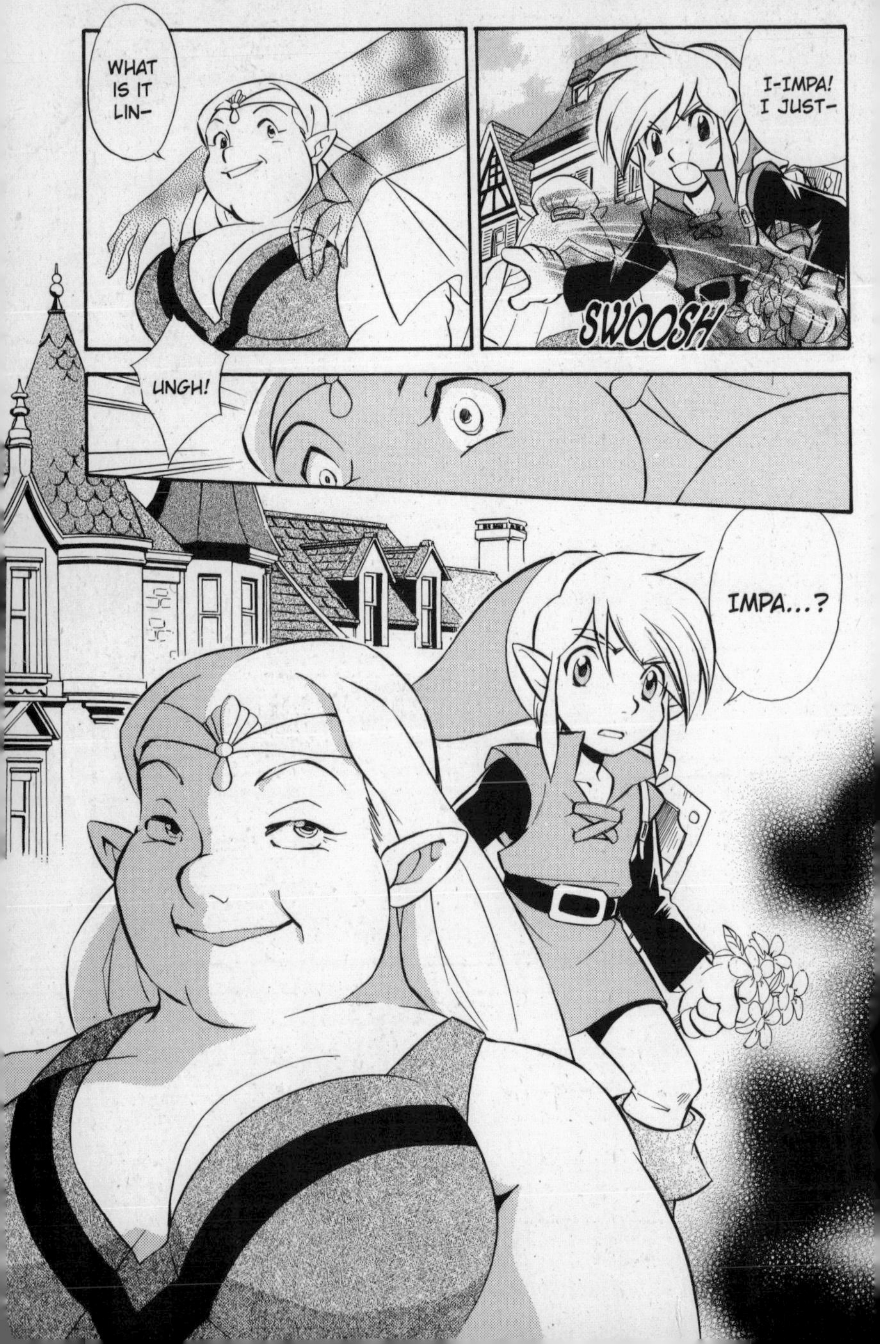
I-IMPA! I JUST-
SWOOSH
WHAT IS IT LIN-
UNGH!
IMPA...?

CHAPTER 2

SORCERESS OF SHADOWS: VERAN

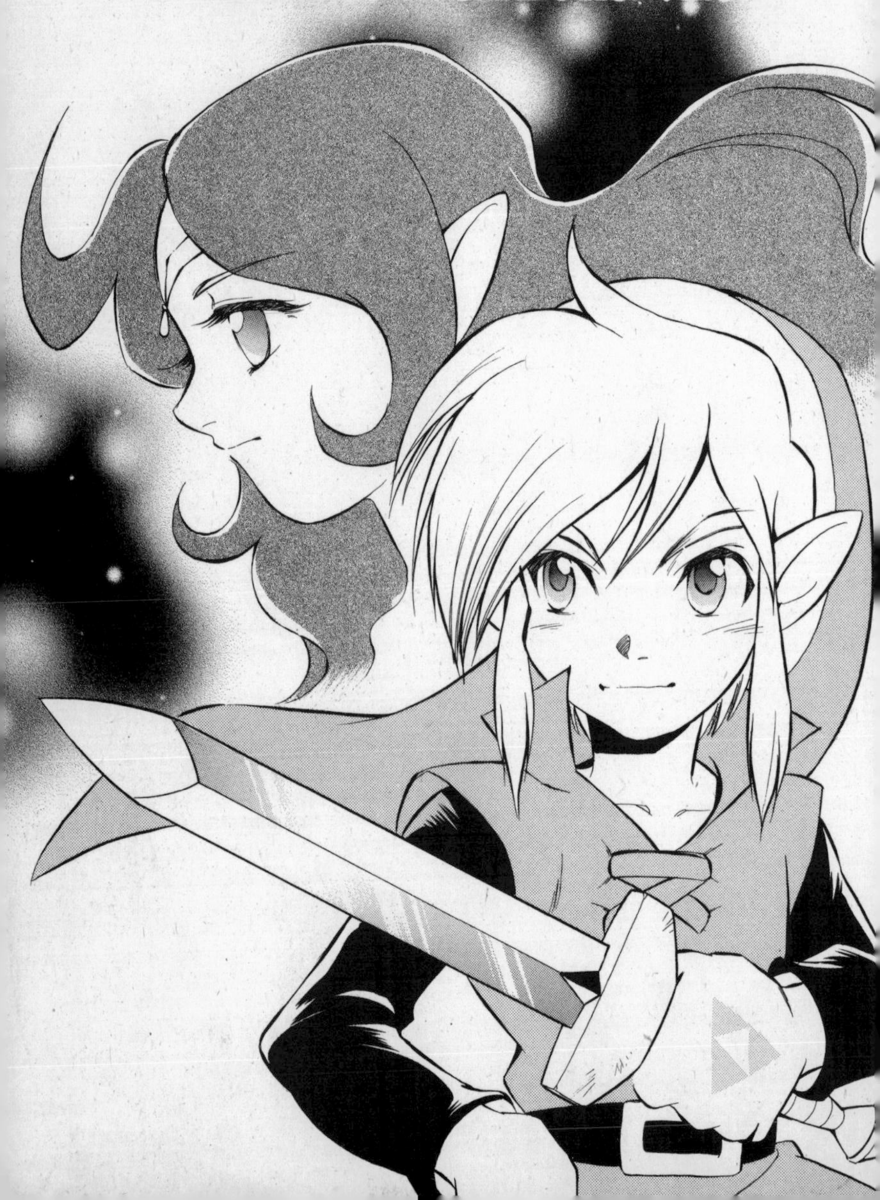

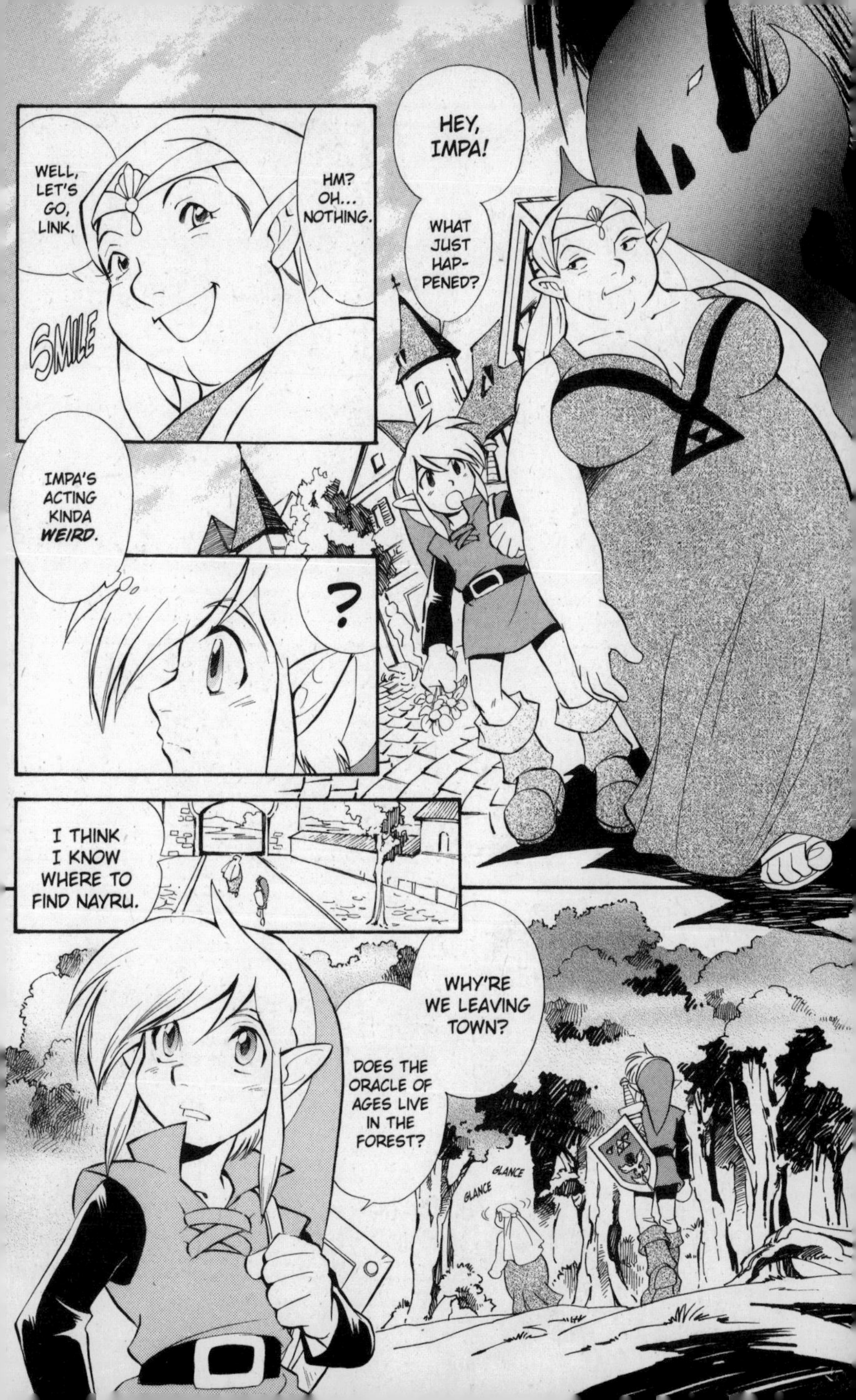
HEY, IMPA!
WHAT JUST HAPPENED?
HM? OH... NOTHING.
WELL, LET'S GO, LINK.
SMILE
?
IMPA'S ACTING KINDA WEIRD.
I THINK I KNOW WHERE TO FIND NAYRU.
WHY'RE WE LEAVING TOWN?
DOES THE ORACLE OF AGES LIVE IN THE FOREST?
GLANCE
GLANCE

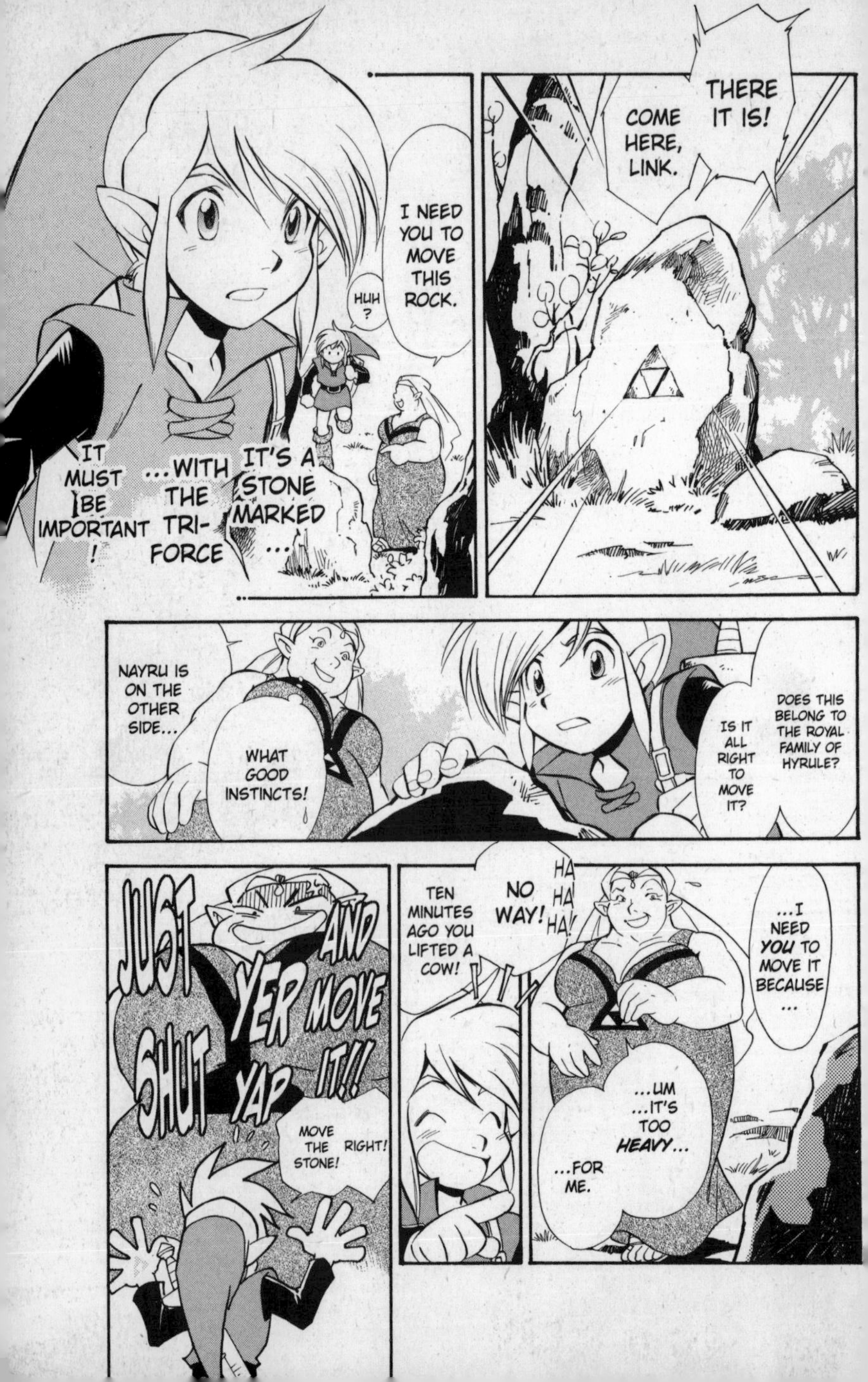
THERE IT IS!
COME HERE, LINK.
I NEED YOU TO MOVE THIS ROCK.
HUH?
IT'S A STONE MARKED...
...WITH THE TRI-FORCE
IT MUST BE IMPORTANT!
DOES THIS BELONG TO THE ROYAL FAMILY OF HYRULE?
IS IT ALL RIGHT TO MOVE IT?
...
WHAT GOOD INSTINCTS!
NAYRU IS ON THE OTHER SIDE...
...I NEED *YOU* TO MOVE IT BECAUSE...
...UM ...IT'S TOO *HEAVY*...
...FOR ME.
HA HA HA!
NO WAY!
TEN MINUTES AGO YOU LIFTED A COW!
JUST SHUT YER YAP AND MOVE IT!!
RIGHT!
MOVE THE STONE!

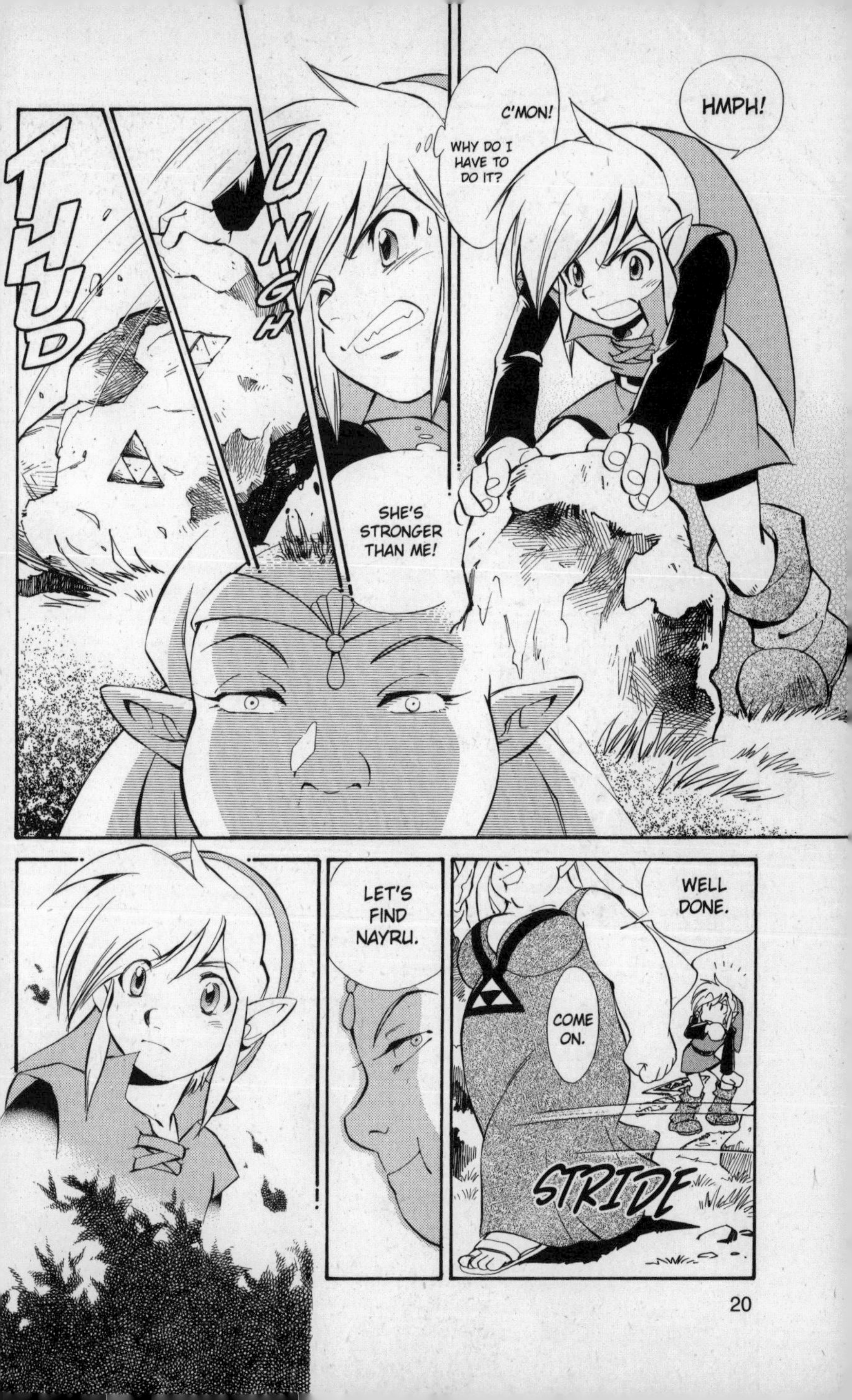
HMPH!
C'MON!
WHY DO I HAVE TO DO IT?
UNGH
THUD
SHE'S STRONGER THAN ME!
WELL DONE.
COME ON.
STRIDE
LET'S FIND NAYRU.

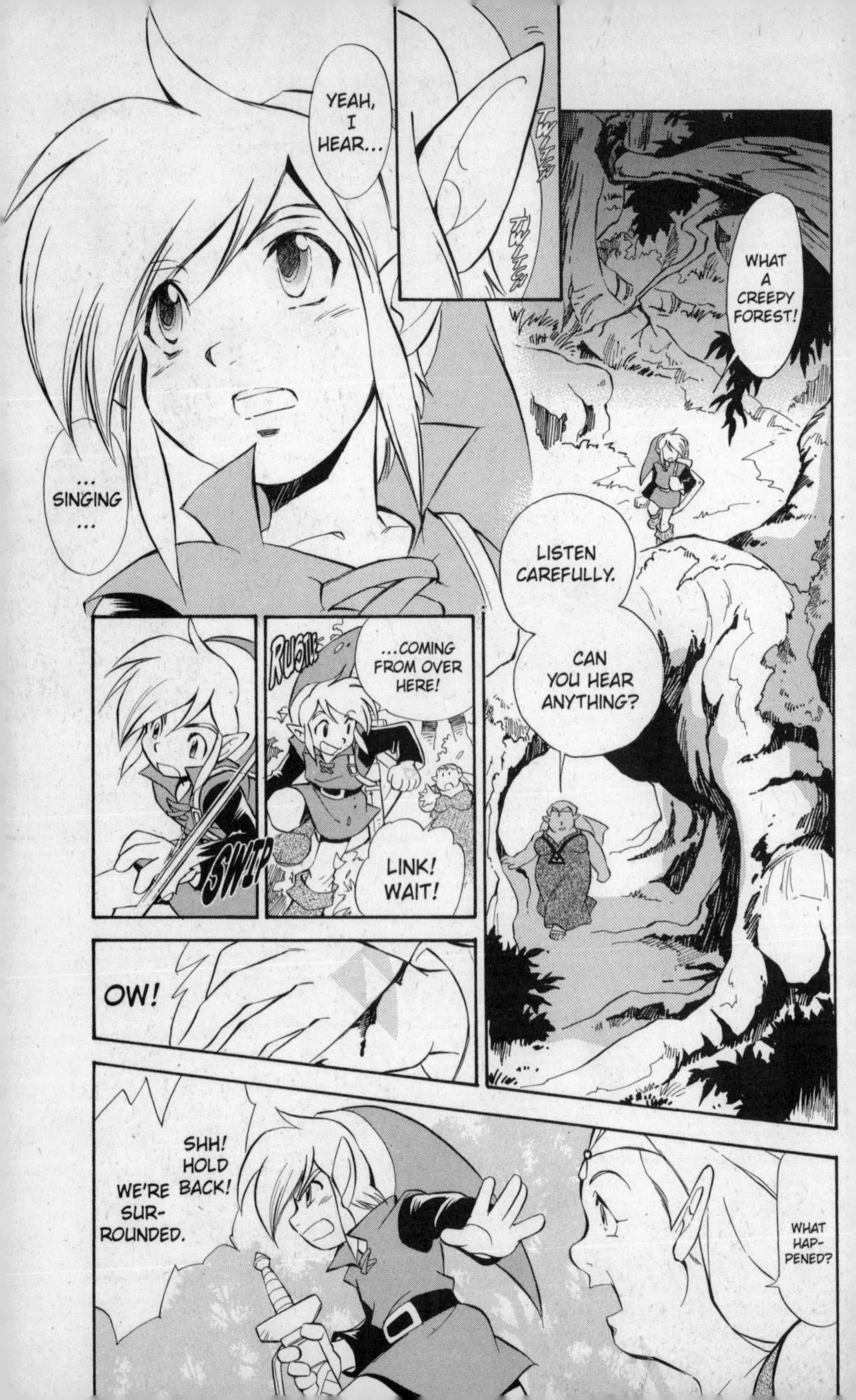
WHAT A CREEPY FOREST!
LISTEN CAREFULLY.
CAN YOU HEAR ANYTHING?
YEAH, I HEAR...
...SINGING...
RUSTLE
...COMING FROM OVER HERE!
LINK! WAIT!
SWIP
OW!
WHAT HAPPENED?
SHH! HOLD BACK!
WE'RE SURROUNDED.

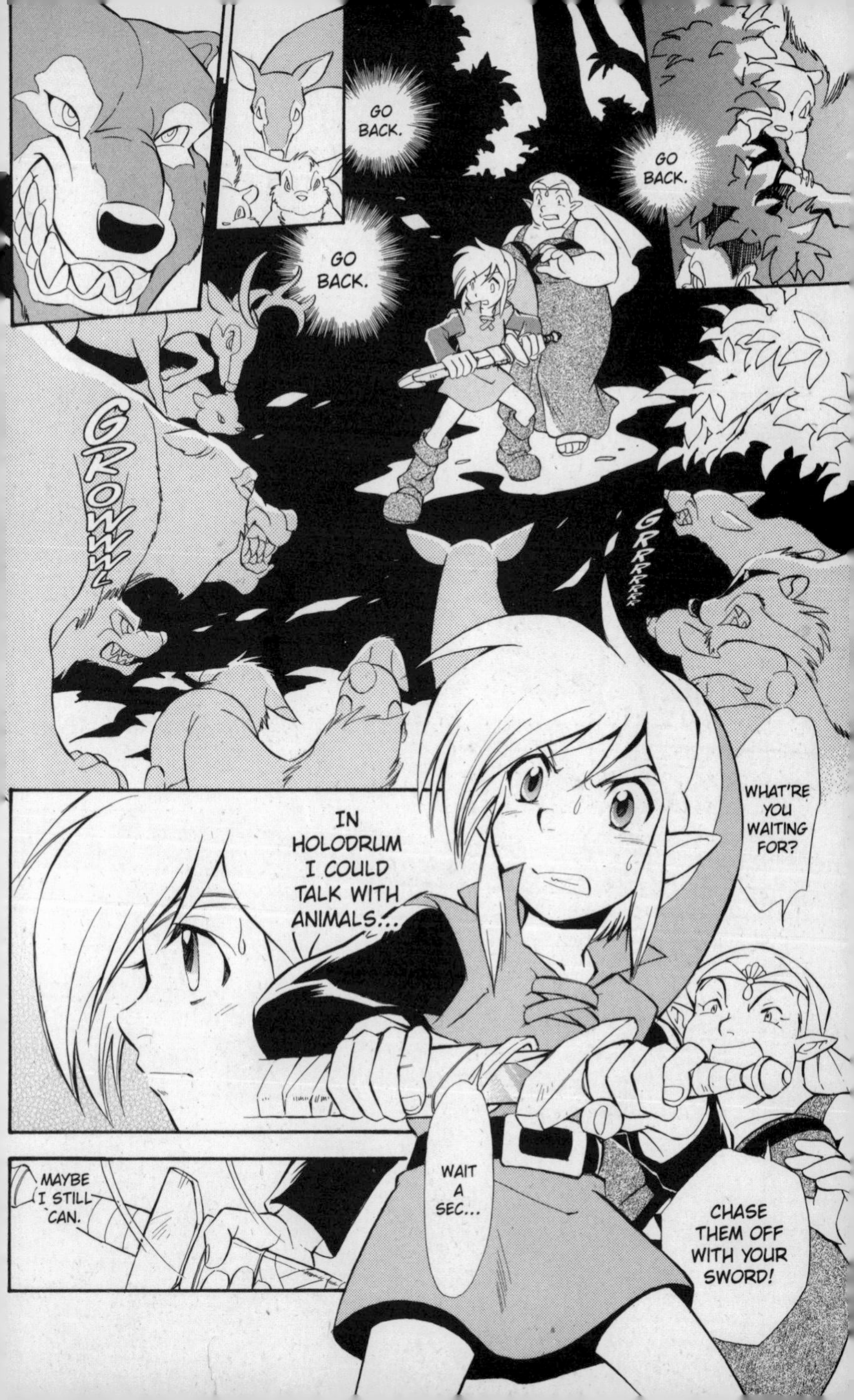
GO BACK.
GO BACK.
GO BACK.
GRRRRRR
GROWWW
WHAT'RE YOU WAITING FOR?
IN HOLODRUM I COULD TALK WITH ANIMALS...
CHASE THEM OFF WITH YOUR SWORD!
WAIT A SEC...
MAYBE I STILL CAN.

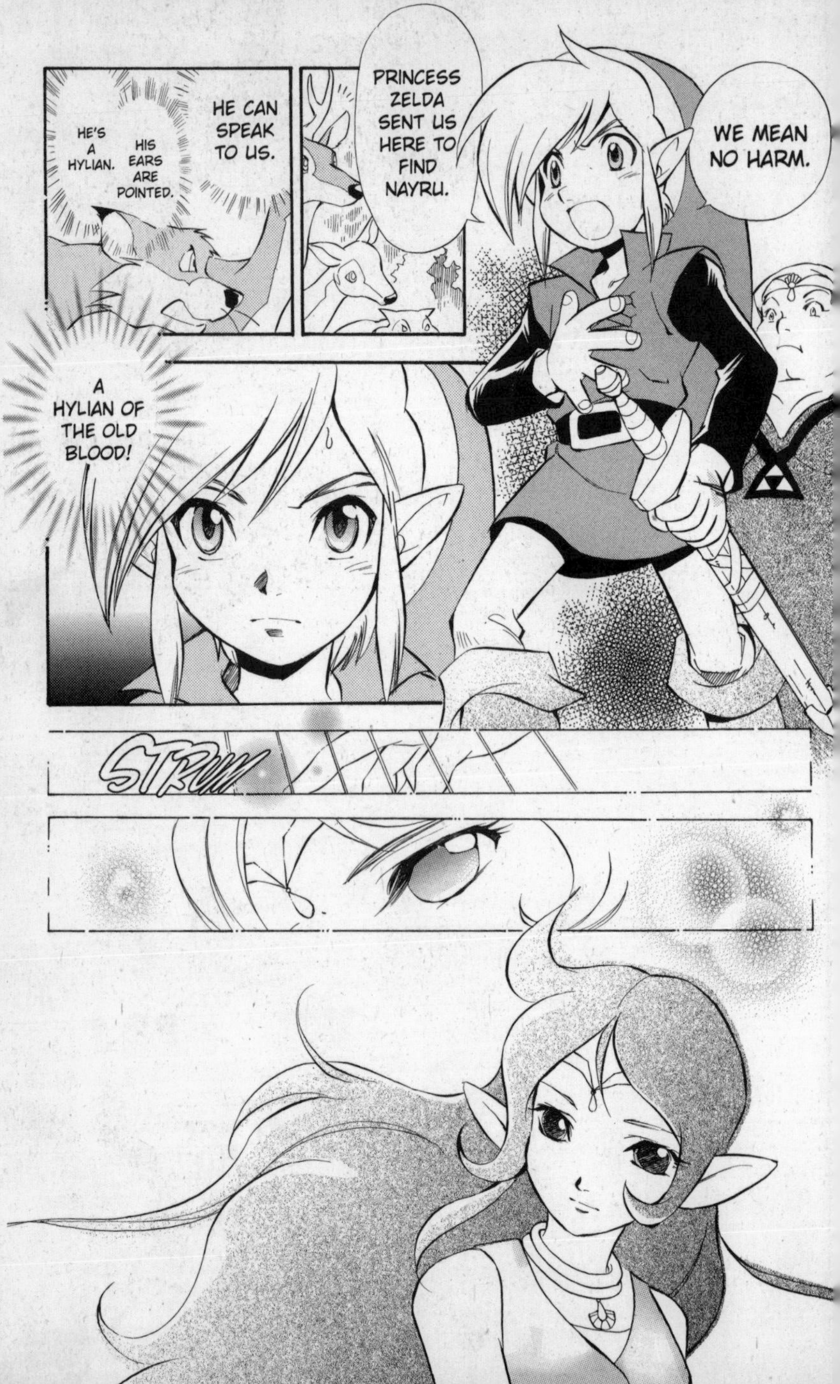
WE MEAN NO HARM.
PRINCESS ZELDA SENT US HERE TO FIND NAYRU.
HE CAN SPEAK TO US.
HIS EARS ARE POINTED.
HE'S A HYLIAN.
A HYLIAN OF THE OLD BLOOD!
STRUM

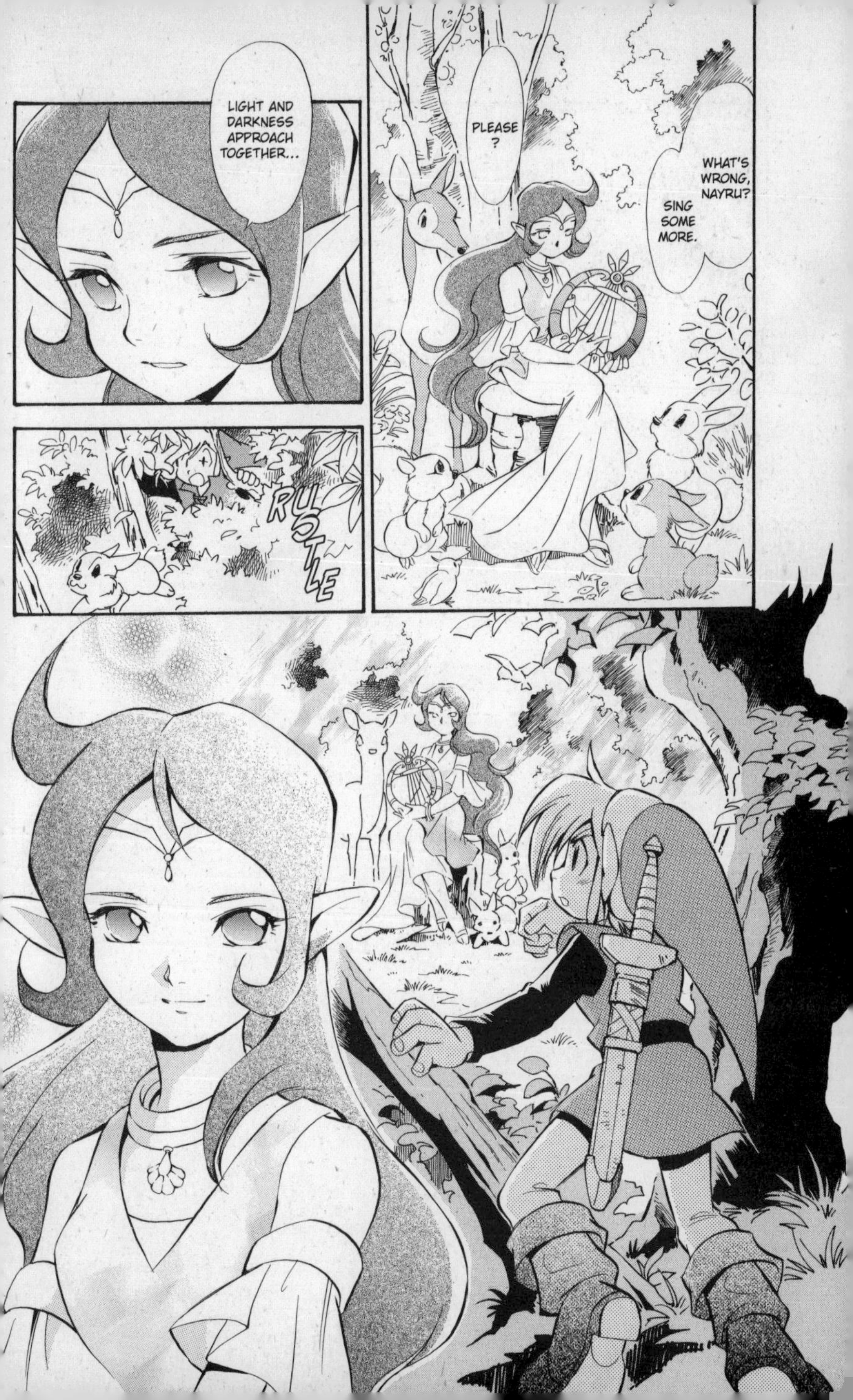
WHAT'S WRONG, NAYRU?
SING SOME MORE.
PLEASE?
LIGHT AND DARKNESS APPROACH TOGETHER...
RUSTLE

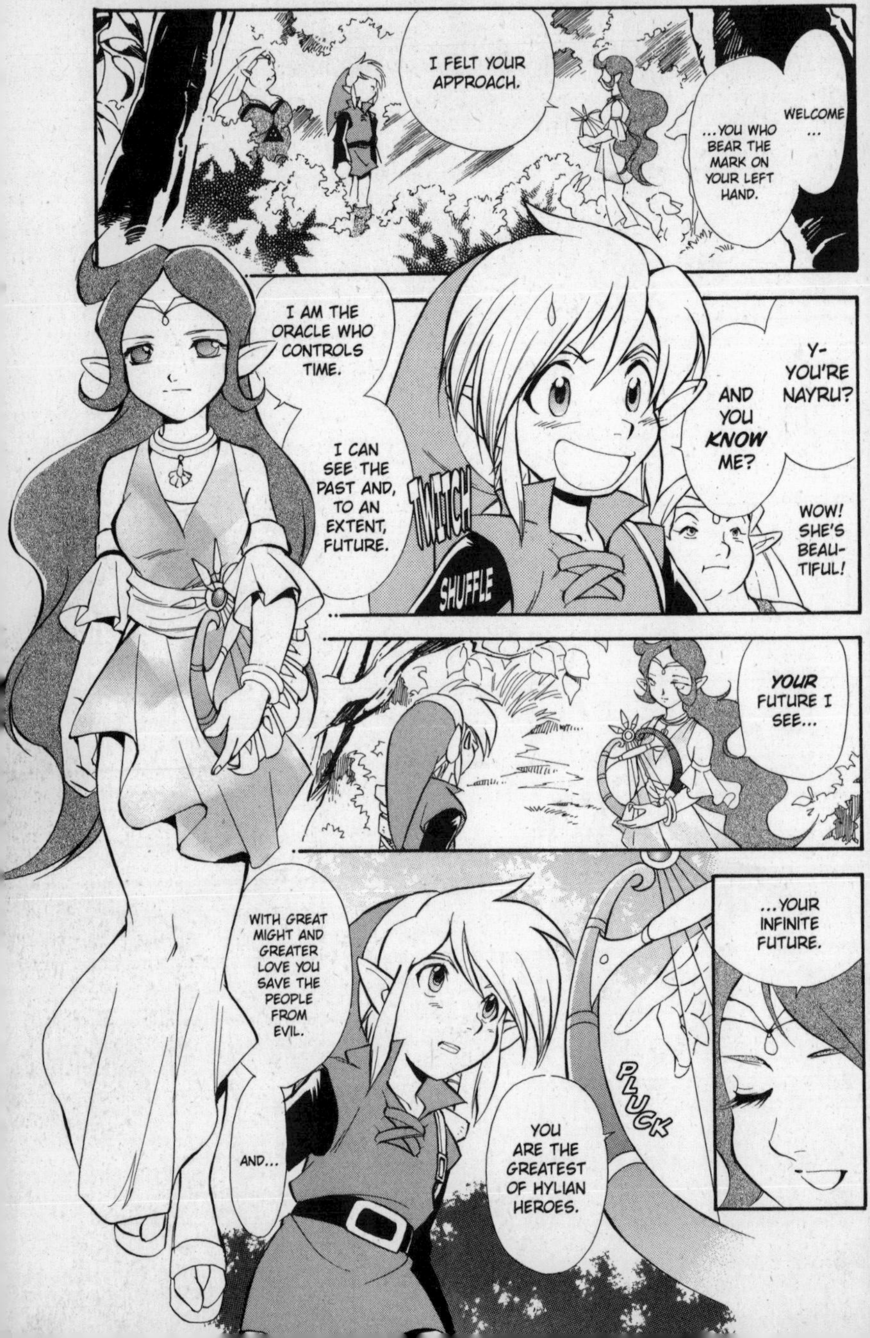
WELCOME ...
...YOU WHO BEAR THE MARK ON YOUR LEFT HAND.
I FELT YOUR APPROACH.
Y- YOU'RE NAYRU?
AND YOU KNOW ME?
TWITCH
SHUFFLE
WOW! SHE'S BEAU-TIFUL!
I AM THE ORACLE WHO CONTROLS TIME.
I CAN SEE THE PAST AND, TO AN EXTENT, FUTURE.
YOUR FUTURE I SEE...
...YOUR INFINITE FUTURE.
PLUCK
WITH GREAT MIGHT AND GREATER LOVE YOU SAVE THE PEOPLE FROM EVIL.
AND...
YOU ARE THE GREATEST OF HYLIAN HEROES.

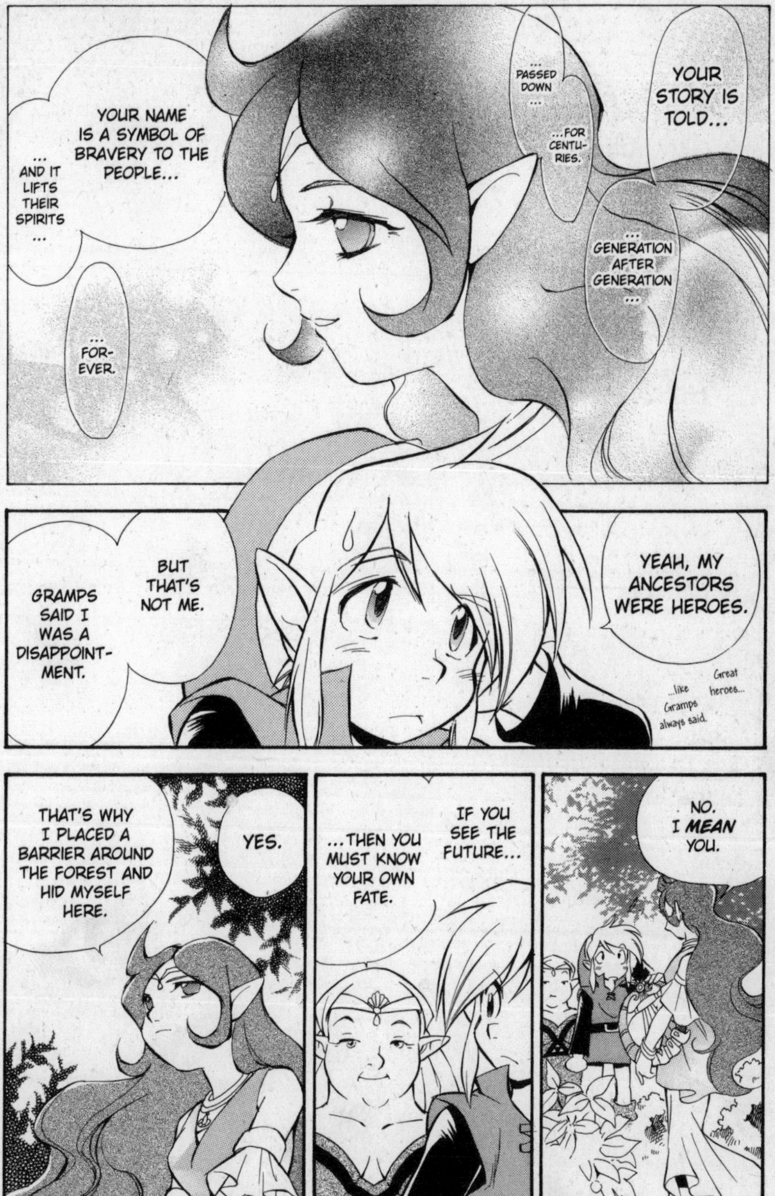
YOUR STORY IS TOLD...
...PASSED DOWN...
...FOR CENTU-RIES.
...GENERATION AFTER GENERATION...
YOUR NAME IS A SYMBOL OF BRAVERY TO THE PEOPLE...
...AND IT LIFTS THEIR SPIRITS...
...FOR-EVER.
YEAH, MY ANCESTORS WERE HEROES.
Great heroes...
...like Gramps always said.
BUT THAT'S NOT ME.
GRAMPS SAID I WAS A DISAPPOINT-MENT.
NO. I *MEAN* YOU.
IF YOU SEE THE FUTURE...
...THEN YOU MUST KNOW YOUR OWN FATE.
YES.
THAT'S WHY I PLACED A BARRIER AROUND THE FOREST AND HID MYSELF HERE.

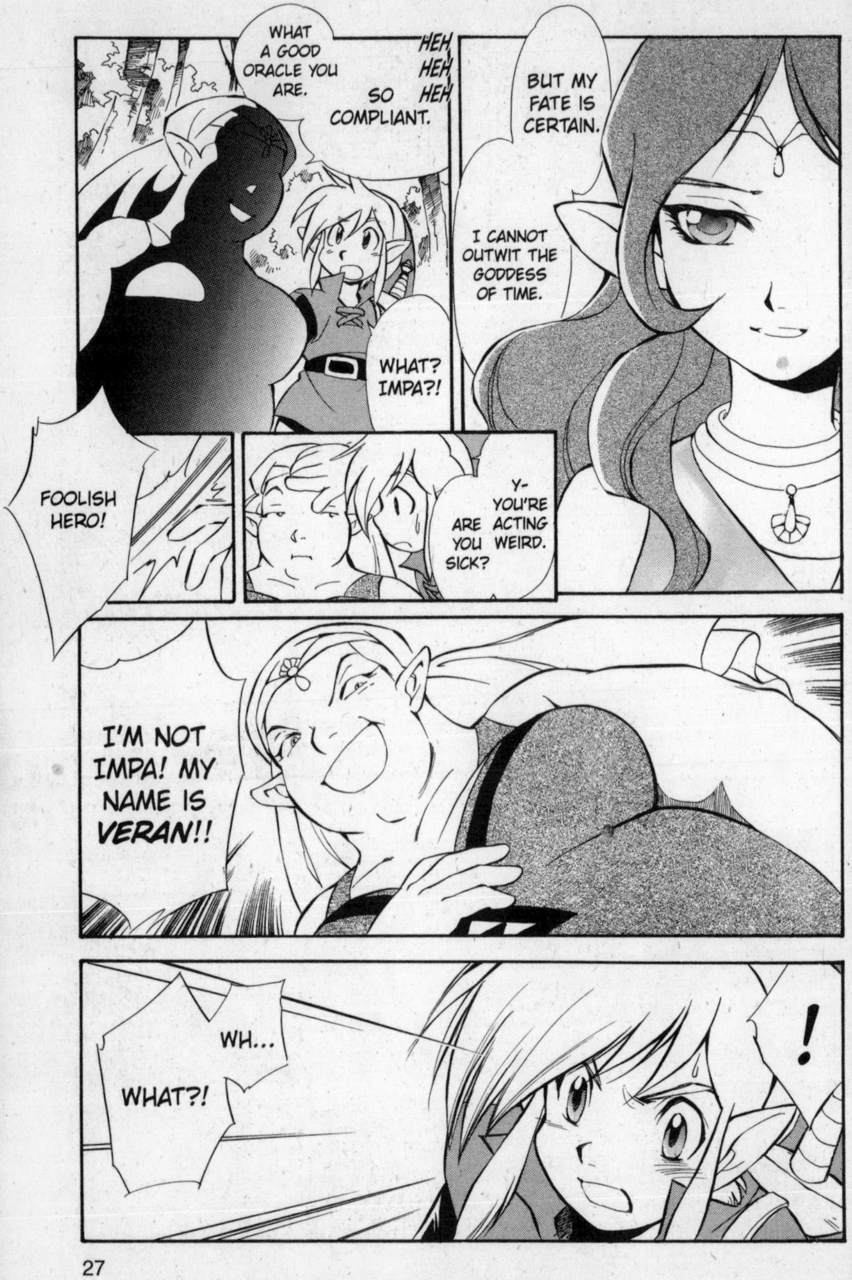
BUT MY FATE IS CERTAIN.
I CANNOT OUTWIT THE GODDESS OF TIME.
WHAT A GOOD ORACLE YOU ARE.
HEH HEH HEH
SO COMPLIANT.
WHAT? IMPA?!
Y- YOU'RE ACTING WEIRD. ARE YOU SICK?
FOOLISH HERO!
I'M NOT IMPA! MY NAME IS **VERAN**!!
!
WH...
WHAT?!

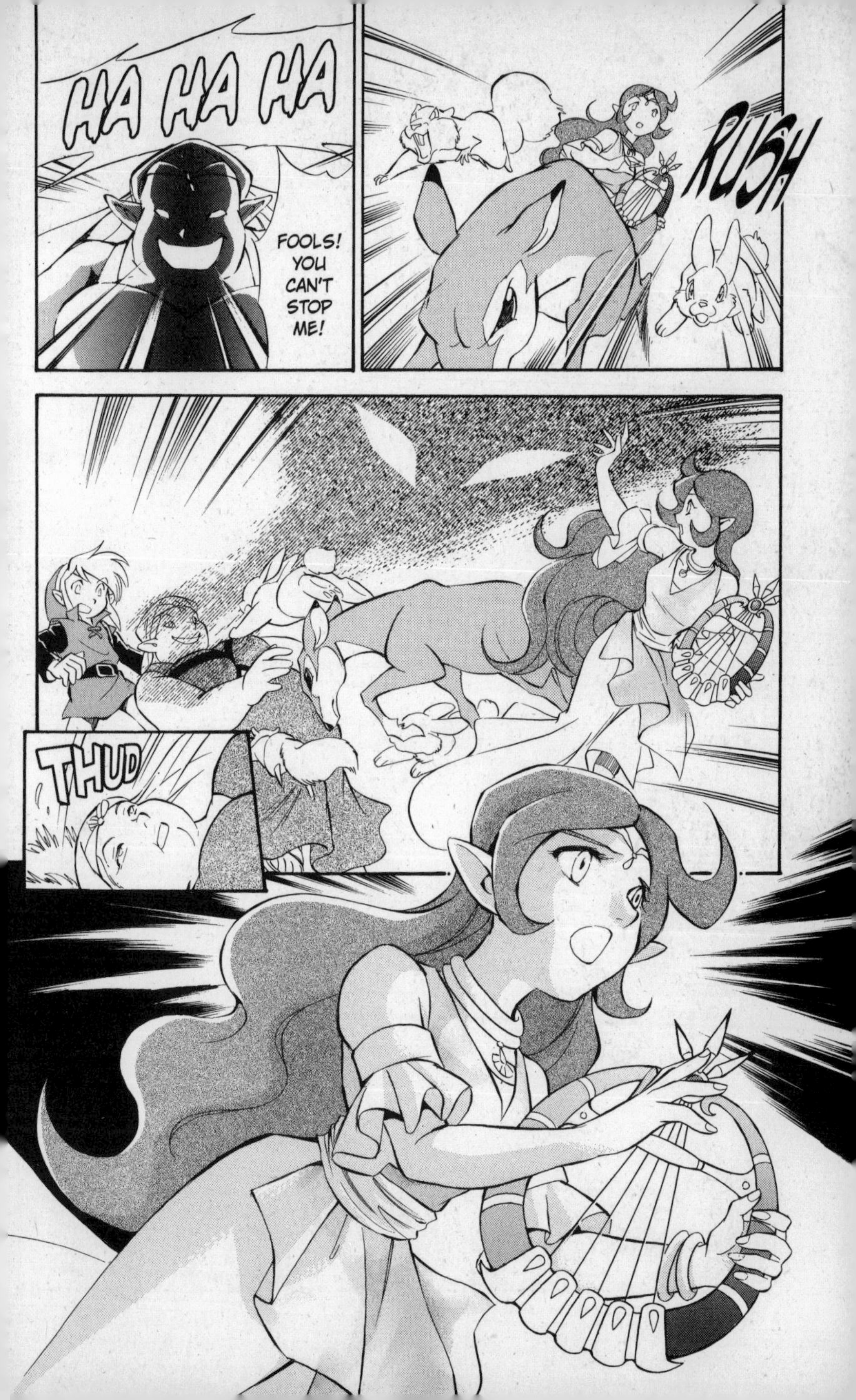
RUSH
HA HA HA
FOOLS! YOU CAN'T STOP ME!
THUD

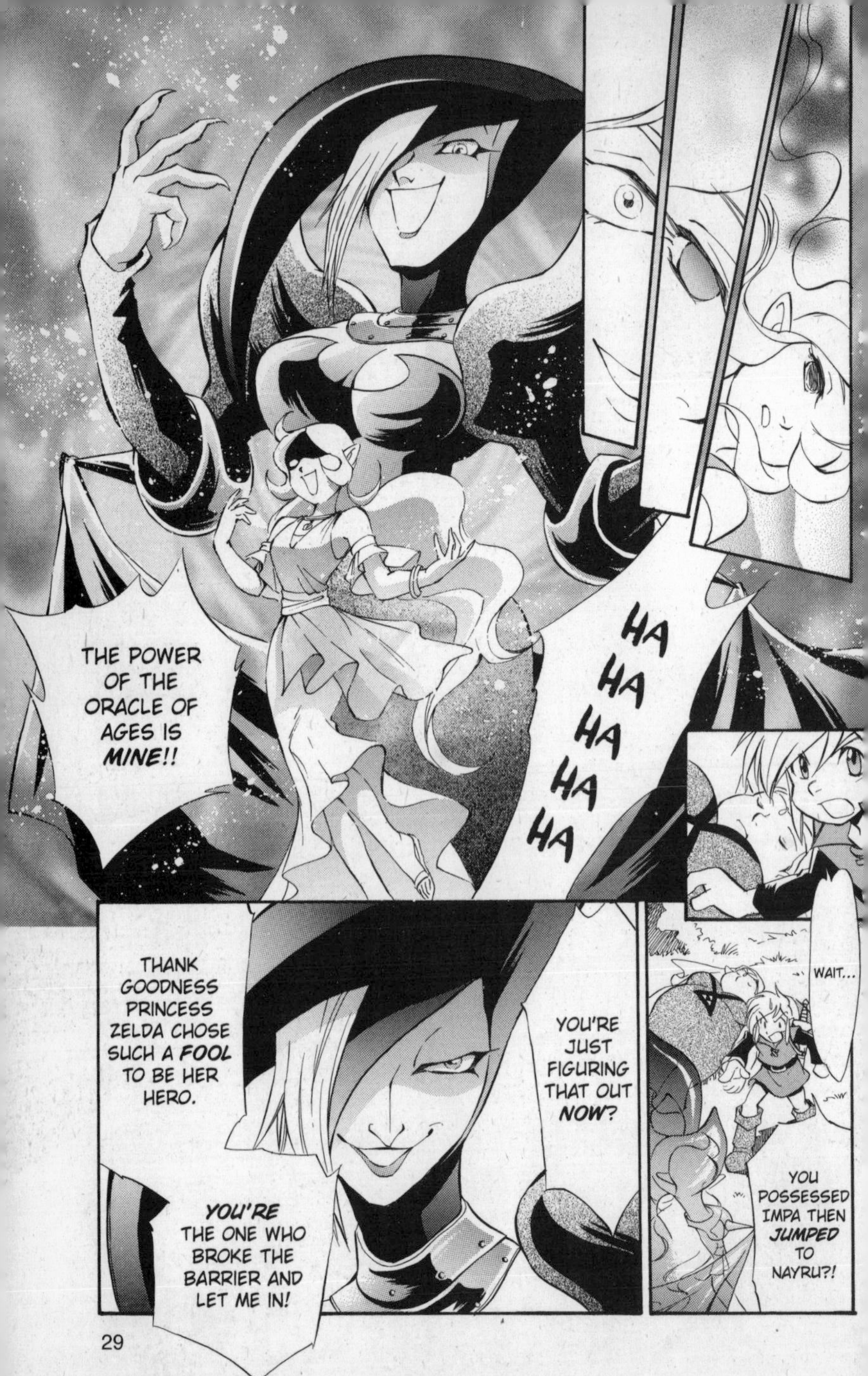
HA HA HA HA HA HA
THE POWER OF THE ORACLE OF AGES IS MINE!!
WAIT...
YOU POSSESSED IMPA THEN JUMPED TO NAYRU?!
YOU'RE JUST FIGURING THAT OUT NOW?
THANK GOODNESS PRINCESS ZELDA CHOSE SUCH A FOOL TO BE HER HERO.
YOU'RE THE ONE WHO BROKE THE BARRIER AND LET ME IN!

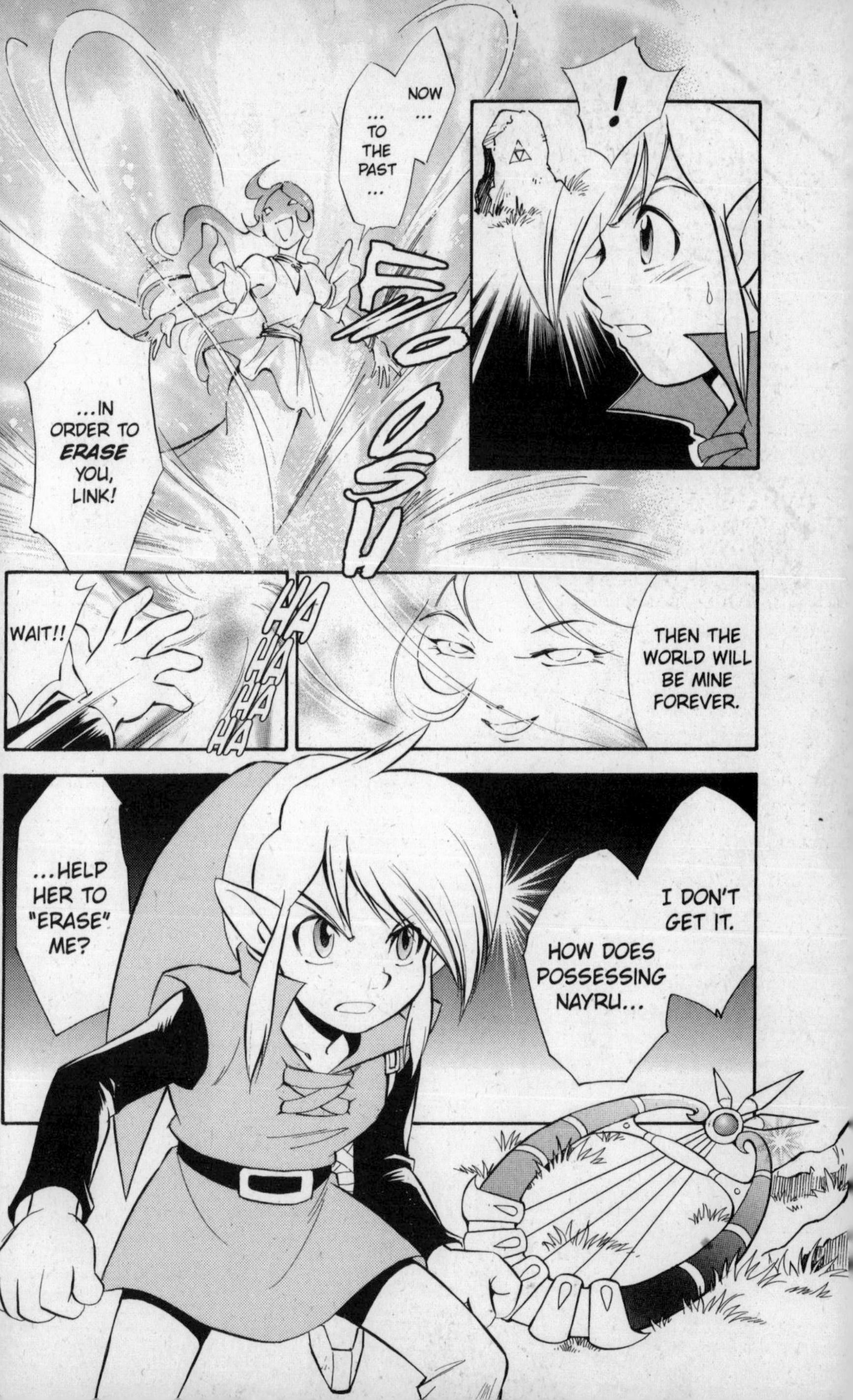
!
NOW... ...TO THE PAST...
...IN ORDER TO *ERASE* YOU, LINK!
FWOOSH
THEN THE WORLD WILL BE MINE FOREVER.
HAHAHAHA
WAIT!!
I DON'T GET IT.
HOW DOES POSSESSING NAYRU...
...HELP HER TO "ERASE" ME?

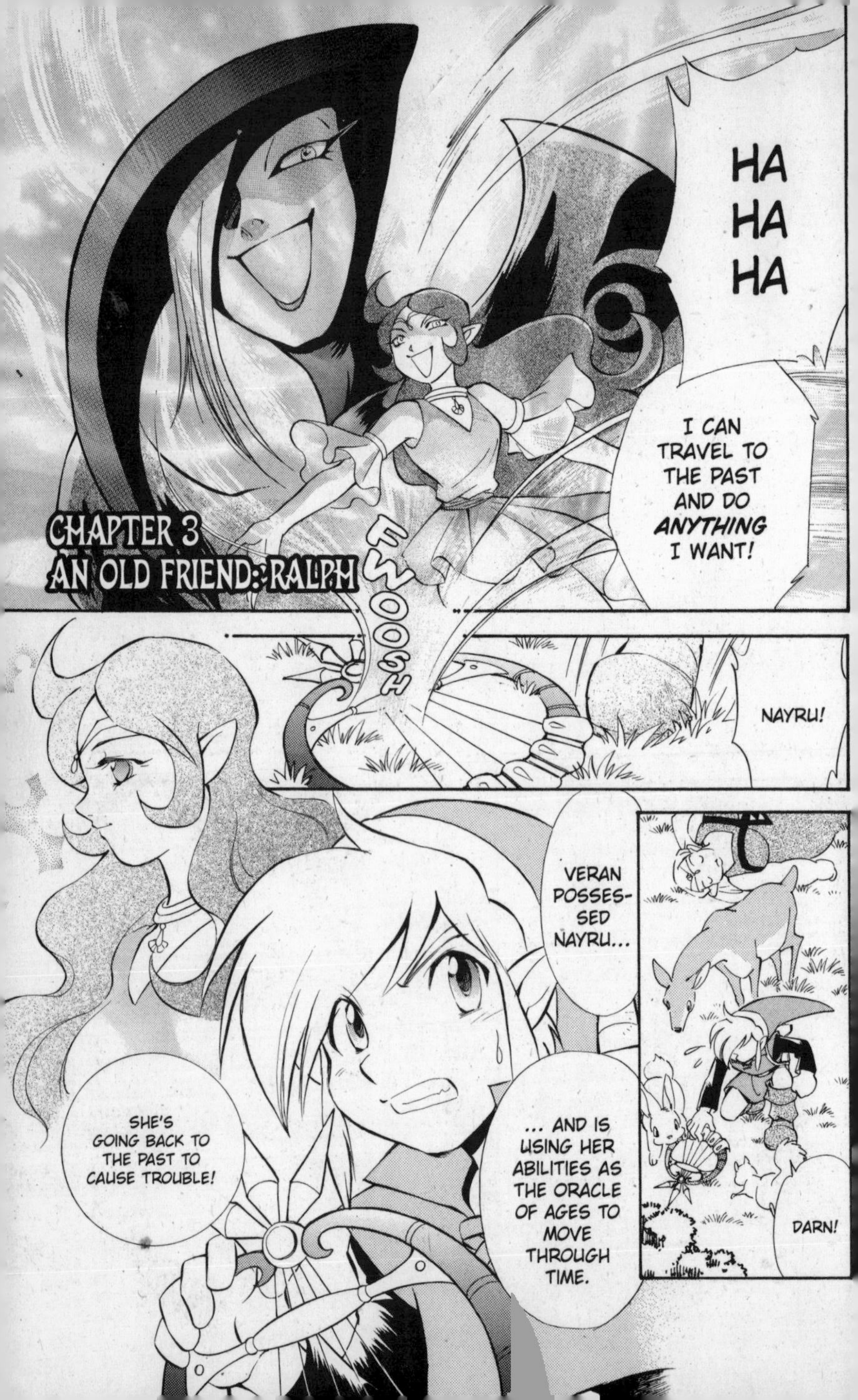
HA HA HA
I CAN TRAVEL TO THE PAST AND DO *ANYTHING* I WANT!
FWOOSH
CHAPTER 3
AN OLD FRIEND: RALPH
NAYRU!
DARN!
VERAN POSSES-SED NAYRU...
... AND IS USING HER ABILITIES AS THE ORACLE OF AGES TO MOVE THROUGH TIME.
SHE'S GOING BACK TO THE PAST TO CAUSE TROUBLE!

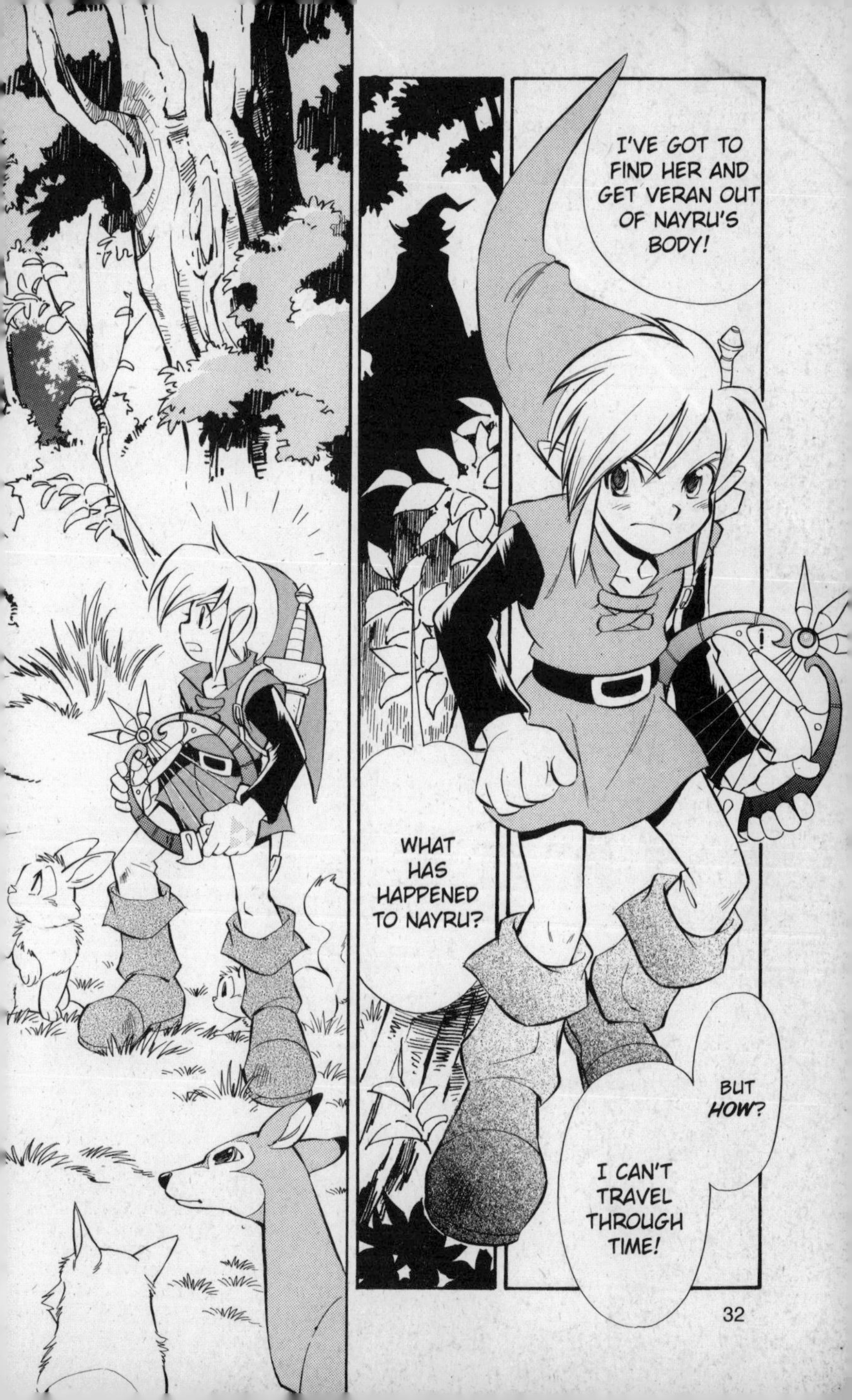
I'VE GOT TO FIND HER AND GET VERAN OUT OF NAYRU'S BODY!
WHAT HAS HAPPENED TO NAYRU?
BUT *HOW?*
I CAN'T TRAVEL THROUGH TIME!

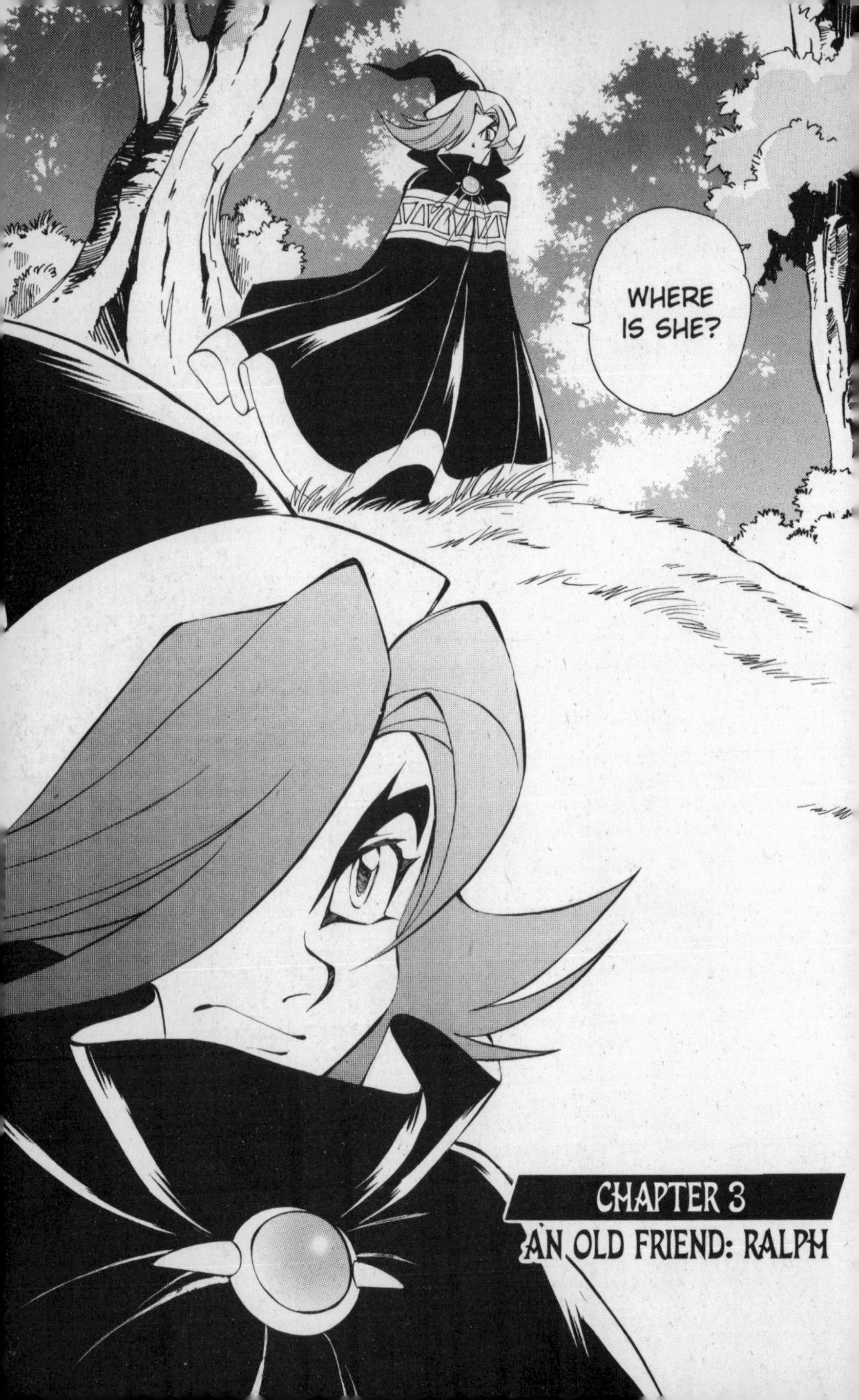
WHERE IS SHE?
CHAPTER 3
AN OLD FRIEND: RALPH

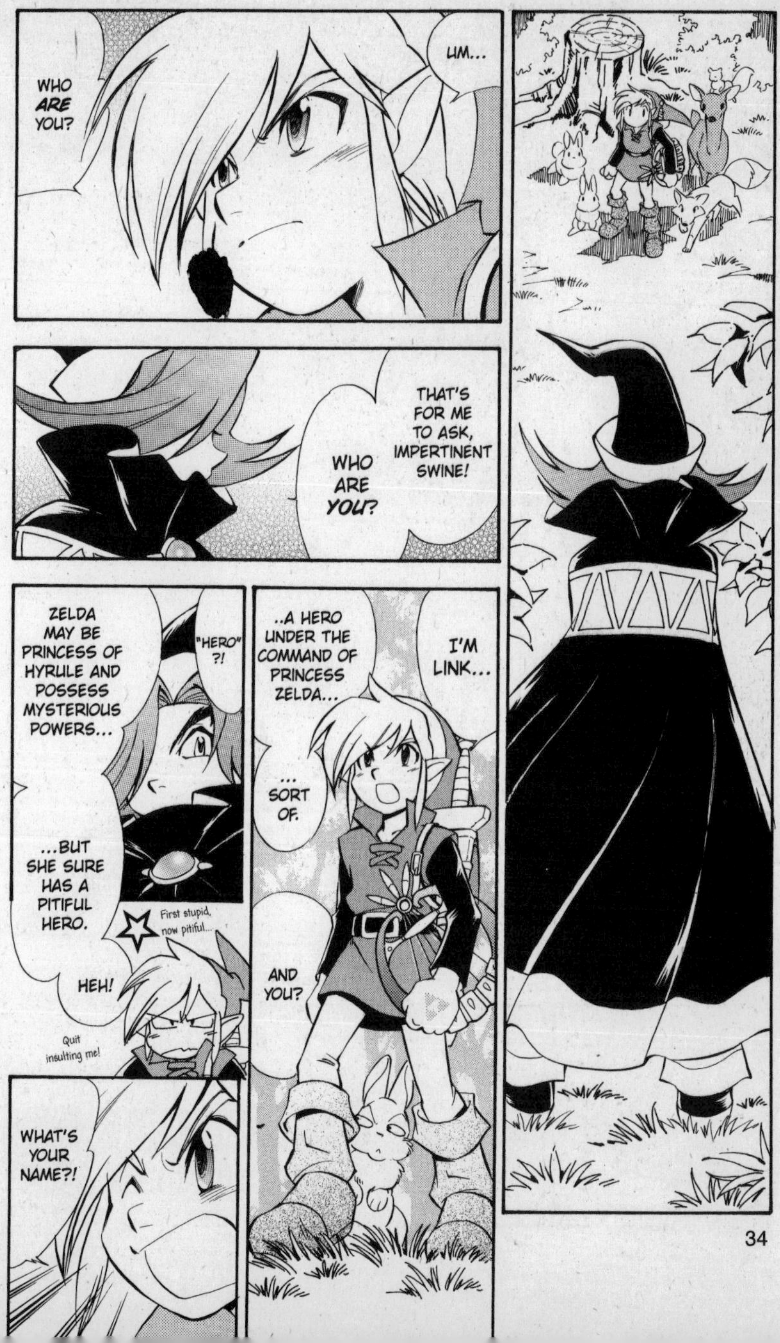
UM...
WHO ARE YOU?
THAT'S FOR ME TO ASK, IMPERTINENT SWINE!
WHO ARE YOU?
I'M LINK...
..A HERO UNDER THE COMMAND OF PRINCESS ZELDA...
... SORT OF.
AND YOU?
"HERO" ?!
ZELDA MAY BE PRINCESS OF HYRULE AND POSSESS MYSTERIOUS POWERS...
...BUT SHE SURE HAS A PITIFUL HERO.
First stupid, now pitiful...
HEH!
Quit insulting me!
WHAT'S YOUR NAME?!

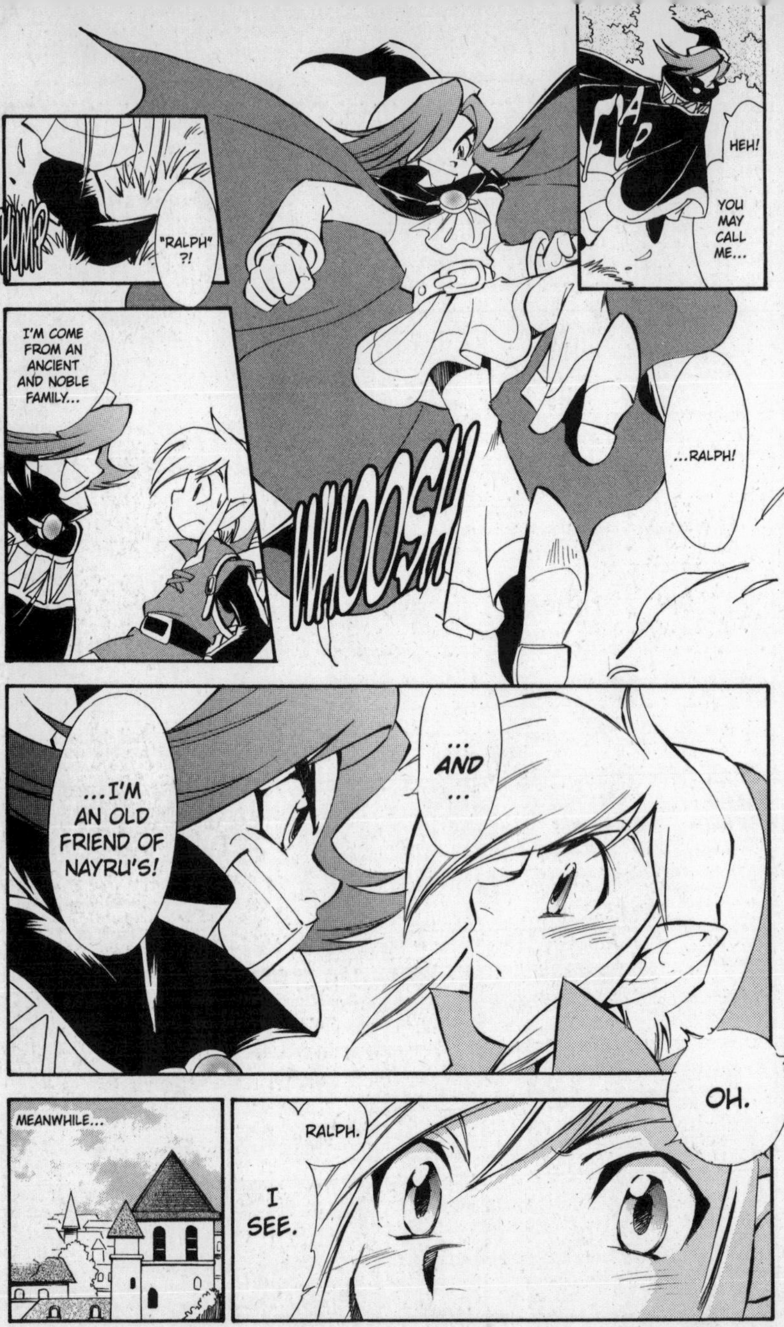
FLAP
HEH!
YOU MAY CALL ME...
...RALPH!
WHOOSH
THUMP
"RALPH" ?!
I'M COME FROM AN ANCIENT AND NOBLE FAMILY...
... AND ...
...I'M AN OLD FRIEND OF NAYRU'S!
OH.
RALPH.
I SEE.
MEANWHILE...

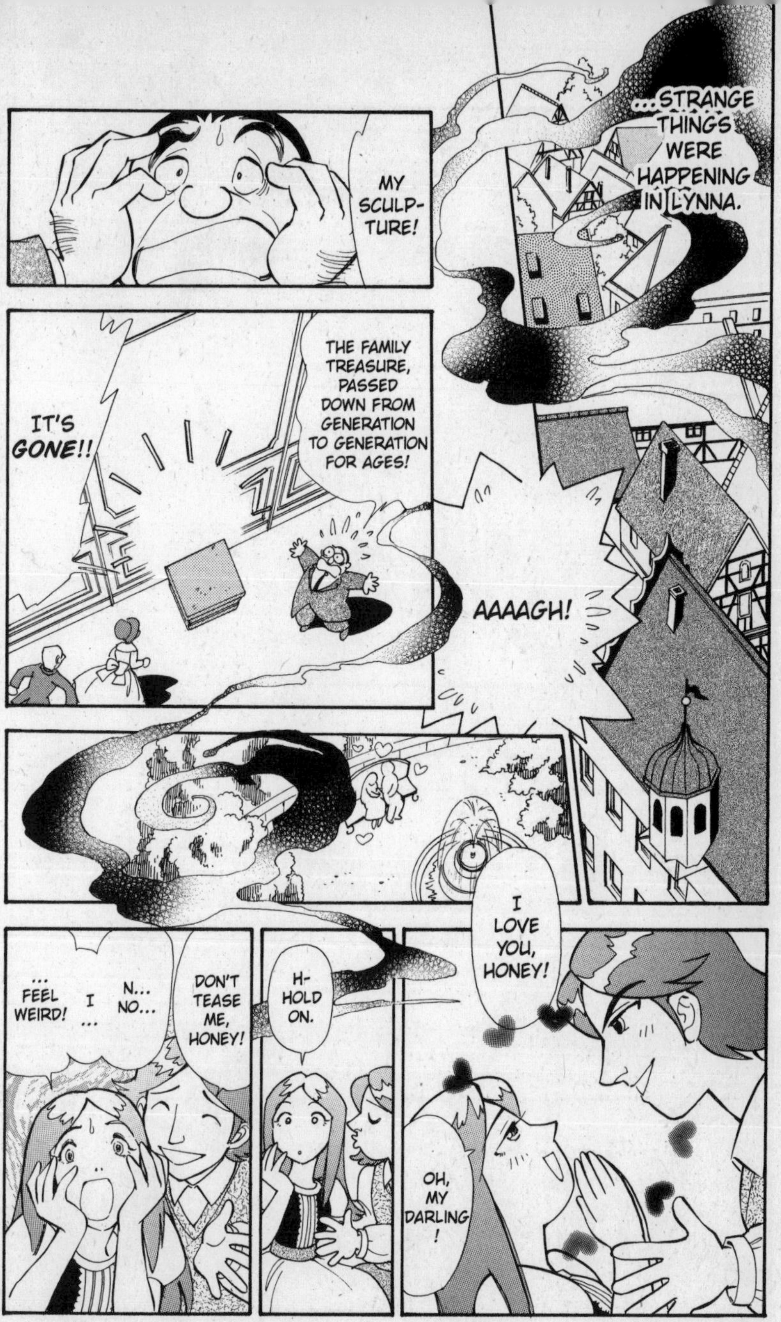
...STRANGE THINGS WERE HAPPENING IN LYNNA.
MY SCULPTURE!
THE FAMILY TREASURE, PASSED DOWN FROM GENERATION TO GENERATION FOR AGES!
IT'S *GONE*!!
AAAAGH!
I LOVE YOU, HONEY!
OH, MY DARLING!
H-HOLD ON.
DON'T TEASE ME, HONEY!
N... NO...
I...
...FEEL WEIRD!

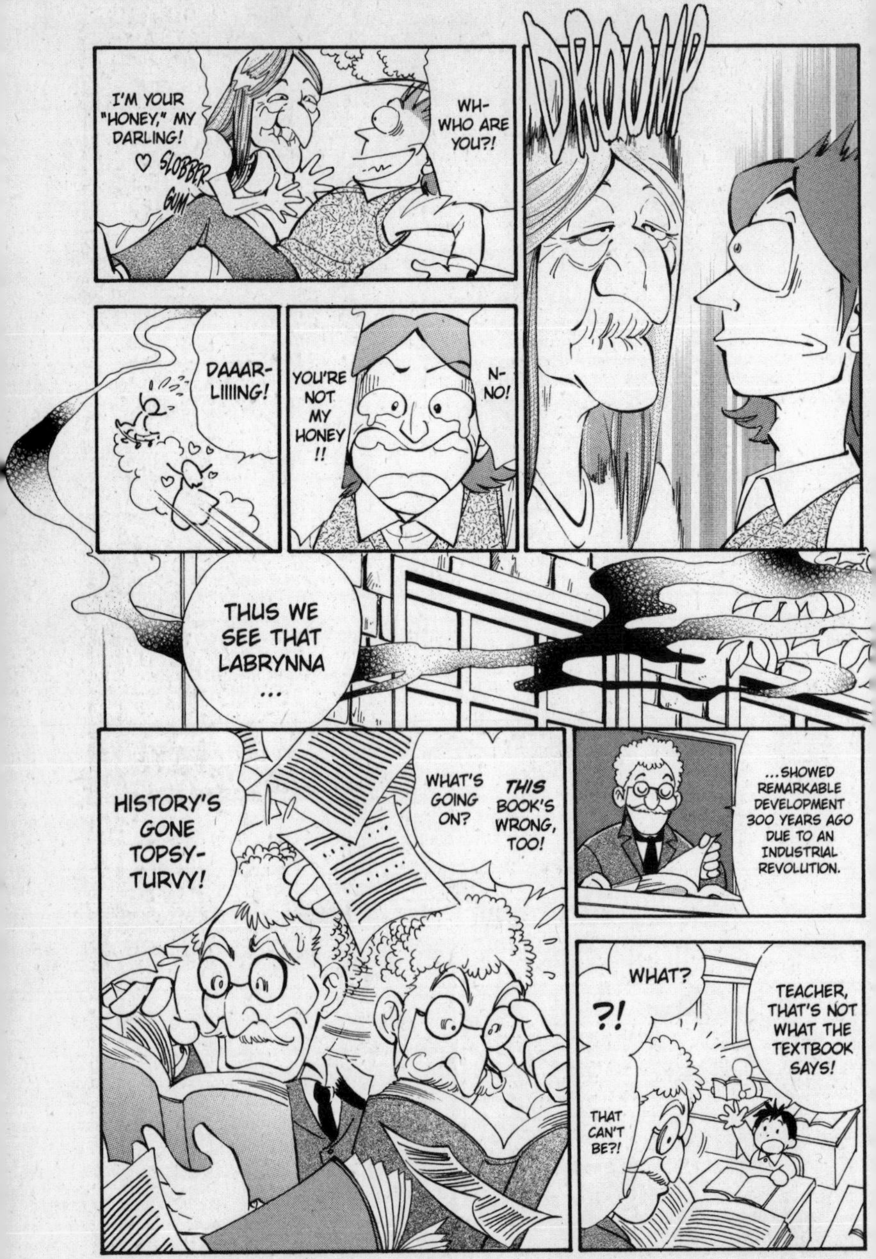
DROOMP
WH- WHO ARE YOU?!
I'M YOUR "HONEY," MY DARLING!
♡ SLOBBER GUM
N- NO!
YOU'RE NOT MY HONEY !!
DAAAR-LIIIING!
THUS WE SEE THAT LABRYNNA ...
...SHOWED REMARKABLE DEVELOPMENT 300 YEARS AGO DUE TO AN INDUSTRIAL REVOLUTION.
TEACHER, THAT'S NOT WHAT THE TEXTBOOK SAYS!
WHAT?
?!
THAT CAN'T BE?!
THIS BOOK'S WRONG, TOO!
WHAT'S GOING ON?
HISTORY'S GONE TOPSY-TURVY!

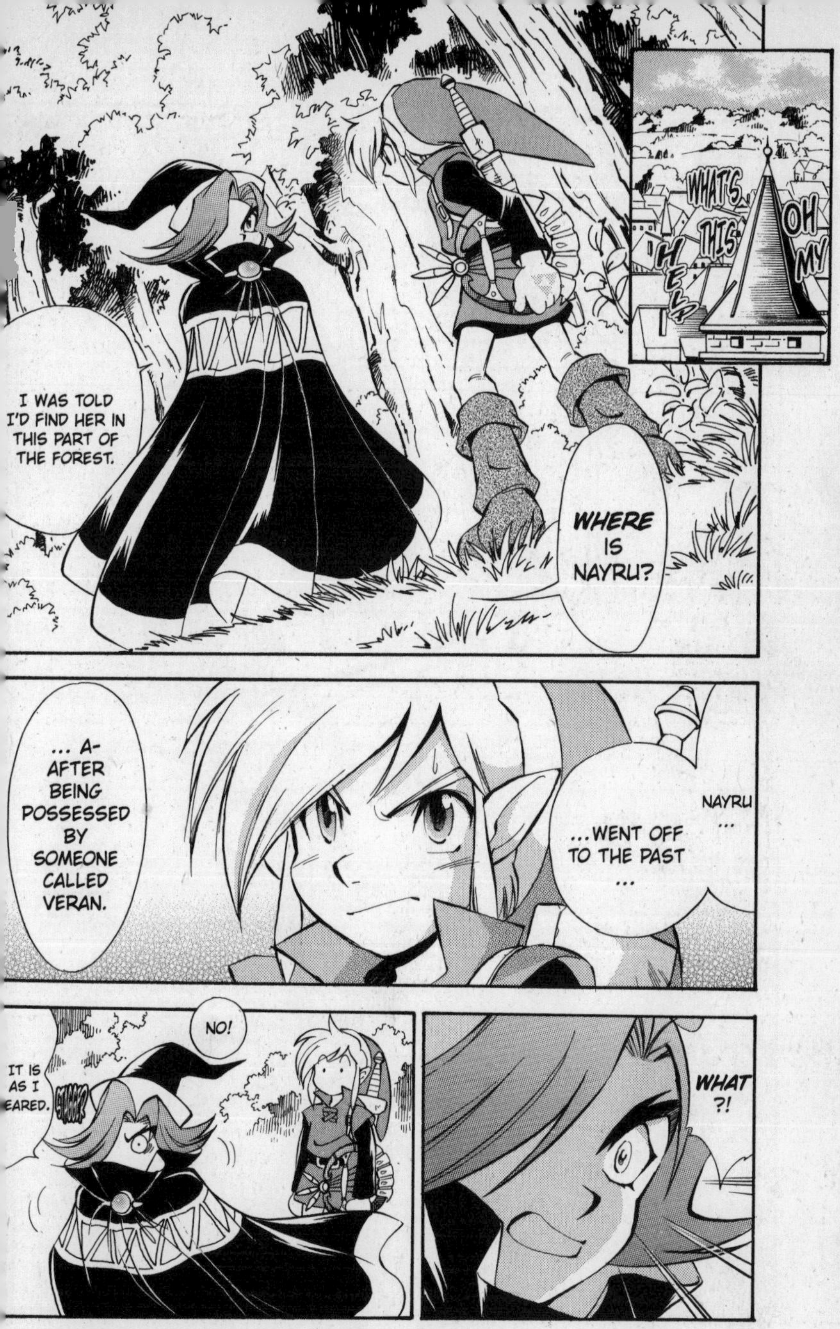
OH MY
WHAT'S THIS
HELP
WHERE IS NAYRU?
I WAS TOLD I'D FIND HER IN THIS PART OF THE FOREST.
NAYRU ...
...WENT OFF TO THE PAST ...
... A- AFTER BEING POSSESSED BY SOMEONE CALLED VERAN.
WHAT ?!
NO!
IT IS AS I EARED.

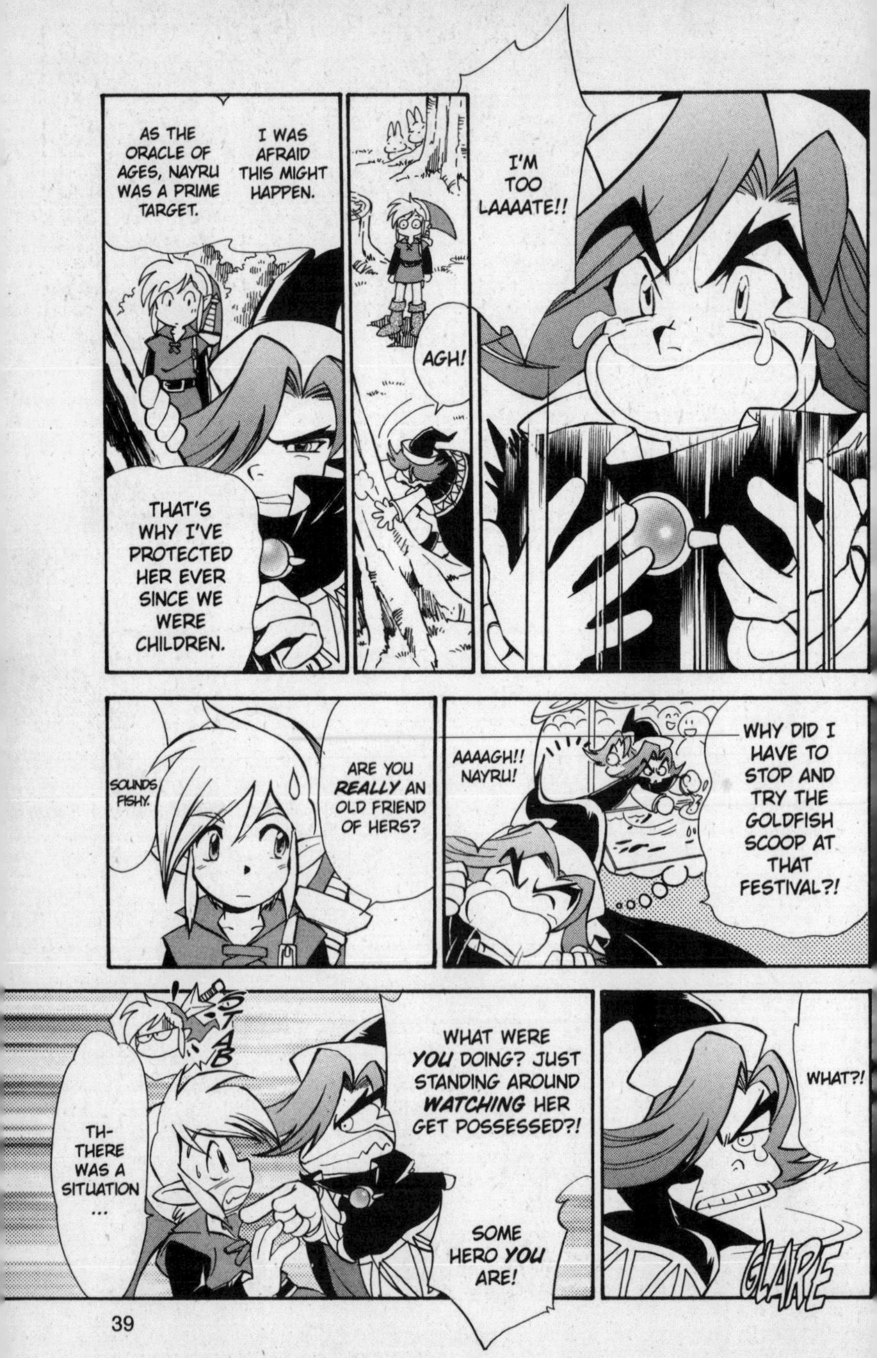
I'M TOO LAAAATE!!
AGH!
I WAS AFRAID THIS MIGHT HAPPEN.
AS THE ORACLE OF AGES, NAYRU WAS A PRIME TARGET.
THAT'S WHY I'VE PROTECTED HER EVER SINCE WE WERE CHILDREN.
WHY DID I HAVE TO STOP AND TRY THE GOLDFISH SCOOP AT THAT FESTIVAL?!
AAAAGH!! NAYRU!
ARE YOU REALLY AN OLD FRIEND OF HERS?
SOUNDS FISHY.
WHAT?!
GLARE
WHAT WERE YOU DOING? JUST STANDING AROUND WATCHING HER GET POSSESSED?!
STAB
TH- THERE WAS A SITUATION ...
SOME HERO YOU ARE!

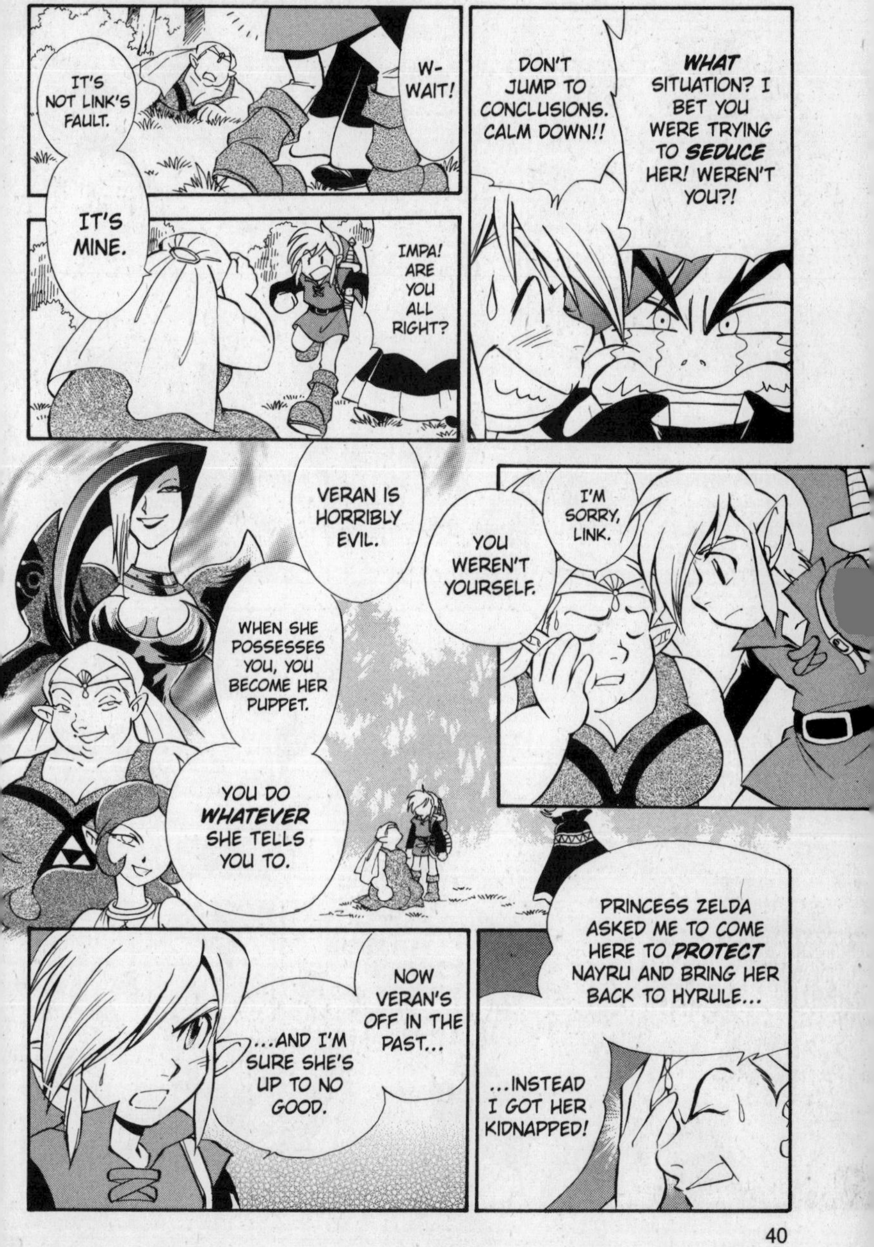
WHAT SITUATION? I BET YOU WERE TRYING TO SEDUCE HER! WEREN'T YOU?!
DON'T JUMP TO CONCLUSIONS. CALM DOWN!!
W-WAIT!
IT'S NOT LINK'S FAULT.
IT'S MINE.
IMPA! ARE YOU ALL RIGHT?
I'M SORRY, LINK.
YOU WEREN'T YOURSELF.
VERAN IS HORRIBLY EVIL.
WHEN SHE POSSESSES YOU, YOU BECOME HER PUPPET.
YOU DO WHATEVER SHE TELLS YOU TO.
PRINCESS ZELDA ASKED ME TO COME HERE TO PROTECT NAYRU AND BRING HER BACK TO HYRULE...
...INSTEAD I GOT HER KIDNAPPED!
NOW VERAN'S OFF IN THE PAST...
...AND I'M SURE SHE'S UP TO NO GOOD.

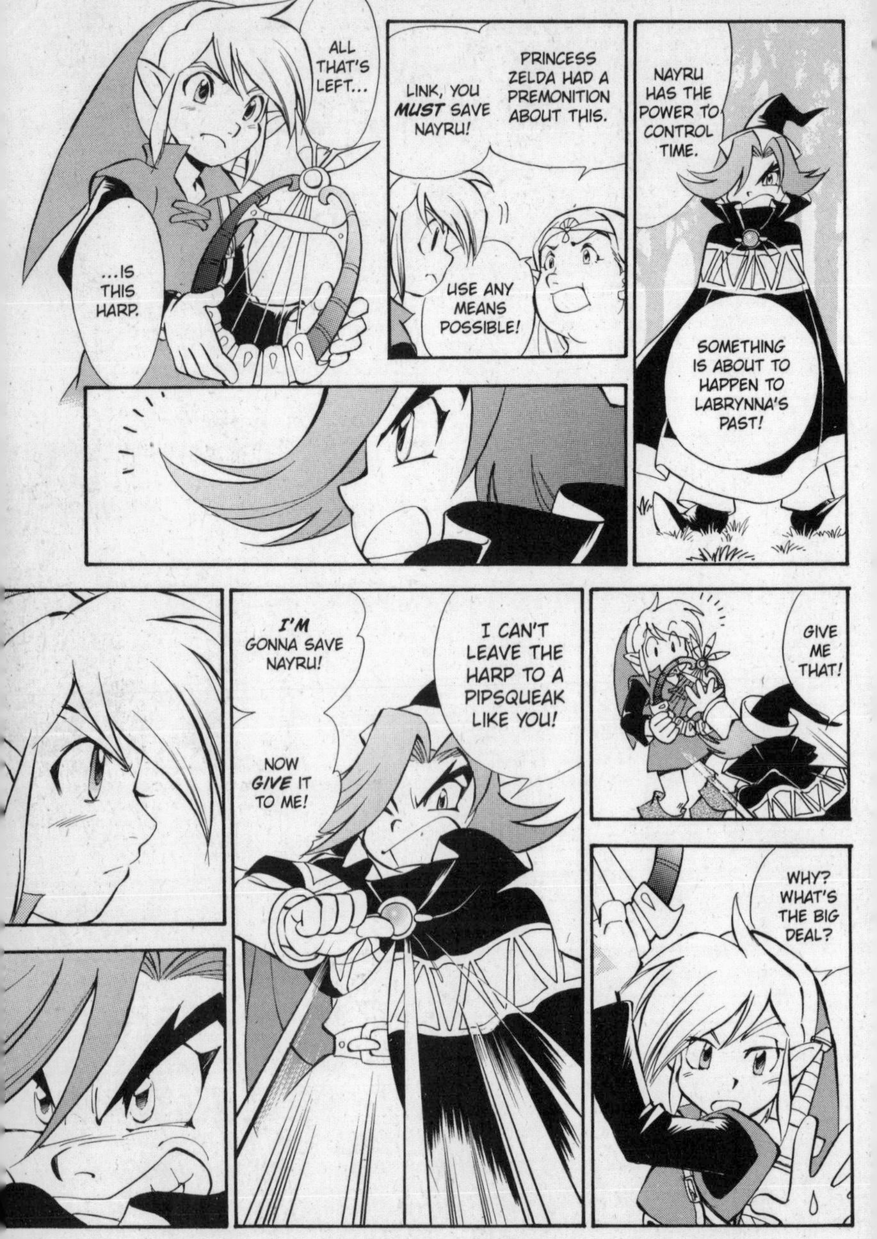
NAYRU HAS THE POWER TO CONTROL TIME.
SOMETHING IS ABOUT TO HAPPEN TO LABRYNNA'S PAST!
PRINCESS ZELDA HAD A PREMONITION ABOUT THIS.
LINK, YOU **MUST** SAVE NAYRU!
USE ANY MEANS POSSIBLE!
ALL THAT'S LEFT...
...IS THIS HARP.
GIVE ME THAT!
WHY? WHAT'S THE BIG DEAL?
I CAN'T LEAVE THE HARP TO A PIPSQUEAK LIKE YOU!
I'M GONNA SAVE NAYRU!
NOW ***GIVE*** IT TO ME!

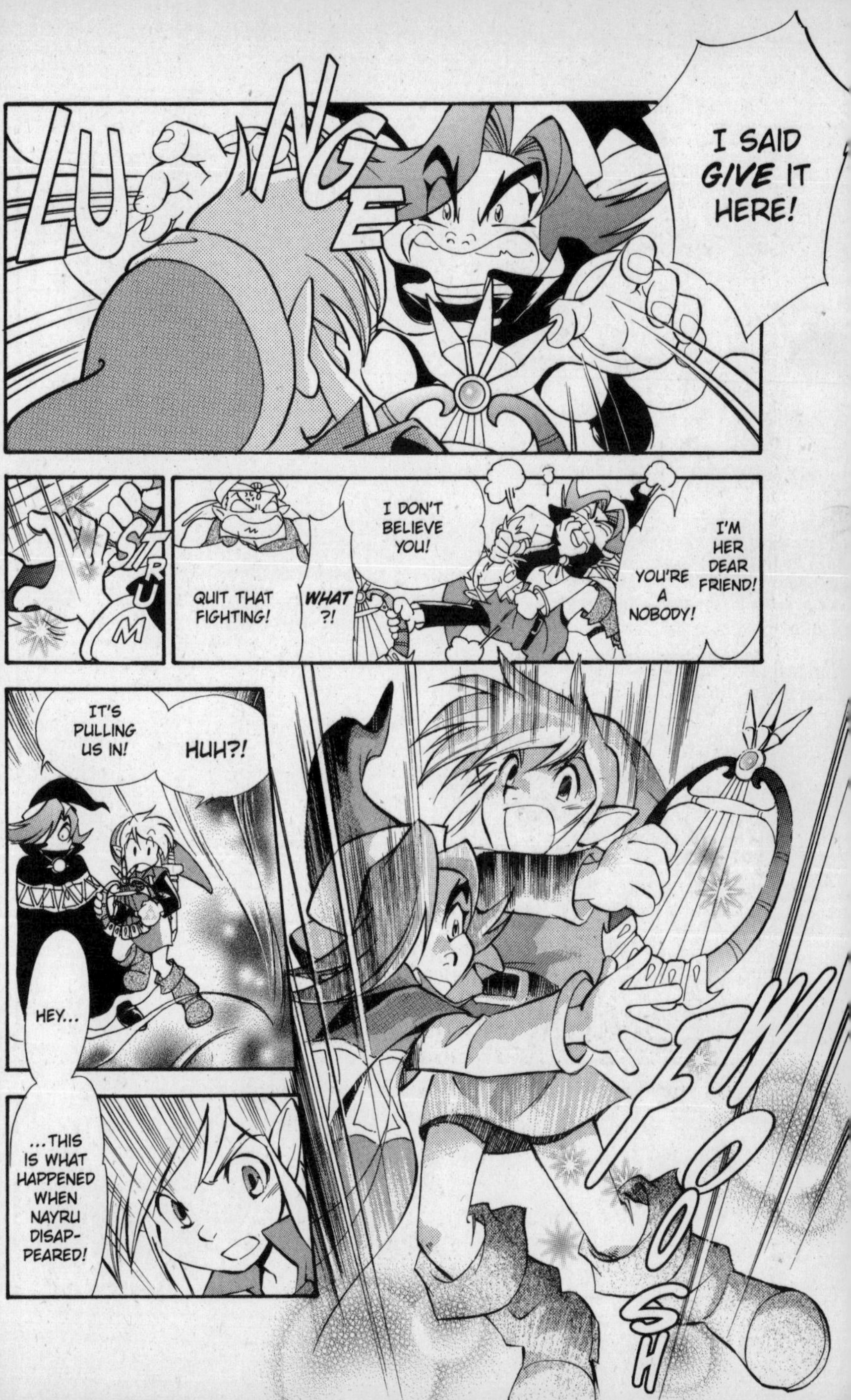
I SAID *GIVE* IT HERE!
LUNGE
I'M HER DEAR FRIEND!
YOU'RE A NOBODY!
I DON'T BELIEVE YOU!
WHAT?!
QUIT THAT FIGHTING!
STRUM
WHOOSH
HUH?!
IT'S PULLING US IN!
HEY...
...THIS IS WHAT HAPPENED WHEN NAYRU DISAP-PEARED!

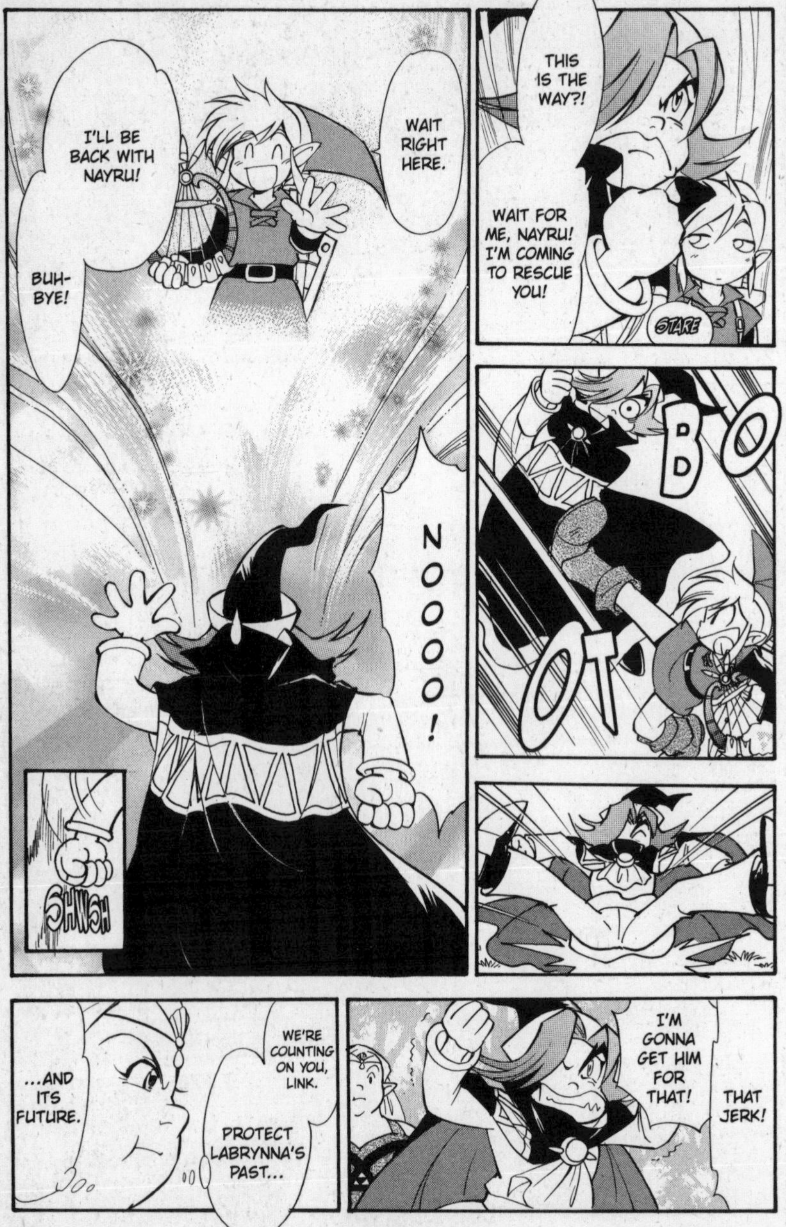
THIS IS THE WAY?!
WAIT FOR ME, NAYRU! I'M COMING TO RESCUE YOU!
STARE
BOOT
WAIT RIGHT HERE.
I'LL BE BACK WITH NAYRU!
BUH-BYE!
NOOOOO!
SHWSH
THAT JERK!
I'M GONNA GET HIM FOR THAT!
WE'RE COUNTING ON YOU, LINK.
PROTECT LABRYNNA'S PAST...
...AND ITS FUTURE.

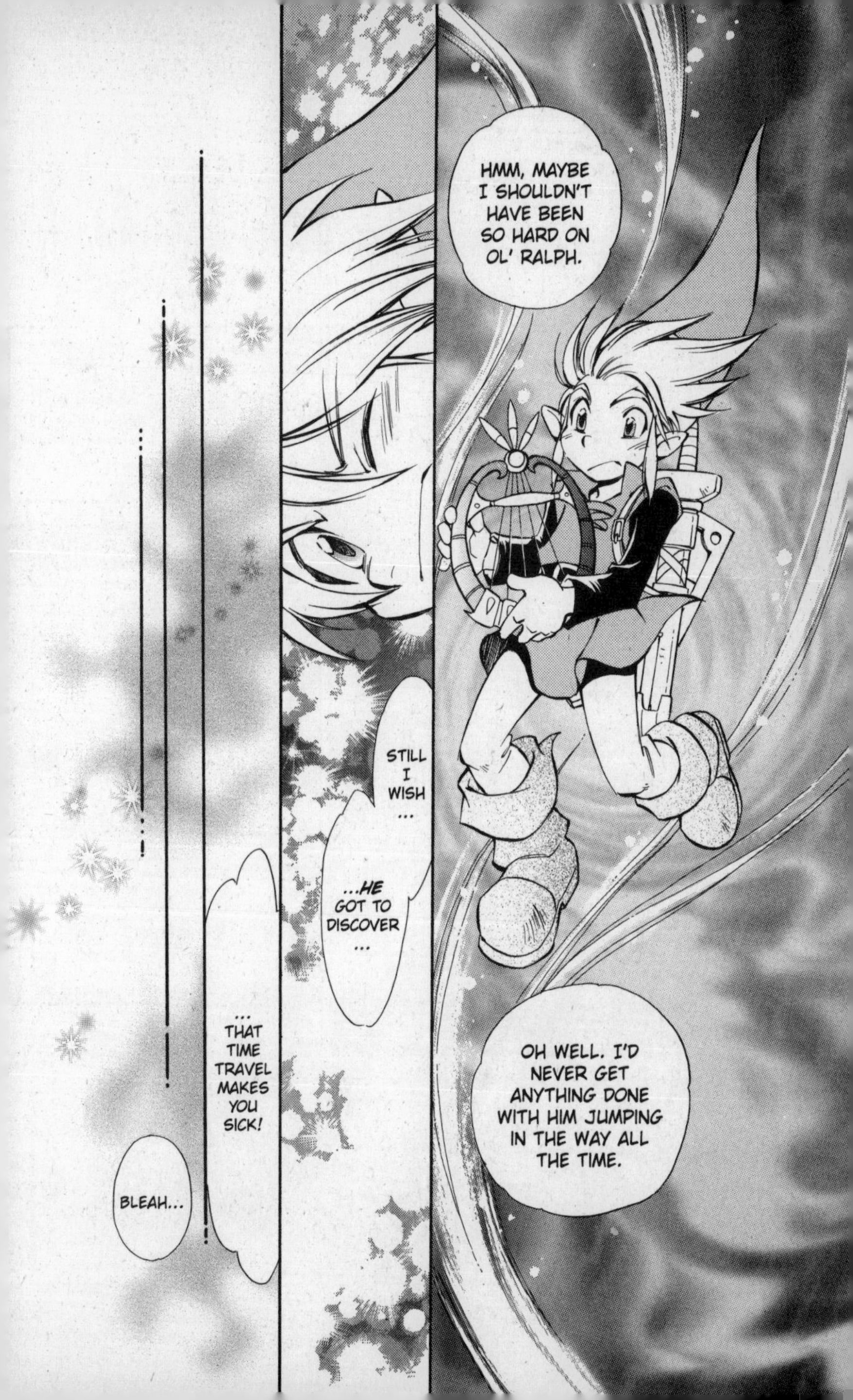
HMM, MAYBE I SHOULDN'T HAVE BEEN SO HARD ON OL' RALPH.
OH WELL. I'D NEVER GET ANYTHING DONE WITH HIM JUMPING IN THE WAY ALL THE TIME.
STILL I WISH ...
...*HE* GOT TO DISCOVER ...
... THAT TIME TRAVEL MAKES YOU SICK!
BLEAH...

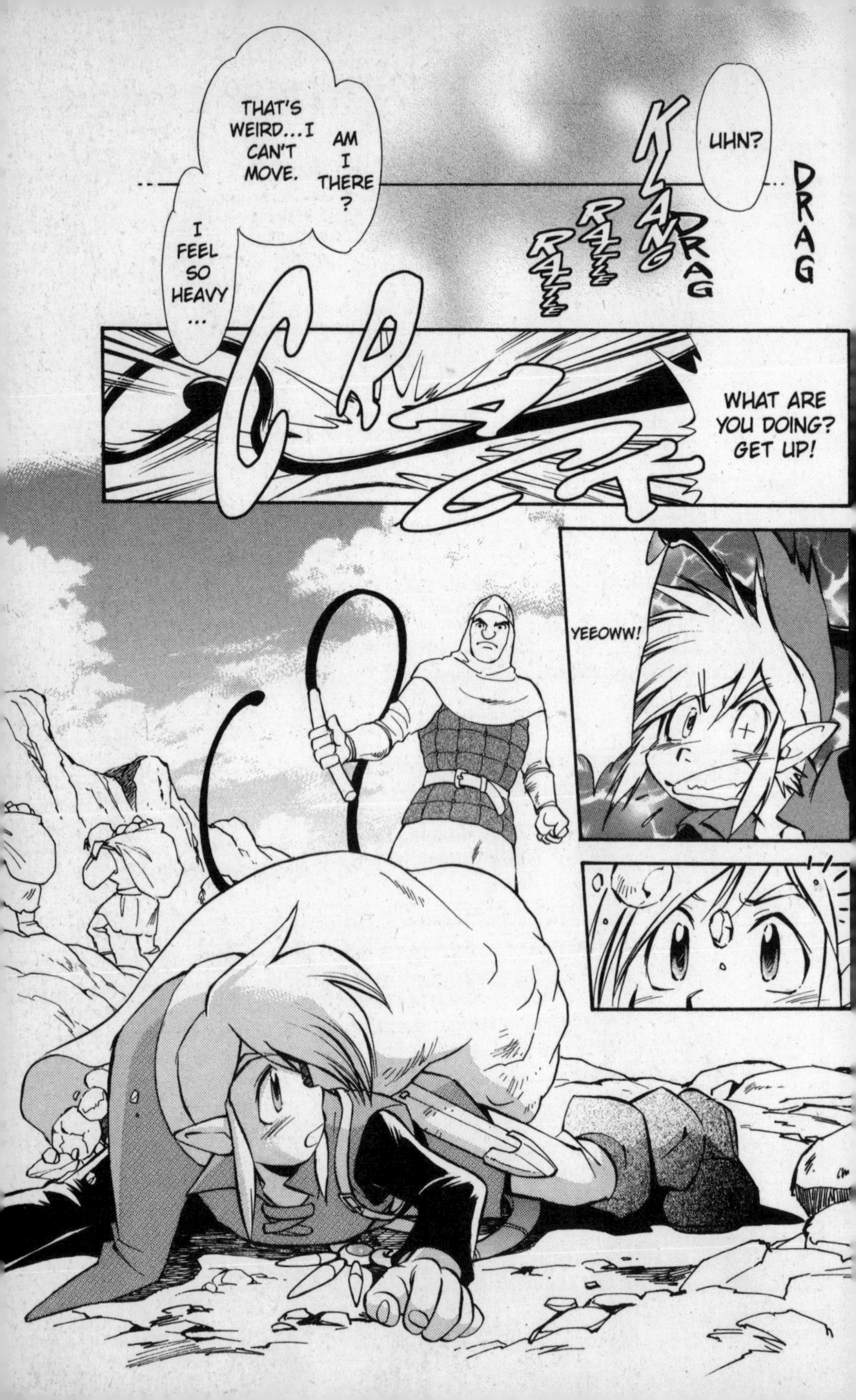
DRAG
UHN?
DRAG
KLANG
RATTLE
RATTLE
THAT'S WEIRD...I CAN'T MOVE.
AM I THERE?
I FEEL SO HEAVY...
CRACK
WHAT ARE YOU DOING? GET UP!
YEEOWW!
!!

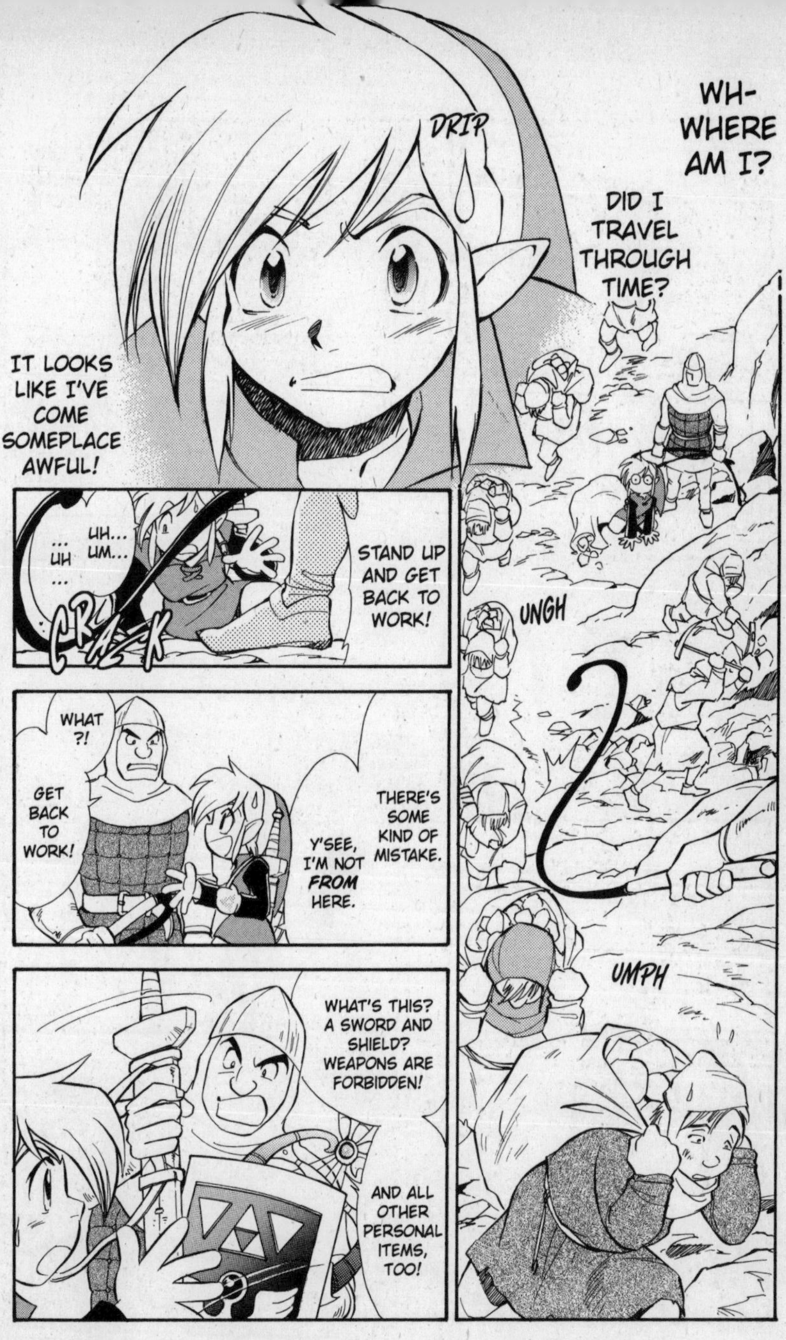
DRIP
WH- WHERE AM I?
DID I TRAVEL THROUGH TIME?
IT LOOKS LIKE I'VE COME SOMEPLACE AWFUL!
UNGH
UMPH
STAND UP AND GET BACK TO WORK!
UH... UM...
... UH ...
CRACK
THERE'S SOME KIND OF MISTAKE.
Y'SEE, I'M NOT *FROM* HERE.
WHAT ?!
GET BACK TO WORK!
WHAT'S THIS? A SWORD AND SHIELD? WEAPONS ARE FORBIDDEN!
AND ALL OTHER PERSONAL ITEMS, TOO!

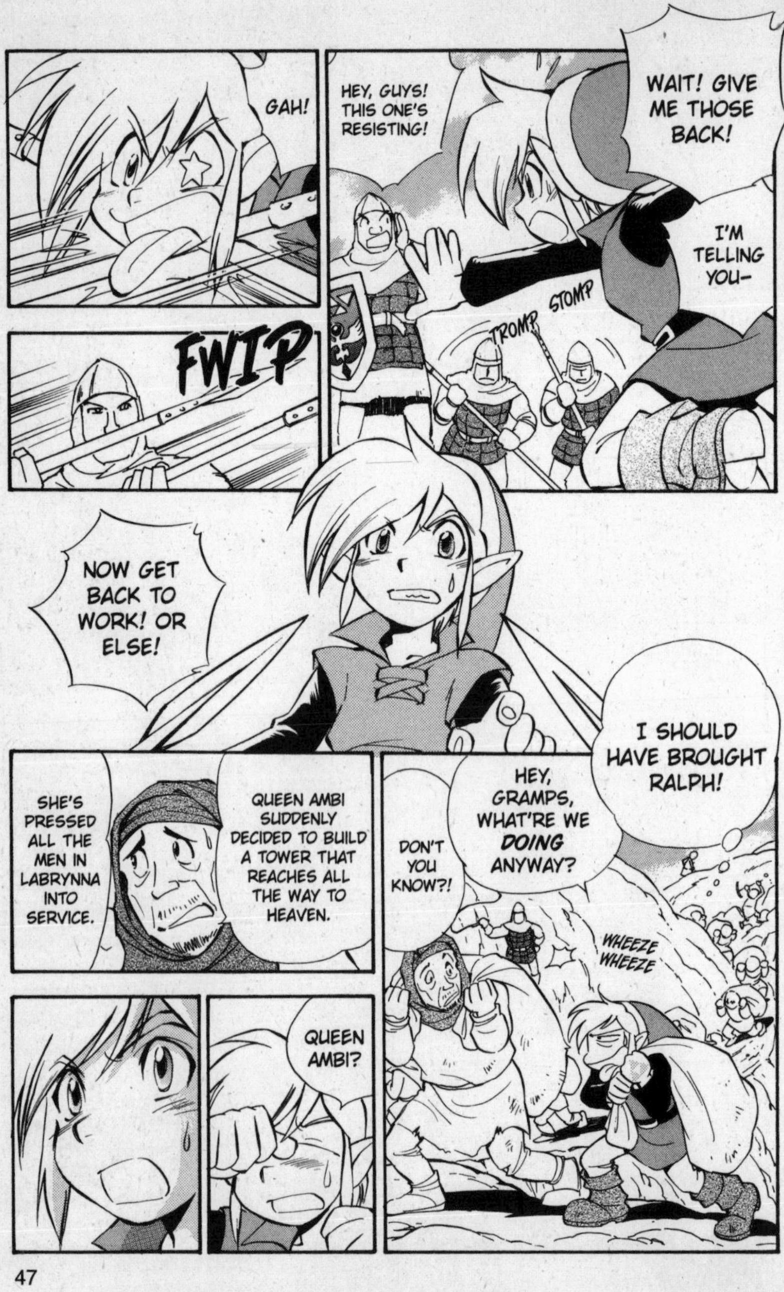
WAIT! GIVE ME THOSE BACK!
I'M TELLING YOU-
HEY, GUYS! THIS ONE'S RESISTING!
STOMP
TROMP
GAH!
FWIP
I SHOULD HAVE BROUGHT RALPH!
NOW GET BACK TO WORK! OR ELSE!
HEY, GRAMPS, WHAT'RE WE *DOING* ANYWAY?
DON'T YOU KNOW?!
WHEEZE WHEEZE
QUEEN AMBI SUDDENLY DECIDED TO BUILD A TOWER THAT REACHES ALL THE WAY TO HEAVEN.
SHE'S PRESSED ALL THE MEN IN LABRYNNA INTO SERVICE.
QUEEN AMBI?

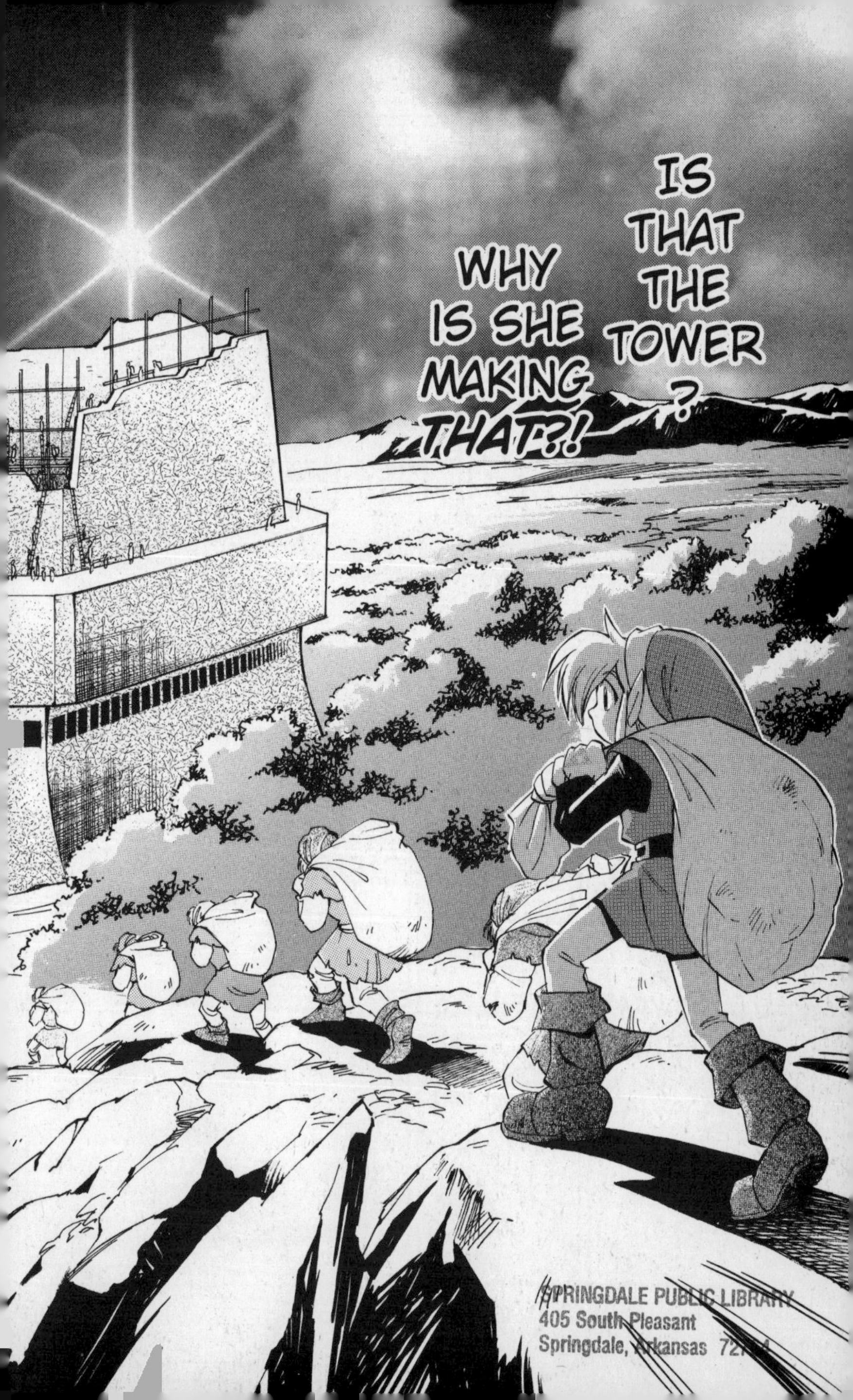
IS THAT THE TOWER?
WHY IS SHE MAKING THAT?!

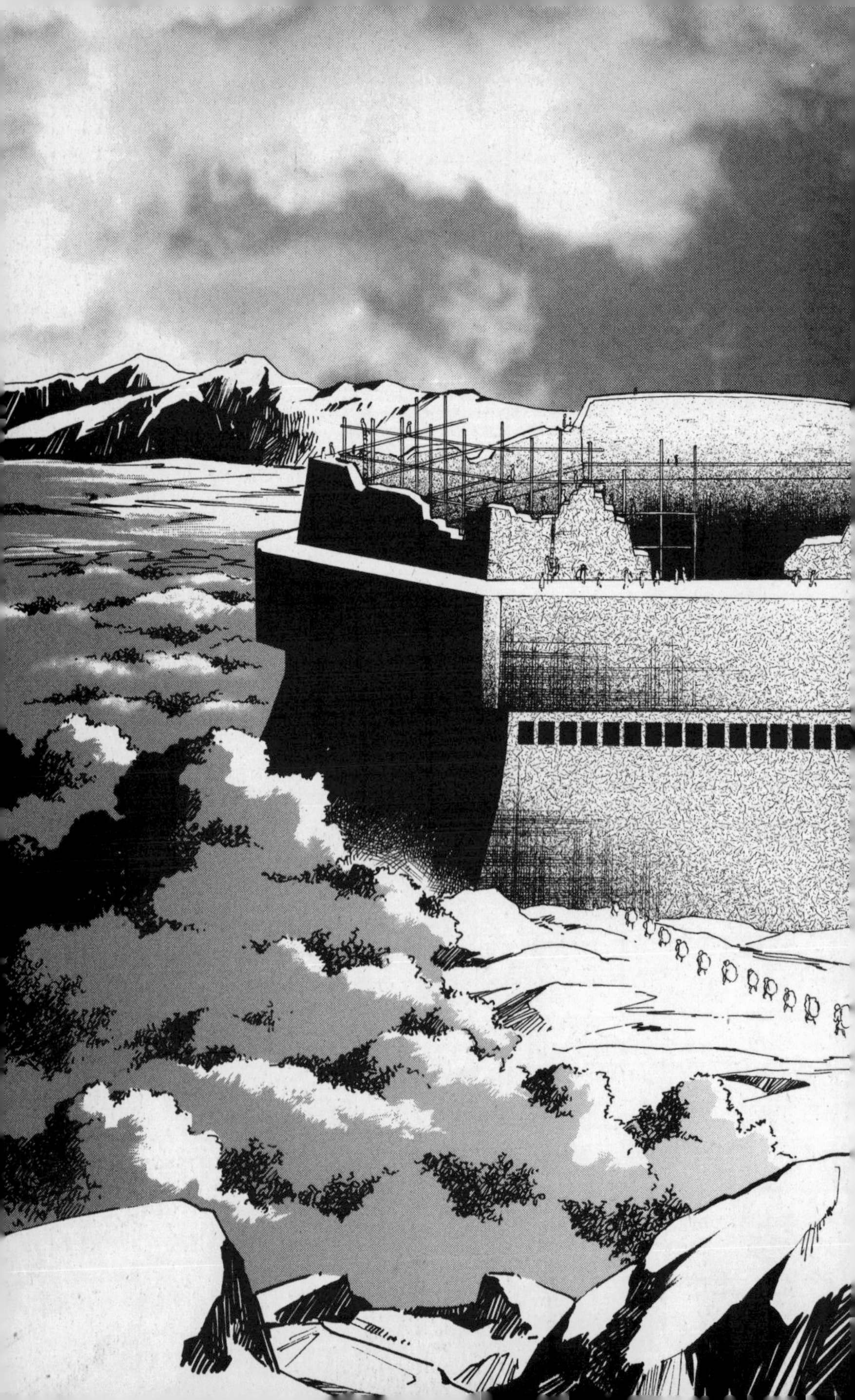

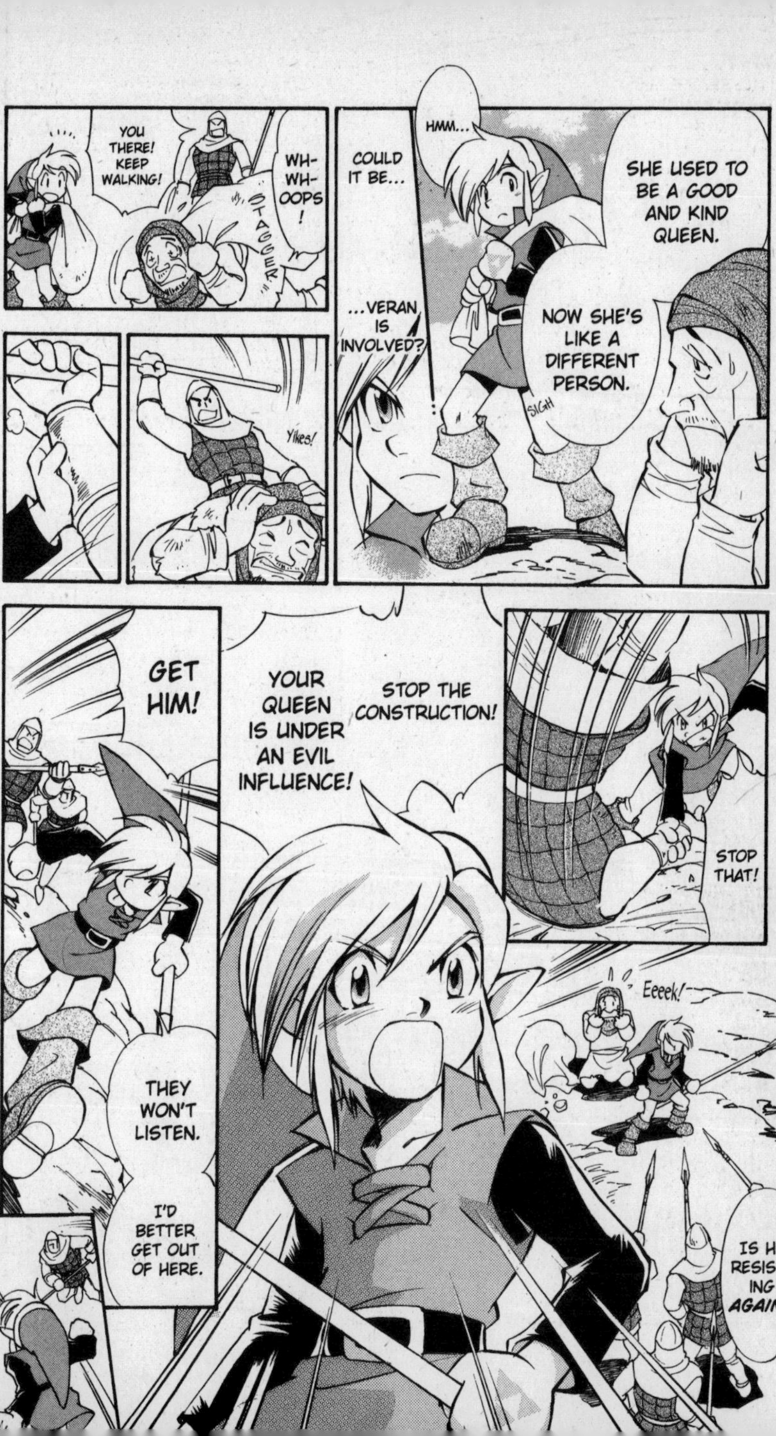
SHE USED TO BE A GOOD AND KIND QUEEN.
HMM...
NOW SHE'S LIKE A DIFFERENT PERSON.
SIGH
COULD IT BE...
...VERAN IS INVOLVED?
WH-WH-OOPS!
STAGGER
YOU THERE! KEEP WALKING!
Yikes!
STOP THAT!
STOP THE CONSTRUCTION!
YOUR QUEEN IS UNDER AN EVIL INFLUENCE!
Eeeek!
IS HE RESIST-ING AGAIN?
GET HIM!
THEY WON'T LISTEN.
I'D BETTER GET OUT OF HERE.

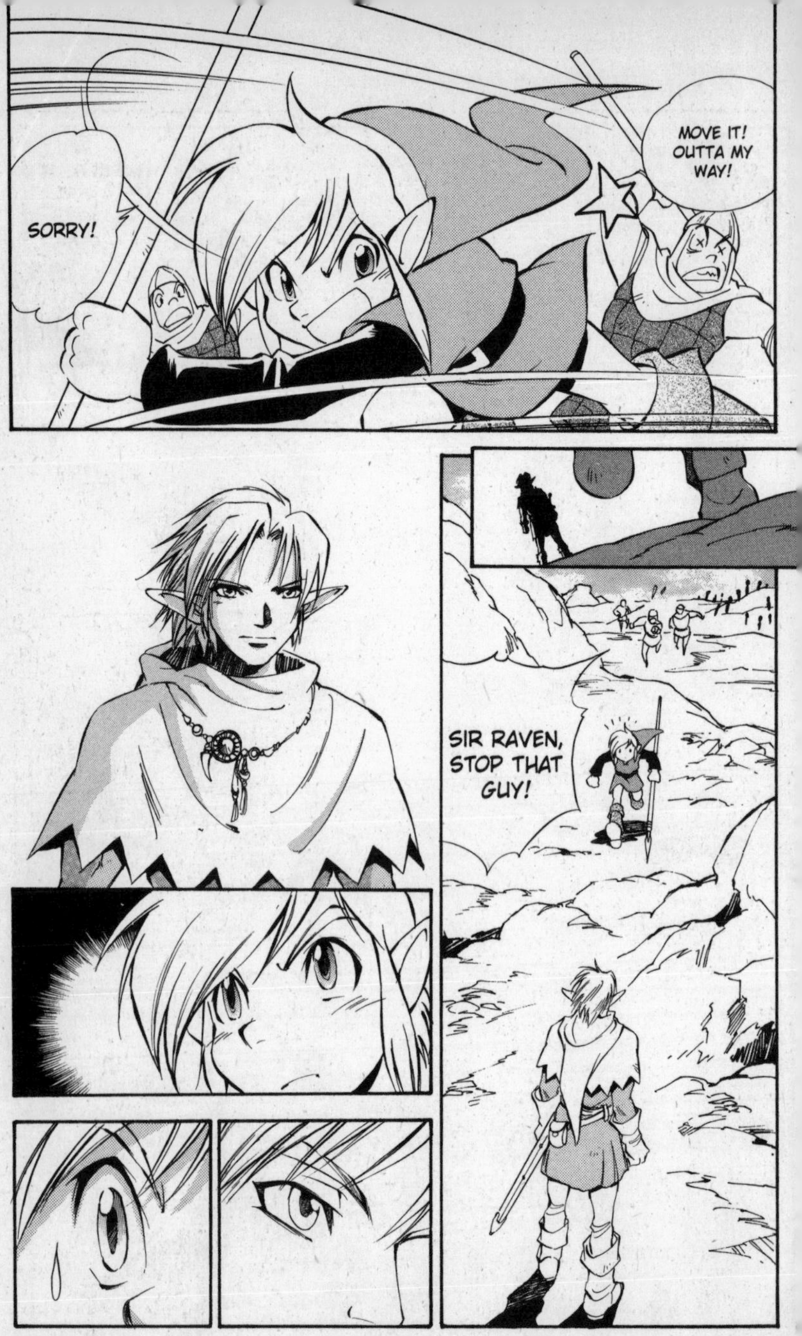
MOVE IT! OUTTA MY WAY!
SORRY!
SIR RAVEN, STOP THAT GUY!

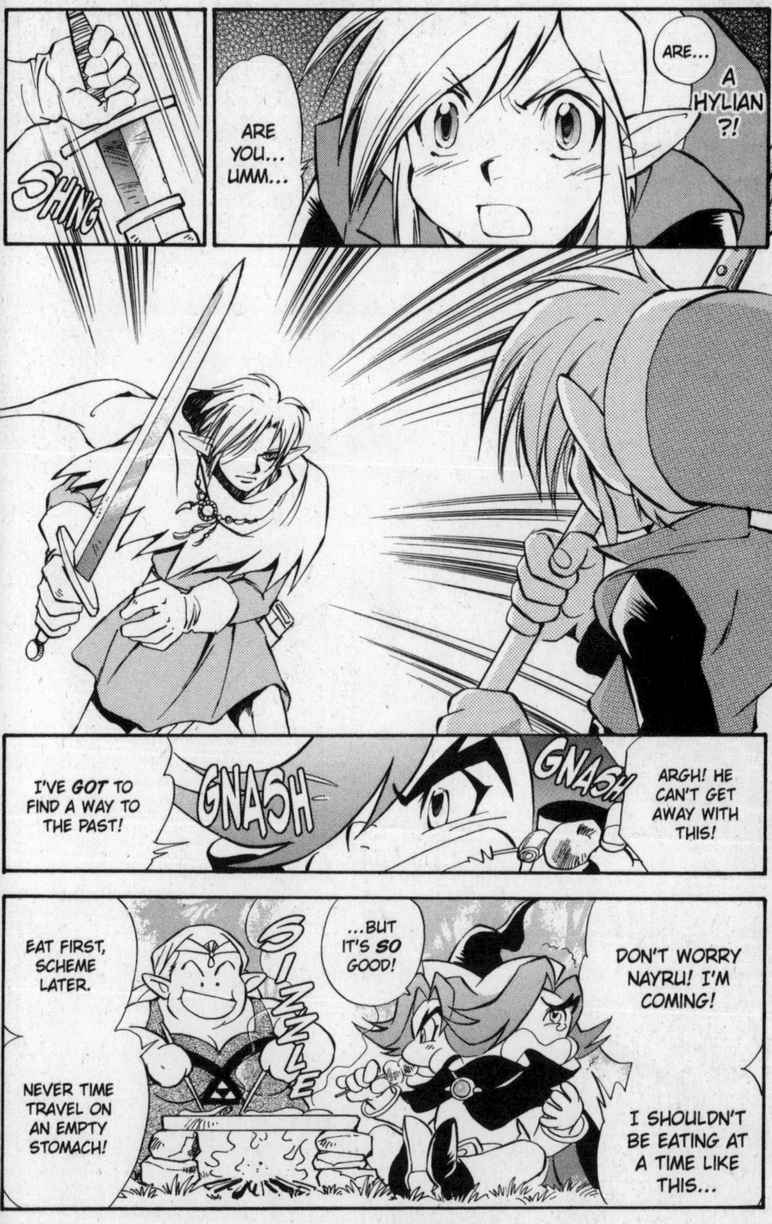
ARE...
A HYLIAN ?!
ARE YOU... UMM...
SHING
ARGH! HE CAN'T GET AWAY WITH THIS!
GNASH
GNASH
I'VE **GOT** TO FIND A WAY TO THE PAST!
DON'T WORRY NAYRU! I'M COMING!
I SHOULDN'T BE EATING AT A TIME LIKE THIS...
...BUT IT'S **SO** GOOD!
SIZZLE
EAT FIRST, SCHEME LATER.
NEVER TIME TRAVEL ON AN EMPTY STOMACH!

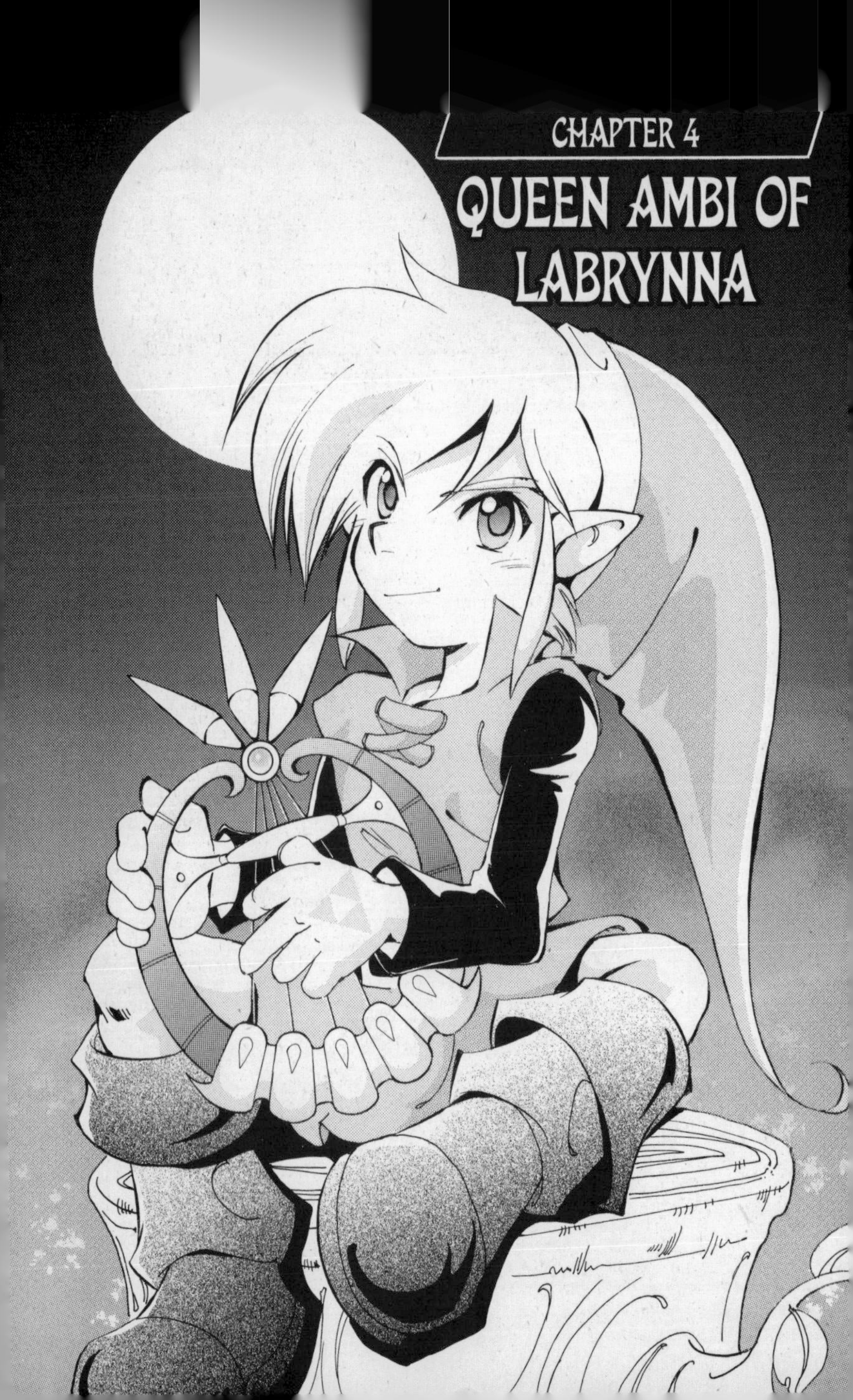
CHAPTER 4
QUEEN AMBI OF LABRYNNA

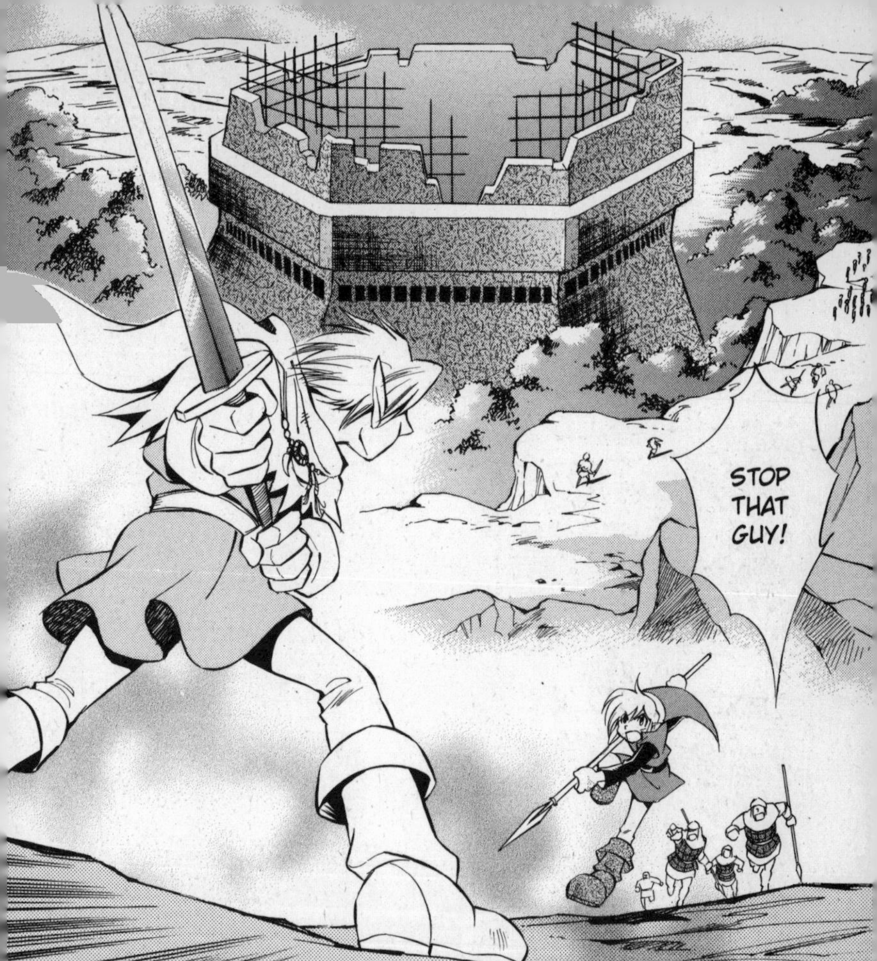
STOP THAT GUY!
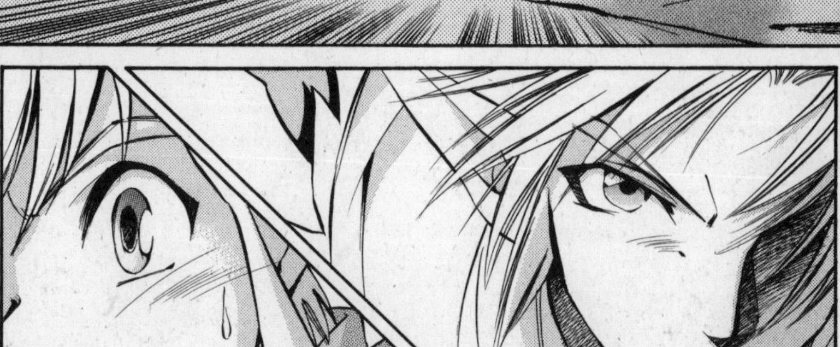

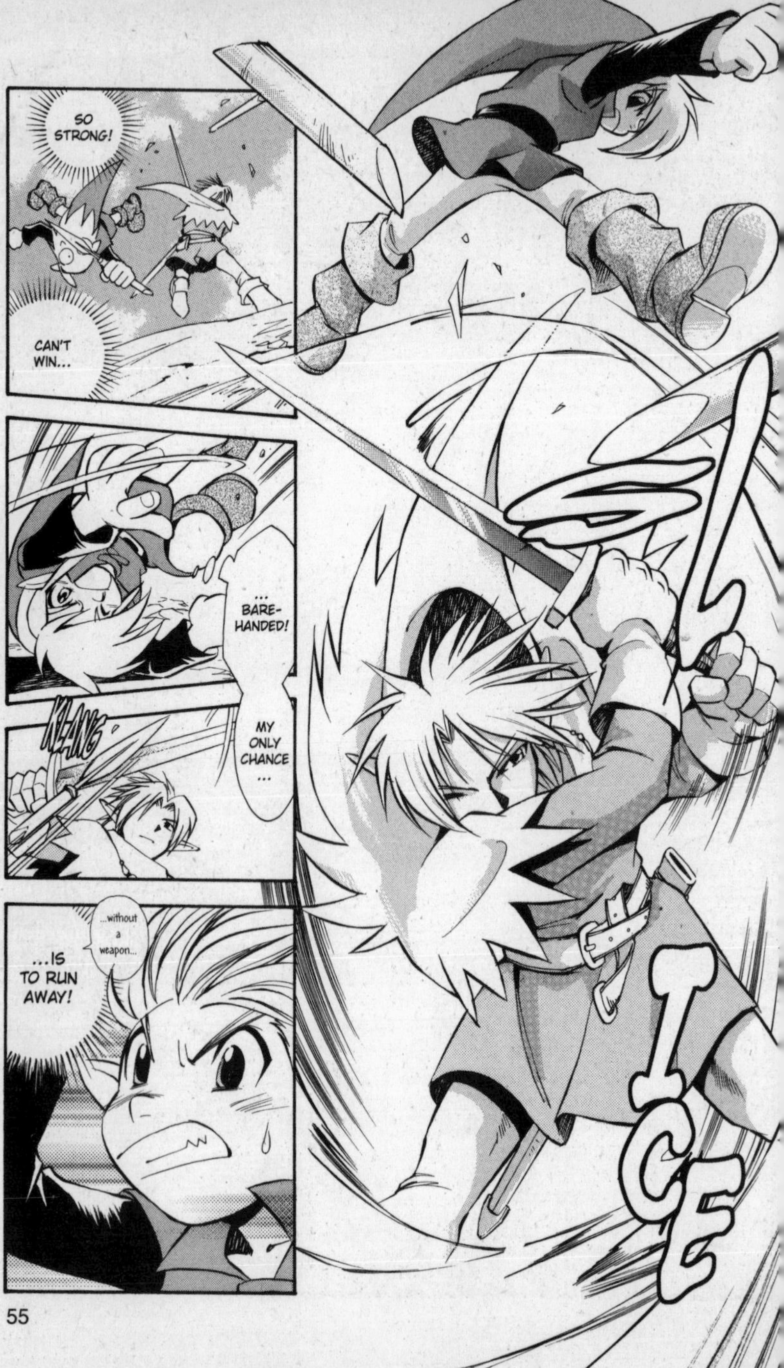
SLICE
SO STRONG!
CAN'T WIN...
...BARE-HANDED!
MY ONLY CHANCE...
KLANG
...without a weapon...
...IS TO RUN AWAY!

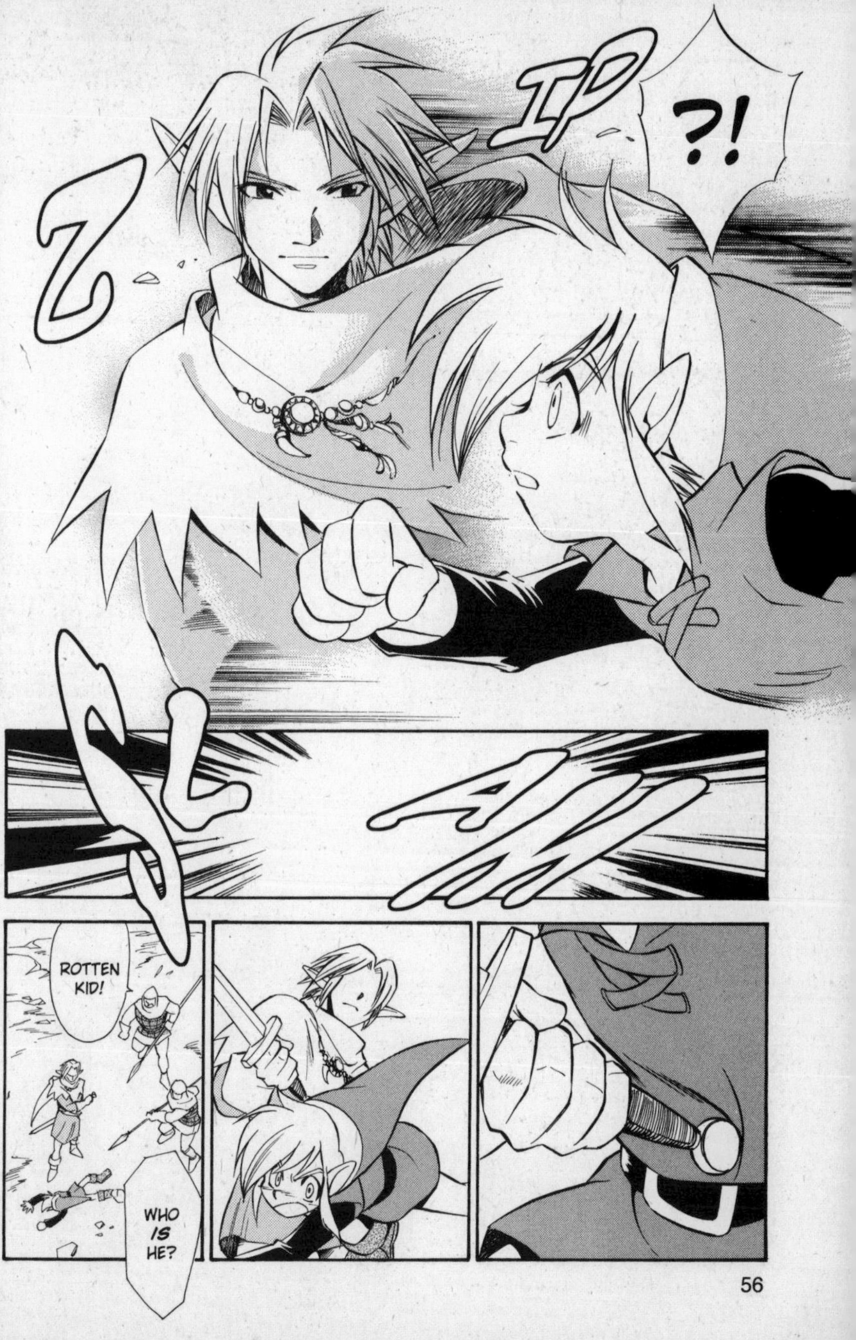
?!
ZIP
SLAM
ROTTEN KID!
WHO *IS* HE?

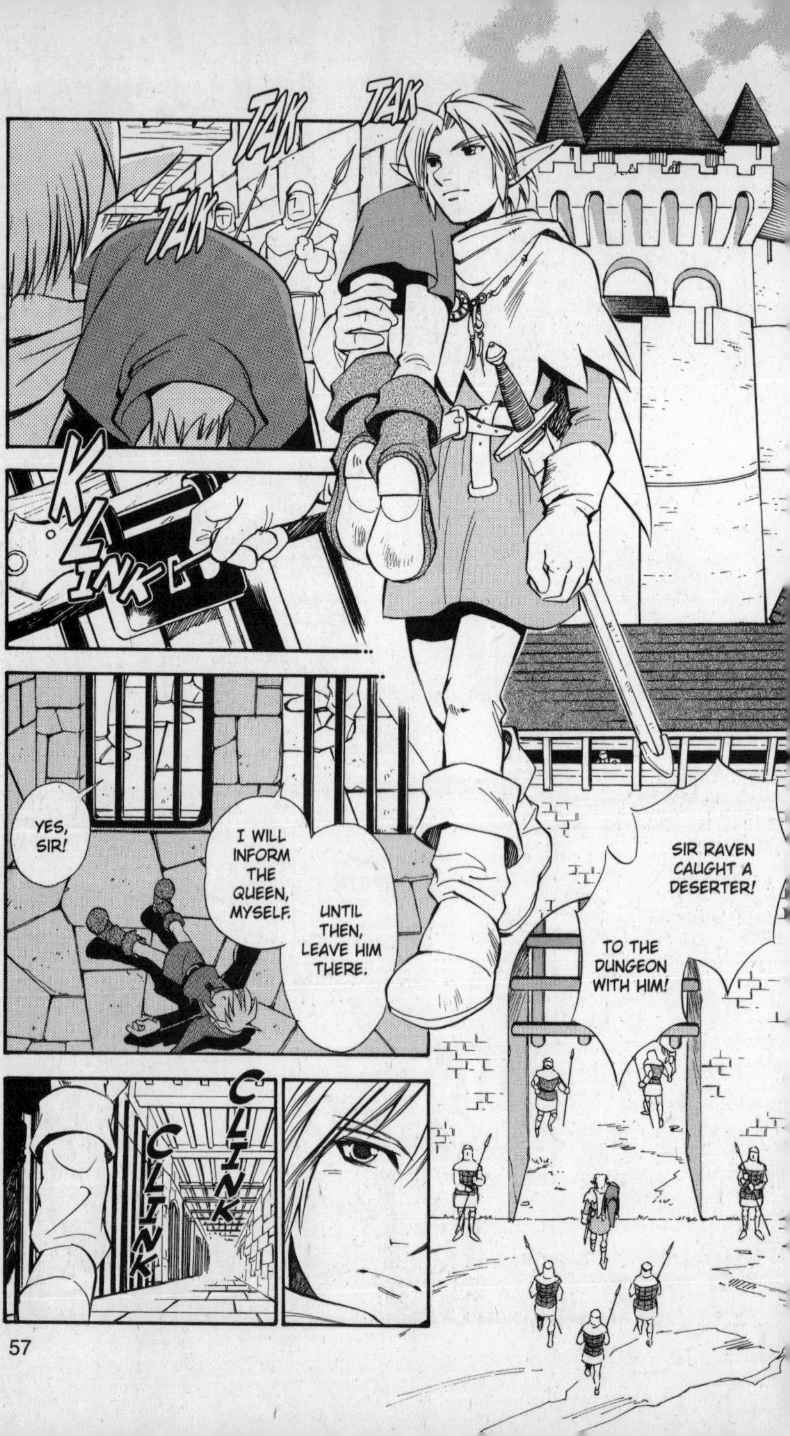
SIR RAVEN CAUGHT A DESERTER!
TO THE DUNGEON WITH HIM!
TAK TAK
TAK
KLINK
I WILL INFORM THE QUEEN, MYSELF.
UNTIL THEN, LEAVE HIM THERE.
YES, SIR!
CLINK
CLINK

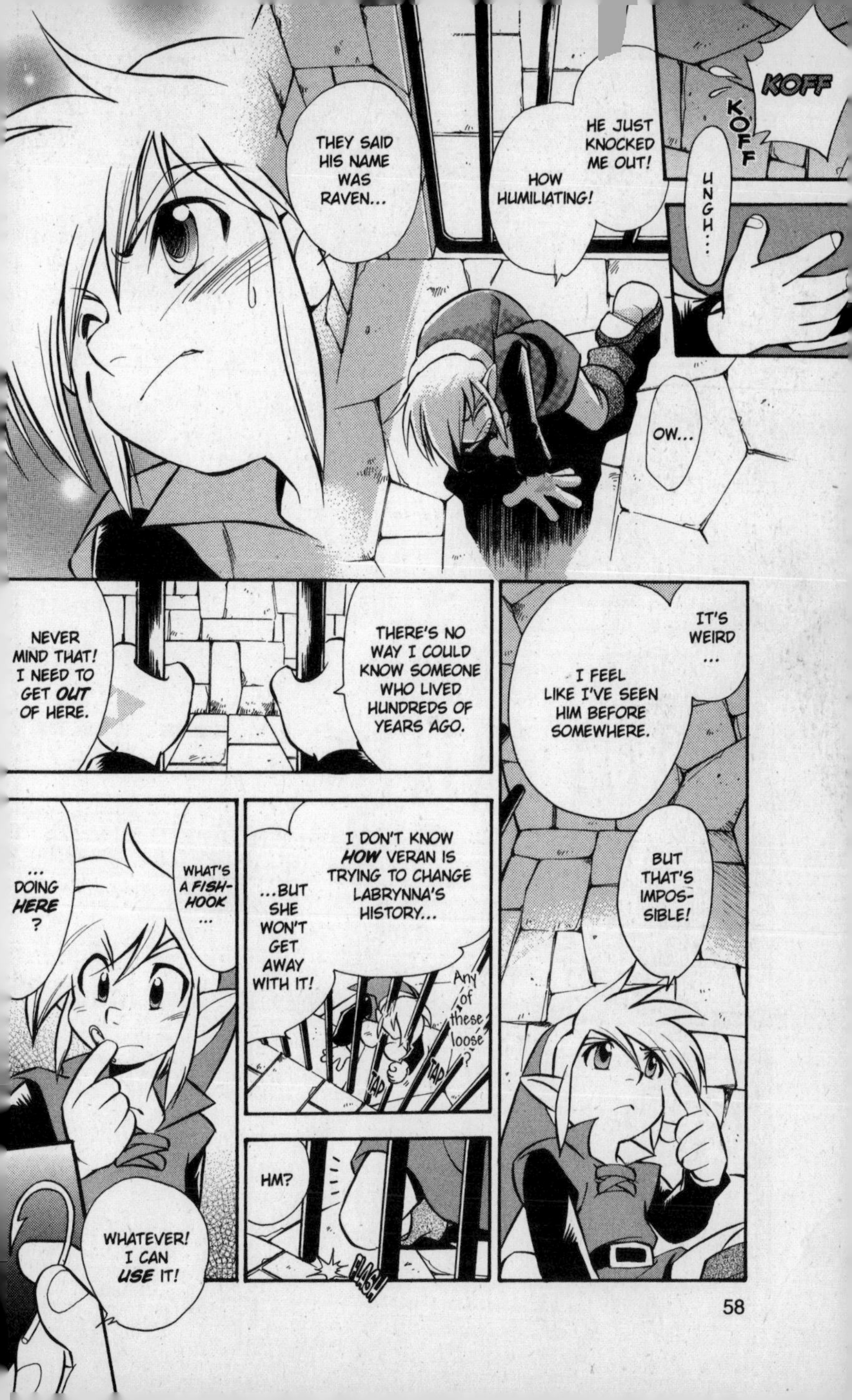
KOFF
KOFF
UNGH...
OW...
HE JUST KNOCKED ME OUT!
HOW HUMILIATING!
THEY SAID HIS NAME WAS RAVEN...
IT'S WEIRD...
I FEEL LIKE I'VE SEEN HIM BEFORE SOMEWHERE.
BUT THAT'S IMPOSSIBLE!
THERE'S NO WAY I COULD KNOW SOMEONE WHO LIVED HUNDREDS OF YEARS AGO.
NEVER MIND THAT! I NEED TO GET OUT OF HERE.
I DON'T KNOW HOW VERAN IS TRYING TO CHANGE LABRYNNA'S HISTORY...
...BUT SHE WON'T GET AWAY WITH IT!
Any of these loose?
TAP
TAP
HM?
FLASH
WHAT'S A FISH-HOOK...
...DOING HERE?
WHATEVER! I CAN USE IT!

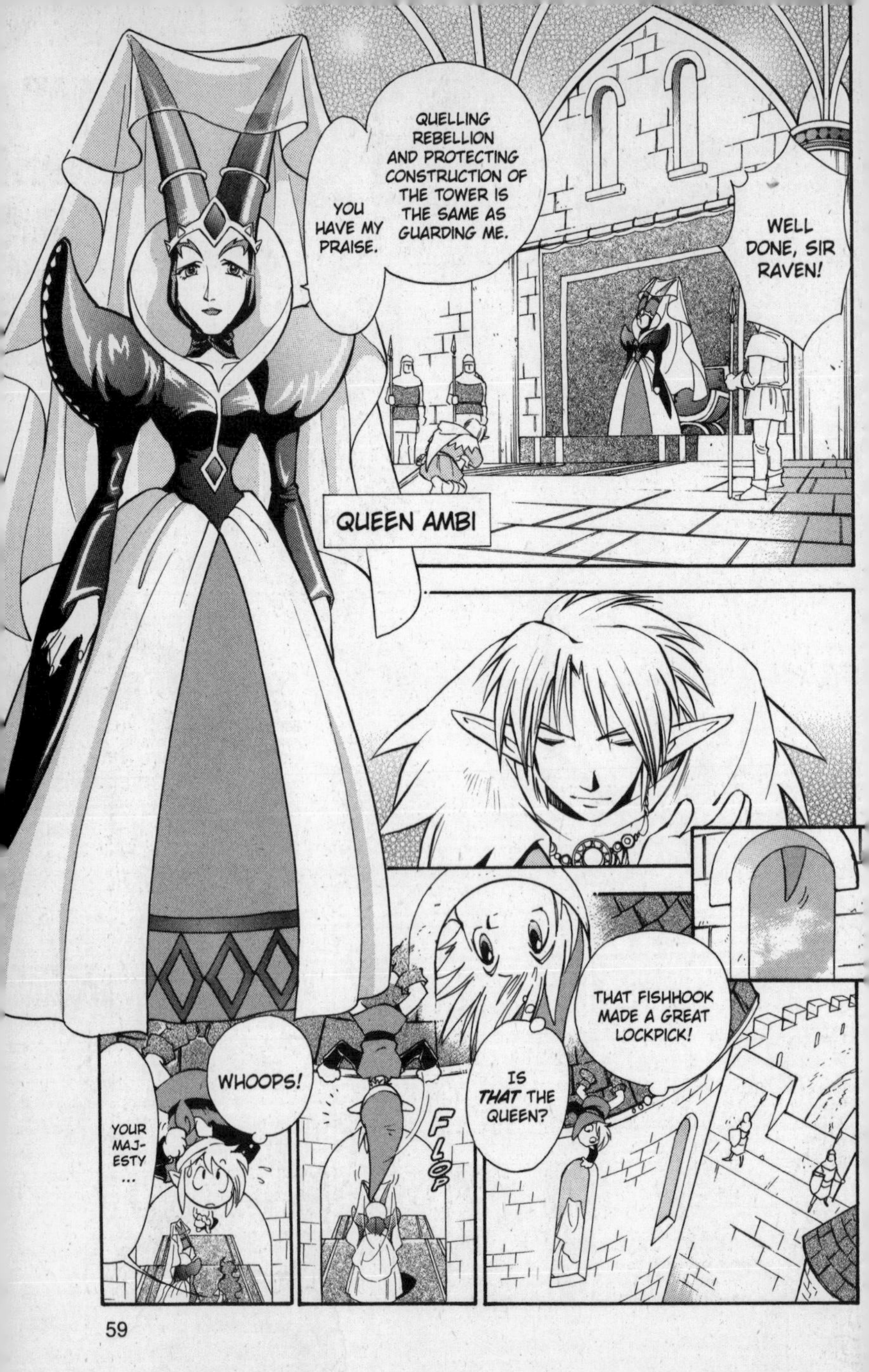
WELL DONE, SIR RAVEN!
QUEEN AMBI
YOU HAVE MY PRAISE. QUELLING REBELLION AND PROTECTING CONSTRUCTION OF THE TOWER IS THE SAME AS GUARDING ME.
THAT FISHHOOK MADE A GREAT LOCKPICK!
IS *THAT* THE QUEEN?
FLOP
WHOOPS!
YOUR MAJ-ESTY ...

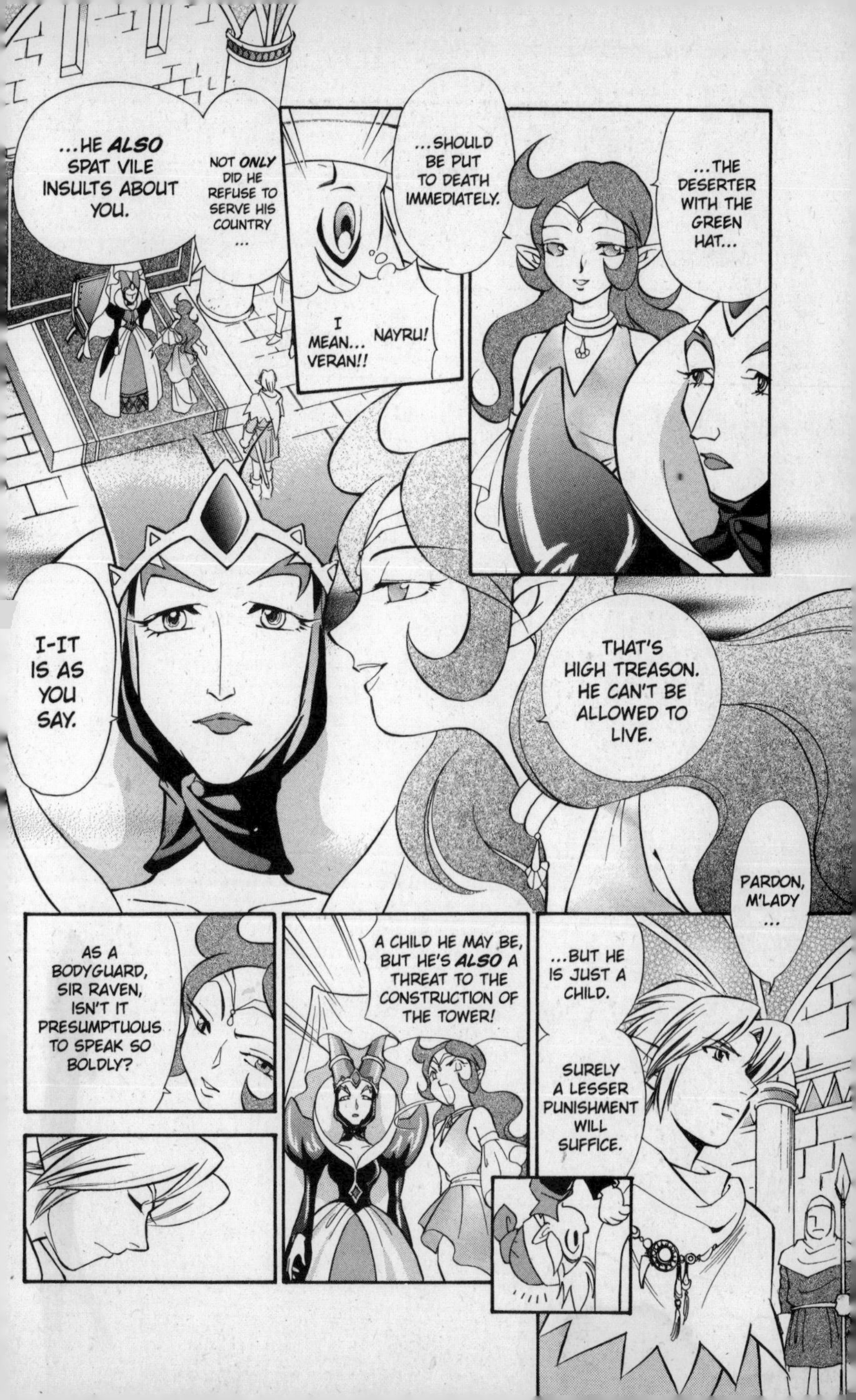
...THE DESERTER WITH THE GREEN HAT...
...SHOULD BE PUT TO DEATH IMMEDIATELY.
NAYRU!
I MEAN... VERAN!!
NOT ONLY DID HE REFUSE TO SERVE HIS COUNTRY...
...HE ALSO SPAT VILE INSULTS ABOUT YOU.
THAT'S HIGH TREASON. HE CAN'T BE ALLOWED TO LIVE.
I-IT IS AS YOU SAY.
PARDON, M'LADY...
...BUT HE IS JUST A CHILD.
SURELY A LESSER PUNISHMENT WILL SUFFICE.
A CHILD HE MAY BE, BUT HE'S ALSO A THREAT TO THE CONSTRUCTION OF THE TOWER!
AS A BODYGUARD, SIR RAVEN, ISN'T IT PRESUMPTUOUS TO SPEAK SO BOLDLY?

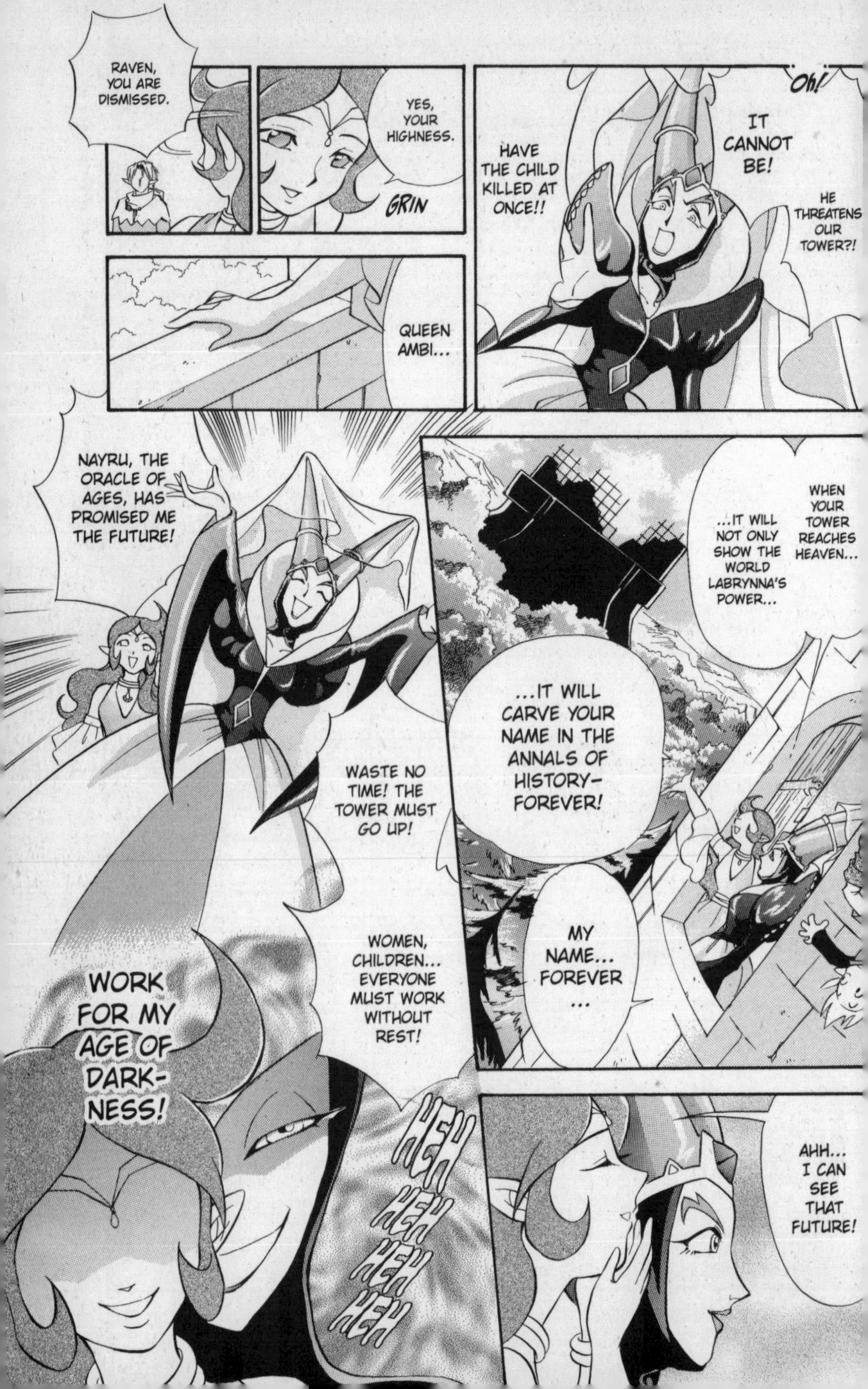
Oh!
IT CANNOT BE!
HE THREATENS OUR TOWER?!
HAVE THE CHILD KILLED AT ONCE!!
YES, YOUR HIGHNESS.
GRIN
RAVEN, YOU ARE DISMISSED.
QUEEN AMBI...
WHEN YOUR TOWER REACHES HEAVEN...
...IT WILL NOT ONLY SHOW THE WORLD LABRYNNA'S POWER...
...IT WILL CARVE YOUR NAME IN THE ANNALS OF HISTORY—FOREVER!
MY NAME... FOREVER ...
AHH... I CAN SEE THAT FUTURE!
NAYRU, THE ORACLE OF AGES, HAS PROMISED ME THE FUTURE!
WASTE NO TIME! THE TOWER MUST GO UP!
WOMEN, CHILDREN... EVERYONE MUST WORK WITHOUT REST!
WORK FOR MY AGE OF DARK-NESS!
HEH HEH HEH HEH HEH

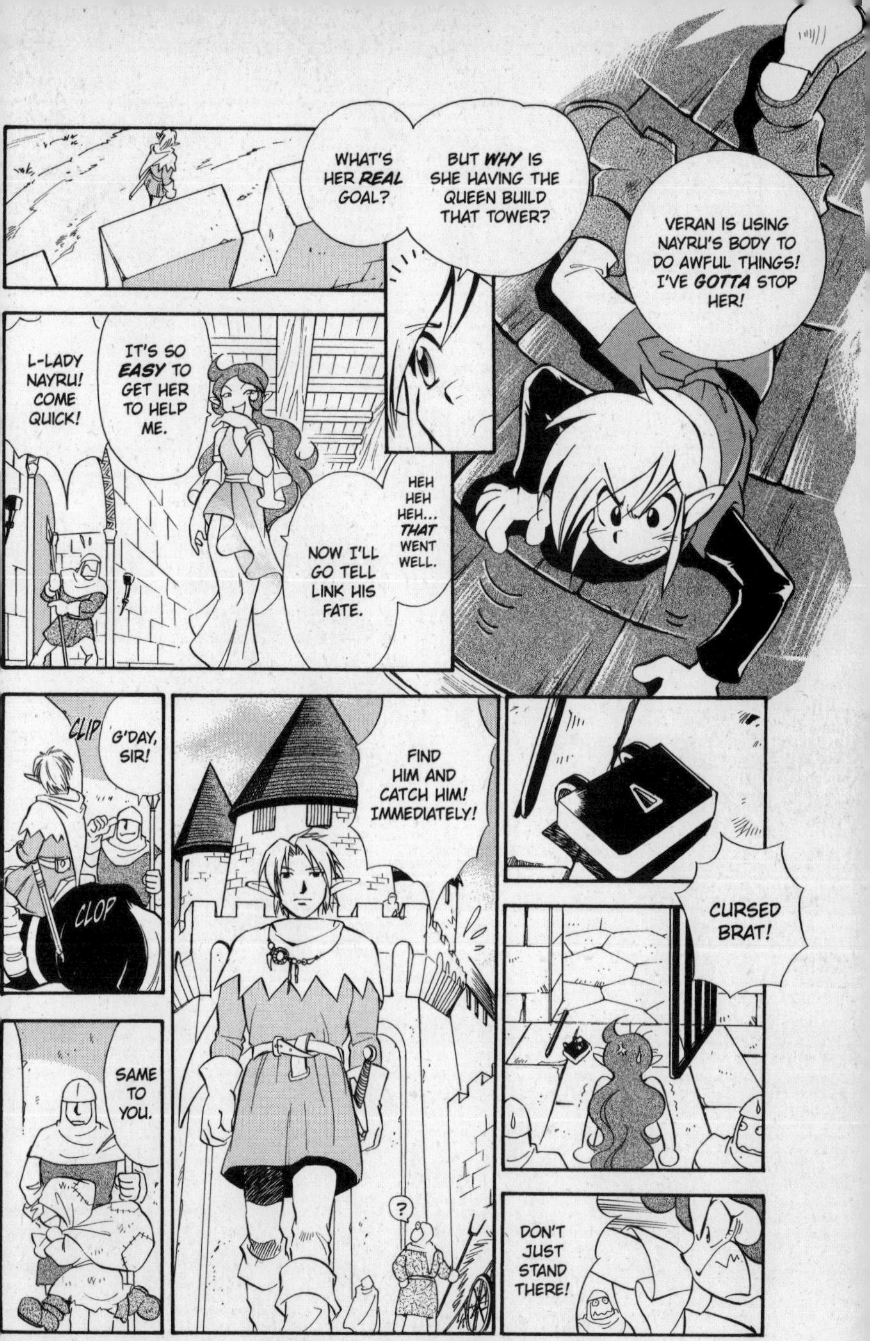
VERAN IS USING NAYRU'S BODY TO DO AWFUL THINGS! I'VE GOTTA STOP HER!
BUT WHY IS SHE HAVING THE QUEEN BUILD THAT TOWER?
WHAT'S HER REAL GOAL?
HEH HEH HEH... THAT WENT WELL.
NOW I'LL GO TELL LINK HIS FATE.
IT'S SO EASY TO GET HER TO HELP ME.
L-LADY NAYRU! COME QUICK!
CURSED BRAT!
DON'T JUST STAND THERE!
FIND HIM AND CATCH HIM! IMMEDIATELY!
?
CLIP
G'DAY, SIR!
CLOP
SAME TO YOU.

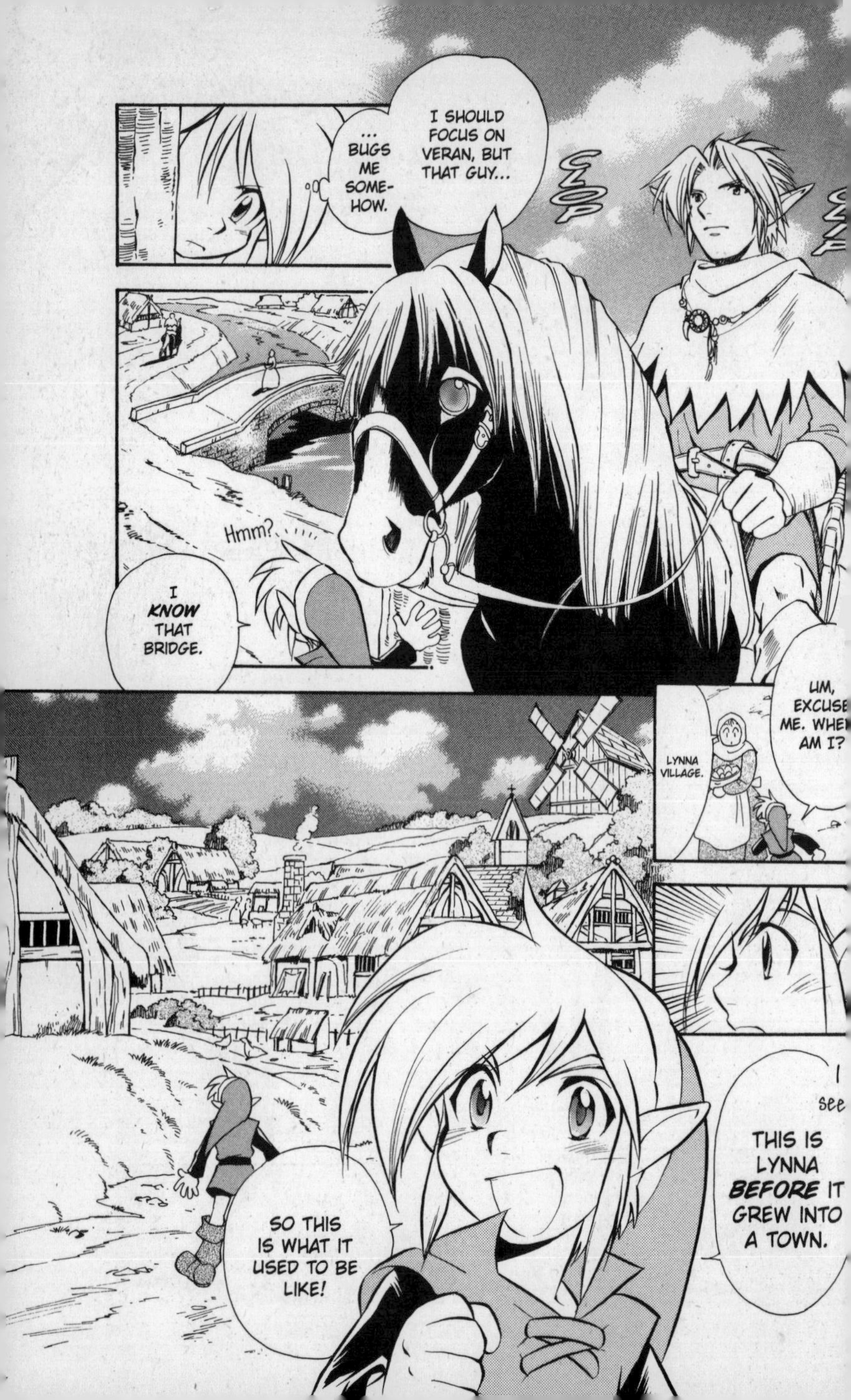

CLOP
I SHOULD FOCUS ON VERAN, BUT THAT GUY...
... BUGS ME SOME-HOW.
Hmm?
I *KNOW* THAT BRIDGE.
UM, EXCUSE ME. WHE AM I?
LYNNA VILLAGE.
I see
THIS IS LYNNA *BEFORE* IT GREW INTO A TOWN.
SO THIS IS WHAT IT USED TO BE LIKE!

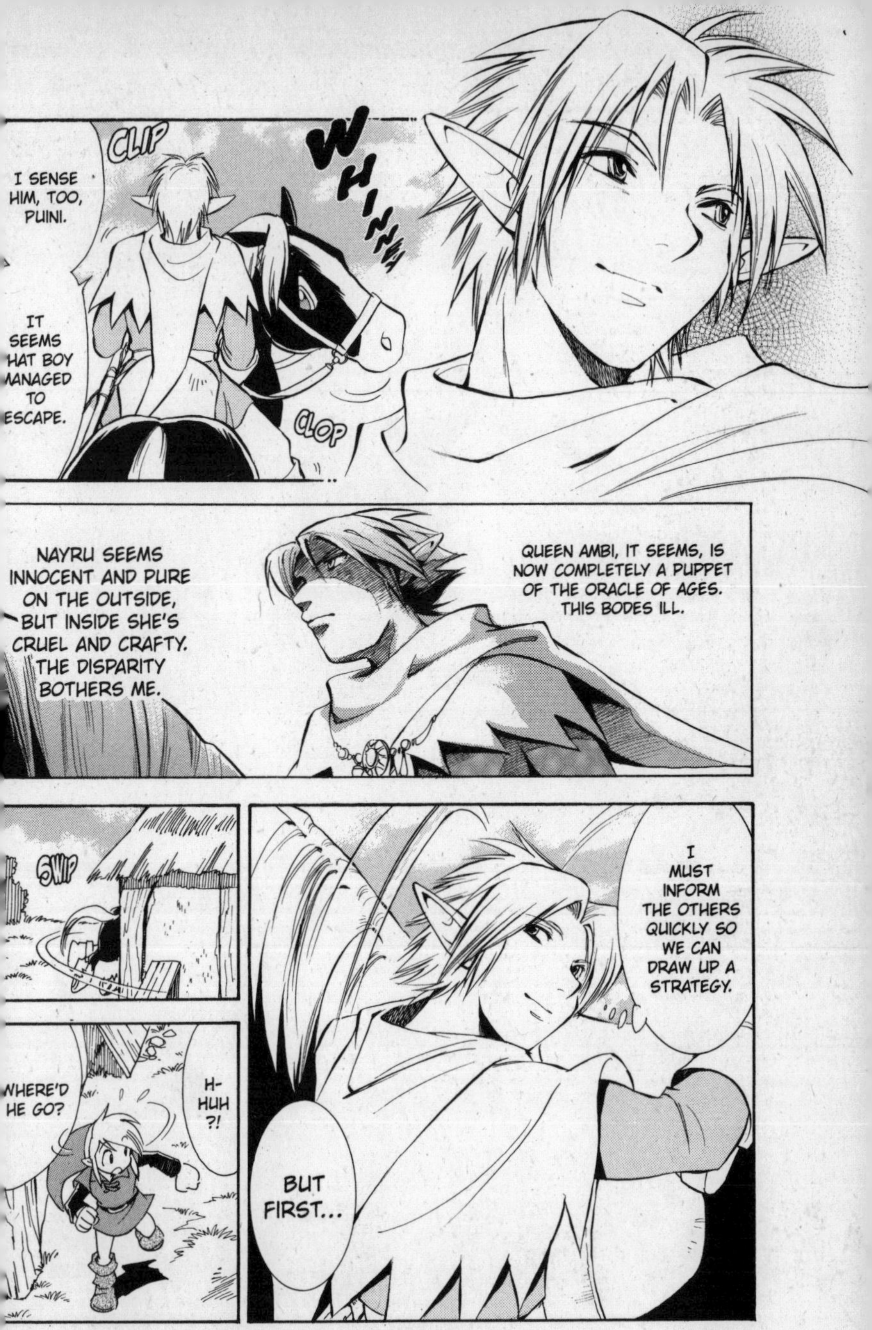
WHINNY
CLIP
I SENSE HIM, TOO, PUINI.
CLOP
IT SEEMS HAT BOY MANAGED TO ESCAPE.
QUEEN AMBI, IT SEEMS, IS NOW COMPLETELY A PUPPET OF THE ORACLE OF AGES. THIS BODES ILL.
NAYRU SEEMS INNOCENT AND PURE ON THE OUTSIDE, BUT INSIDE SHE'S CRUEL AND CRAFTY. THE DISPARITY BOTHERS ME.
I MUST INFORM THE OTHERS QUICKLY SO WE CAN DRAW UP A STRATEGY.
BUT FIRST...
SWIP
H-HUH?!
WHERE'D HE GO?

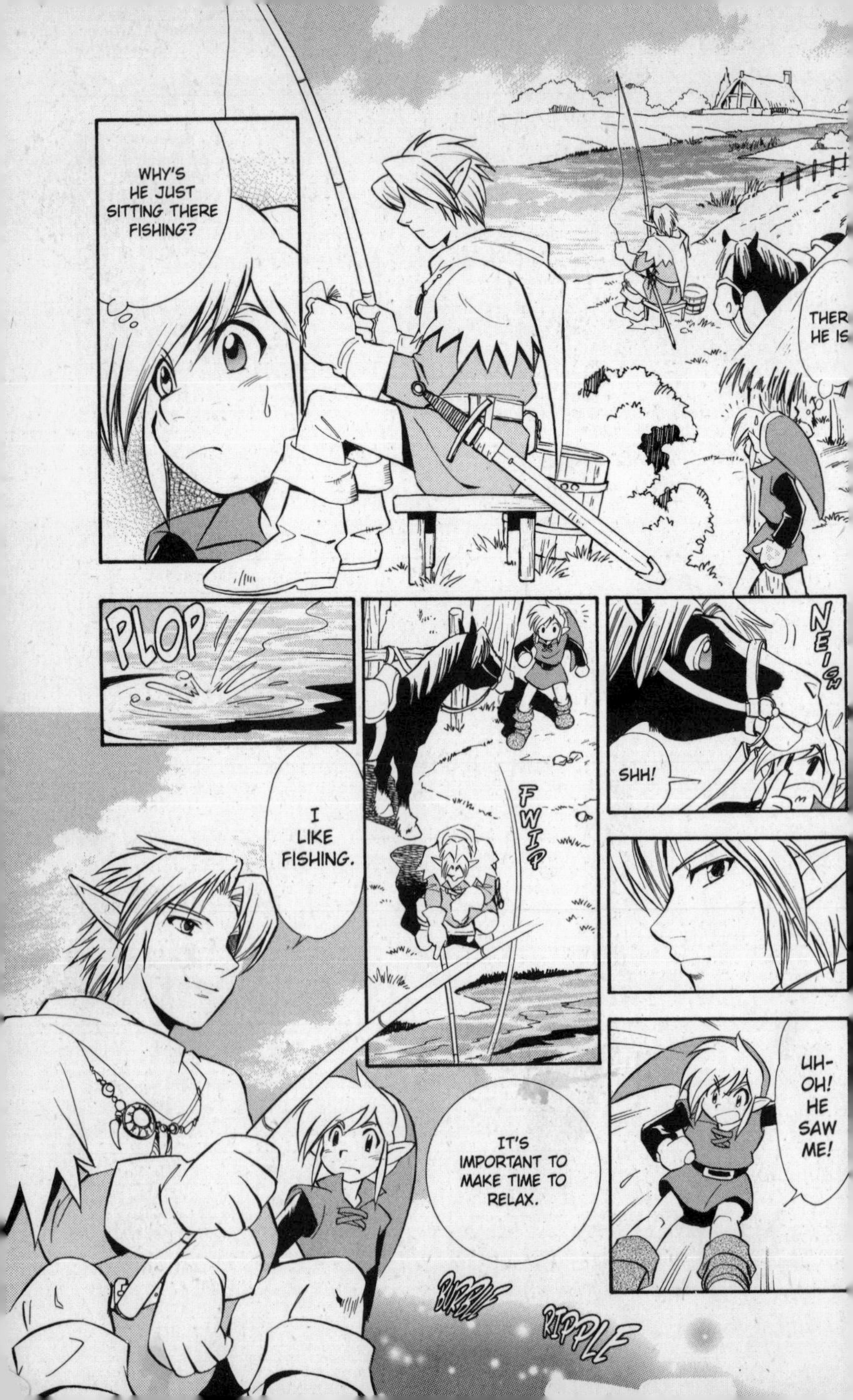
THER HE IS
WHY'S HE JUST SITTING THERE FISHING?
NEIGH
SHH!
UH-OH! HE SAW ME!
FWIP
PLOP
I LIKE FISHING.
IT'S IMPORTANT TO MAKE TIME TO RELAX.
BUBBLE
RIPPLE

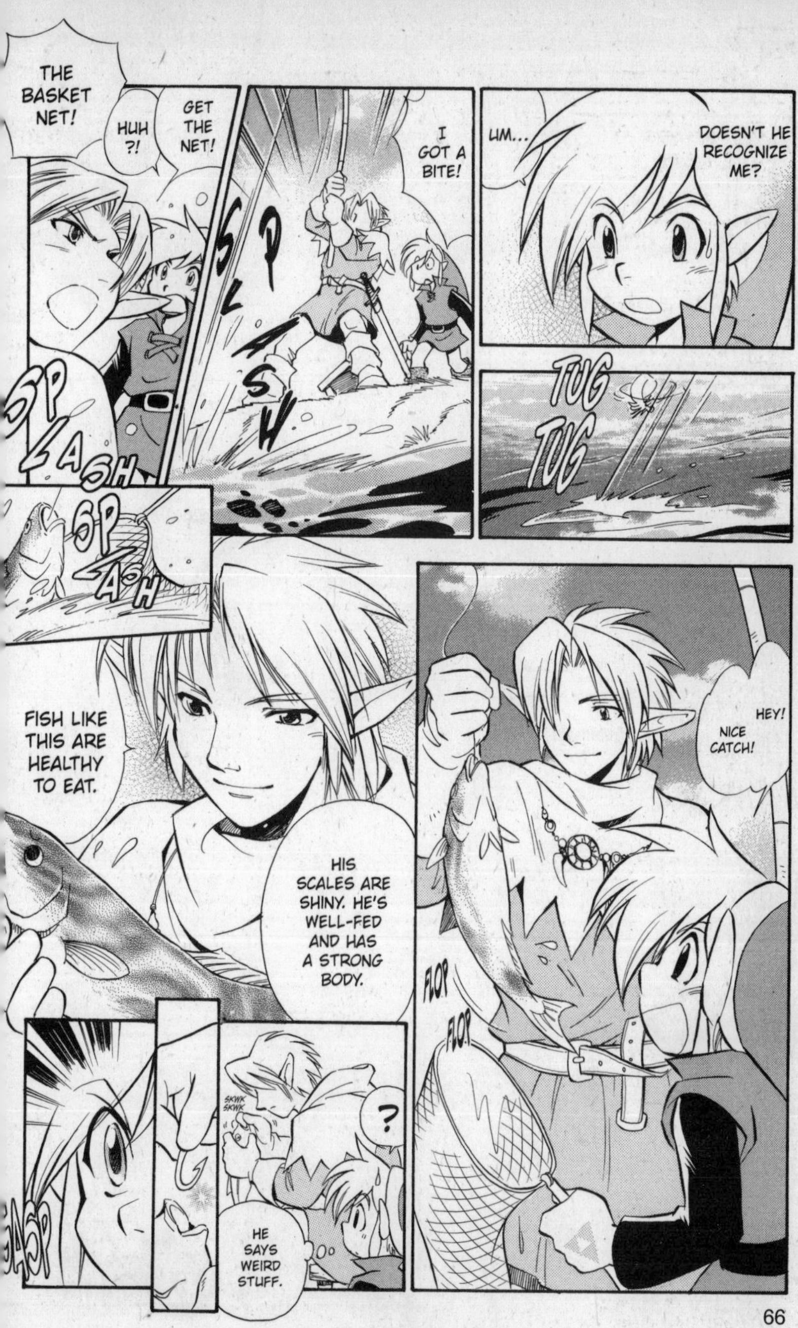
DOESN'T HE RECOGNIZE ME?
UM...
TUG TUG
I GOT A BITE!
SPLASH
GET THE NET!
HUH ?!
THE BASKET NET!
SPLASH
SPLASH
HEY! NICE CATCH!
FLOP FLOP
FISH LIKE THIS ARE HEALTHY TO EAT.
HIS SCALES ARE SHINY. HE'S WELL-FED AND HAS A STRONG BODY.
?
SKWK SKWK
HE SAYS WEIRD STUFF.
GASP

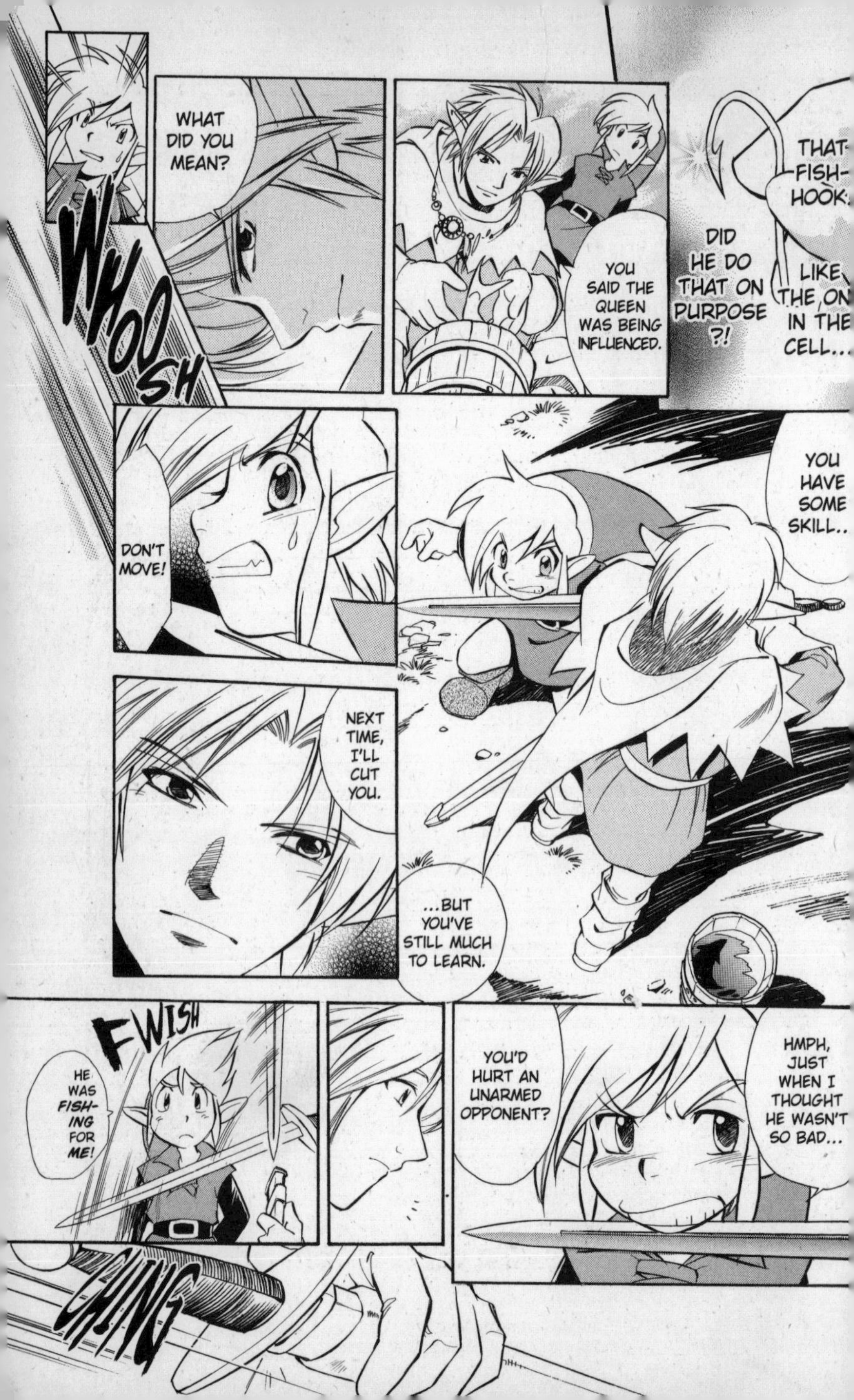
THAT FISH-HOOK!
LIKE THE ONE IN THE CELL...
DID HE DO THAT ON PURPOSE?!
YOU SAID THE QUEEN WAS BEING INFLUENCED.
WHAT DID YOU MEAN?
WHOOSH
YOU HAVE SOME SKILL...
...BUT YOU'VE STILL MUCH TO LEARN.
DON'T MOVE!
NEXT TIME, I'LL CUT YOU.
HMPH, JUST WHEN I THOUGHT HE WASN'T SO BAD...
YOU'D HURT AN UNARMED OPPONENT?
...
FWISH
HE WAS *FISHING* FOR *ME*!
CHING

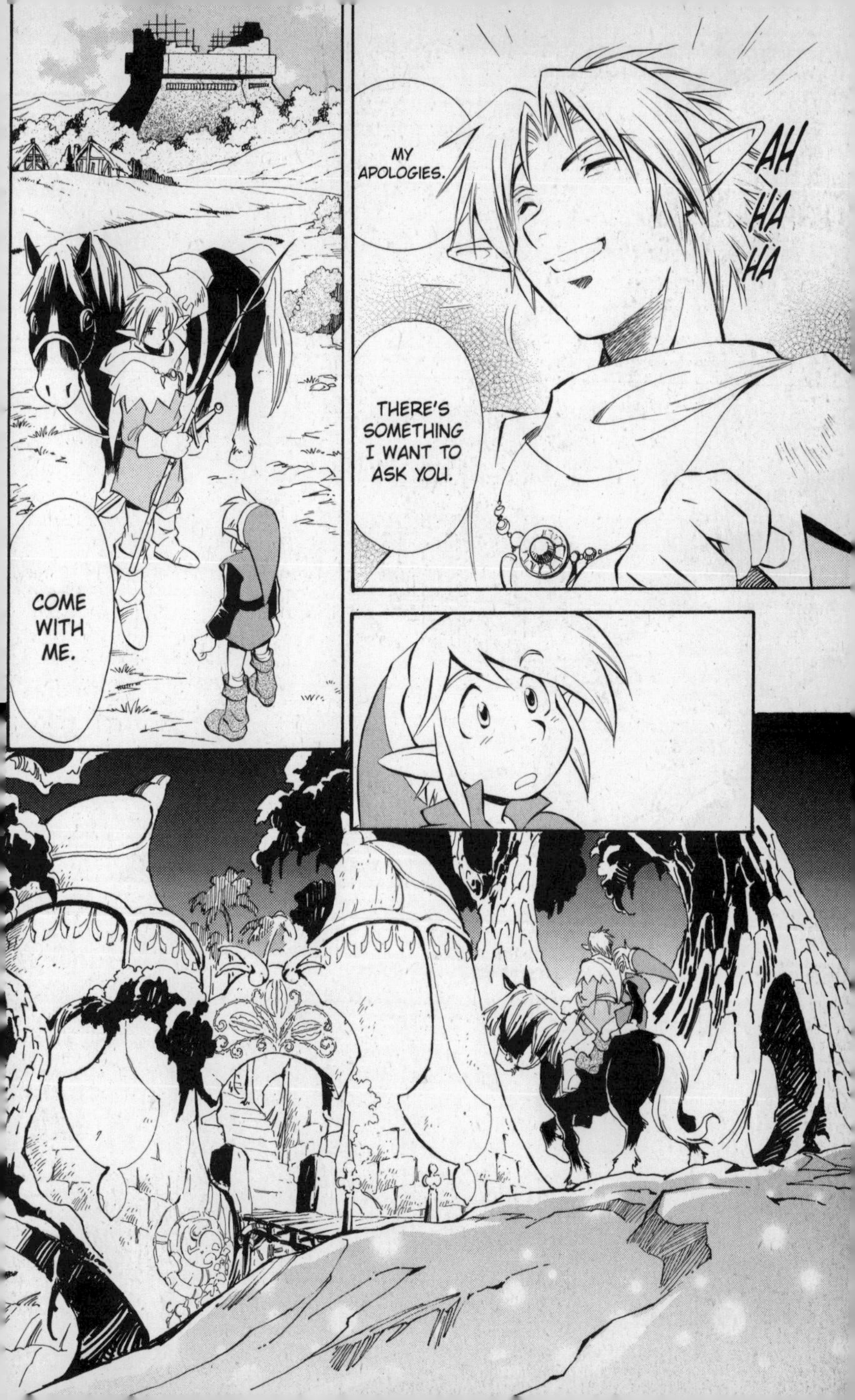
AH HA HA HA
MY APOLOGIES.
THERE'S SOMETHING I WANT TO ASK YOU.
COME WITH ME.

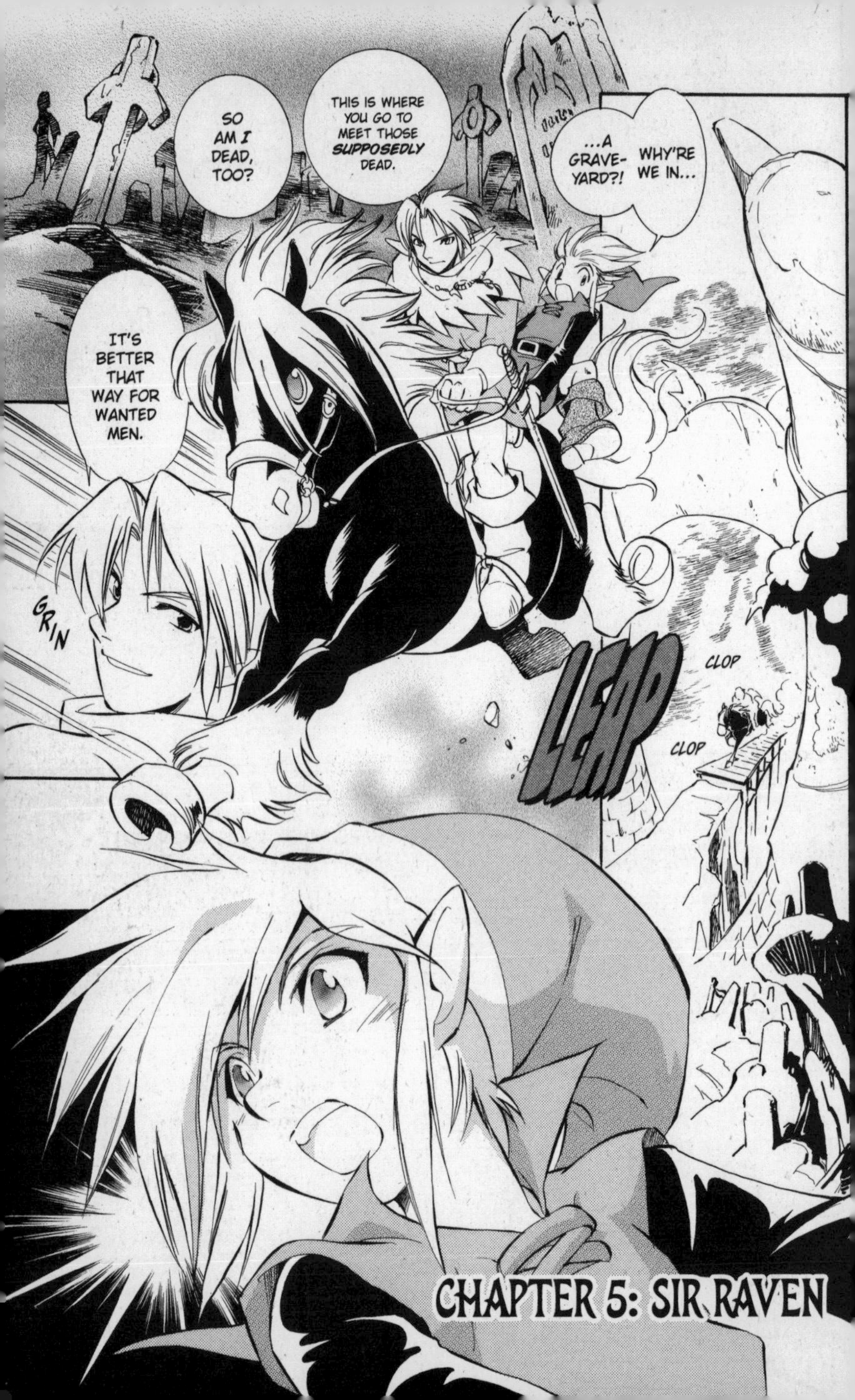
WHY'RE WE IN... ...A GRAVE-YARD?!
THIS IS WHERE YOU GO TO MEET THOSE SUPPOSEDLY DEAD.
SO AM I DEAD, TOO?
CLOP
CLOP
LEAP
IT'S BETTER THAT WAY FOR WANTED MEN.
GRIN
CHAPTER 5: SIR RAVEN

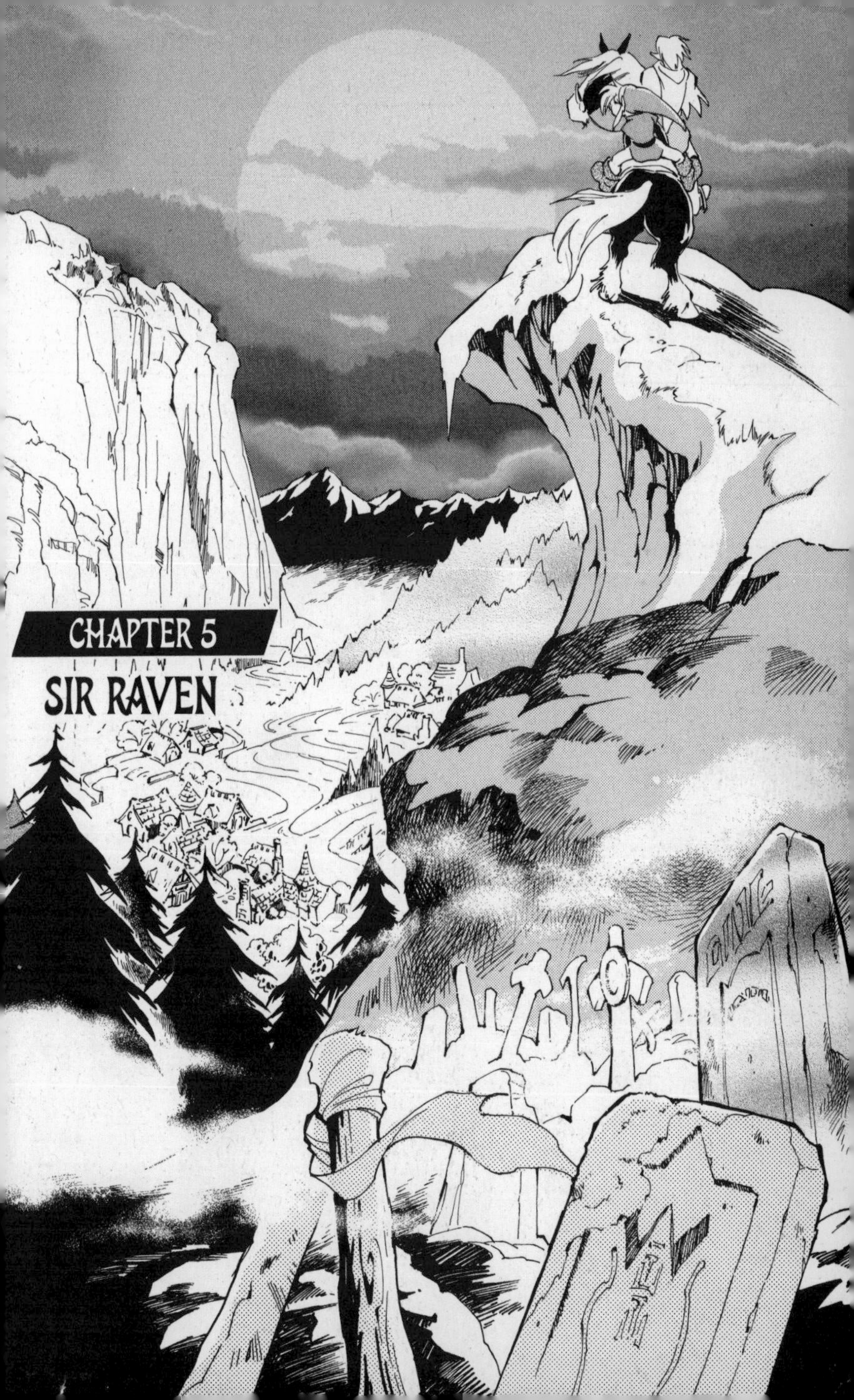
CHAPTER 5
SIR RAVEN

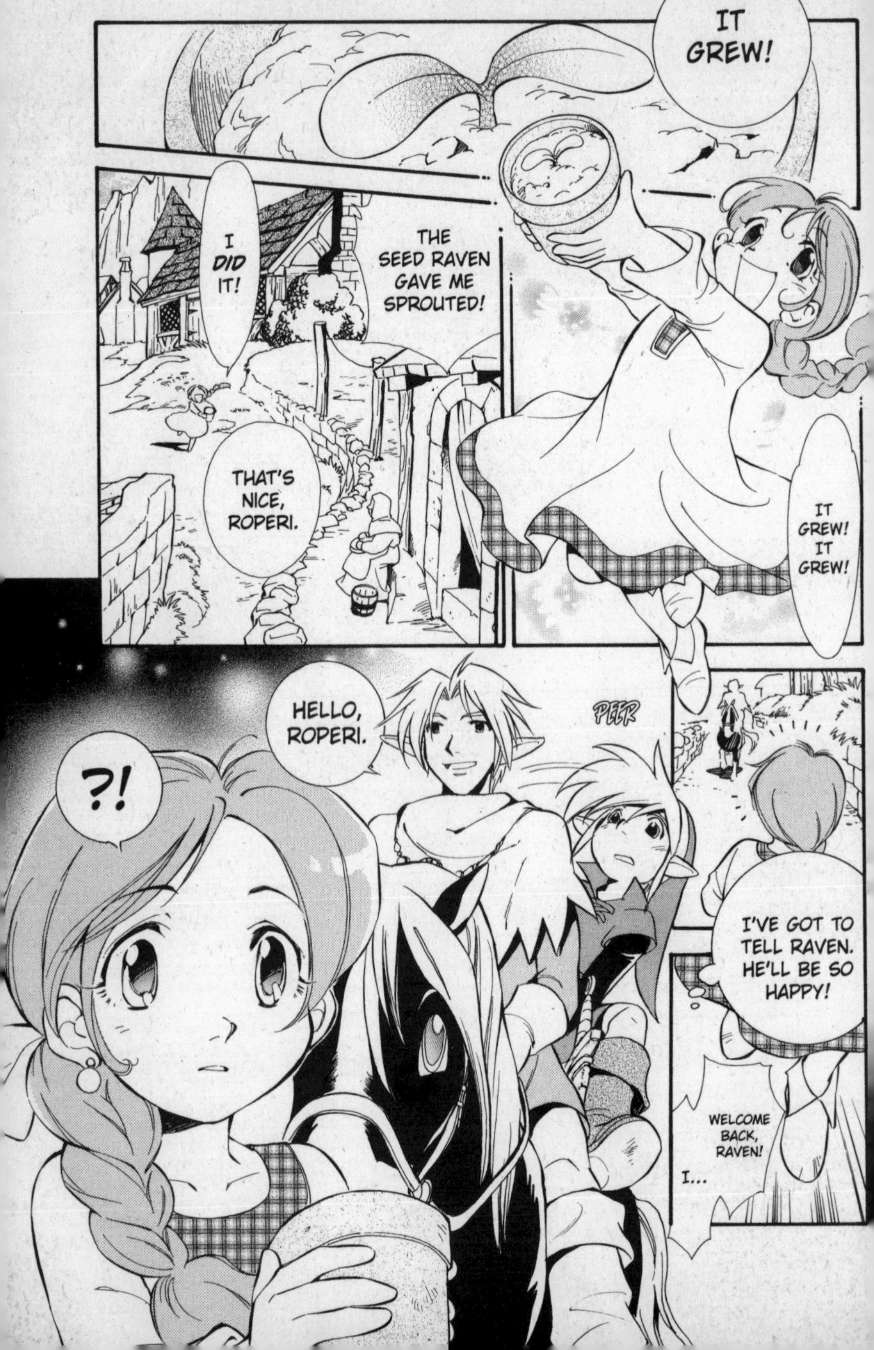
IT GREW!
IT GREW! IT GREW!
THE SEED RAVEN GAVE ME SPROUTED!
I DID IT!
THAT'S NICE, ROPERI.
I'VE GOT TO TELL RAVEN. HE'LL BE SO HAPPY!
WELCOME BACK, RAVEN!
I...
PEER
HELLO, ROPERI.
?!

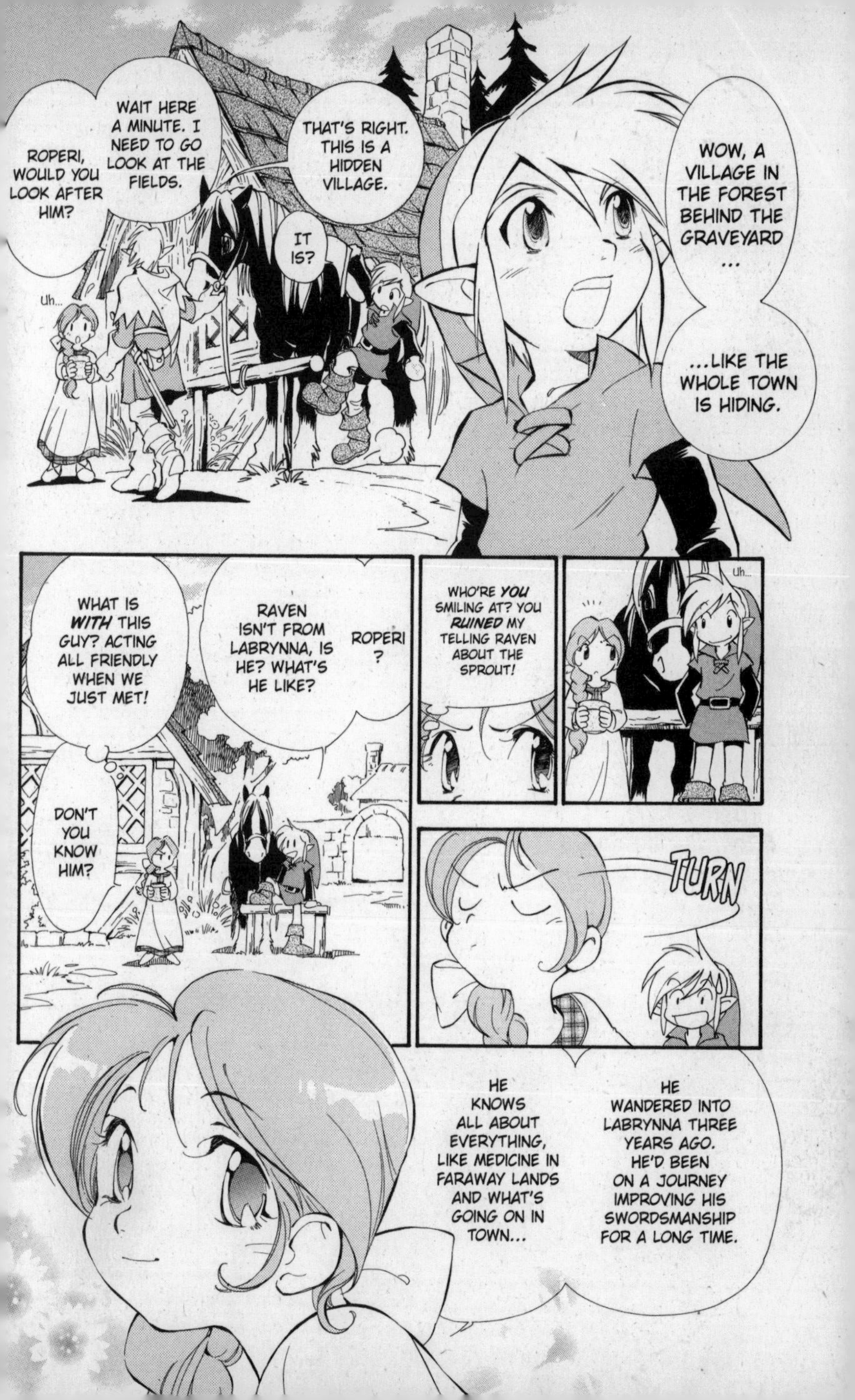
WOW, A VILLAGE IN THE FOREST BEHIND THE GRAVEYARD ...
...LIKE THE WHOLE TOWN IS HIDING.
THAT'S RIGHT. THIS IS A HIDDEN VILLAGE.
IT IS?
WAIT HERE A MINUTE. I NEED TO GO LOOK AT THE FIELDS.
ROPERI, WOULD YOU LOOK AFTER HIM?
Uh...
Uh...
WHO'RE *YOU* SMILING AT? YOU *RUINED* MY TELLING RAVEN ABOUT THE SPROUT!
TURN
ROPERI?
RAVEN ISN'T FROM LABRYNNA, IS HE? WHAT'S HE LIKE?
WHAT IS *WITH* THIS GUY? ACTING ALL FRIENDLY WHEN WE JUST MET!
DON'T YOU KNOW HIM?
HE WANDERED INTO LABRYNNA THREE YEARS AGO. HE'D BEEN ON A JOURNEY IMPROVING HIS SWORDSMANSHIP FOR A LONG TIME.
HE KNOWS ALL ABOUT EVERYTHING, LIKE MEDICINE IN FARAWAY LANDS AND WHAT'S GOING ON IN TOWN...

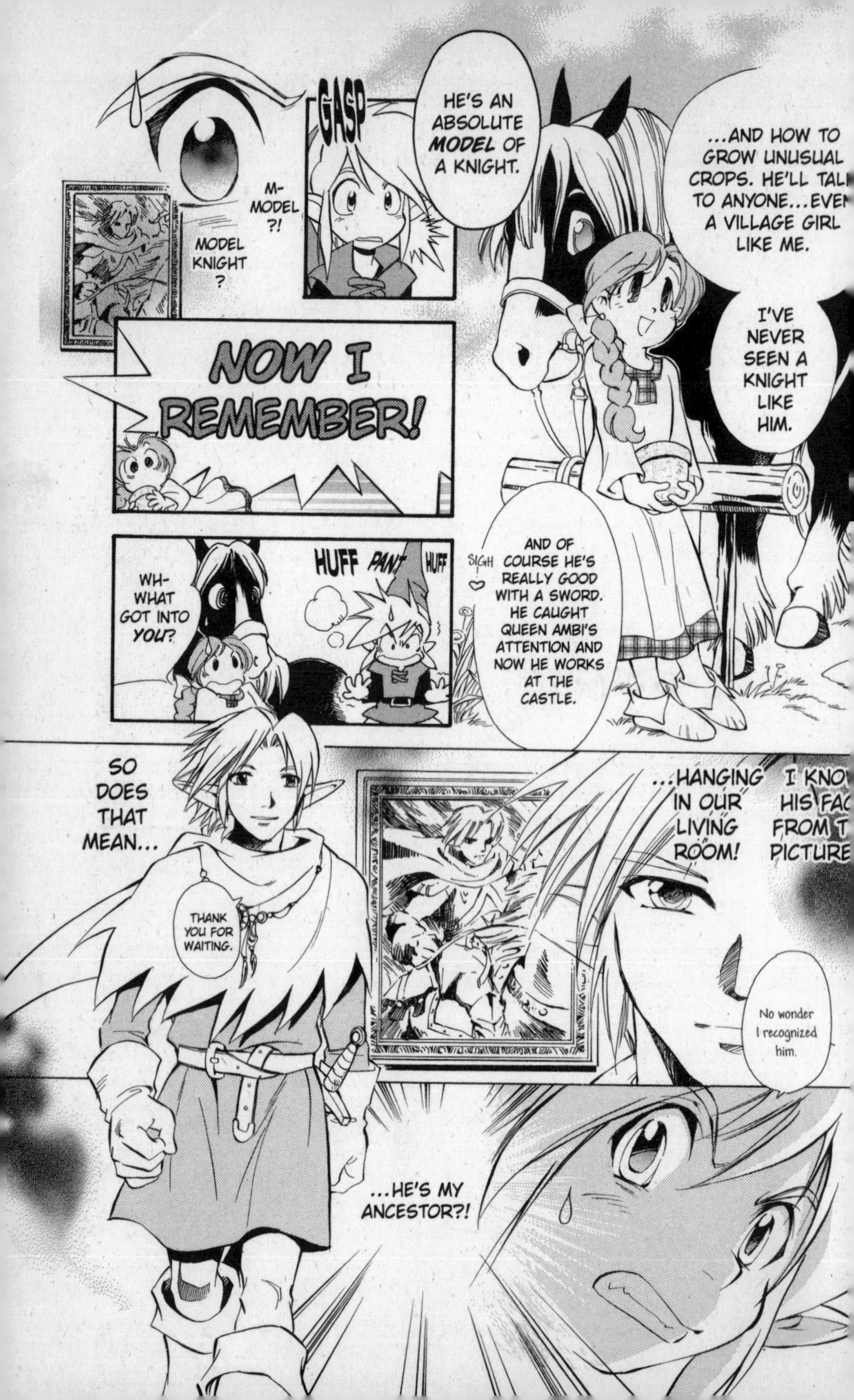

...AND HOW TO GROW UNUSUAL CROPS. HE'LL TAL TO ANYONE...EVE A VILLAGE GIRL LIKE ME.
I'VE NEVER SEEN A KNIGHT LIKE HIM.
SIGH
AND OF COURSE HE'S REALLY GOOD WITH A SWORD. HE CAUGHT QUEEN AMBI'S ATTENTION AND NOW HE WORKS AT THE CASTLE.
HE'S AN ABSOLUTE MODEL OF A KNIGHT.
GASP
M-MODEL?!
MODEL KNIGHT?
NOW I REMEMBER!
HUFF PANT HUFF
WH-WHAT GOT INTO YOU?
I KNO HIS FAC FROM T PICTURE
...HANGING IN OUR LIVING ROOM!
No wonder I recognized him.
SO DOES THAT MEAN...
THANK YOU FOR WAITING.
...HE'S MY ANCESTOR?!

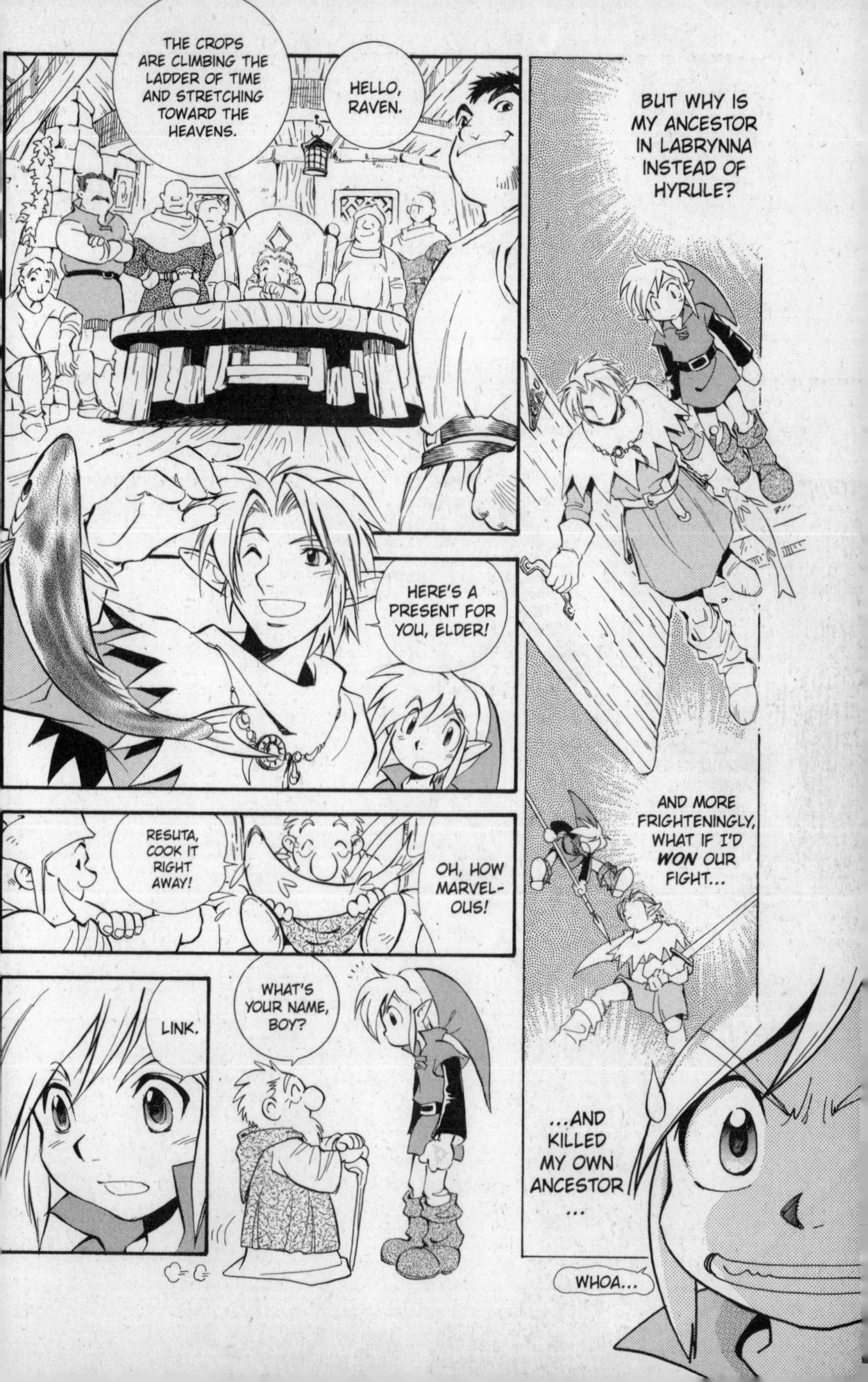
BUT WHY IS MY ANCESTOR IN LABRYNNA INSTEAD OF HYRULE?
AND MORE FRIGHTENINGLY, WHAT IF I'D *WON* OUR FIGHT...
...AND KILLED MY OWN ANCESTOR ...
WHOA...
HELLO, RAVEN.
THE CROPS ARE CLIMBING THE LADDER OF TIME AND STRETCHING TOWARD THE HEAVENS.
HERE'S A PRESENT FOR YOU, ELDER!
OH, HOW MARVEL-OUS!
RESUTA, COOK IT RIGHT AWAY!
WHAT'S YOUR NAME, BOY?
LINK.

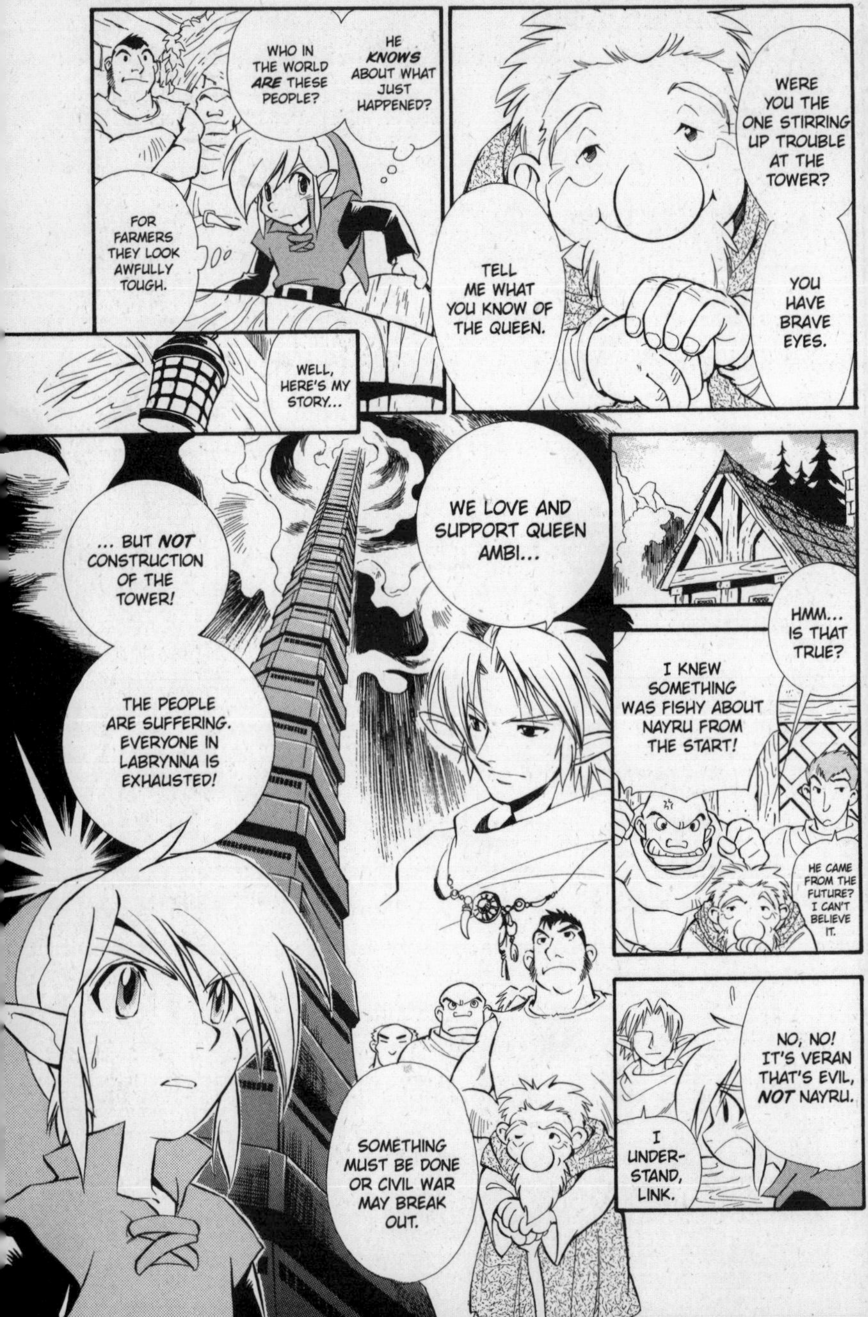
WERE YOU THE ONE STIRRING UP TROUBLE AT THE TOWER?
YOU HAVE BRAVE EYES.
TELL ME WHAT YOU KNOW OF THE QUEEN.
HE *KNOWS* ABOUT WHAT JUST HAPPENED?
WHO IN THE WORLD *ARE* THESE PEOPLE?
FOR FARMERS THEY LOOK AWFULLY TOUGH.
WELL, HERE'S MY STORY...
HMM... IS THAT TRUE?
I KNEW SOMETHING WAS FISHY ABOUT NAYRU FROM THE START!
HE CAME FROM THE FUTURE? I CAN'T BELIEVE IT.
NO, NO! IT'S VERAN THAT'S EVIL, *NOT* NAYRU.
I UNDERSTAND, LINK.
WE LOVE AND SUPPORT QUEEN AMBI...
... BUT *NOT* CONSTRUCTION OF THE TOWER!
THE PEOPLE ARE SUFFERING. EVERYONE IN LABRYNNA IS EXHAUSTED!
SOMETHING MUST BE DONE OR CIVIL WAR MAY BREAK OUT.

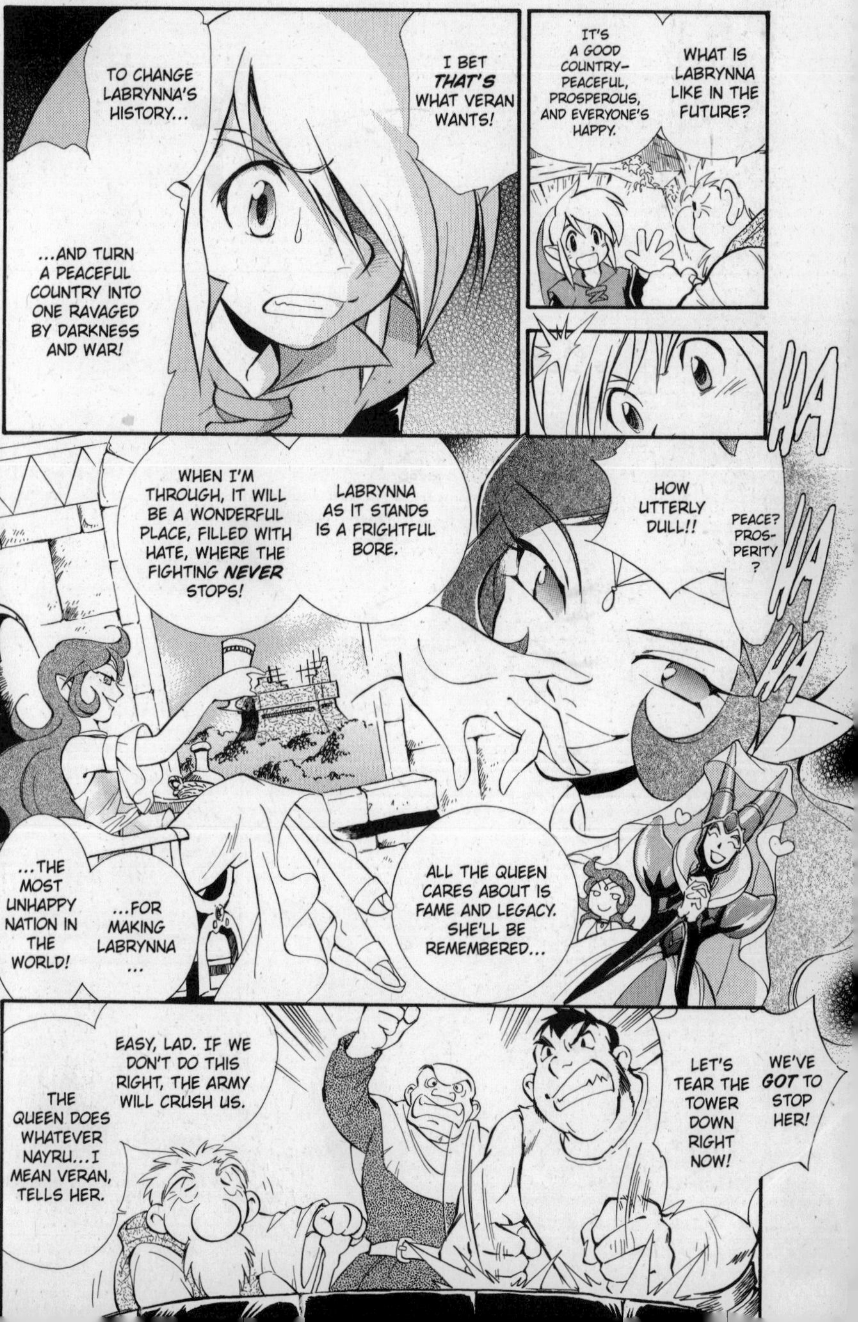
WHAT IS LABRYNNA LIKE IN THE FUTURE?
IT'S A GOOD COUNTRY—PEACEFUL, PROSPEROUS, AND EVERYONE'S HAPPY.
I BET **THAT'S** WHAT VERAN WANTS!
TO CHANGE LABRYNNA'S HISTORY...
...AND TURN A PEACEFUL COUNTRY INTO ONE RAVAGED BY DARKNESS AND WAR!
HA HA HA HA
PEACE? PROS-PERITY?
HOW UTTERLY DULL!!
LABRYNNA AS IT STANDS IS A FRIGHTFUL BORE.
WHEN I'M THROUGH, IT WILL BE A WONDERFUL PLACE, FILLED WITH HATE, WHERE THE FIGHTING **NEVER** STOPS!
ALL THE QUEEN CARES ABOUT IS FAME AND LEGACY. SHE'LL BE REMEMBERED...
...FOR MAKING LABRYNNA...
...THE MOST UNHAPPY NATION IN THE WORLD!
WE'VE **GOT** TO STOP HER!
LET'S TEAR THE TOWER DOWN RIGHT NOW!
EASY, LAD. IF WE DON'T DO THIS RIGHT, THE ARMY WILL CRUSH US.
THE QUEEN DOES WHATEVER NAYRU...I MEAN VERAN, TELLS HER.

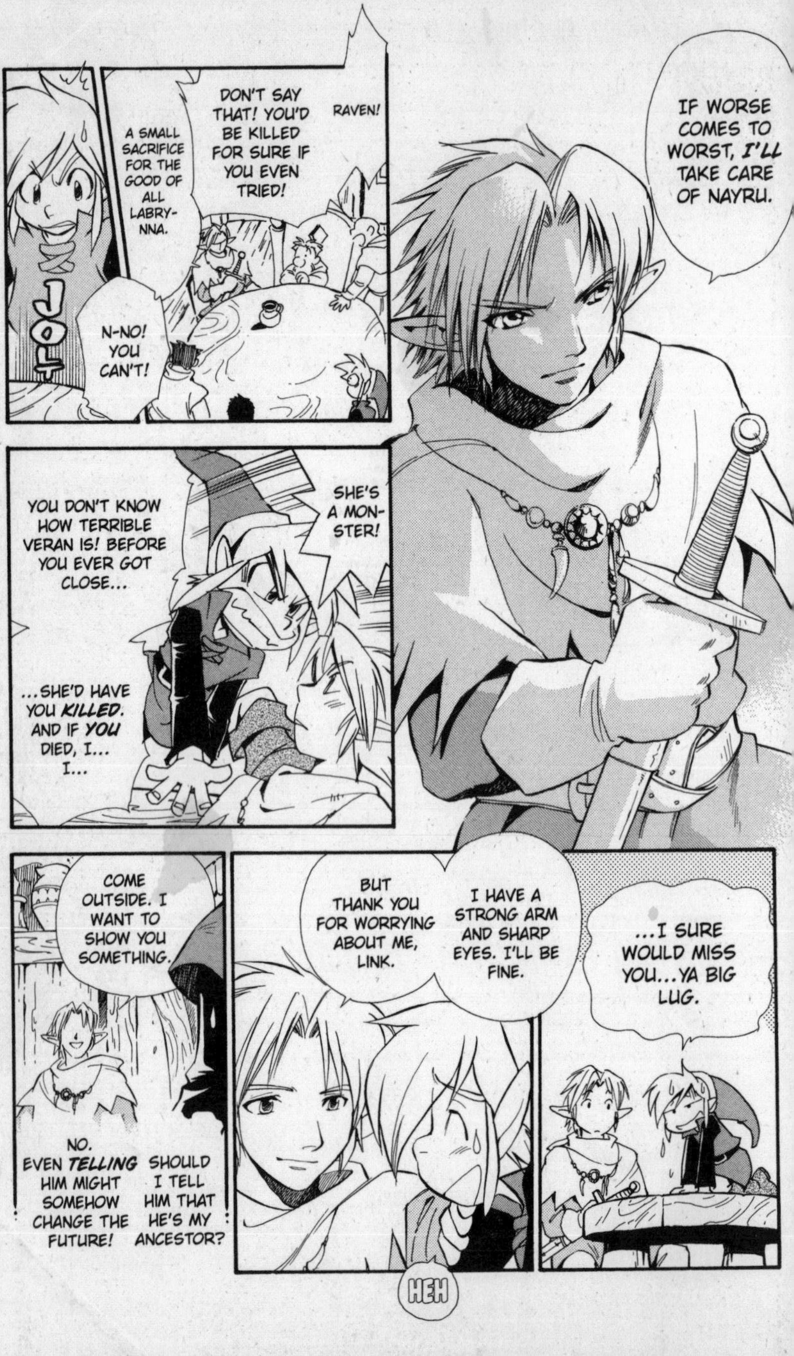
IF WORSE COMES TO WORST, *I'LL* TAKE CARE OF NAYRU.
RAVEN!
DON'T SAY THAT! YOU'D BE KILLED FOR SURE IF YOU EVEN TRIED!
A SMALL SACRIFICE FOR THE GOOD OF ALL LABRY-NNA.
JOLT
N-NO! YOU CAN'T!
SHE'S A MON-STER!
YOU DON'T KNOW HOW TERRIBLE VERAN IS! BEFORE YOU EVER GOT CLOSE...
...SHE'D HAVE YOU *KILLED*. AND IF *YOU* DIED, I... I...
...I SURE WOULD MISS YOU...YA BIG LUG.
HEH
I HAVE A STRONG ARM AND SHARP EYES. I'LL BE FINE.
BUT THANK YOU FOR WORRYING ABOUT ME, LINK.
COME OUTSIDE. I WANT TO SHOW YOU SOMETHING.
SHOULD I TELL HIM THAT HE'S MY ANCESTOR?
NO. EVEN *TELLING* HIM MIGHT SOMEHOW CHANGE THE FUTURE!

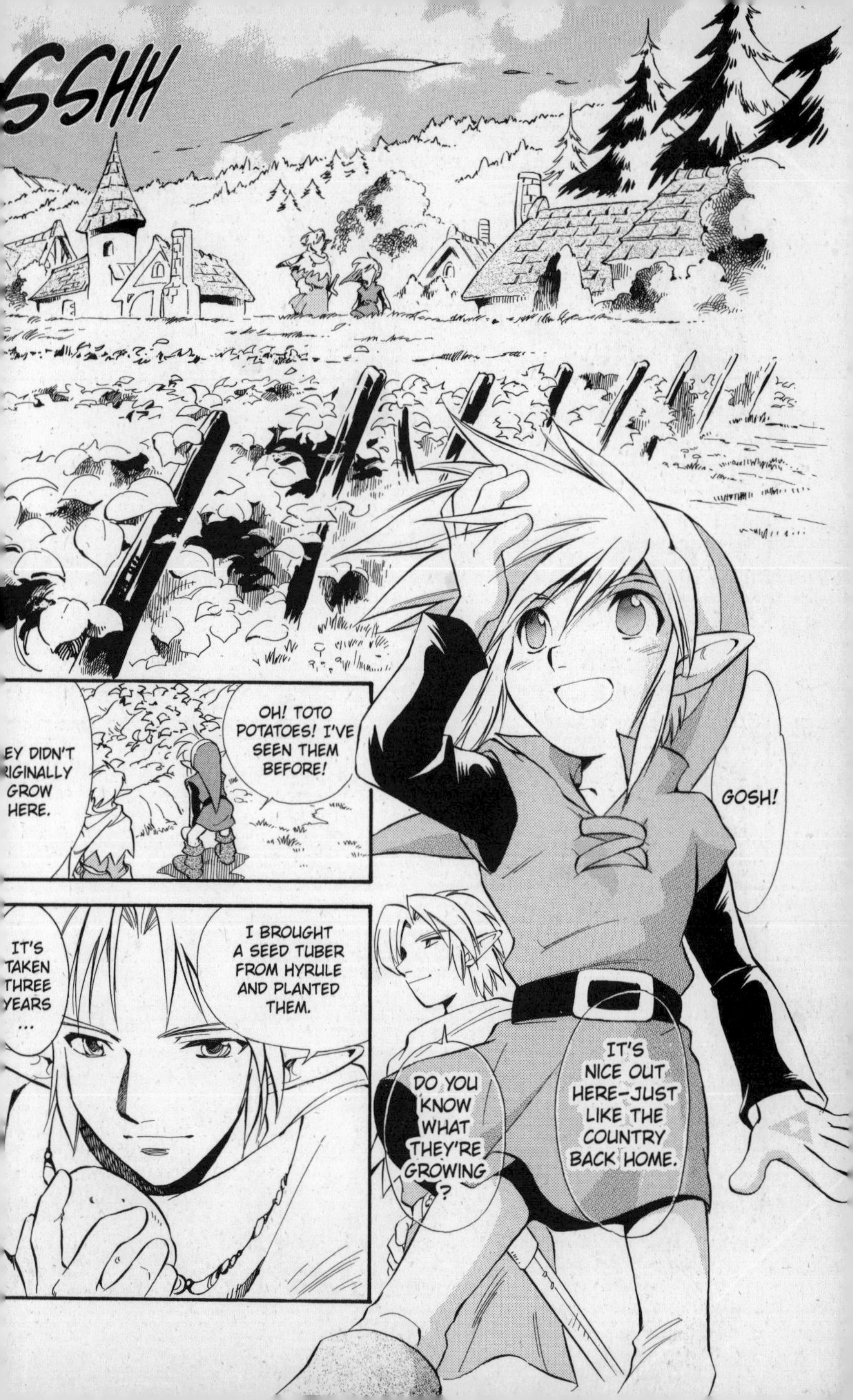
SSHH
GOSH!
IT'S NICE OUT HERE—JUST LIKE THE COUNTRY BACK HOME.
DO YOU KNOW WHAT THEY'RE GROWING?
OH! TOTO POTATOES! I'VE SEEN THEM BEFORE!
EY DIDN'T RIGINALLY GROW HERE.
I BROUGHT A SEED TUBER FROM HYRULE AND PLANTED THEM.
IT'S TAKEN THREE YEARS ...

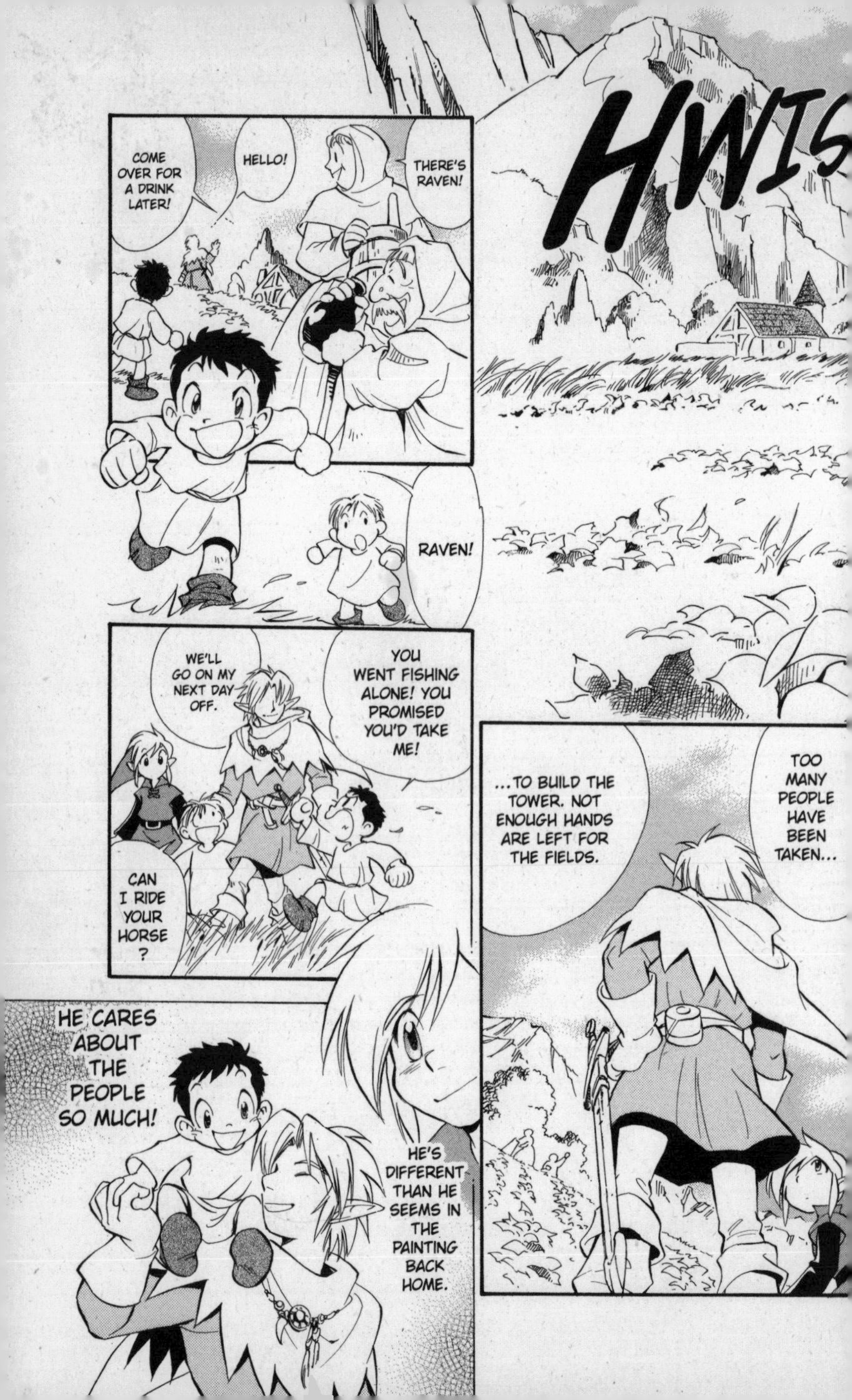
HWIS
THERE'S RAVEN!
HELLO!
COME OVER FOR A DRINK LATER!
RAVEN!
YOU WENT FISHING ALONE! YOU PROMISED YOU'D TAKE ME!
WE'LL GO ON MY NEXT DAY OFF.
CAN I RIDE YOUR HORSE?
TOO MANY PEOPLE HAVE BEEN TAKEN...
...TO BUILD THE TOWER. NOT ENOUGH HANDS ARE LEFT FOR THE FIELDS.
HE'S DIFFERENT THAN HE SEEMS IN THE PAINTING BACK HOME.
HE CARES ABOUT THE PEOPLE SO MUCH!

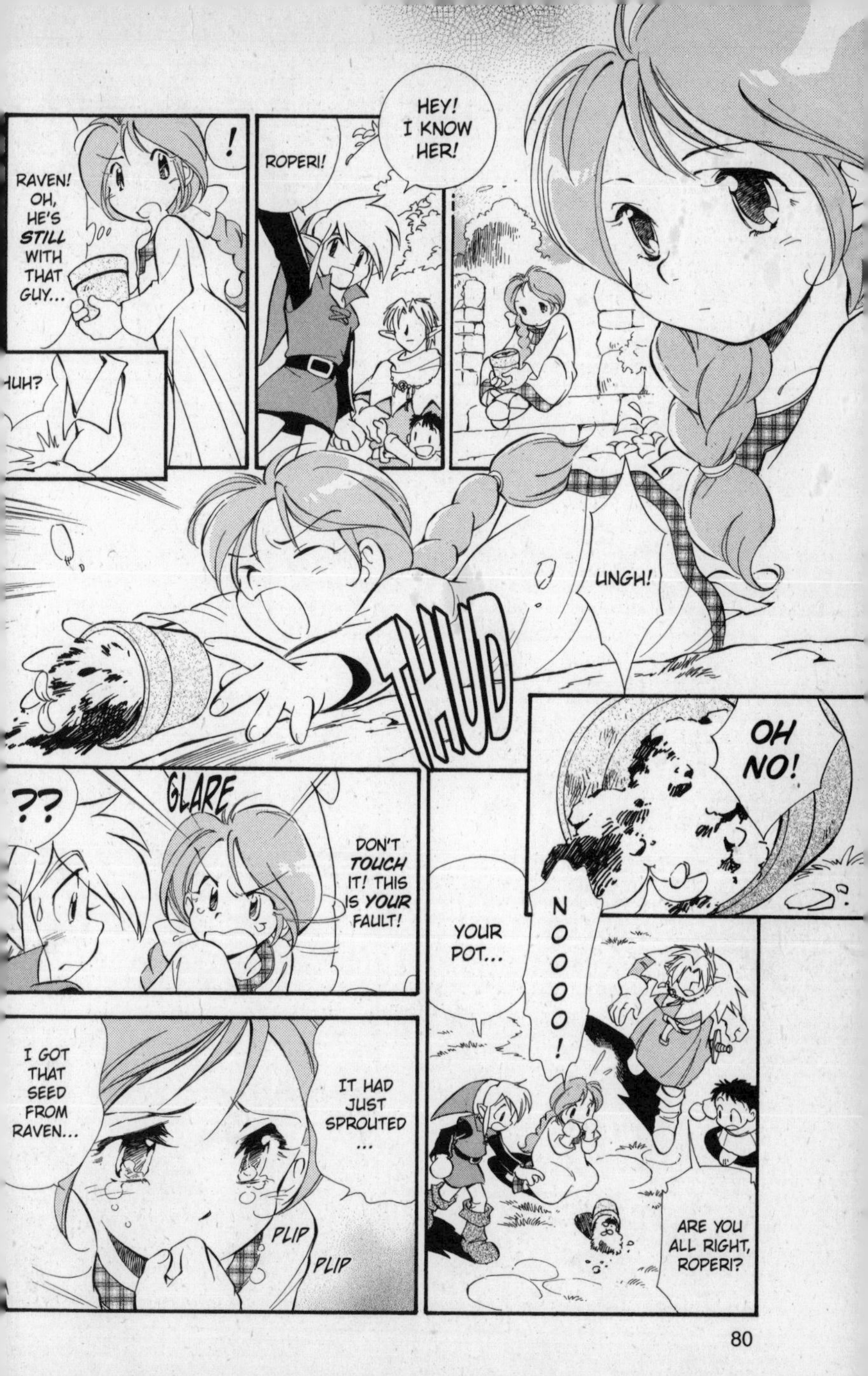
HEY! I KNOW HER!
ROPERI!
!
RAVEN! OH, HE'S STILL WITH THAT GUY...
HUH?
UNGH!
THUD
OH NO!
YOUR POT...
DON'T TOUCH IT! THIS IS YOUR FAULT!
GLARE
??
NOOOOO!
ARE YOU ALL RIGHT, ROPERI?
IT HAD JUST SPROUTED...
I GOT THAT SEED FROM RAVEN...
PLIP
PLIP

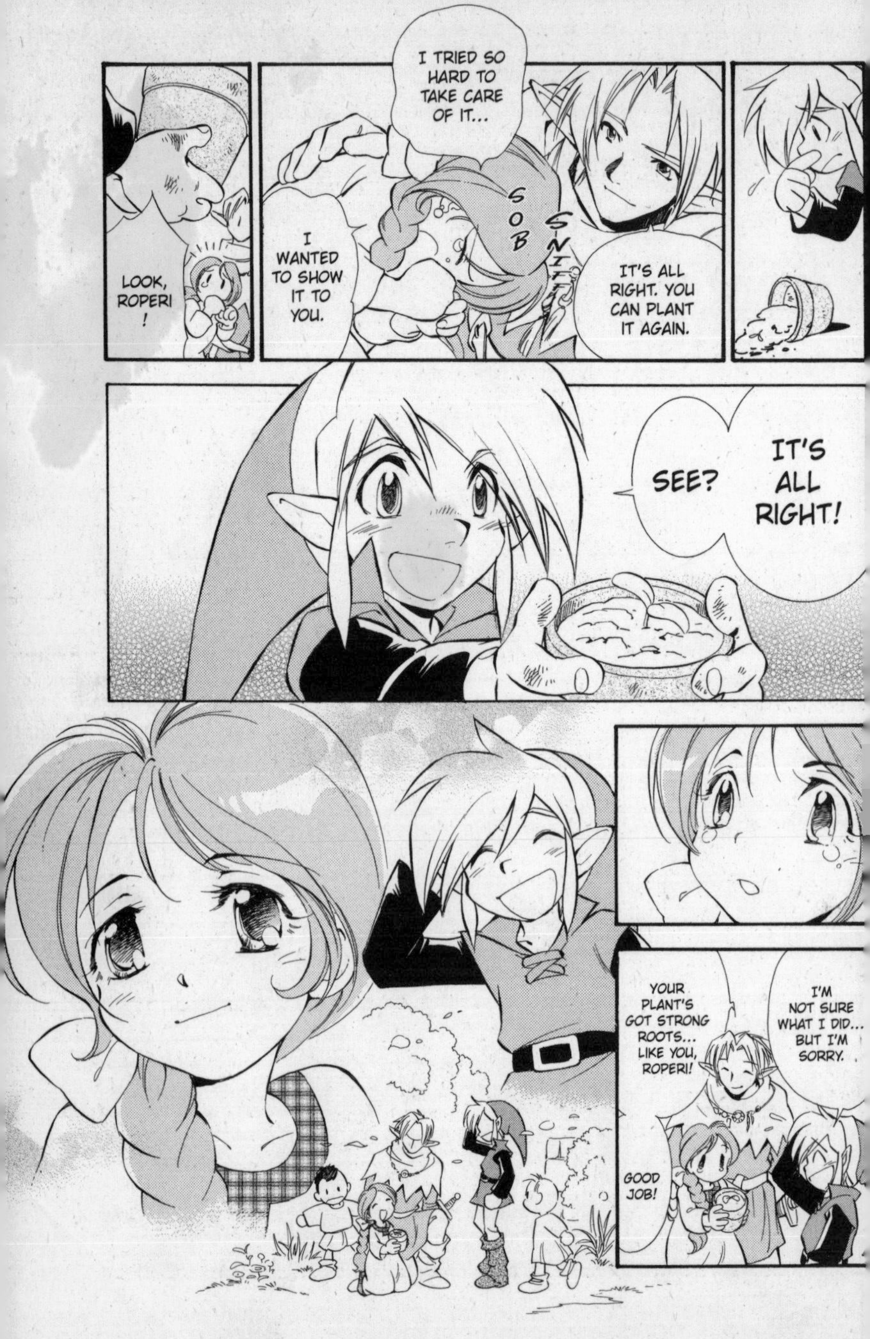

I TRIED SO HARD TO TAKE CARE OF IT...
I WANTED TO SHOW IT TO YOU.
SOB
SNIFF
IT'S ALL RIGHT. YOU CAN PLANT IT AGAIN.
LOOK, ROPERI!
SEE? IT'S ALL RIGHT!
I'M NOT SURE WHAT I DID... BUT I'M SORRY.
YOUR PLANT'S GOT STRONG ROOTS... LIKE YOU, ROPERI!
GOOD JOB!

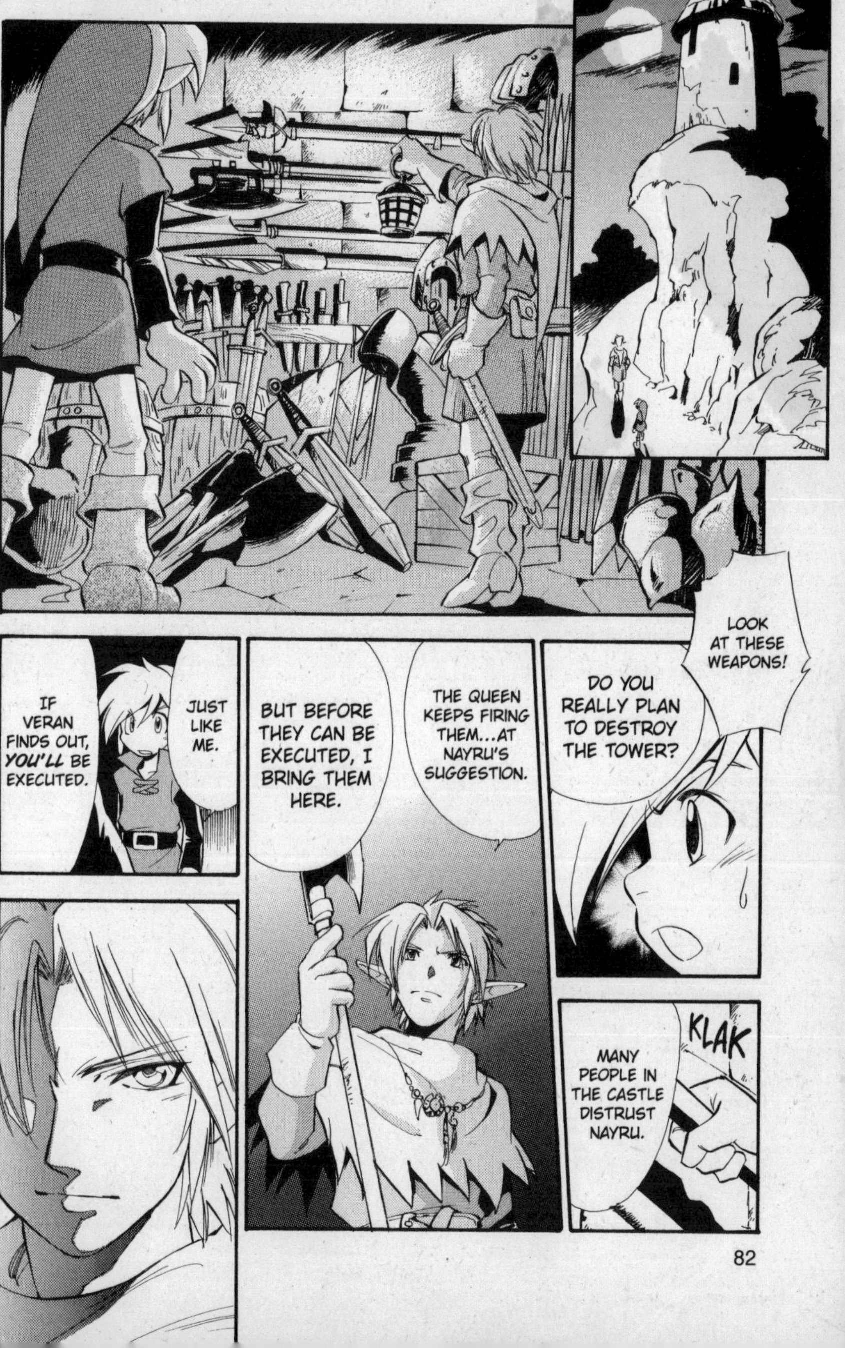
LOOK AT THESE WEAPONS!
DO YOU REALLY PLAN TO DESTROY THE TOWER?
KLAK
MANY PEOPLE IN THE CASTLE DISTRUST NAYRU.
THE QUEEN KEEPS FIRING THEM...AT NAYRU'S SUGGESTION.
BUT BEFORE THEY CAN BE EXECUTED, I BRING THEM HERE.
JUST LIKE ME.
IF VERAN FINDS OUT, *YOU'LL* BE EXECUTED.

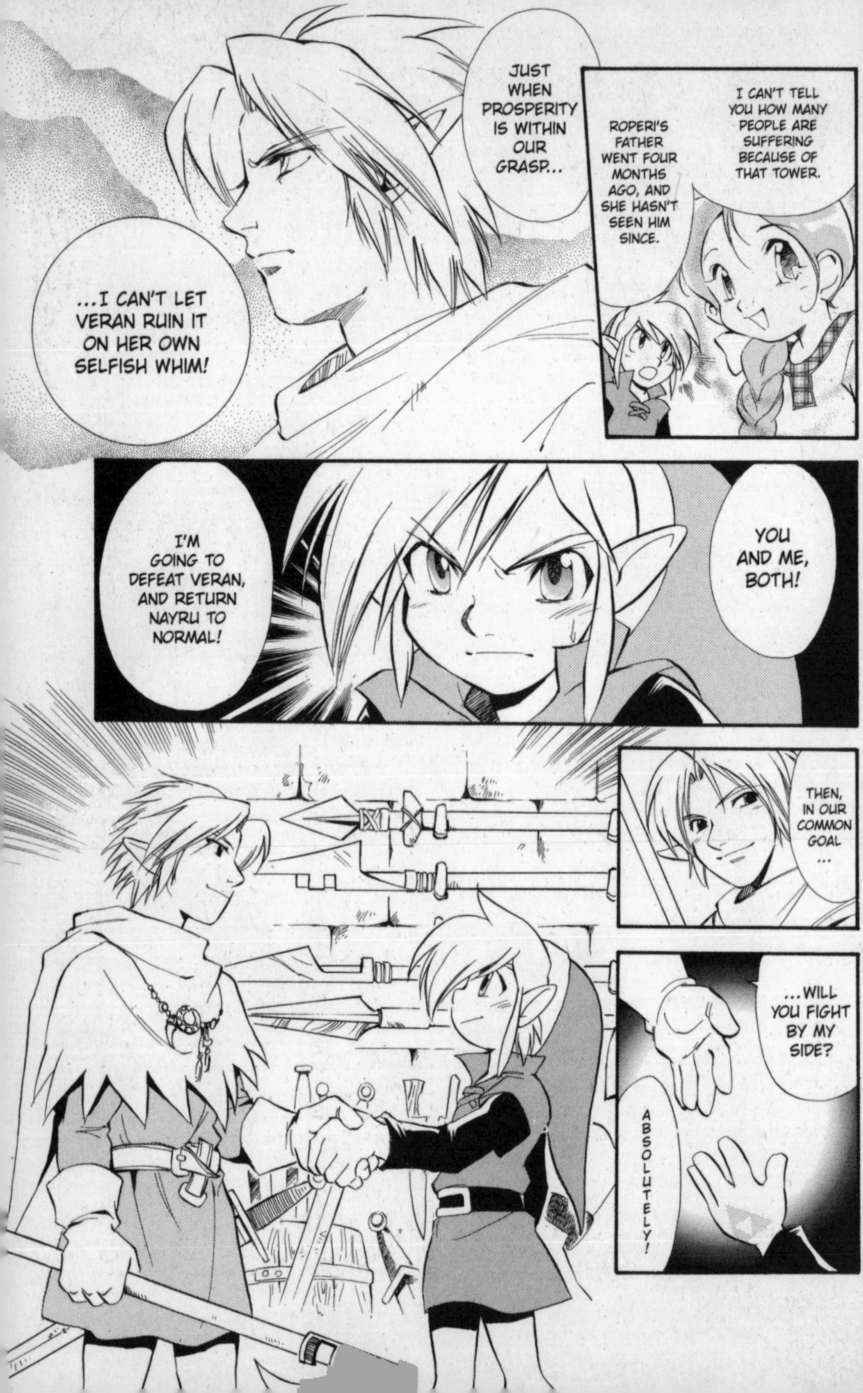

I CAN'T TELL YOU HOW MANY PEOPLE ARE SUFFERING BECAUSE OF THAT TOWER.
ROPERI'S FATHER WENT FOUR MONTHS AGO, AND SHE HASN'T SEEN HIM SINCE.
JUST WHEN PROSPERITY IS WITHIN OUR GRASP...
...I CAN'T LET VERAN RUIN IT ON HER OWN SELFISH WHIM!
I'M GOING TO DEFEAT VERAN, AND RETURN NAYRU TO NORMAL!
YOU AND ME, BOTH!
THEN, IN OUR COMMON GOAL ...
...WILL YOU FIGHT BY MY SIDE?
ABSOLUTELY!

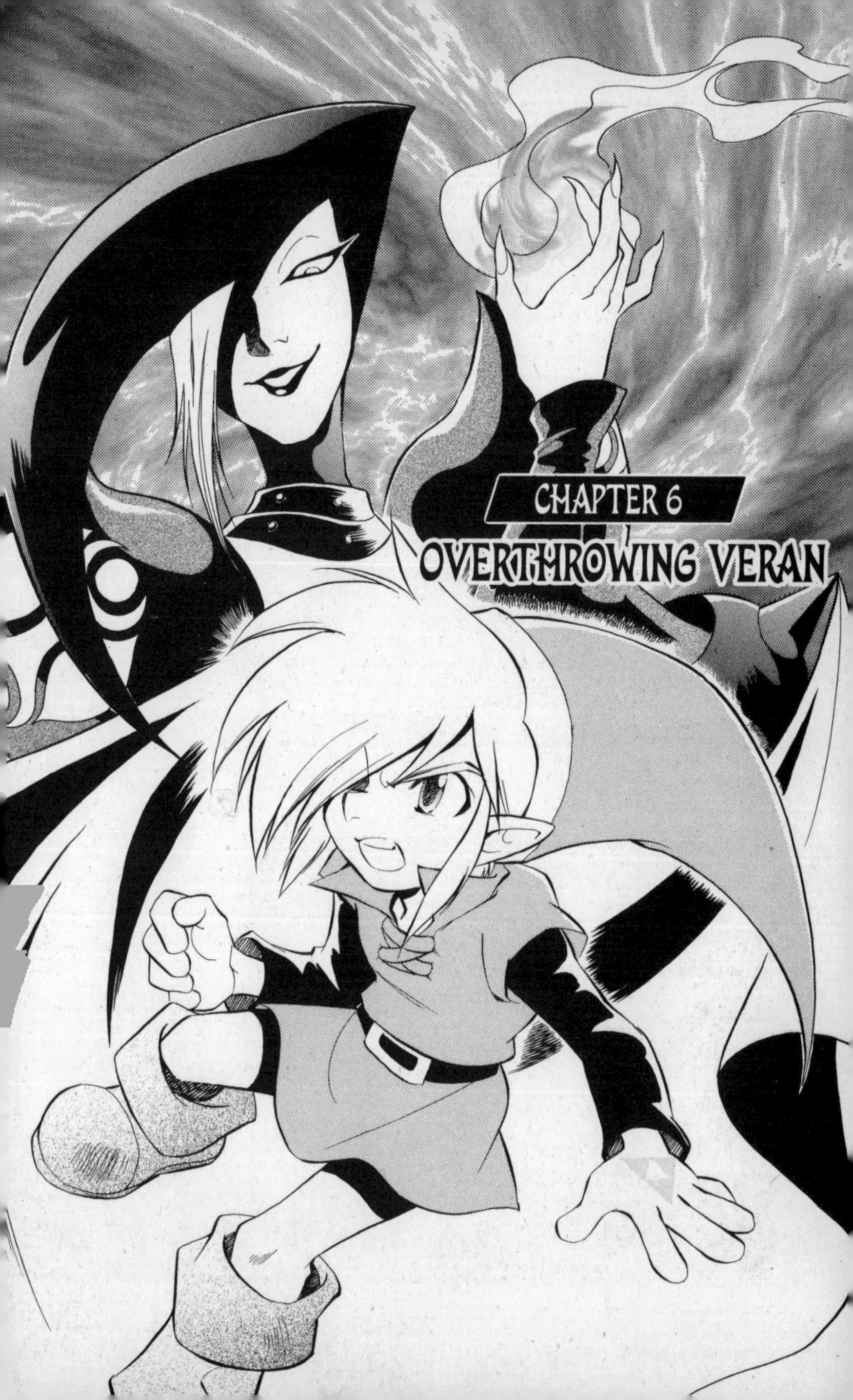
CHAPTER 6
OVERTHROWING VERAN

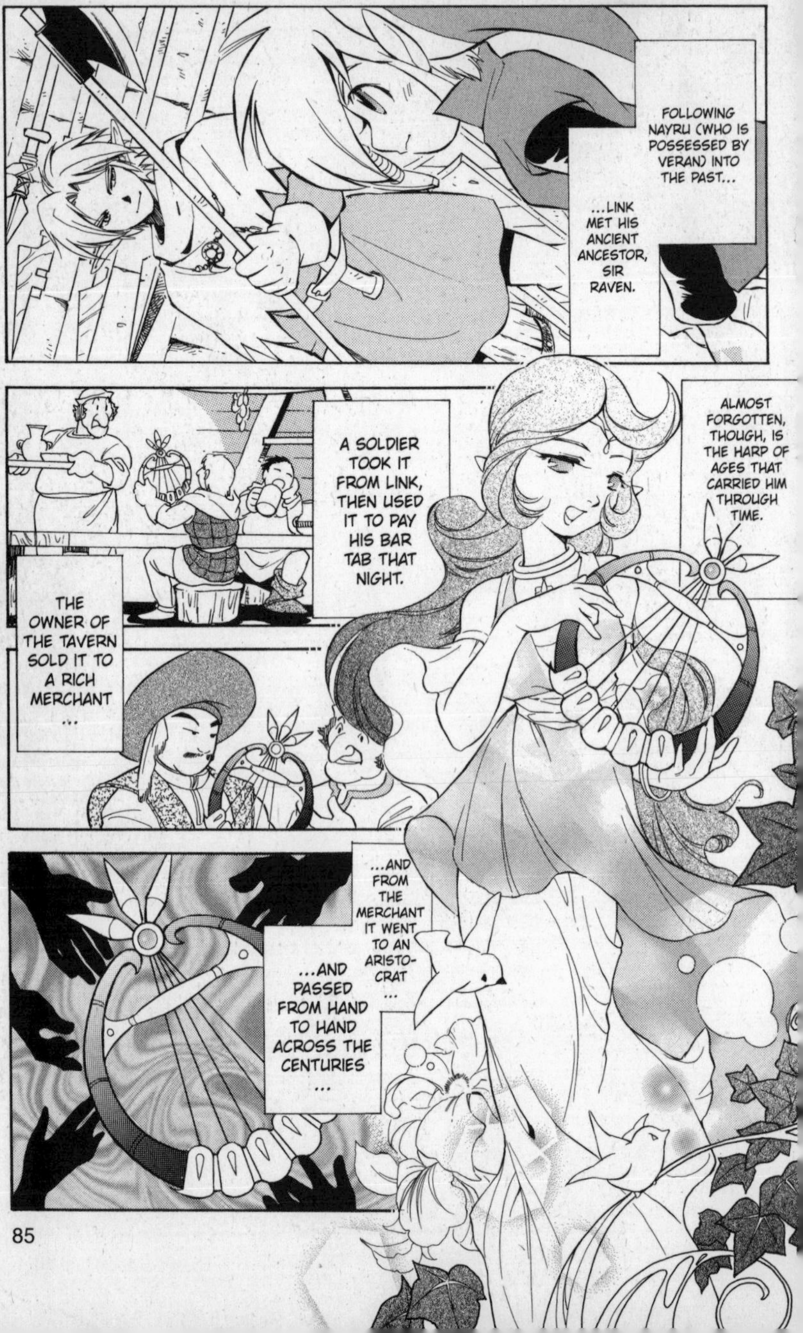
FOLLOWING NAYRU (WHO IS POSSESSED BY VERAN) INTO THE PAST...
...LINK MET HIS ANCIENT ANCESTOR, SIR RAVEN.
ALMOST FORGOTTEN, THOUGH, IS THE HARP OF AGES THAT CARRIED HIM THROUGH TIME.
A SOLDIER TOOK IT FROM LINK, THEN USED IT TO PAY HIS BAR TAB THAT NIGHT.
THE OWNER OF THE TAVERN SOLD IT TO A RICH MERCHANT ...
...AND FROM THE MERCHANT IT WENT TO AN ARISTO-CRAT ...
...AND PASSED FROM HAND TO HAND ACROSS THE CENTURIES ...

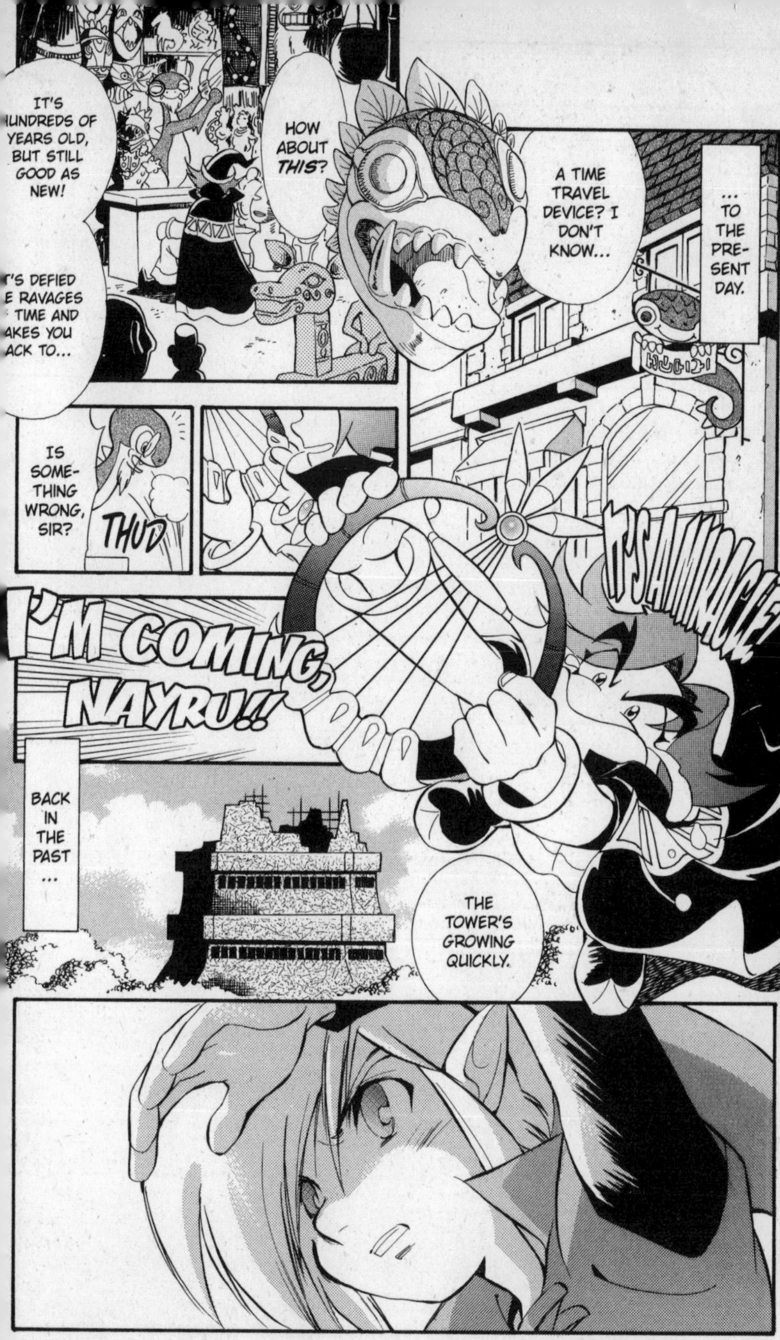

... TO THE PRESENT DAY.
A TIME TRAVEL DEVICE? I DON'T KNOW...
HOW ABOUT *THIS*?
IT'S UNDREDS OF YEARS OLD, BUT STILL GOOD AS NEW!
'S DEFIED E RAVAGES TIME AND AKES YOU ACK TO...
IT'S A MIRACLE!
IS SOMETHING WRONG, SIR?
THUD
I'M COMING, NAYRU!!
BACK IN THE PAST ...
THE TOWER'S GROWING QUICKLY.

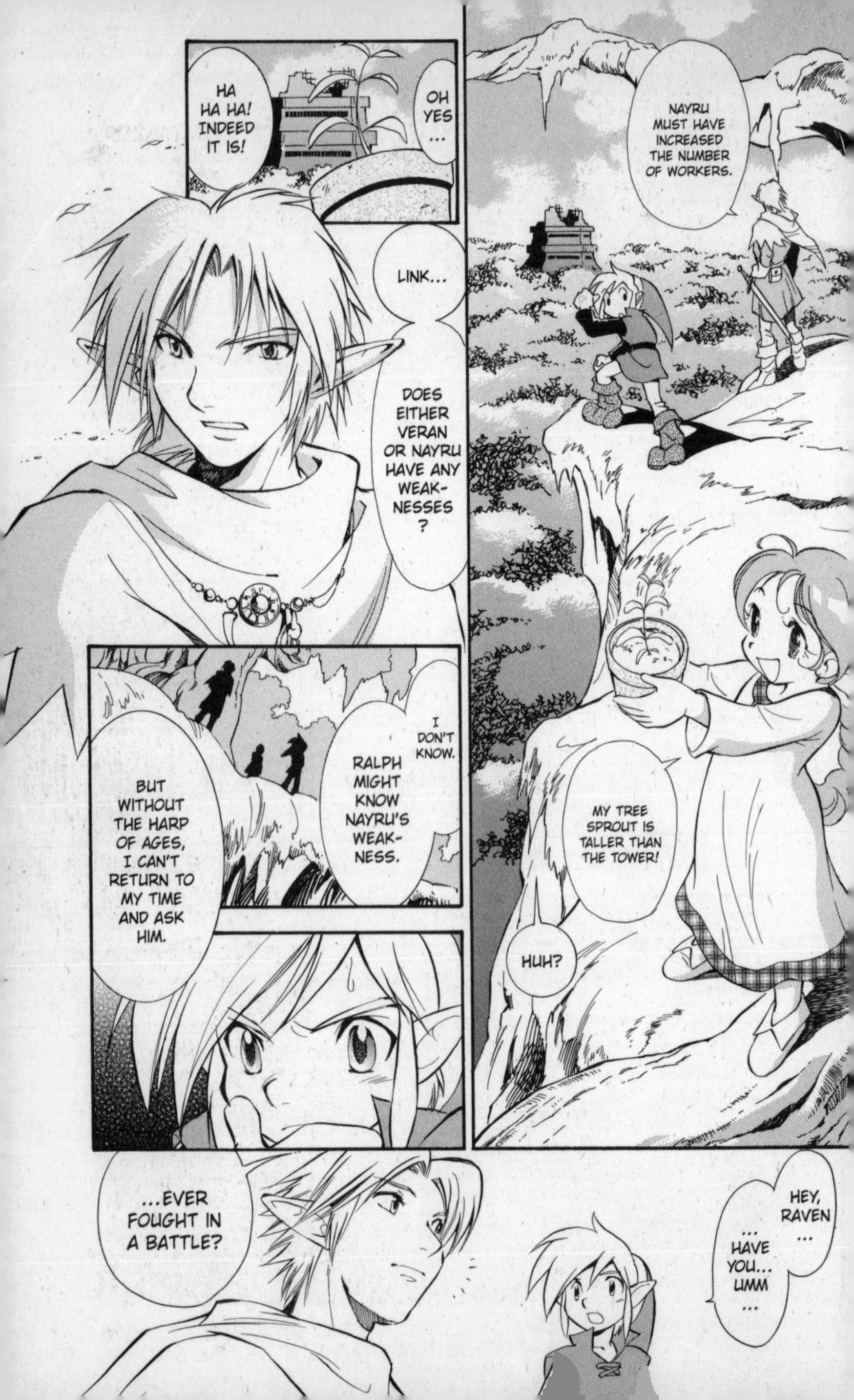
NAYRU MUST HAVE INCREASED THE NUMBER OF WORKERS.
MY TREE SPROUT IS TALLER THAN THE TOWER!
HUH?
OH YES ...
HA HA HA! INDEED IT IS!
LINK...
DOES EITHER VERAN OR NAYRU HAVE ANY WEAK-NESSES ?
I DON'T KNOW.
RALPH MIGHT KNOW NAYRU'S WEAK-NESS.
BUT WITHOUT THE HARP OF AGES, I CAN'T RETURN TO MY TIME AND ASK HIM.
HEY, RAVEN ...
... HAVE YOU... UMM ...
...EVER FOUGHT IN A BATTLE?

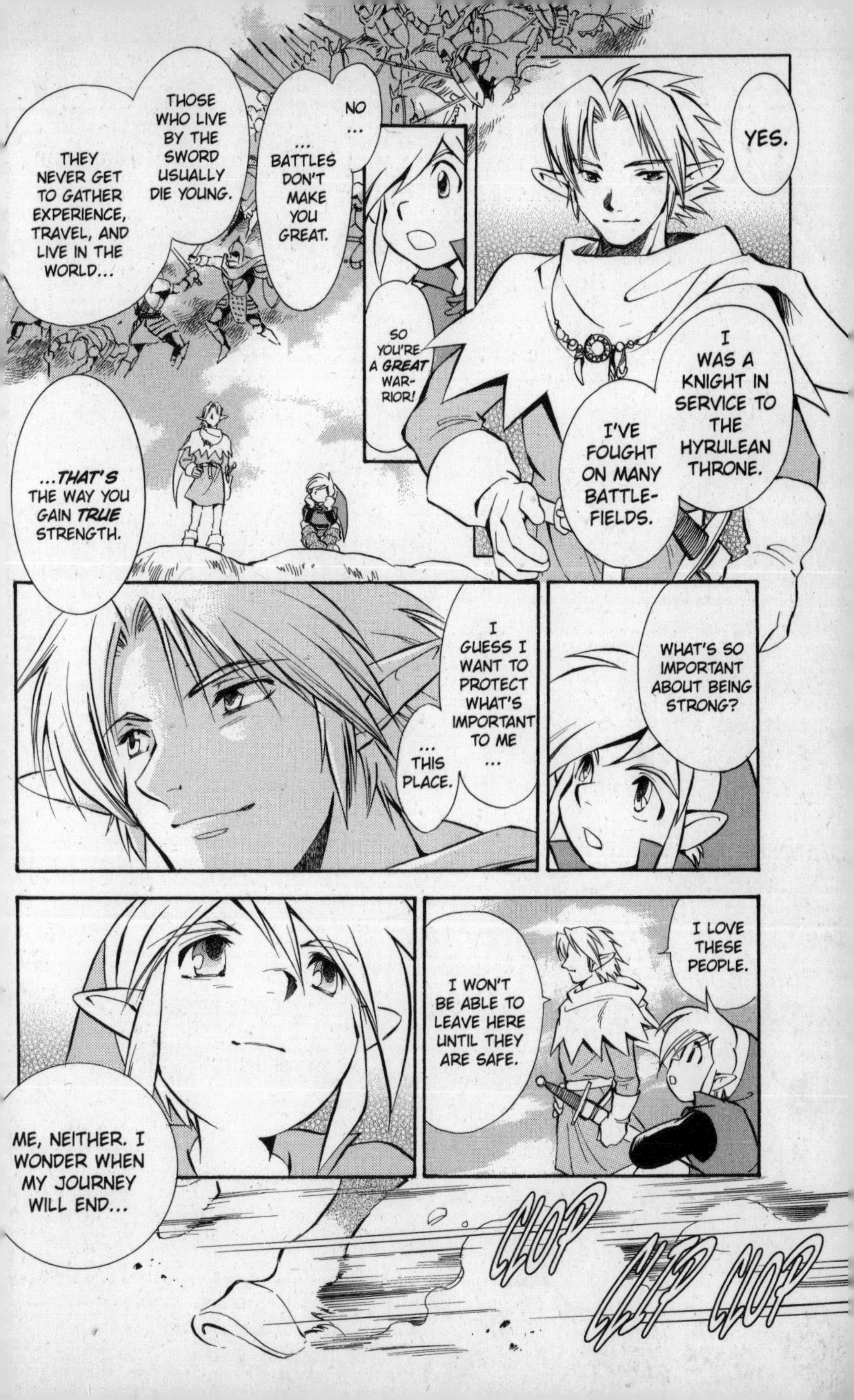
YES.
I WAS A KNIGHT IN SERVICE TO THE HYRULEAN THRONE.
I'VE FOUGHT ON MANY BATTLE-FIELDS.
SO YOU'RE A *GREAT* WAR-RIOR!
NO ... ... BATTLES DON'T MAKE YOU GREAT.
THOSE WHO LIVE BY THE SWORD USUALLY DIE YOUNG.
THEY NEVER GET TO GATHER EXPERIENCE, TRAVEL, AND LIVE IN THE WORLD...
...*THAT'S* THE WAY YOU GAIN *TRUE* STRENGTH.
WHAT'S SO IMPORTANT ABOUT BEING STRONG?
I GUESS I WANT TO PROTECT WHAT'S IMPORTANT TO ME ...
... THIS PLACE.
I LOVE THESE PEOPLE.
I WON'T BE ABLE TO LEAVE HERE UNTIL THEY ARE SAFE.
ME, NEITHER. I WONDER WHEN MY JOURNEY WILL END...
CLOP
CLIP CLOP

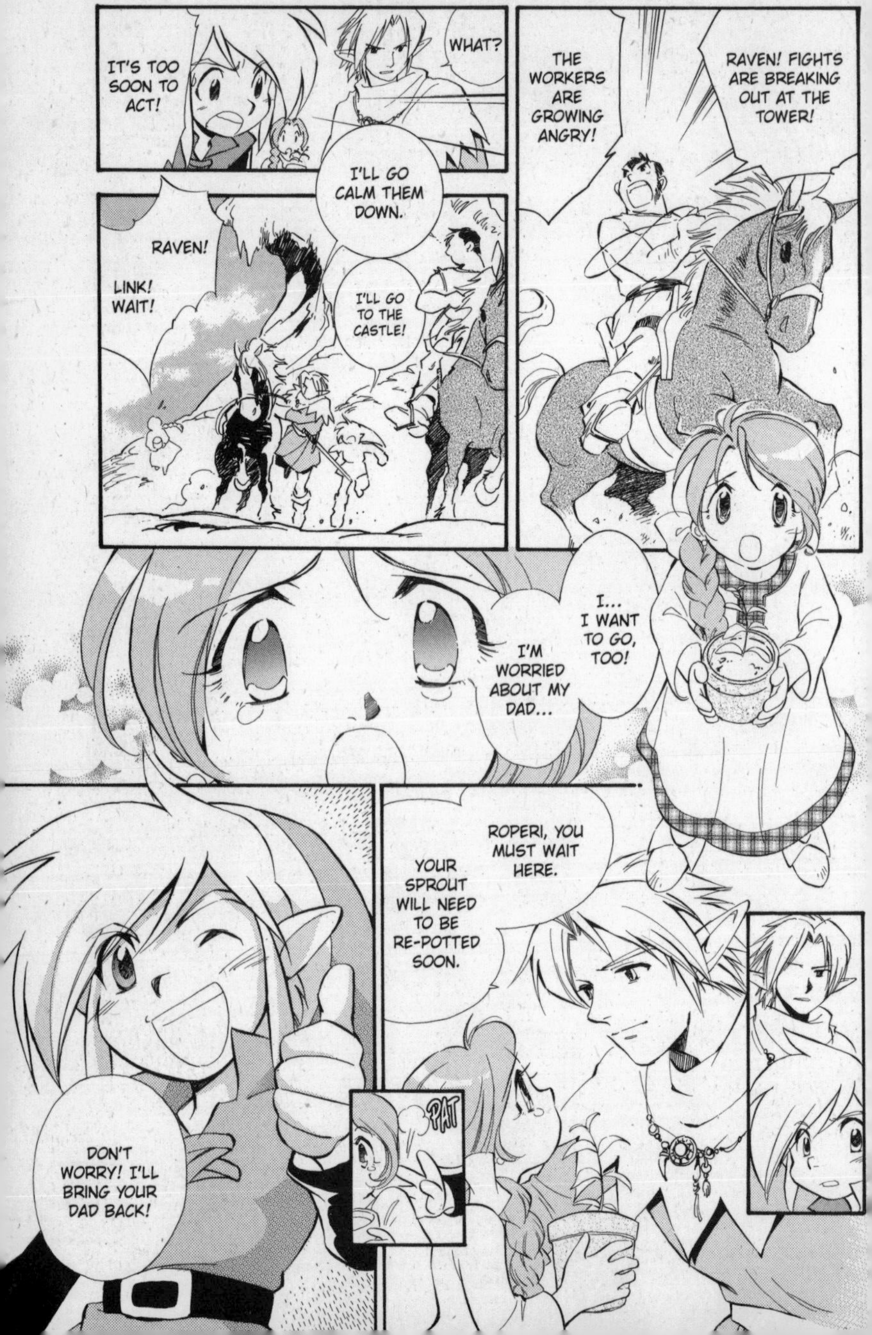
RAVEN! FIGHTS ARE BREAKING OUT AT THE TOWER!
THE WORKERS ARE GROWING ANGRY!
WHAT?
IT'S TOO SOON TO ACT!
I'LL GO CALM THEM DOWN.
I'LL GO TO THE CASTLE!
RAVEN!
LINK! WAIT!
I... I WANT TO GO, TOO!
I'M WORRIED ABOUT MY DAD...
ROPERI, YOU MUST WAIT HERE.
YOUR SPROUT WILL NEED TO BE RE-POTTED SOON.
PAT
DON'T WORRY! I'LL BRING YOUR DAD BACK!

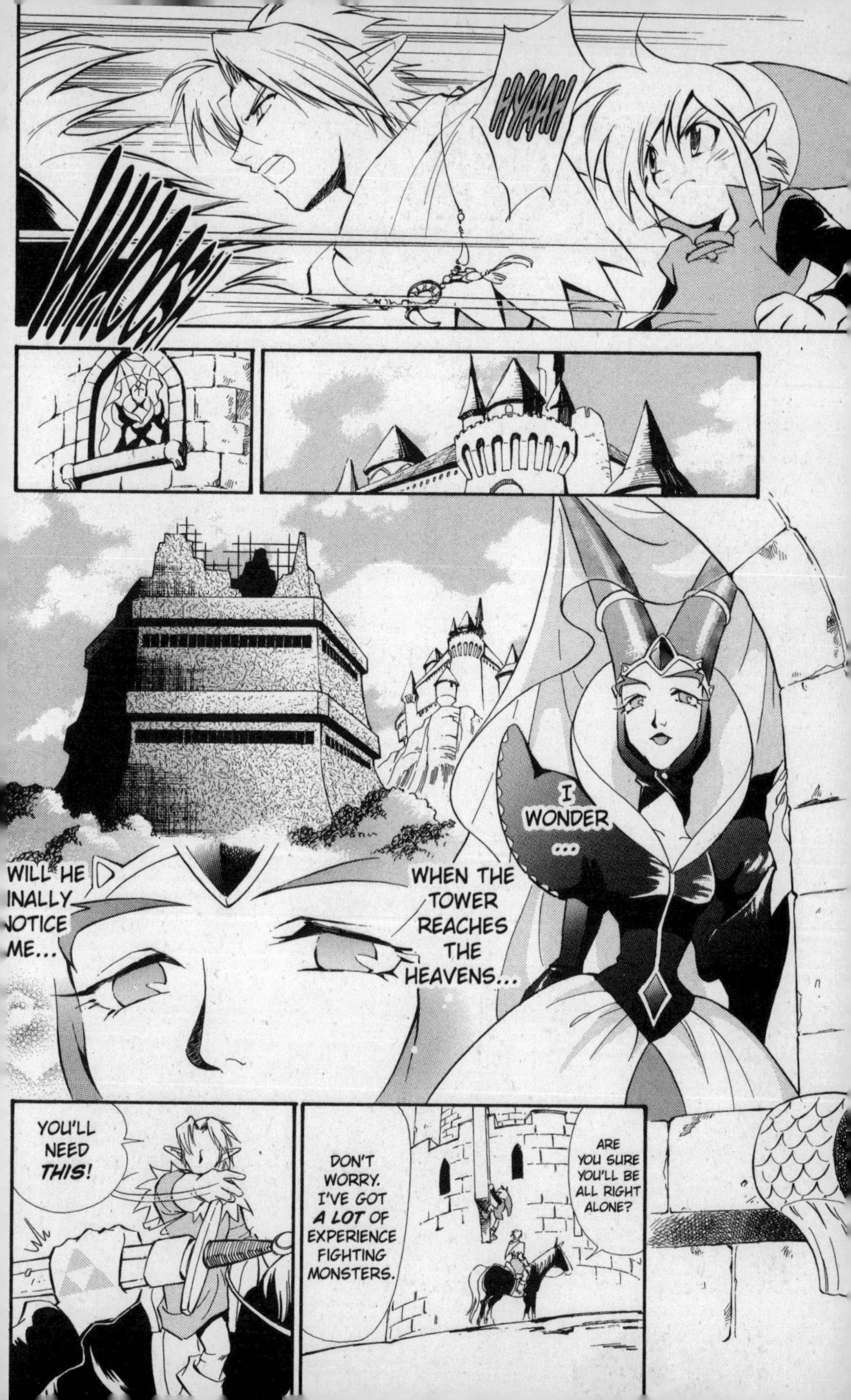

HYAAH
WHOOSH
I WONDER...
WHEN THE TOWER REACHES THE HEAVENS...
WILL HE INALLY NOTICE ME...
ARE YOU SURE YOU'LL BE ALL RIGHT ALONE?
DON'T WORRY. I'VE GOT **A LOT** OF EXPERIENCE FIGHTING MONSTERS.
YOU'LL NEED **THIS**!

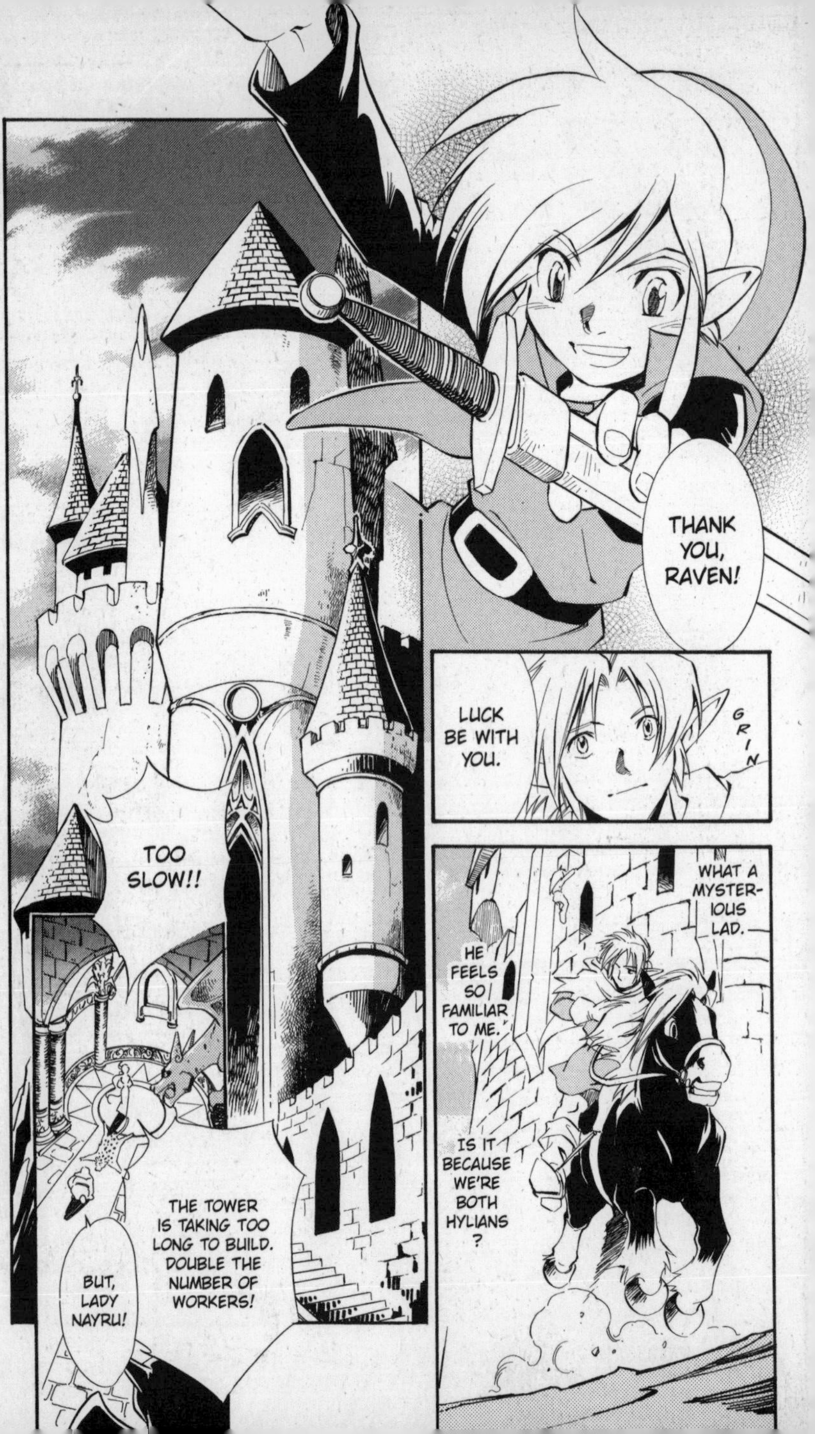
THANK YOU, RAVEN!
LUCK BE WITH YOU.
GRIN
WHAT A MYSTERIOUS LAD.
HE FEELS SO FAMILIAR TO ME.
IS IT BECAUSE WE'RE BOTH HYLIANS?
TOO SLOW!!
THE TOWER IS TAKING TOO LONG TO BUILD. DOUBLE THE NUMBER OF WORKERS!
BUT, LADY NAYRU!

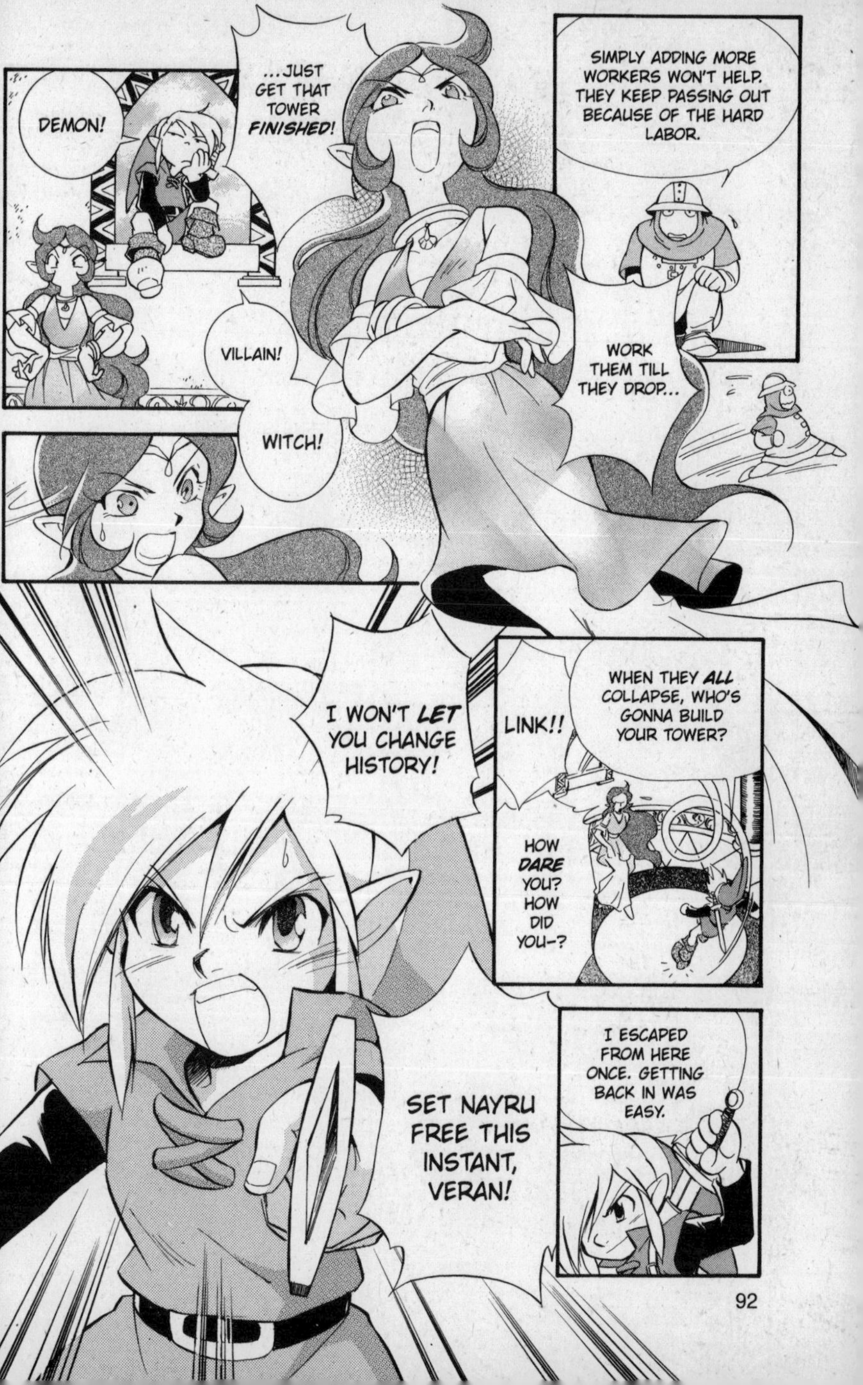
SIMPLY ADDING MORE WORKERS WON'T HELP. THEY KEEP PASSING OUT BECAUSE OF THE HARD LABOR.
WORK THEM TILL THEY DROP...
...JUST GET THAT TOWER *FINISHED*!
DEMON!
VILLAIN!
WITCH!
WHEN THEY *ALL* COLLAPSE, WHO'S GONNA BUILD YOUR TOWER?
LINK!!
HOW *DARE* YOU? HOW DID YOU-?
I WON'T *LET* YOU CHANGE HISTORY!
I ESCAPED FROM HERE ONCE. GETTING BACK IN WAS EASY.
SET NAYRU FREE THIS INSTANT, VERAN!

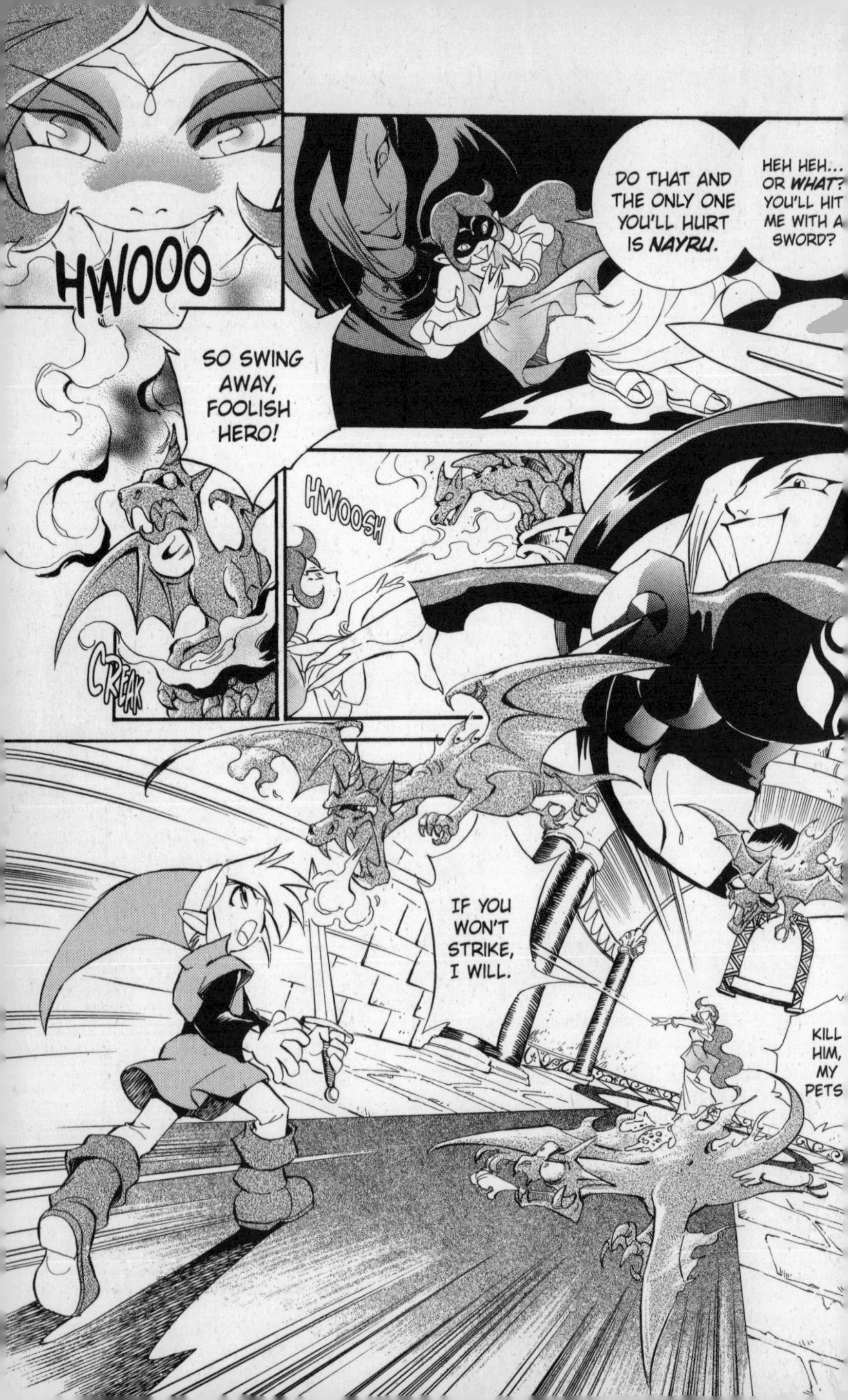
HEH HEH... OR WHAT? YOU'LL HIT ME WITH A SWORD?
DO THAT AND THE ONLY ONE YOU'LL HURT IS NAYRU.
HWOOO
SO SWING AWAY, FOOLISH HERO!
HWOOSH
CREAK
IF YOU WON'T STRIKE, I WILL.
KILL HIM, MY PETS

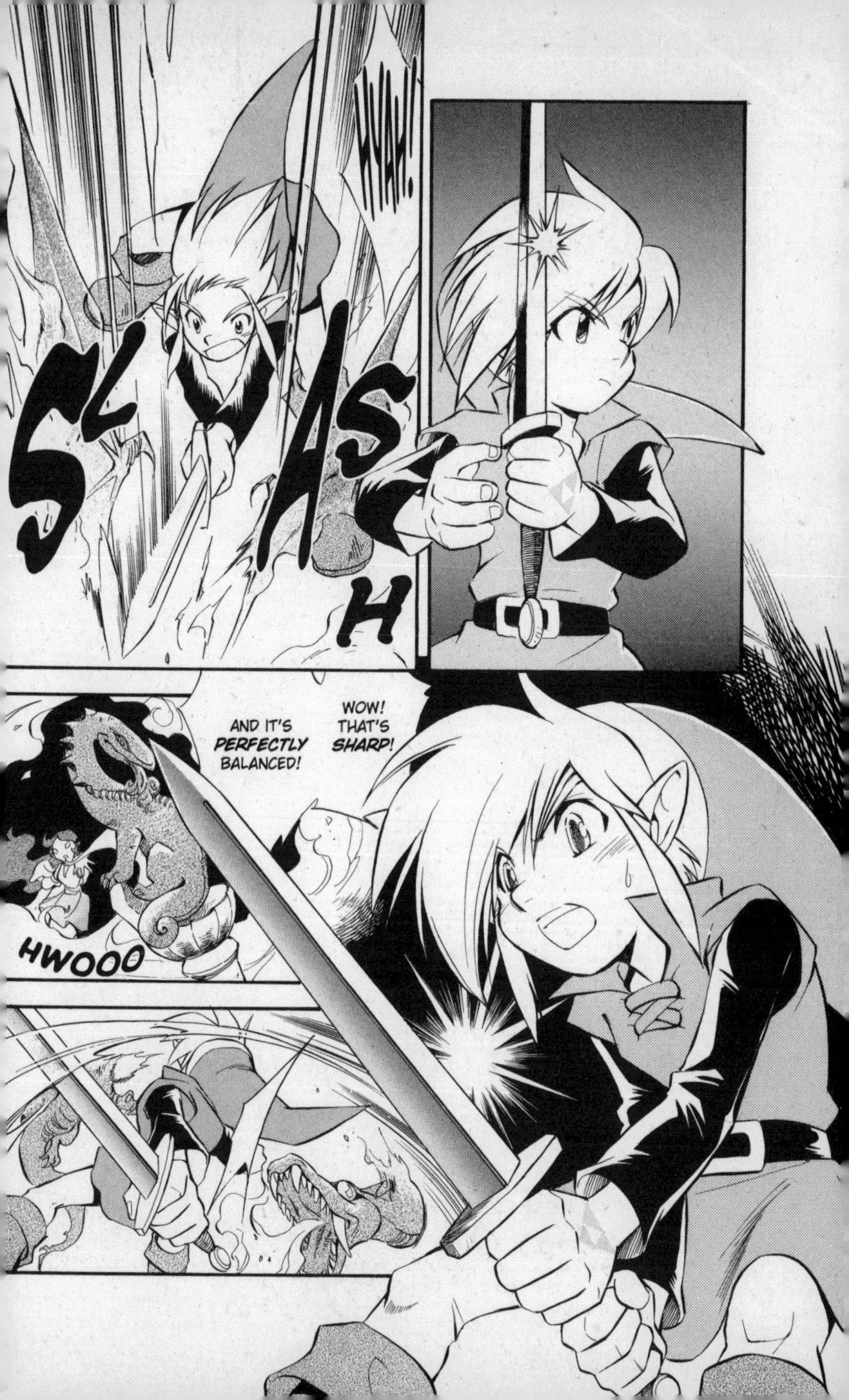
HYAH!
SLASH
WOW! THAT'S *SHARP!*
AND IT'S *PERFECTLY* BALANCED!
HWOOO

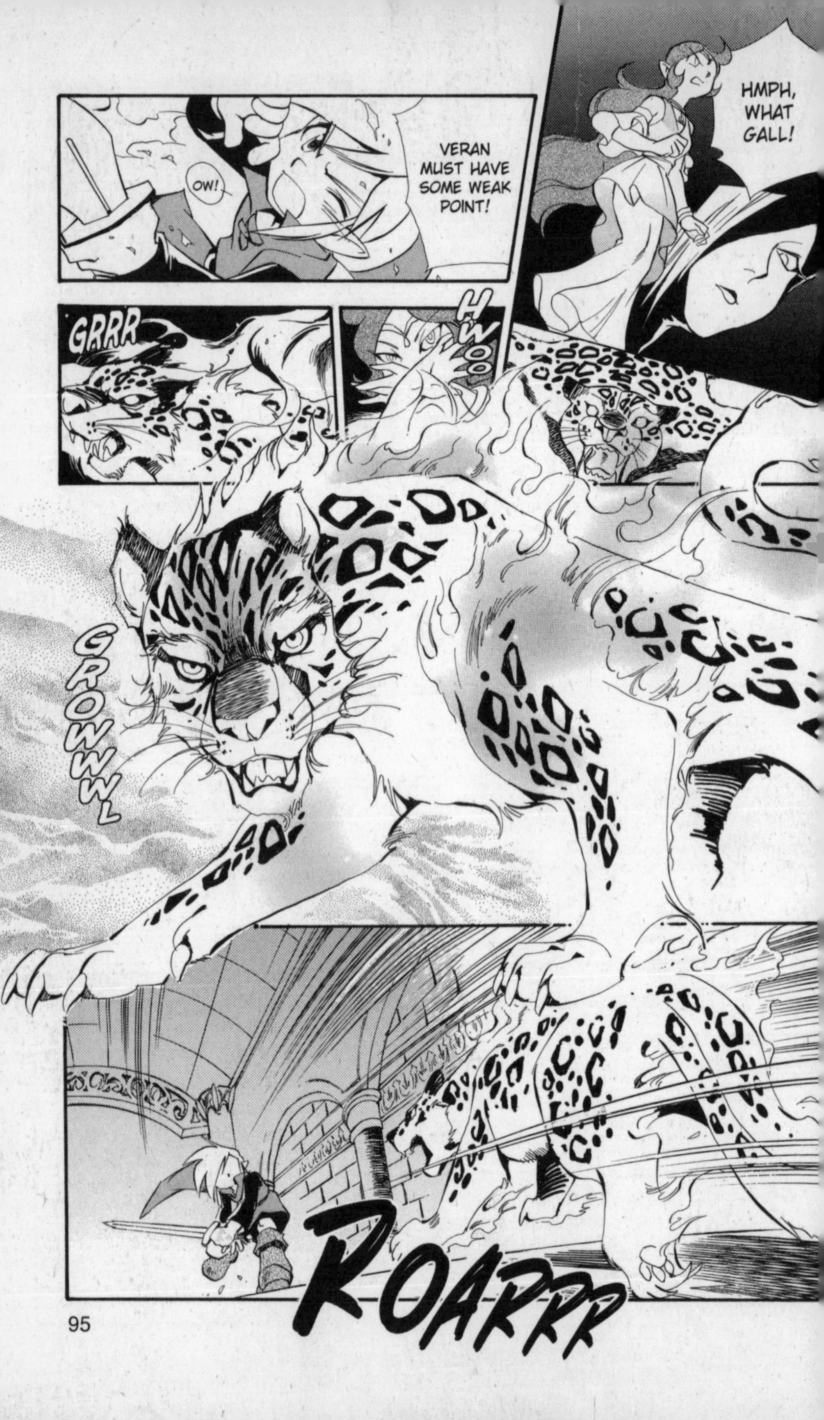
HMPH, WHAT GALL!
VERAN MUST HAVE SOME WEAK POINT!
OW!
HWOO
GRRR
GROWWWL
ROARRR

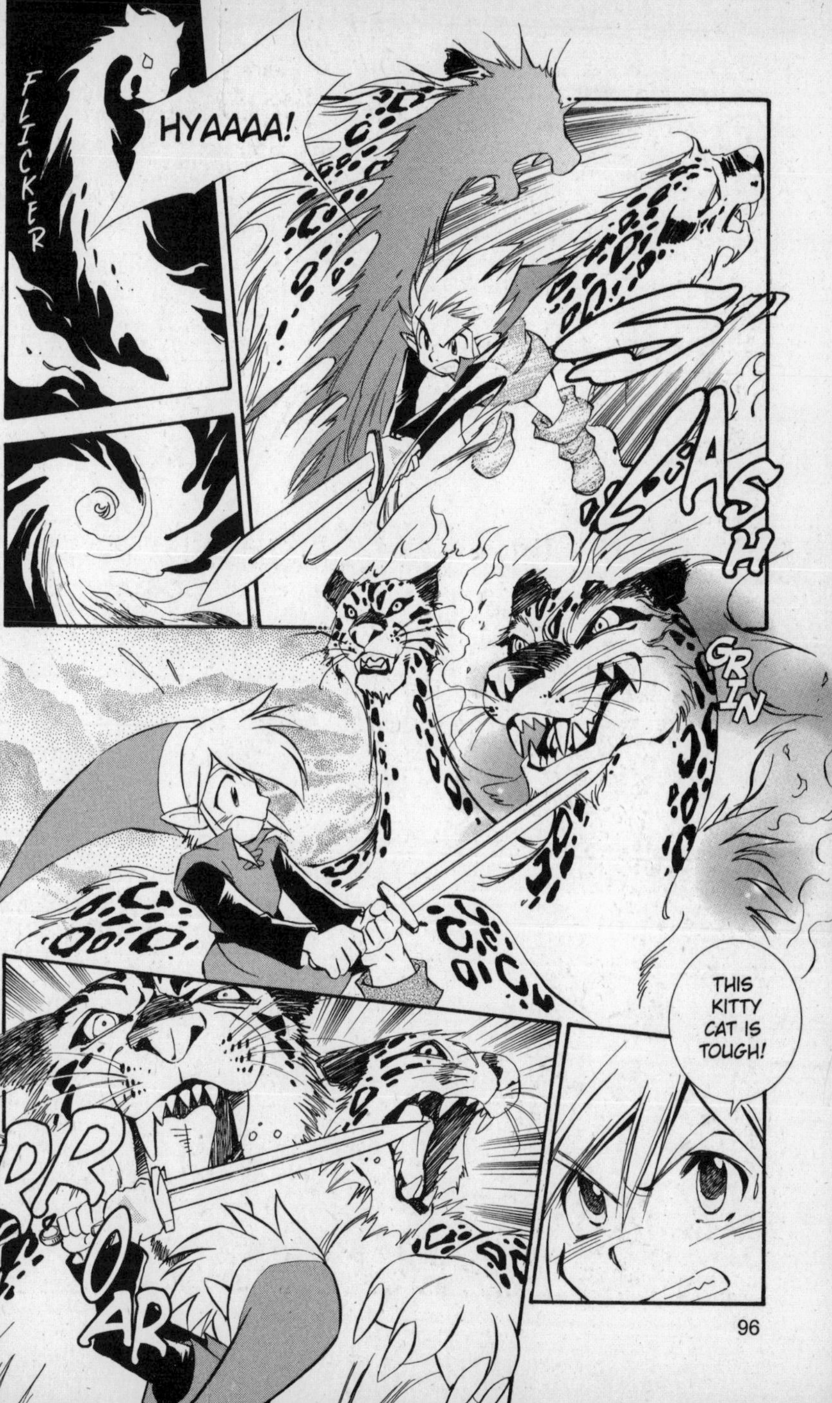
HYAAAA!
SLASH
FLICKER
GRIN
THIS KITTY CAT IS TOUGH!
RROOAR

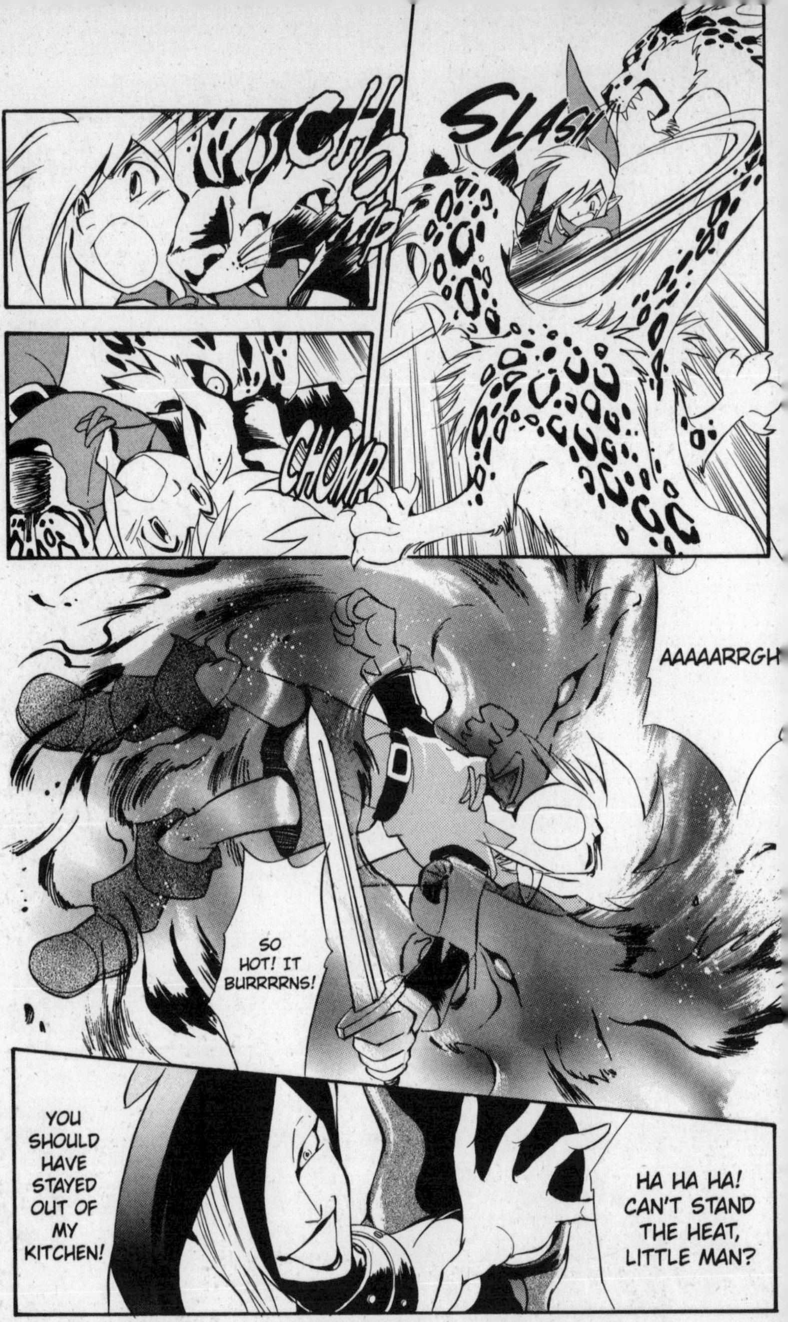
SLASH
CHOMP
AAAAARRGH
SO HOT! IT BURRRRNS!
HA HA HA! CAN'T STAND THE HEAT, LITTLE MAN?
YOU SHOULD HAVE STAYED OUT OF MY KITCHEN!

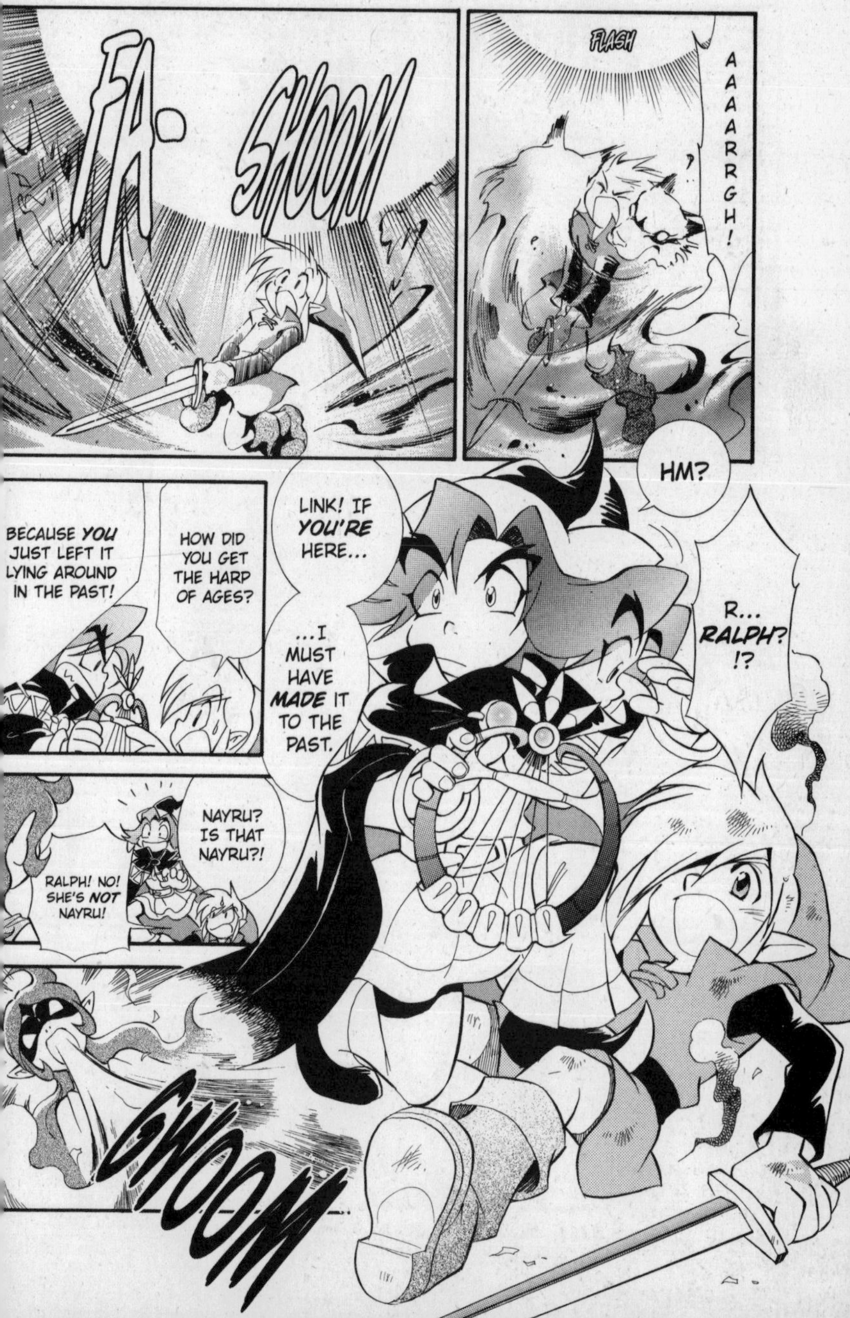
FLASH
AAAAARRGH!
FA-SHOOM
HM?
R... RALPH?!?
LINK! IF YOU'RE HERE...
...I MUST HAVE MADE IT TO THE PAST.
GWOOM
HOW DID YOU GET THE HARP OF AGES?
BECAUSE YOU JUST LEFT IT LYING AROUND IN THE PAST!
NAYRU? IS THAT NAYRU?!
RALPH! NO! SHE'S NOT NAYRU!

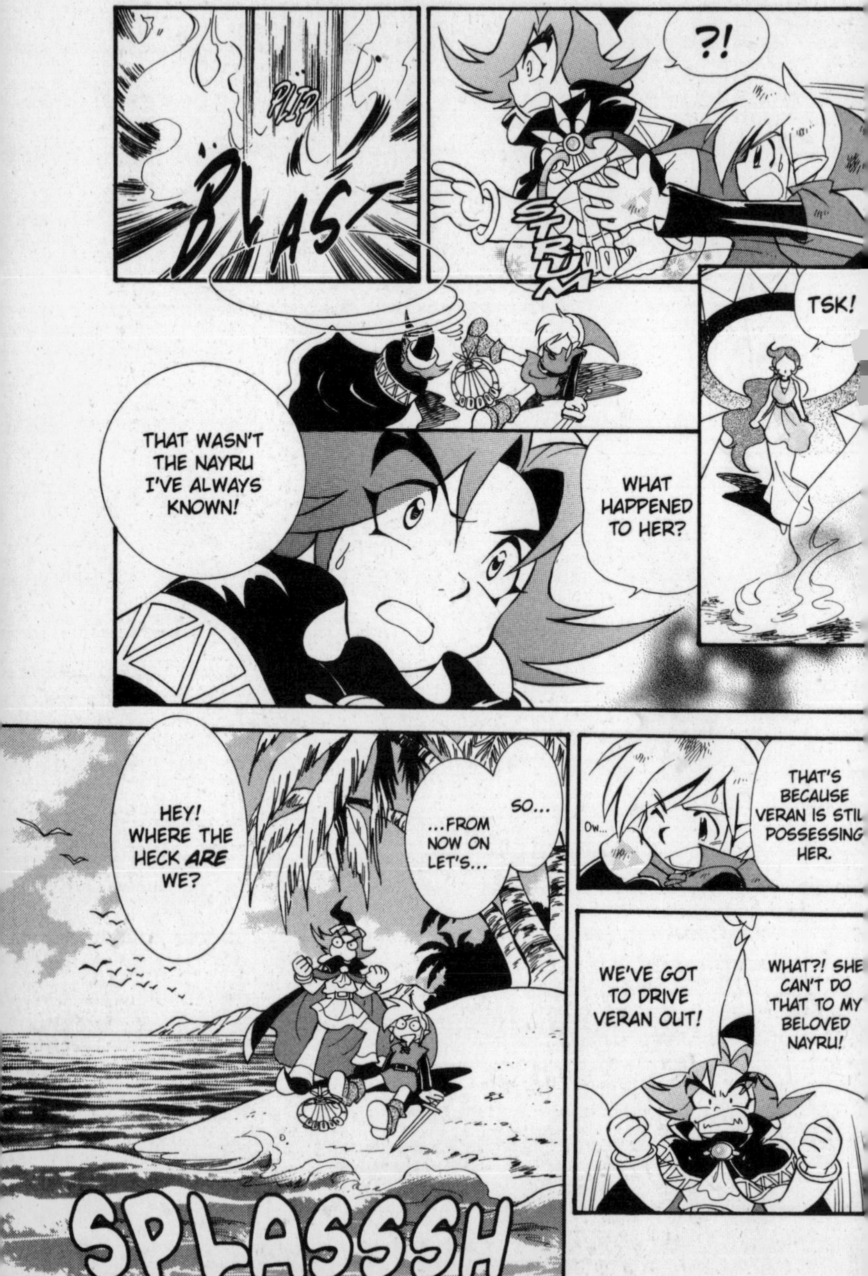
?!
STRUM
PLIP
BLAST
TSK!
THAT WASN'T THE NAYRU I'VE ALWAYS KNOWN!
WHAT HAPPENED TO HER?
OW...
THAT'S BECAUSE VERAN IS STIL POSSESSING HER.
WHAT?! SHE CAN'T DO THAT TO MY BELOVED NAYRU!
WE'VE GOT TO DRIVE VERAN OUT!
SO...
...FROM NOW ON LET'S...
HEY! WHERE THE HECK *ARE* WE?
SPLASSSH

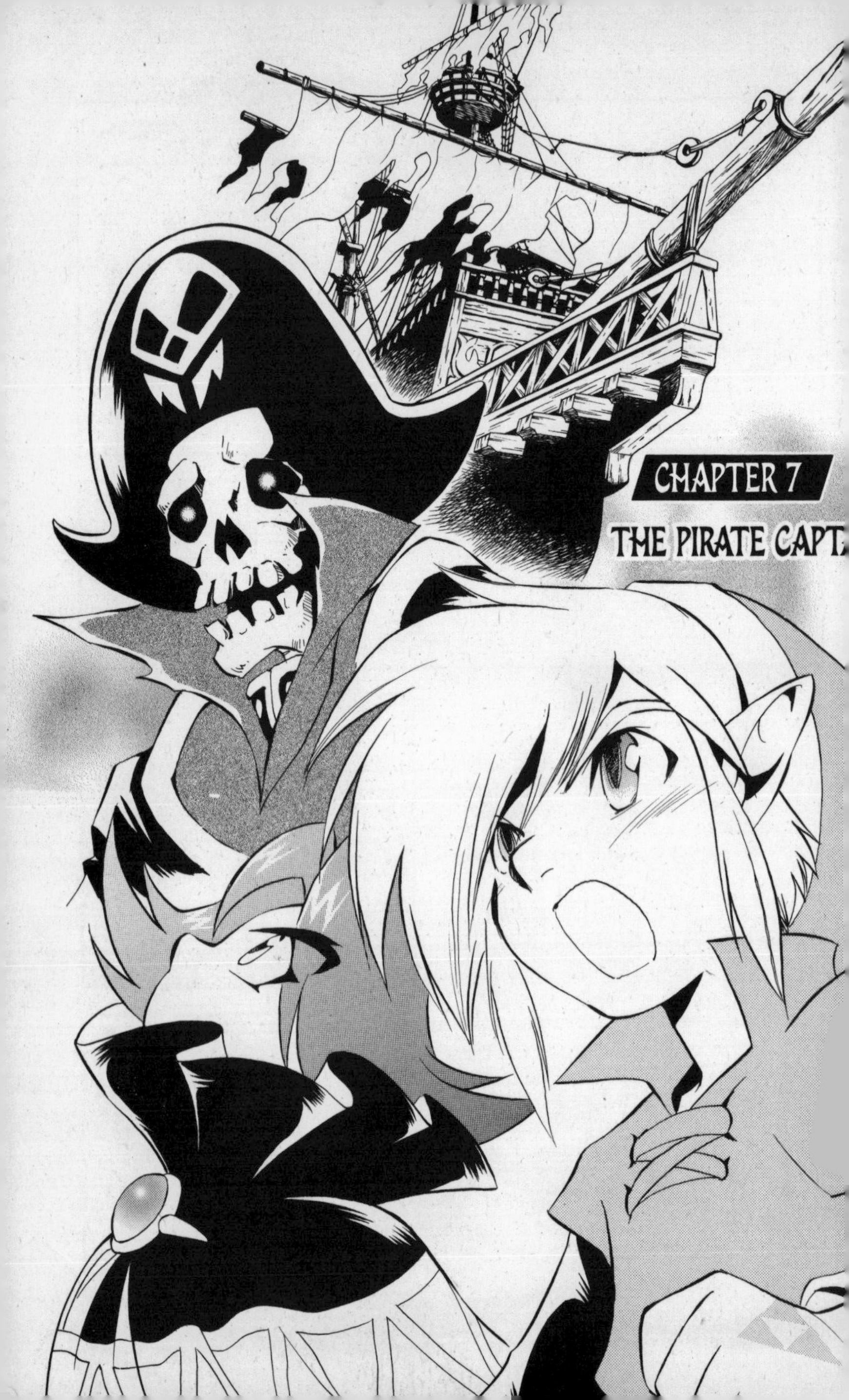
CHAPTER 7
THE PIRATE CAPT

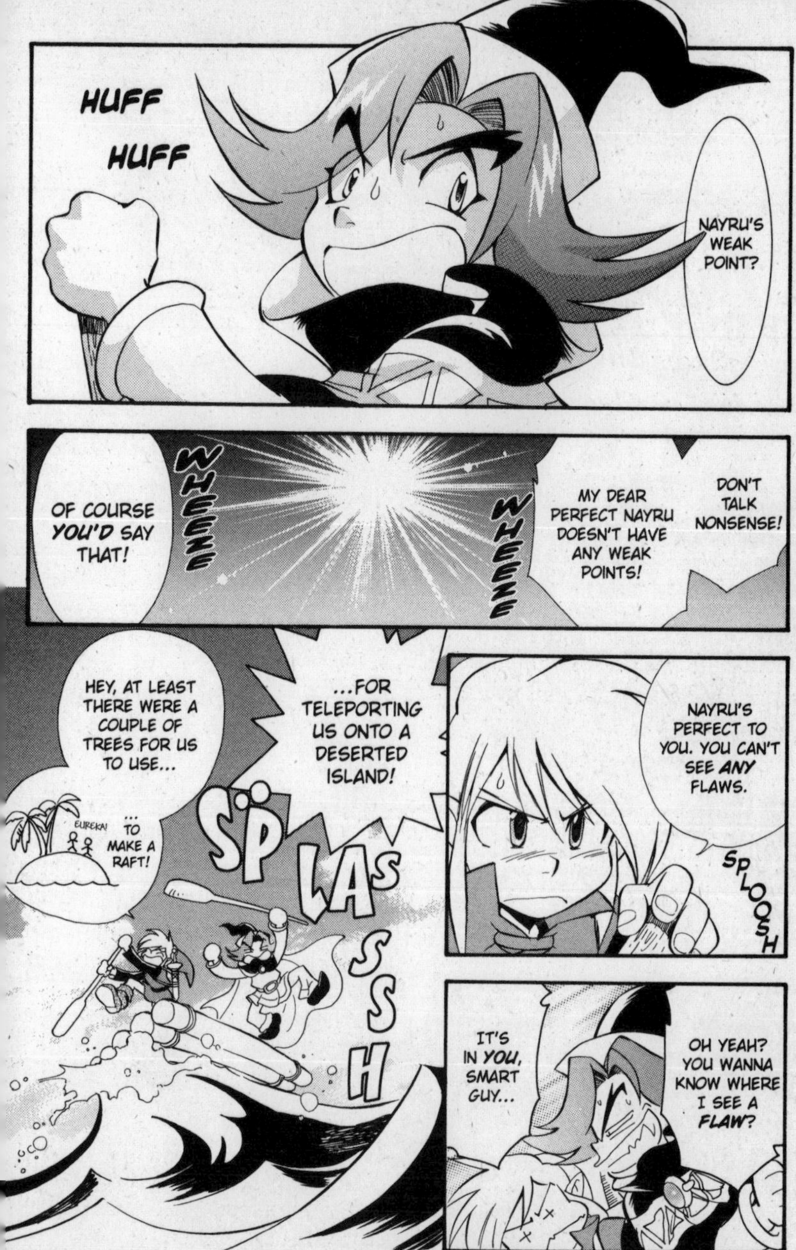
HUFF
HUFF
NAYRU'S WEAK POINT?
DON'T TALK NONSENSE!
MY DEAR PERFECT NAYRU DOESN'T HAVE ANY WEAK POINTS!
WHEEZE
WHEEZE
OF COURSE *YOU'D* SAY THAT!
NAYRU'S PERFECT TO YOU. YOU CAN'T SEE *ANY* FLAWS.
SPLOOSH
OH YEAH? YOU WANNA KNOW WHERE I SEE A *FLAW*?
IT'S IN *YOU*, SMART GUY...
...FOR TELEPORTING US ONTO A DESERTED ISLAND!
HEY, AT LEAST THERE WERE A COUPLE OF TREES FOR US TO USE...
EUREKA!
...TO MAKE A RAFT!
SPLASSSH

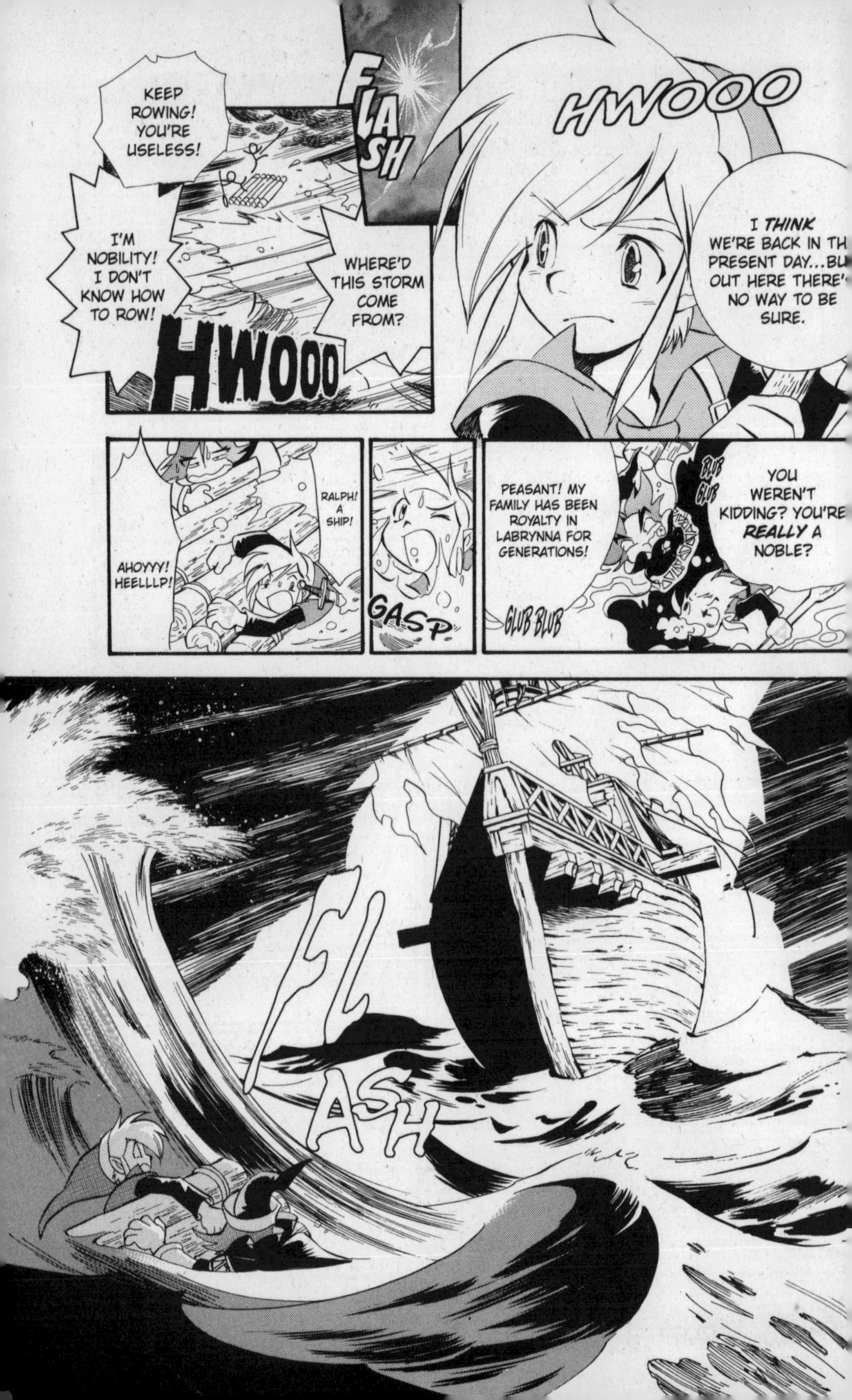
HWOOO
I THINK WE'RE BACK IN TH PRESENT DAY...BU OUT HERE THERE' NO WAY TO BE SURE.
FLASH
KEEP ROWING! YOU'RE USELESS!
I'M NOBILITY! I DON'T KNOW HOW TO ROW!
WHERE'D THIS STORM COME FROM?
HWOOO
YOU WEREN'T KIDDING? YOU'RE REALLY A NOBLE?
BLUB GLUB
PEASANT! MY FAMILY HAS BEEN ROYALTY IN LABRYNNA FOR GENERATIONS!
GLUB BLUB
GASP
RALPH! A SHIP!
AHOYYY! HEELLLP!
FL
ASH

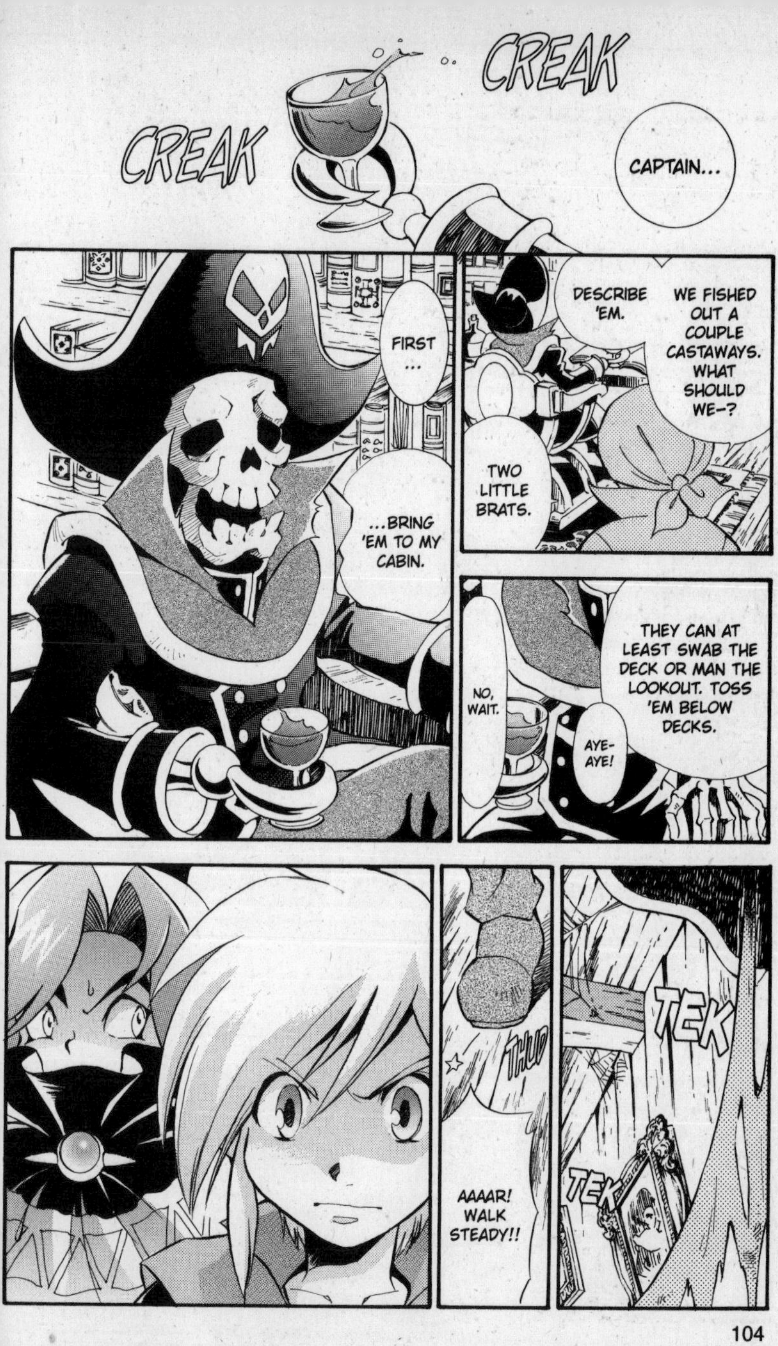
CREAK
CAPTAIN...
CREAK
WE FISHED OUT A COUPLE CASTAWAYS. WHAT SHOULD WE-?
DESCRIBE 'EM.
TWO LITTLE BRATS.
THEY CAN AT LEAST SWAB THE DECK OR MAN THE LOOKOUT. TOSS 'EM BELOW DECKS.
AYE-AYE!
NO, WAIT.
FIRST...
...BRING 'EM TO MY CABIN.
TEK
TEK
THUD
AAAAR! WALK STEADY!!

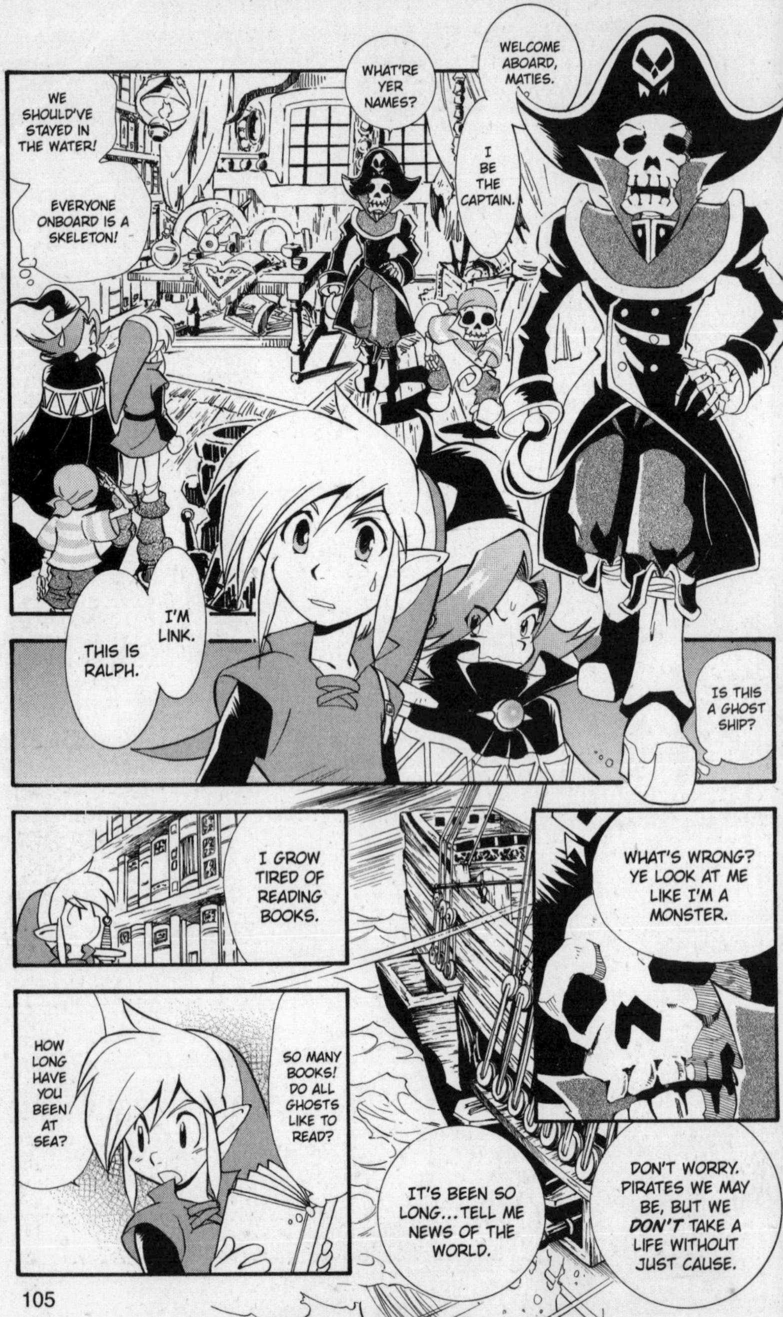
WELCOME ABOARD, MATIES.
I BE THE CAPTAIN.
WHAT'RE YER NAMES?
WE SHOULD'VE STAYED IN THE WATER!
EVERYONE ONBOARD IS A SKELETON!
I'M LINK.
THIS IS RALPH.
IS THIS A GHOST SHIP?
WHAT'S WRONG? YE LOOK AT ME LIKE I'M A MONSTER.
DON'T WORRY. PIRATES WE MAY BE, BUT WE *DON'T* TAKE A LIFE WITHOUT JUST CAUSE.
IT'S BEEN SO LONG...TELL ME NEWS OF THE WORLD.
I GROW TIRED OF READING BOOKS.
SO MANY BOOKS! DO ALL GHOSTS LIKE TO READ?
HOW LONG HAVE YOU BEEN AT SEA?

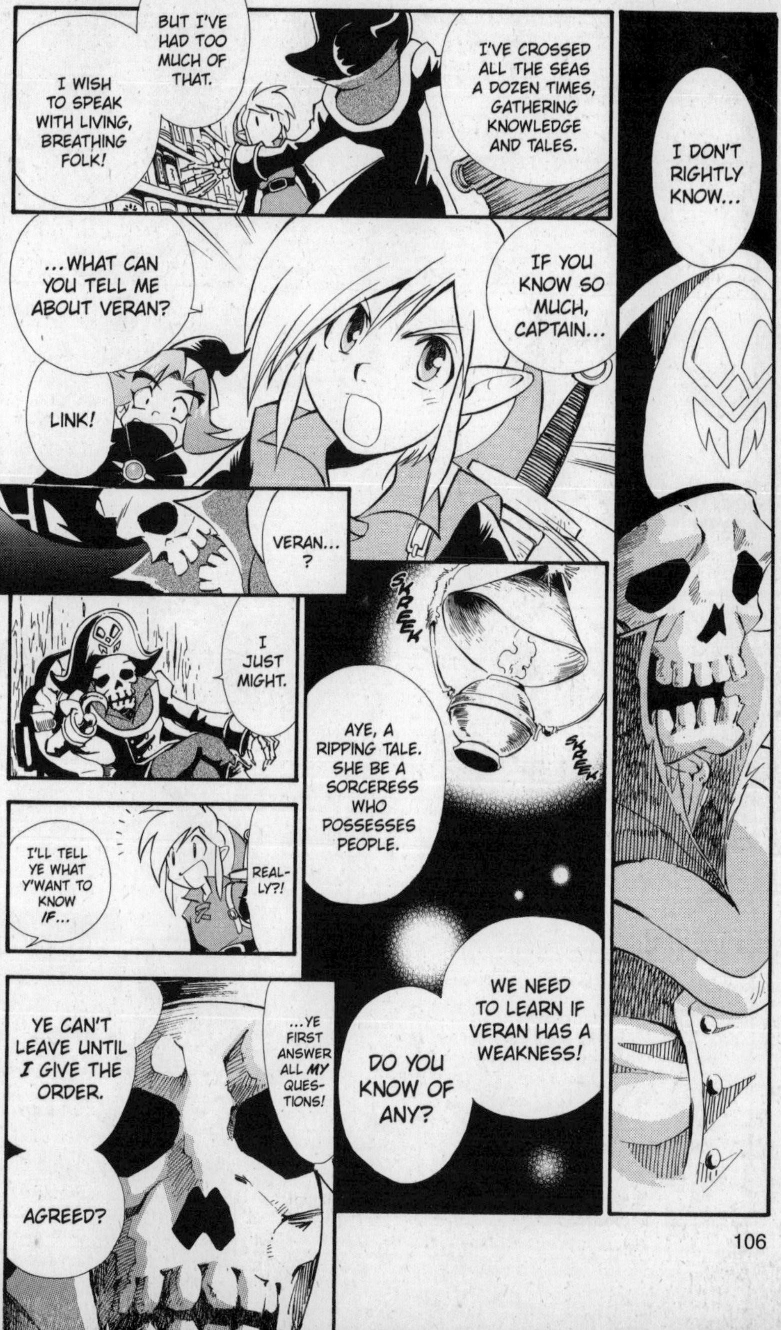
I DON'T RIGHTLY KNOW...
I'VE CROSSED ALL THE SEAS A DOZEN TIMES, GATHERING KNOWLEDGE AND TALES.
BUT I'VE HAD TOO MUCH OF THAT.
I WISH TO SPEAK WITH LIVING, BREATHING FOLK!
IF YOU KNOW SO MUCH, CAPTAIN...
...WHAT CAN YOU TELL ME ABOUT VERAN?
LINK!
VERAN...?
SKREEK
SKREEK
I JUST MIGHT.
AYE, A RIPPING TALE. SHE BE A SORCERESS WHO POSSESSES PEOPLE.
REAL-LY?!
I'LL TELL YE WHAT Y'WANT TO KNOW *IF*...
...YE FIRST ANSWER ALL *MY* QUES-TIONS!
YE CAN'T LEAVE UNTIL *I* GIVE THE ORDER.
AGREED?
WE NEED TO LEARN IF VERAN HAS A WEAKNESS!
DO YOU KNOW OF ANY?

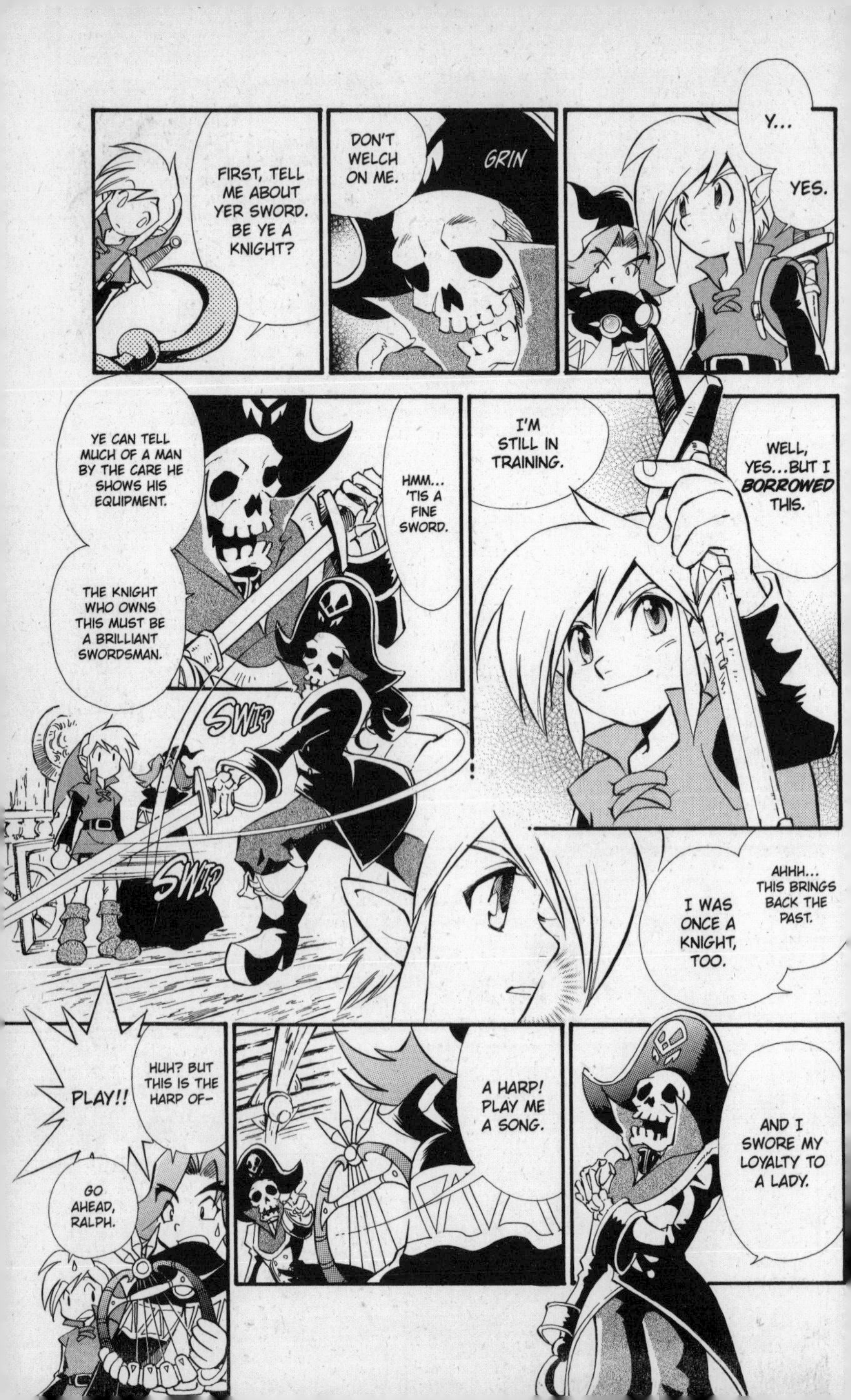
Y...
YES.
GRIN
DON'T WELCH ON ME.
FIRST, TELL ME ABOUT YER SWORD. BE YE A KNIGHT?
WELL, YES...BUT I BORROWED THIS.
I'M STILL IN TRAINING.
HMM... 'TIS A FINE SWORD.
YE CAN TELL MUCH OF A MAN BY THE CARE HE SHOWS HIS EQUIPMENT.
THE KNIGHT WHO OWNS THIS MUST BE A BRILLIANT SWORDSMAN.
SWIP
SWIP
AHHH... THIS BRINGS BACK THE PAST.
I WAS ONCE A KNIGHT, TOO.
AND I SWORE MY LOYALTY TO A LADY.
A HARP! PLAY ME A SONG.
HUH? BUT THIS IS THE HARP OF-
PLAY!!
GO AHEAD, RALPH.

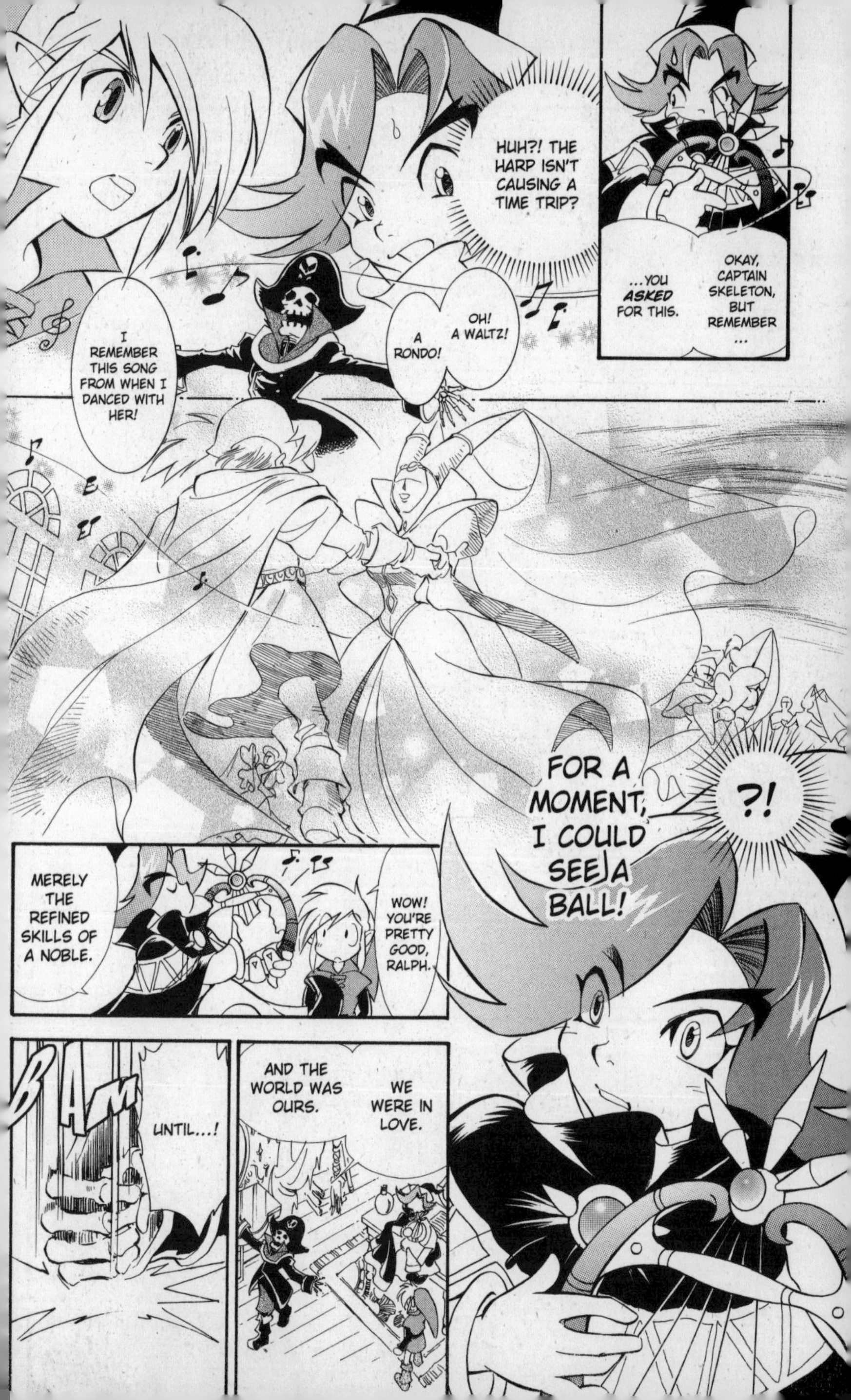

OKAY, CAPTAIN SKELETON, BUT REMEMBER ...
...YOU **ASKED** FOR THIS.
HUH?! THE HARP ISN'T CAUSING A TIME TRIP?
OH! A WALTZ!
A RONDO!
I REMEMBER THIS SONG FROM WHEN I DANCED WITH HER!
?!
FOR A MOMENT, I COULD SEE A BALL!
WOW! YOU'RE PRETTY GOOD, RALPH.
MERELY THE REFINED SKILLS OF A NOBLE.
WE WERE IN LOVE.
AND THE WORLD WAS OURS.
UNTIL...!
BAM

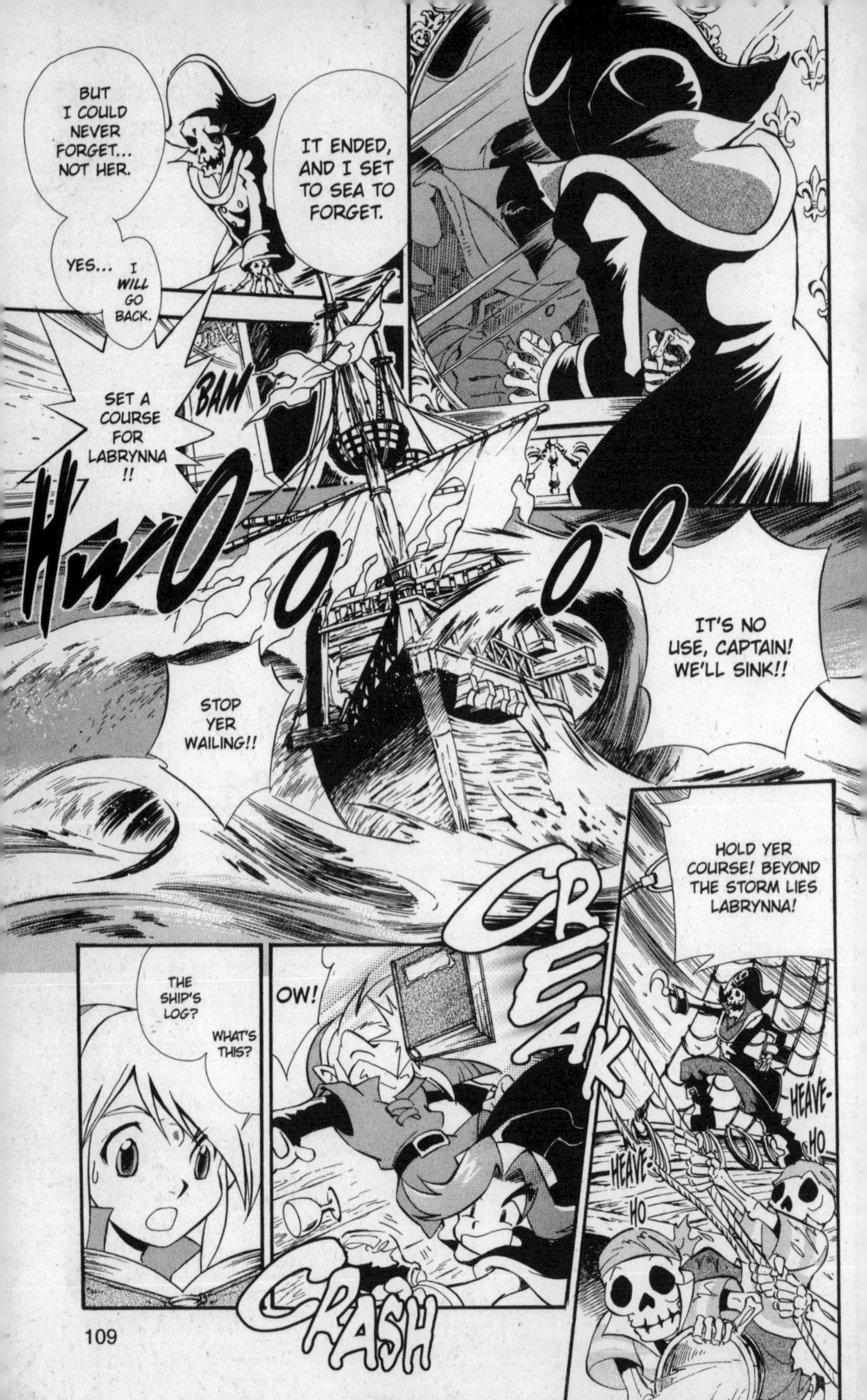
IT ENDED, AND I SET TO SEA TO FORGET.
BUT I COULD NEVER FORGET... NOT HER.
YES... I WILL GO BACK.
BAM
SET A COURSE FOR LABRYNNA!!
HWOOOOO
IT'S NO USE, CAPTAIN! WE'LL SINK!!
STOP YER WAILING!!
HOLD YER COURSE! BEYOND THE STORM LIES LABRYNNA!
CREAK
HEAVE-HO
HEAVE-HO
OW!
CRASH
WHAT'S THIS?
THE SHIP'S LOG?

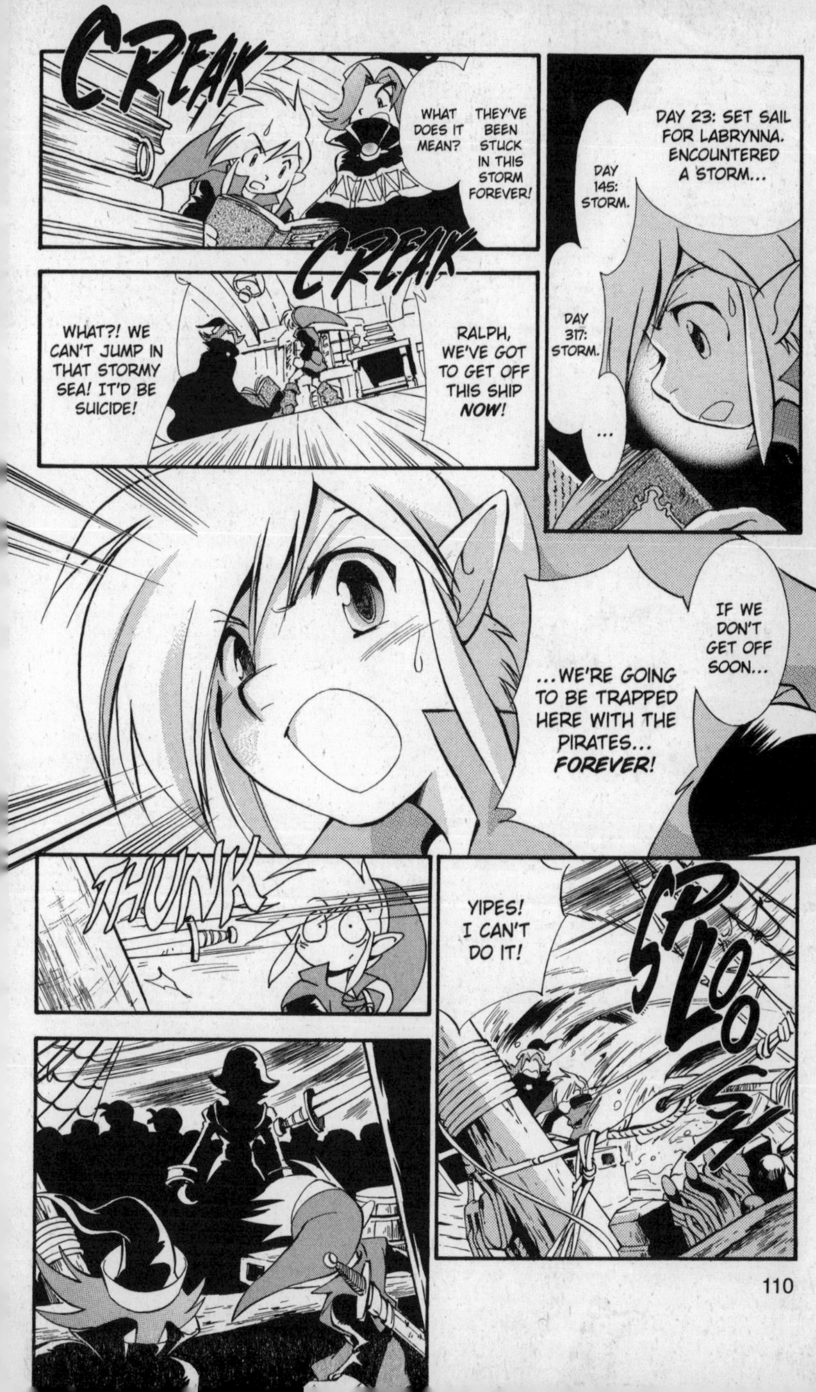

DAY 23: SET SAIL FOR LABRYNNA. ENCOUNTERED A STORM...
DAY 145: STORM.
DAY 317: STORM.
...
CREAK
THEY'VE BEEN STUCK IN THIS STORM FOREVER!
WHAT DOES IT MEAN?
CREAK
RALPH, WE'VE GOT TO GET OFF THIS SHIP NOW!
WHAT?! WE CAN'T JUMP IN THAT STORMY SEA! IT'D BE SUICIDE!
IF WE DON'T GET OFF SOON...
...WE'RE GOING TO BE TRAPPED HERE WITH THE PIRATES... FOREVER!
SPLOOSH
YIPES! I CAN'T DO IT!
THUNK

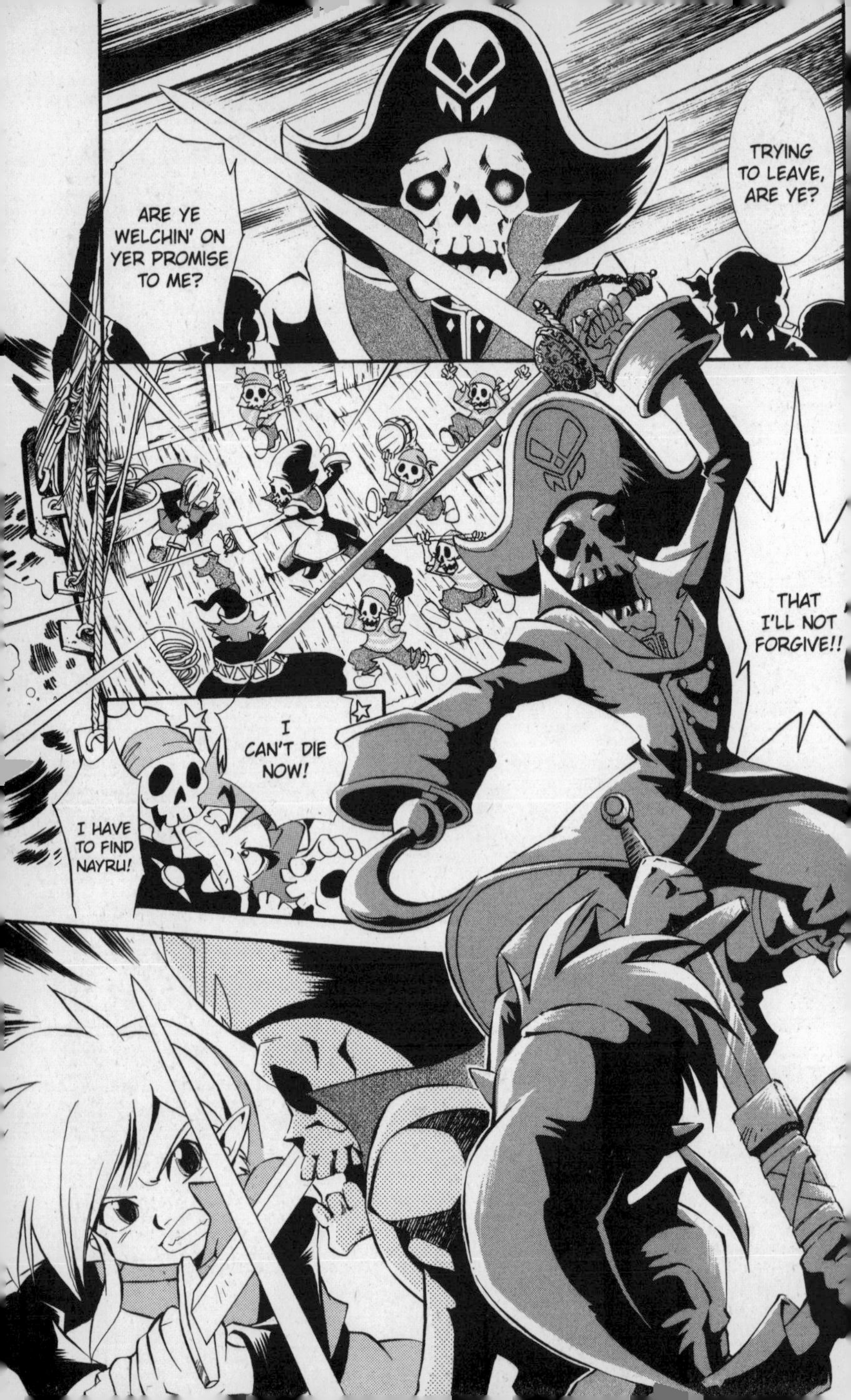
TRYING TO LEAVE, ARE YE?
ARE YE WELCHIN' ON YER PROMISE TO ME?
THAT I'LL NOT FORGIVE!!
I CAN'T DIE NOW!
I HAVE TO FIND NAYRU!

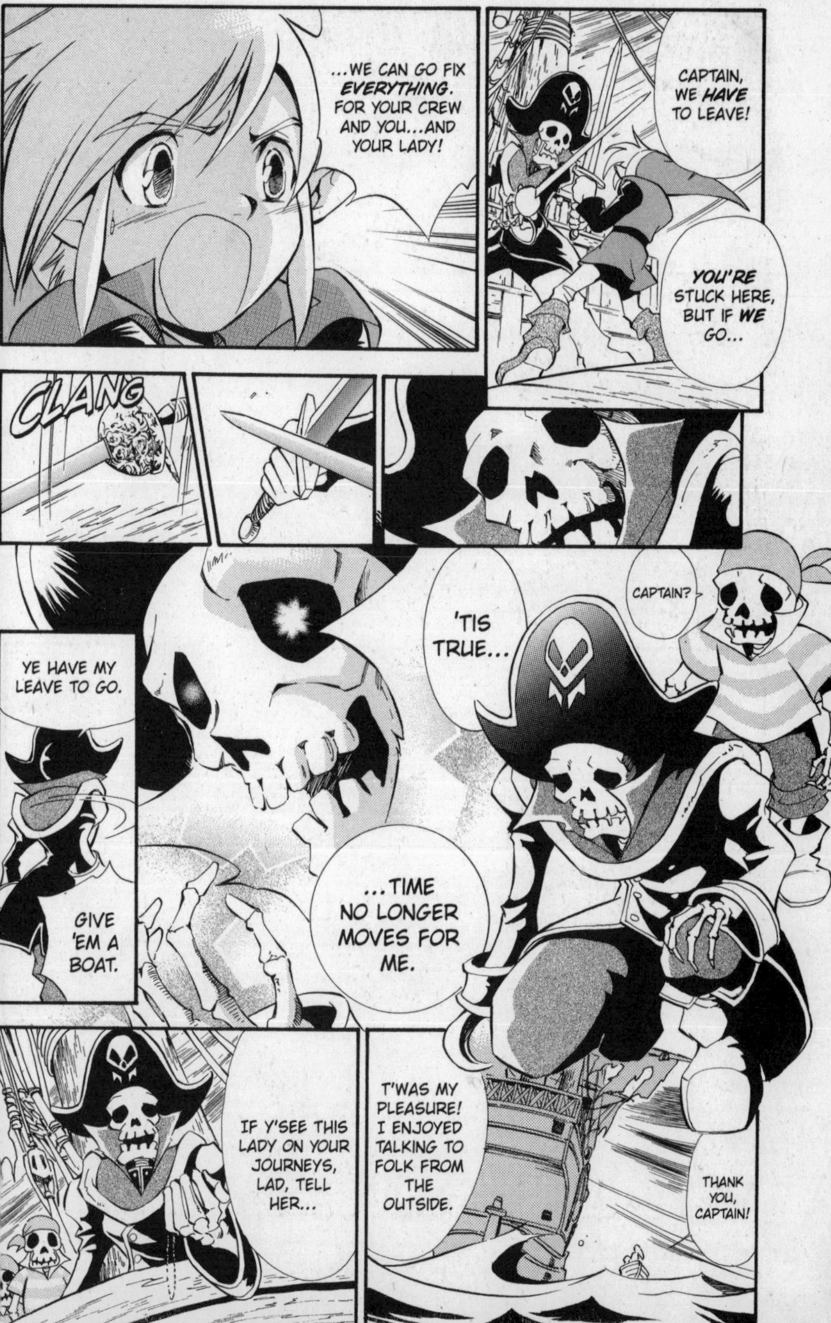
CAPTAIN, WE *HAVE* TO LEAVE!
YOU'RE STUCK HERE, BUT IF *WE* GO...
...WE CAN GO FIX *EVERYTHING*. FOR YOUR CREW AND YOU...AND YOUR LADY!
CLANG
CAPTAIN?
'TIS TRUE...
...TIME NO LONGER MOVES FOR ME.
YE HAVE MY LEAVE TO GO.
GIVE 'EM A BOAT.
THANK YOU, CAPTAIN!
T'WAS MY PLEASURE! I ENJOYED TALKING TO FOLK FROM THE OUTSIDE.
IF Y'SEE THIS LADY ON YOUR JOURNEYS, LAD, TELL HER...

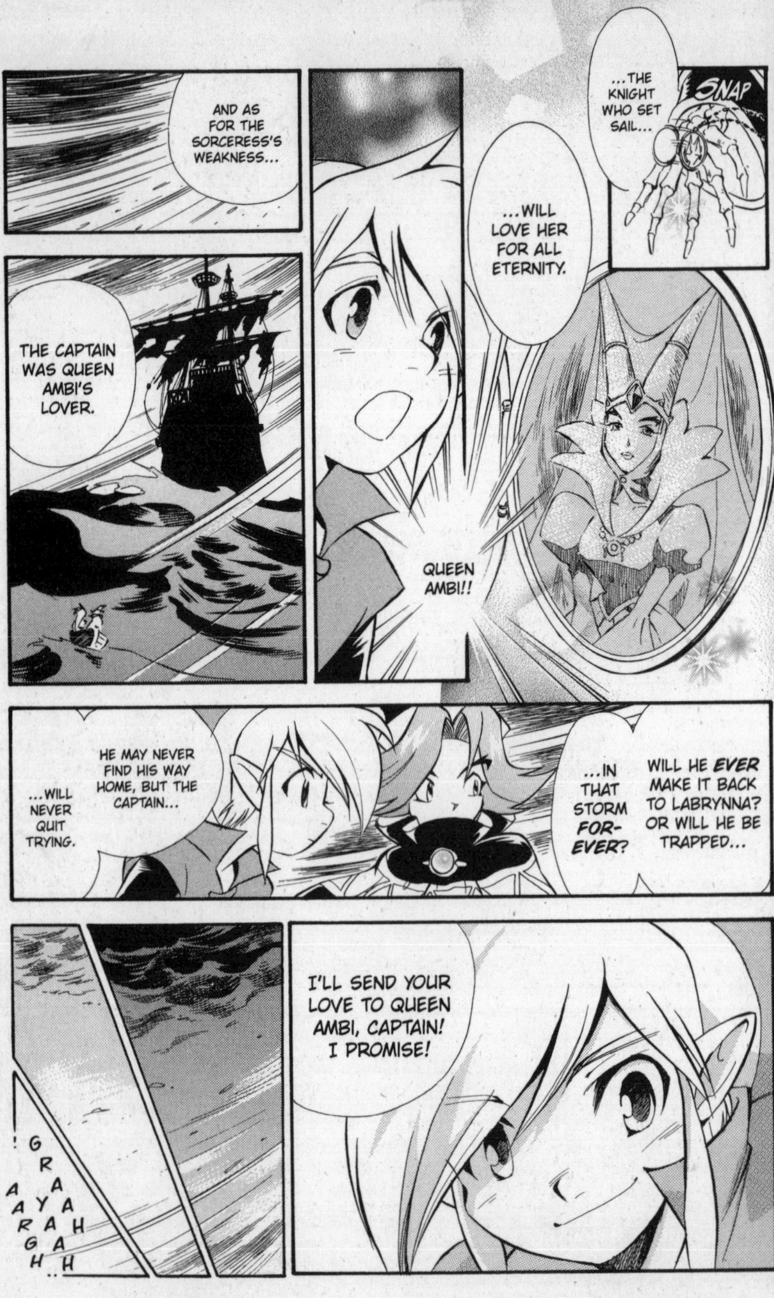
SNAP
...THE KNIGHT WHO SET SAIL...
...WILL LOVE HER FOR ALL ETERNITY.
QUEEN AMBI!!
AND AS FOR THE SORCERESS'S WEAKNESS...
THE CAPTAIN WAS QUEEN AMBI'S LOVER.
WILL HE EVER MAKE IT BACK TO LABRYNNA? OR WILL HE BE TRAPPED...
...IN THAT STORM FOREVER?
HE MAY NEVER FIND HIS WAY HOME, BUT THE CAPTAIN...
...WILL NEVER QUIT TRYING.
I'LL SEND YOUR LOVE TO QUEEN AMBI, CAPTAIN! I PROMISE!
GRAAAAH AAARGH
YAAAHH..!

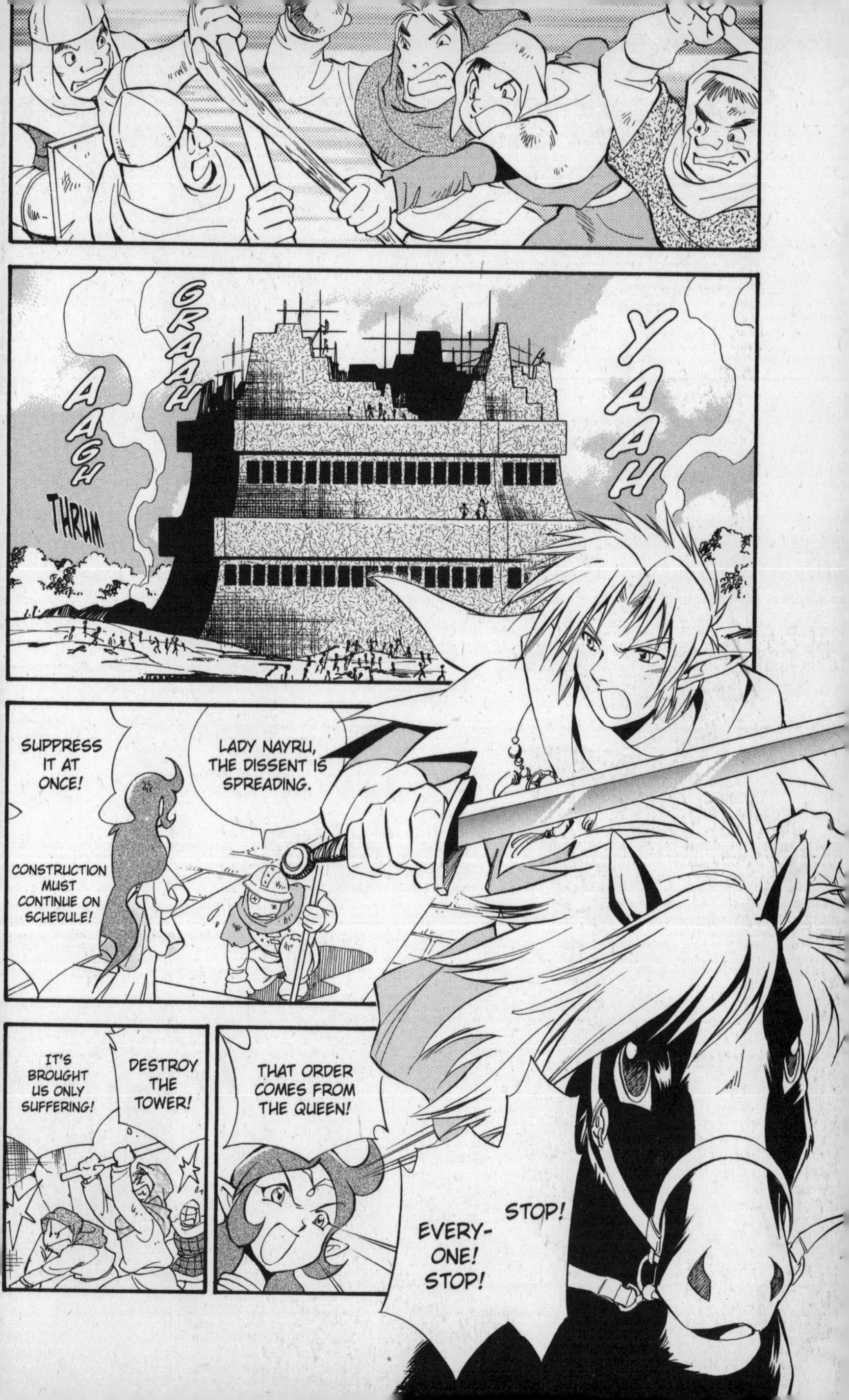
YAAAH
GRAAAH
AAAGH
THRUM
LADY NAYRU, THE DISSENT IS SPREADING.
SUPPRESS IT AT ONCE!
CONSTRUCTION MUST CONTINUE ON SCHEDULE!
THAT ORDER COMES FROM THE QUEEN!
DESTROY THE TOWER!
IT'S BROUGHT US ONLY SUFFERING!
STOP!
EVERY-ONE! STOP!

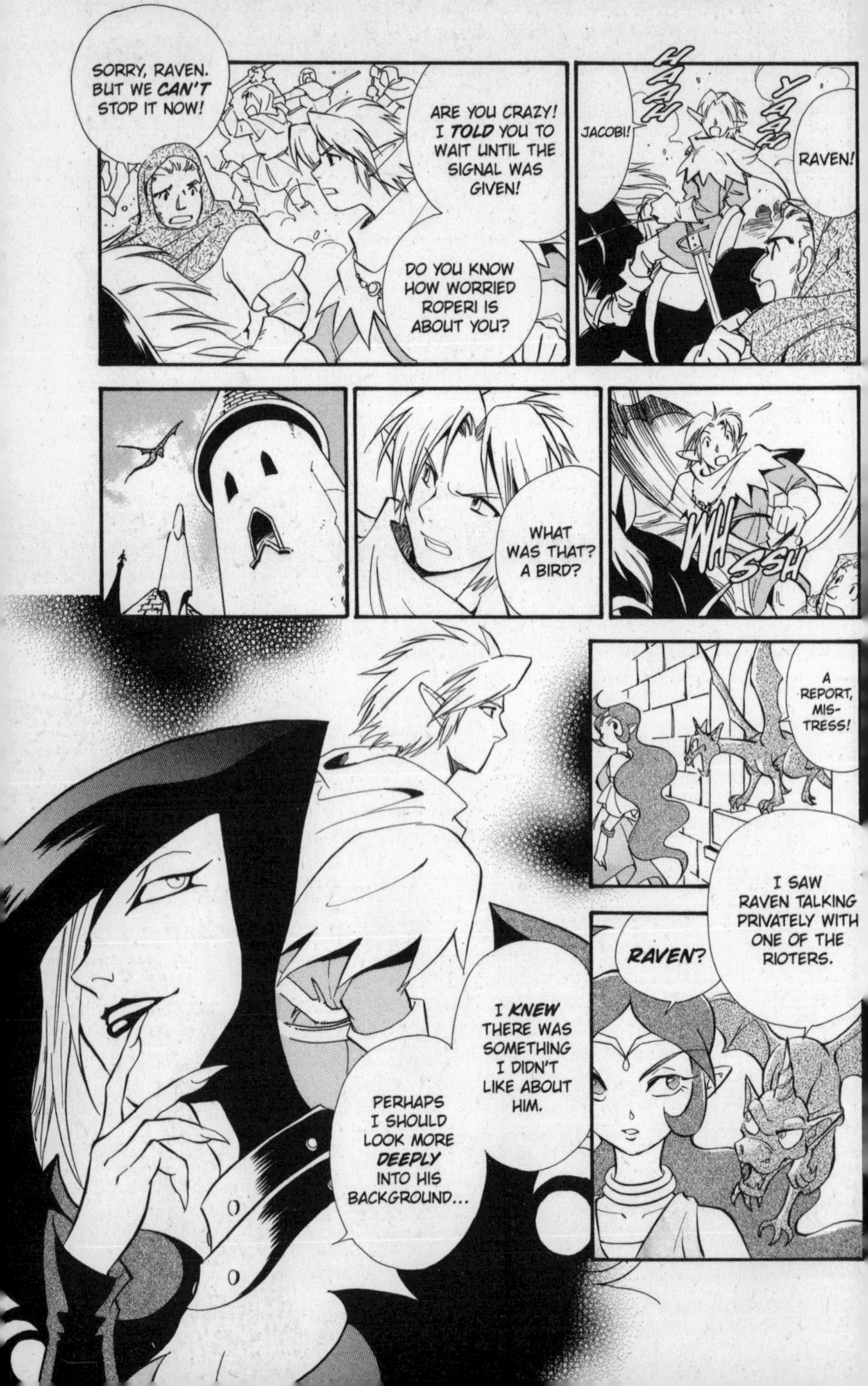
YAAAH
RAVEN!
HAAAH
JACOBI!
ARE YOU CRAZY! I **TOLD** YOU TO WAIT UNTIL THE SIGNAL WAS GIVEN!
DO YOU KNOW HOW WORRIED ROPERI IS ABOUT YOU?
SORRY, RAVEN. BUT WE ***CAN'T*** STOP IT NOW!
WHSSH
WHAT WAS THAT? A BIRD?
A REPORT, MIS-TRESS!
I SAW RAVEN TALKING PRIVATELY WITH ONE OF THE RIOTERS.
RAVEN?
I ***KNEW*** THERE WAS SOMETHING I DIDN'T LIKE ABOUT HIM.
PERHAPS I SHOULD LOOK MORE ***DEEPLY*** INTO HIS BACKGROUND...

CHAPTER 8
RAMROCK

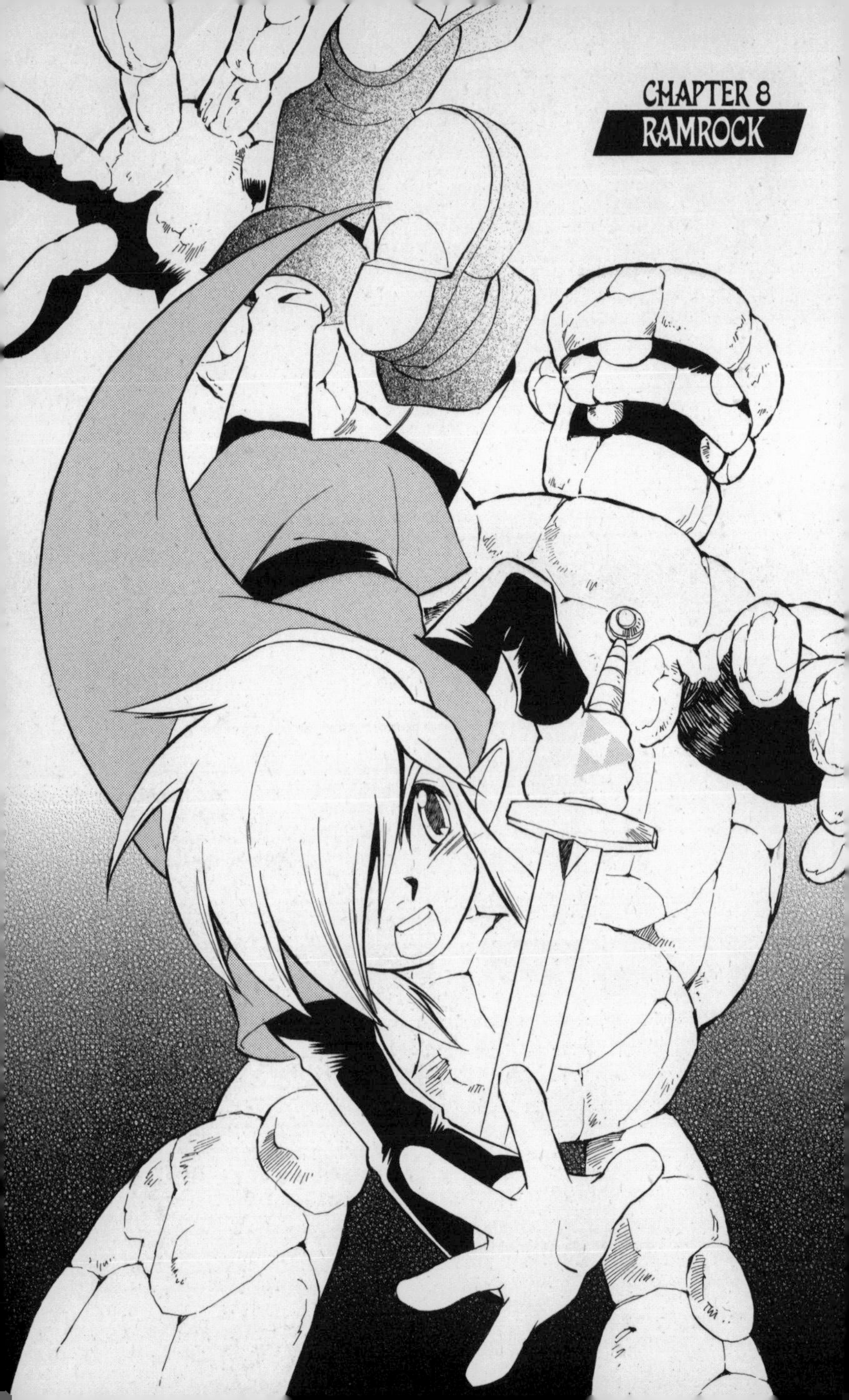

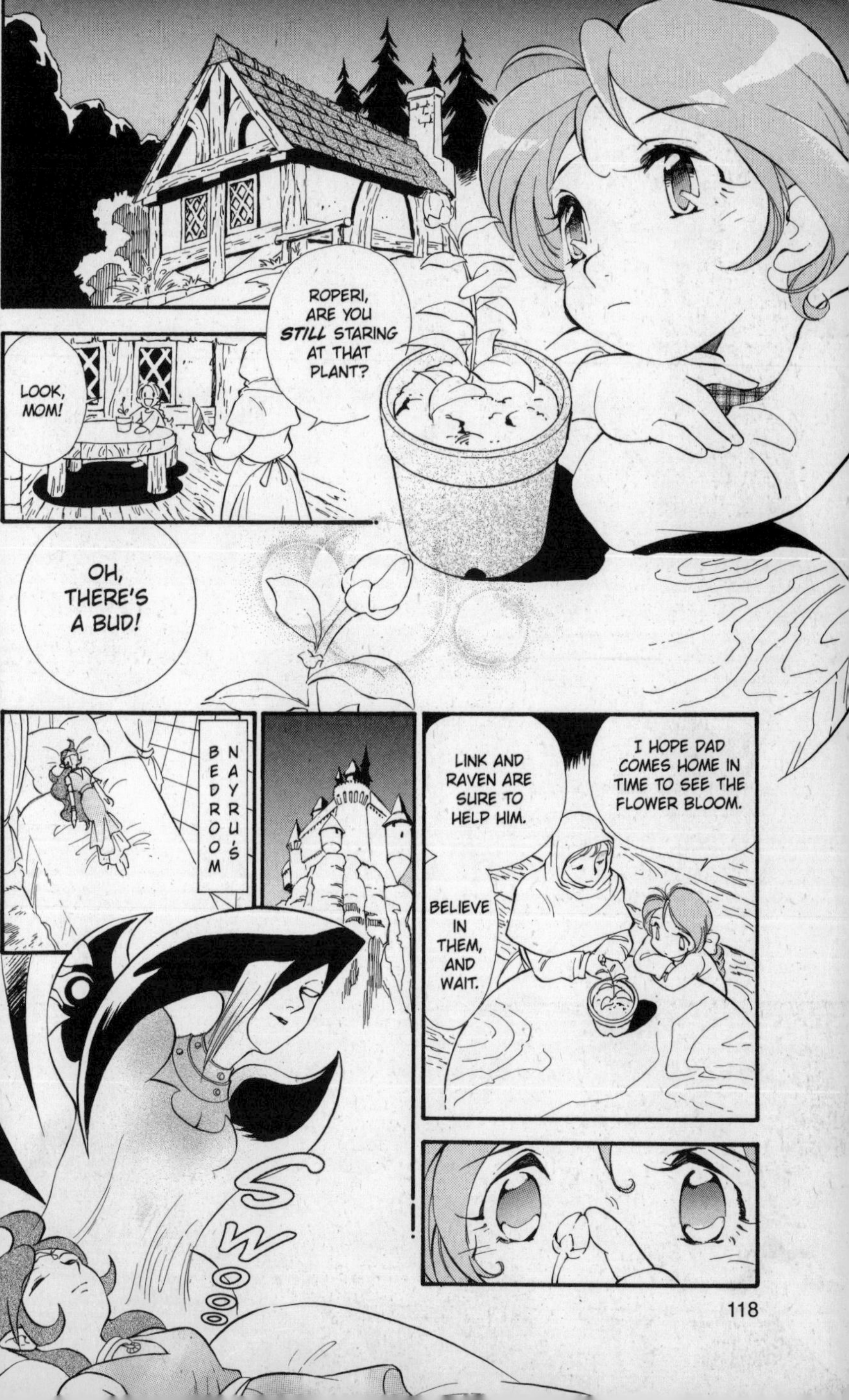
ROPERI, ARE YOU *STILL* STARING AT THAT PLANT?
LOOK, MOM!
OH, THERE'S A BUD!
I HOPE DAD COMES HOME IN TIME TO SEE THE FLOWER BLOOM.
LINK AND RAVEN ARE SURE TO HELP HIM.
BELIEVE IN THEM, AND WAIT.
NAYRU'S BEDROOM
SWOOO

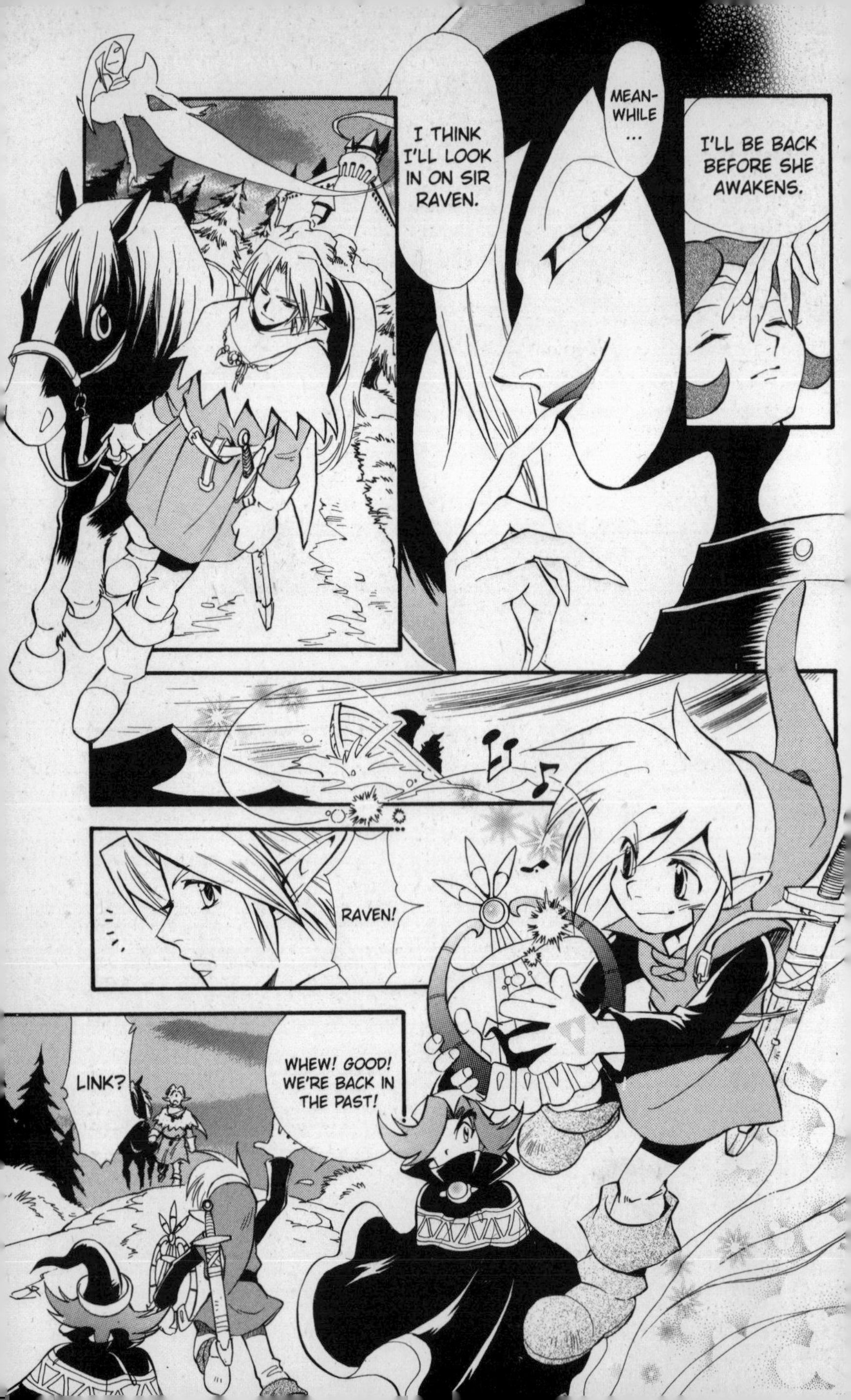
I'LL BE BACK BEFORE SHE AWAKENS.
MEAN-WHILE ...
I THINK I'LL LOOK IN ON SIR RAVEN.
RAVEN!
WHEW! GOOD! WE'RE BACK IN THE PAST!
LINK?

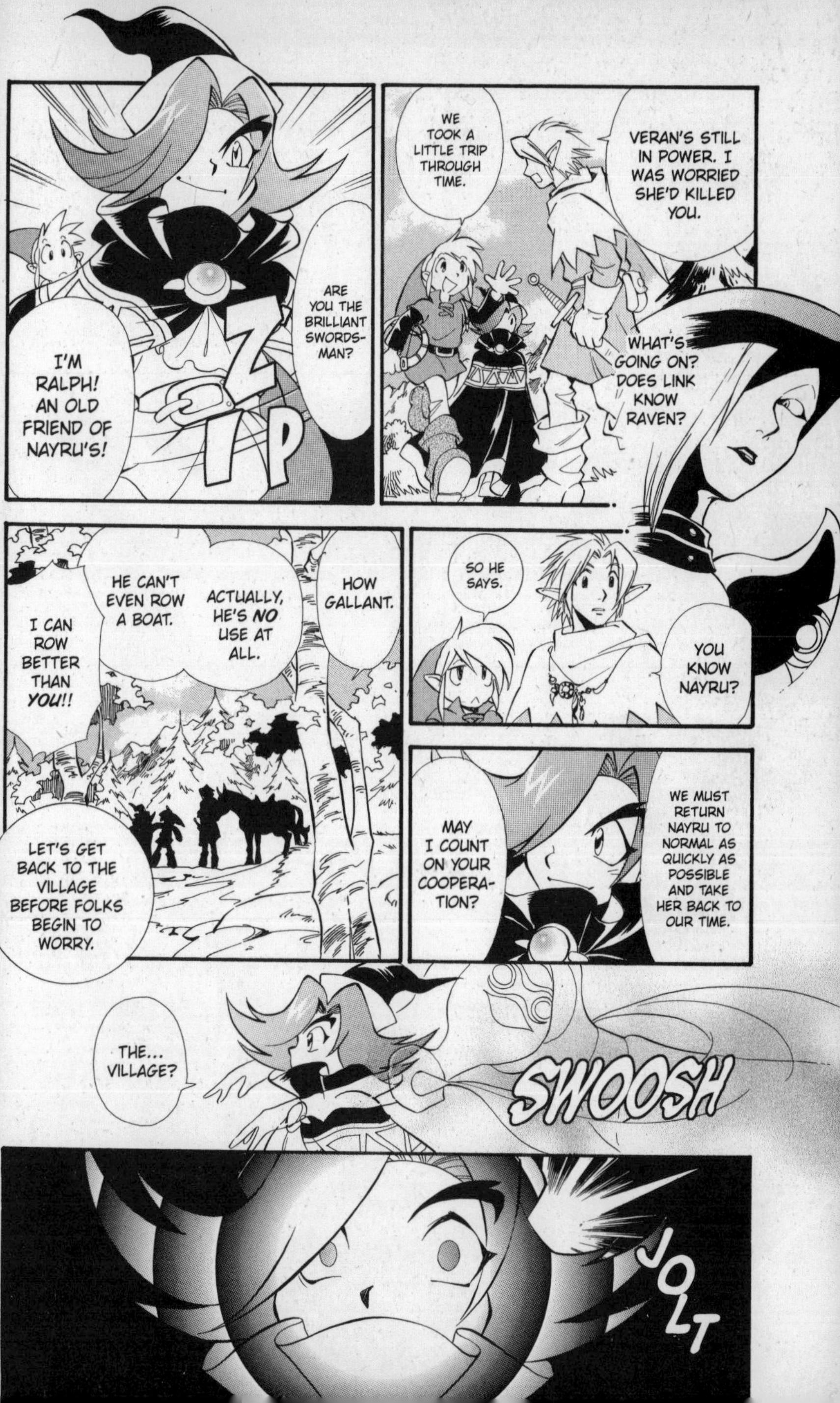
VERAN'S STILL IN POWER. I WAS WORRIED SHE'D KILLED YOU.
WE TOOK A LITTLE TRIP THROUGH TIME.
WHAT'S GOING ON? DOES LINK KNOW RAVEN?
ARE YOU THE BRILLIANT SWORDS-MAN?
ZIP
I'M RALPH! AN OLD FRIEND OF NAYRU'S!
YOU KNOW NAYRU?
SO HE SAYS.
WE MUST RETURN NAYRU TO NORMAL AS QUICKLY AS POSSIBLE AND TAKE HER BACK TO OUR TIME.
MAY I COUNT ON YOUR COOPERA-TION?
HOW GALLANT.
ACTUALLY, HE'S *NO* USE AT ALL.
HE CAN'T EVEN ROW A BOAT.
I CAN ROW BETTER THAN *YOU*!!
LET'S GET BACK TO THE VILLAGE BEFORE FOLKS BEGIN TO WORRY.
SWOOSH
THE... VILLAGE?
JOLT

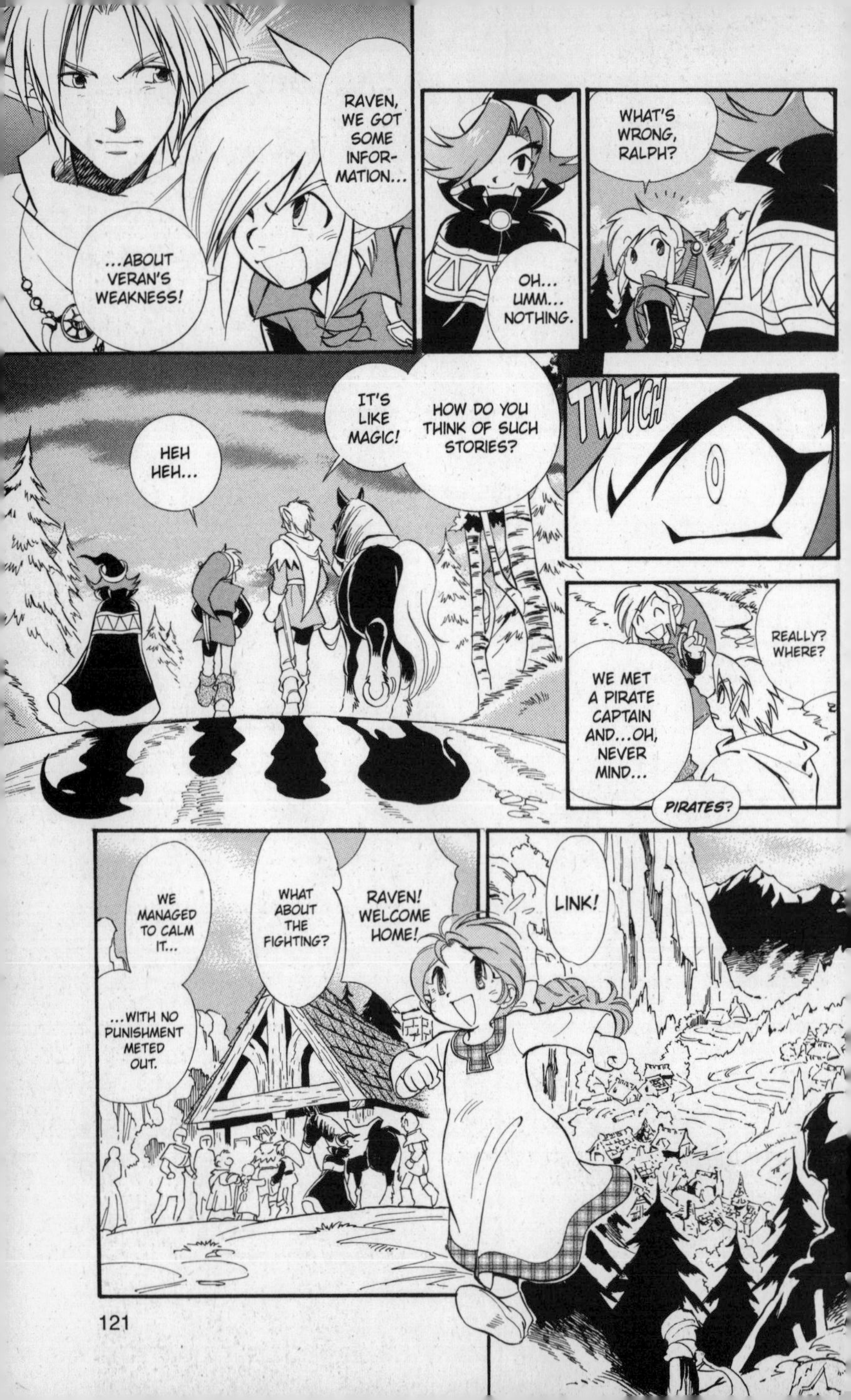
WHAT'S WRONG, RALPH?
OH... UMM... NOTHING.
RAVEN, WE GOT SOME INFORMATION...
...ABOUT VERAN'S WEAKNESS!
TWITCH
REALLY? WHERE?
WE MET A PIRATE CAPTAIN AND...OH, NEVER MIND...
PIRATES?
HOW DO YOU THINK OF SUCH STORIES?
IT'S LIKE MAGIC!
HEH HEH...
LINK!
RAVEN! WELCOME HOME!
WHAT ABOUT THE FIGHTING?
WE MANAGED TO CALM IT...
...WITH NO PUNISHMENT METED OUT.

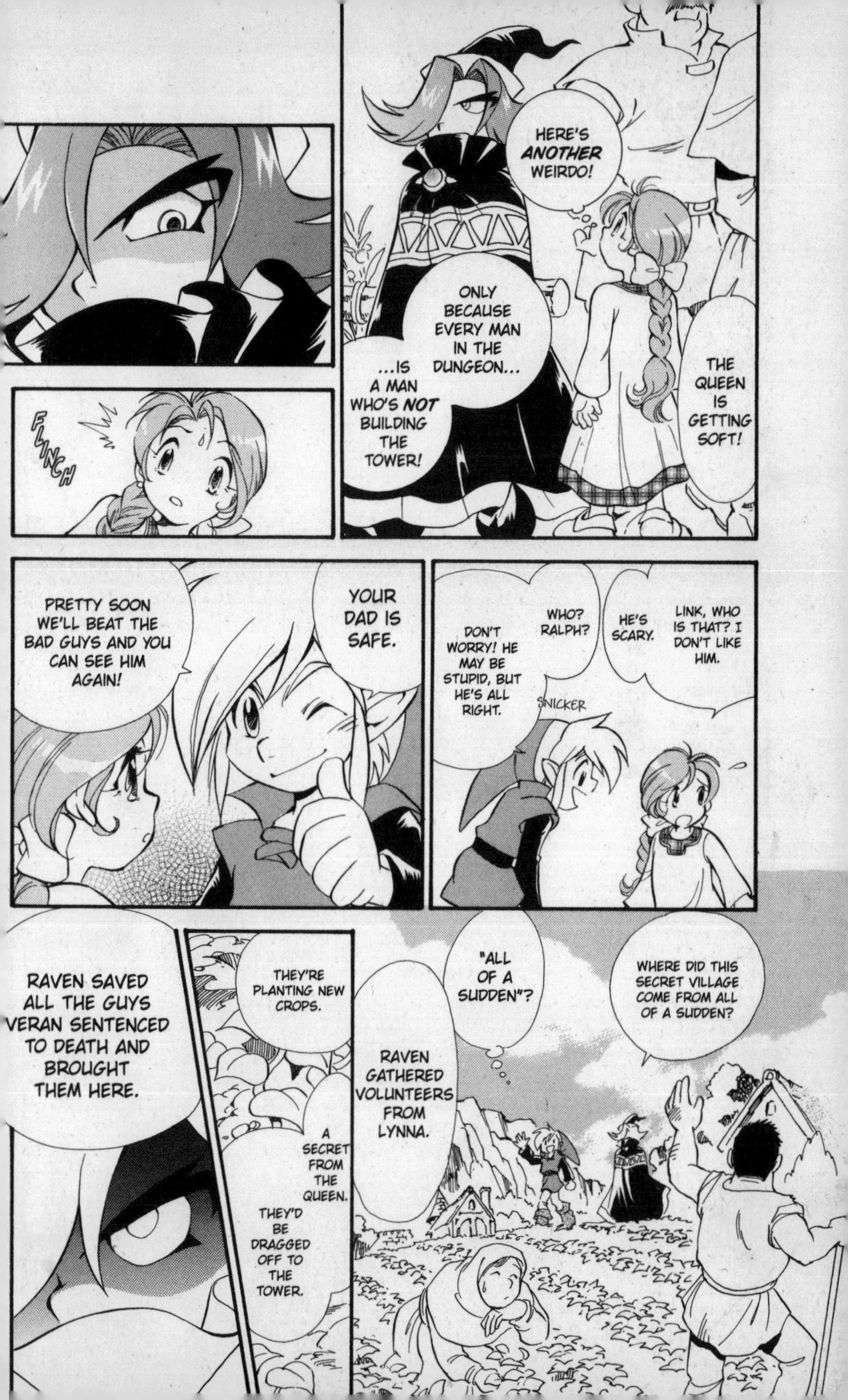
HERE'S ANOTHER WEIRDO!
THE QUEEN IS GETTING SOFT!
ONLY BECAUSE EVERY MAN IN THE DUNGEON...
...IS A MAN WHO'S NOT BUILDING THE TOWER!
FLINCH
LINK, WHO IS THAT? I DON'T LIKE HIM.
HE'S SCARY.
WHO? RALPH?
DON'T WORRY! HE MAY BE STUPID, BUT HE'S ALL RIGHT.
SNICKER
YOUR DAD IS SAFE.
PRETTY SOON WE'LL BEAT THE BAD GUYS AND YOU CAN SEE HIM AGAIN!
WHERE DID THIS SECRET VILLAGE COME FROM ALL OF A SUDDEN?
"ALL OF A SUDDEN"?
RAVEN GATHERED VOLUNTEERS FROM LYNNA.
A SECRET FROM THE QUEEN.
THEY'D BE DRAGGED OFF TO THE TOWER.
THEY'RE PLANTING NEW CROPS.
RAVEN SAVED ALL THE GUYS VERAN SENTENCED TO DEATH AND BROUGHT THEM HERE.

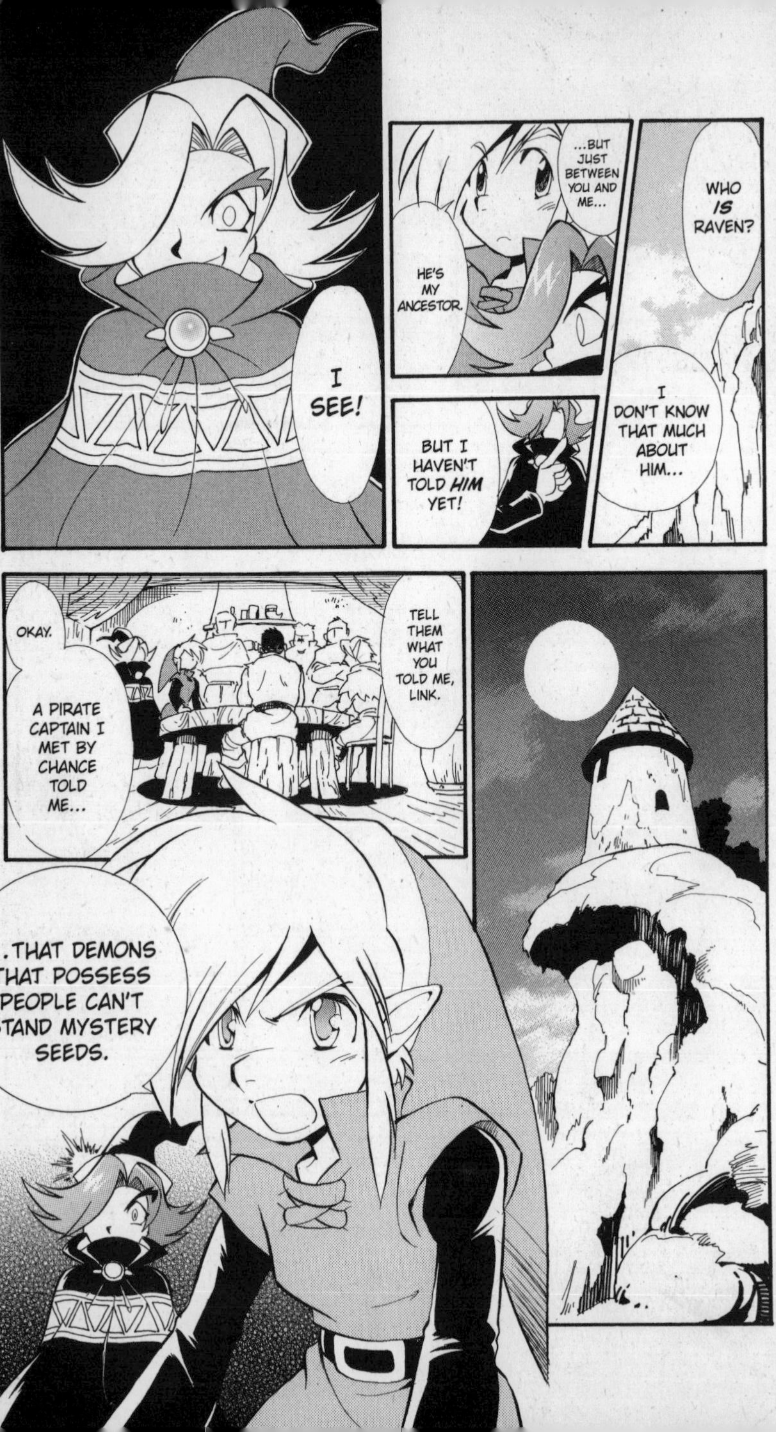
WHO IS RAVEN?
I DON'T KNOW THAT MUCH ABOUT HIM...
...BUT JUST BETWEEN YOU AND ME...
HE'S MY ANCESTOR.
BUT I HAVEN'T TOLD HIM YET!
I SEE!
TELL THEM WHAT YOU TOLD ME, LINK.
OKAY.
A PIRATE CAPTAIN I MET BY CHANCE TOLD ME...
...THAT DEMONS THAT POSSESS PEOPLE CAN'T STAND MYSTERY SEEDS.

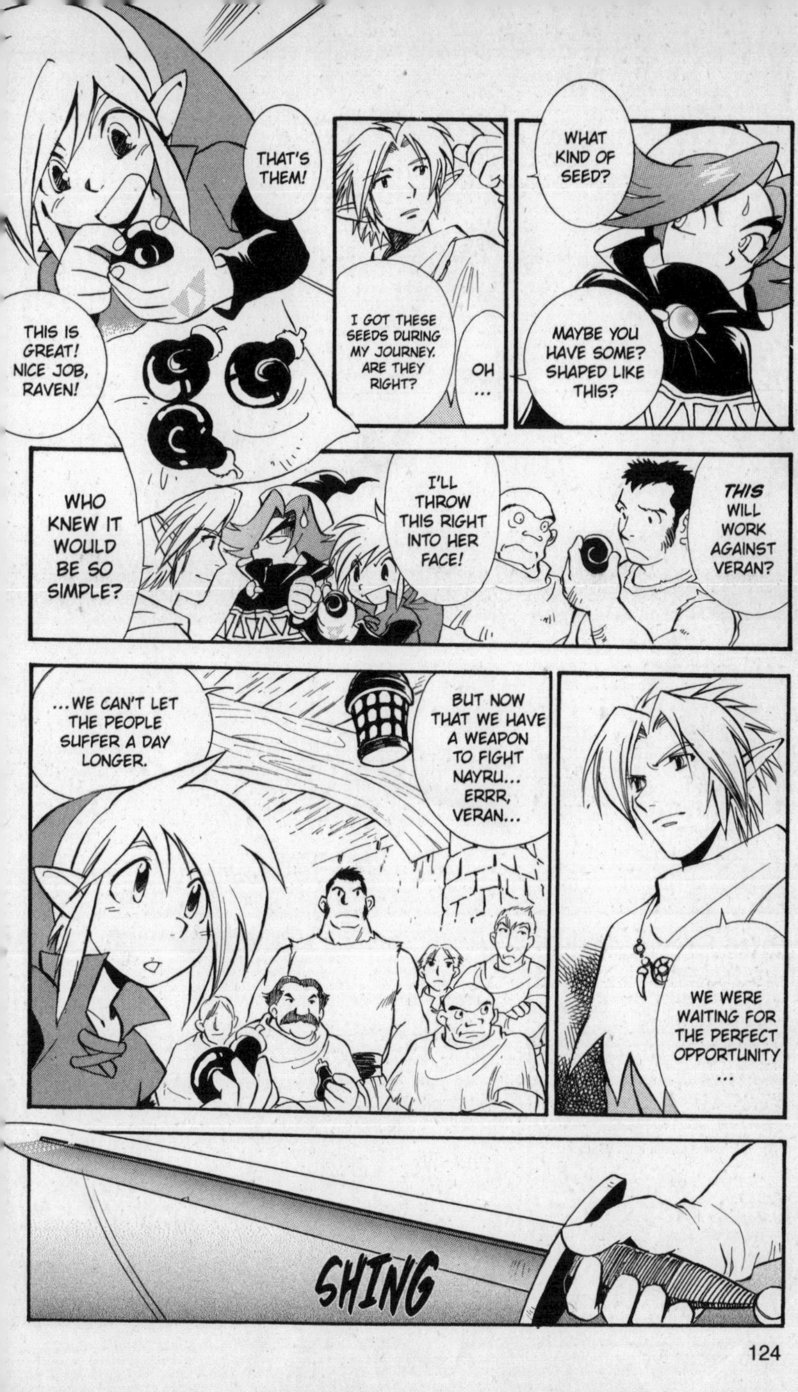
WHAT KIND OF SEED?
MAYBE YOU HAVE SOME? SHAPED LIKE THIS?
OH ...
I GOT THESE SEEDS DURING MY JOURNEY. ARE THEY RIGHT?
THAT'S THEM!
THIS IS GREAT! NICE JOB, RAVEN!
THIS WILL WORK AGAINST VERAN?
I'LL THROW THIS RIGHT INTO HER FACE!
WHO KNEW IT WOULD BE SO SIMPLE?
WE WERE WAITING FOR THE PERFECT OPPORTUNITY ...
BUT NOW THAT WE HAVE A WEAPON TO FIGHT NAYRU... ERRR, VERAN...
...WE CAN'T LET THE PEOPLE SUFFER A DAY LONGER.
SHING

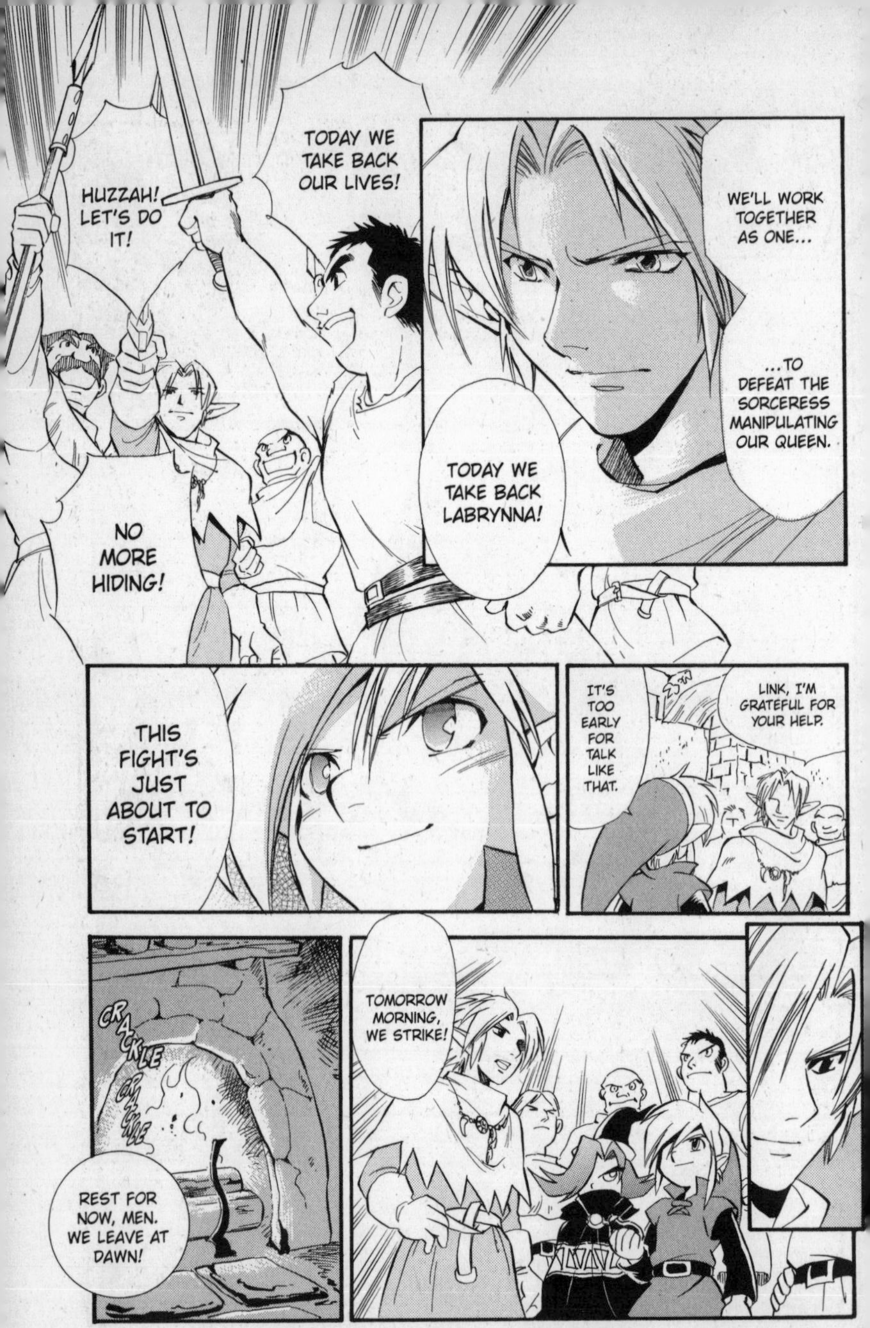
WE'LL WORK TOGETHER AS ONE...
...TO DEFEAT THE SORCERESS MANIPULATING OUR QUEEN.
TODAY WE TAKE BACK LABRYNNA!
TODAY WE TAKE BACK OUR LIVES!
HUZZAH! LET'S DO IT!
NO MORE HIDING!
LINK, I'M GRATEFUL FOR YOUR HELP.
IT'S TOO EARLY FOR TALK LIKE THAT.
THIS FIGHT'S JUST ABOUT TO START!
TOMORROW MORNING, WE STRIKE!
CRACKLE
CRACKLE
REST FOR NOW, MEN. WE LEAVE AT DAWN!

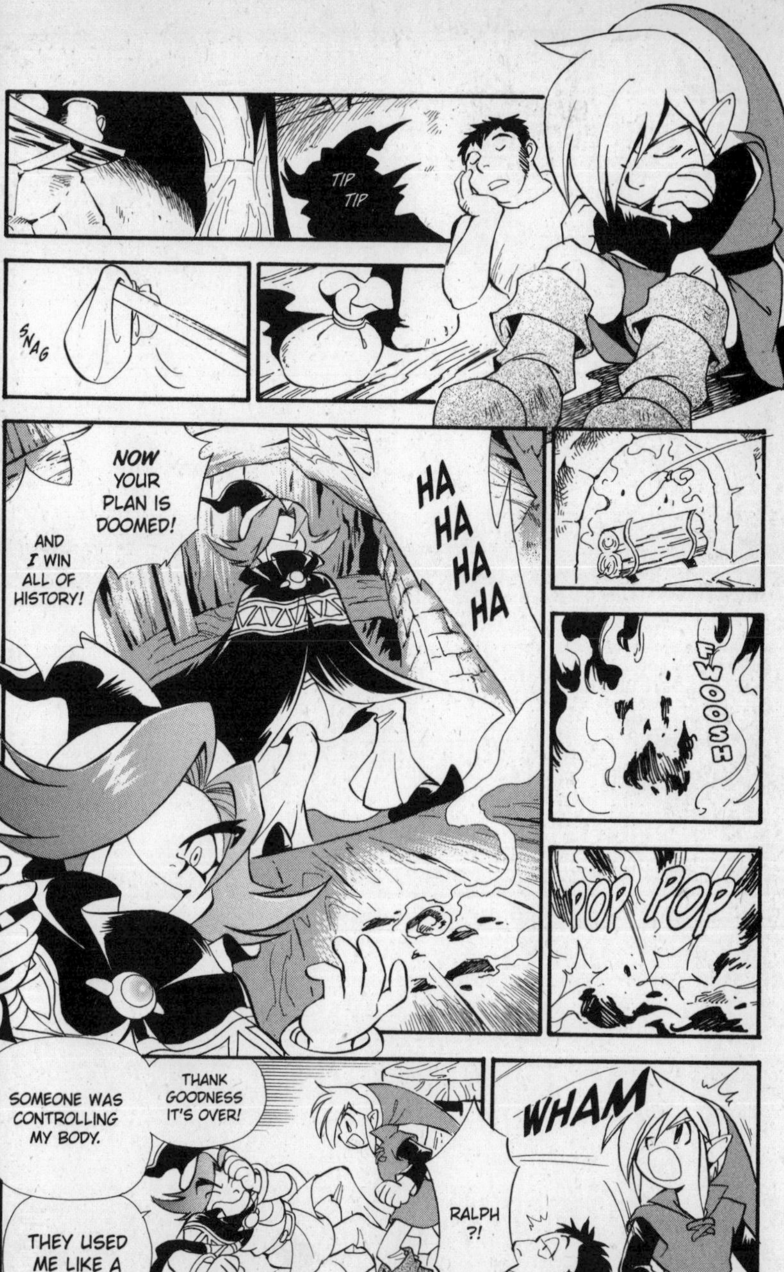
TIP TIP
SNAG
FWOOSH
POP POP
HA HA HA HA HA
NOW YOUR PLAN IS DOOMED!
AND I WIN ALL OF HISTORY!
WHAM
RALPH ?!
THANK GOODNESS IT'S OVER!
SOMEONE WAS CONTROLLING MY BODY.
THEY USED ME LIKE A PUPPET!

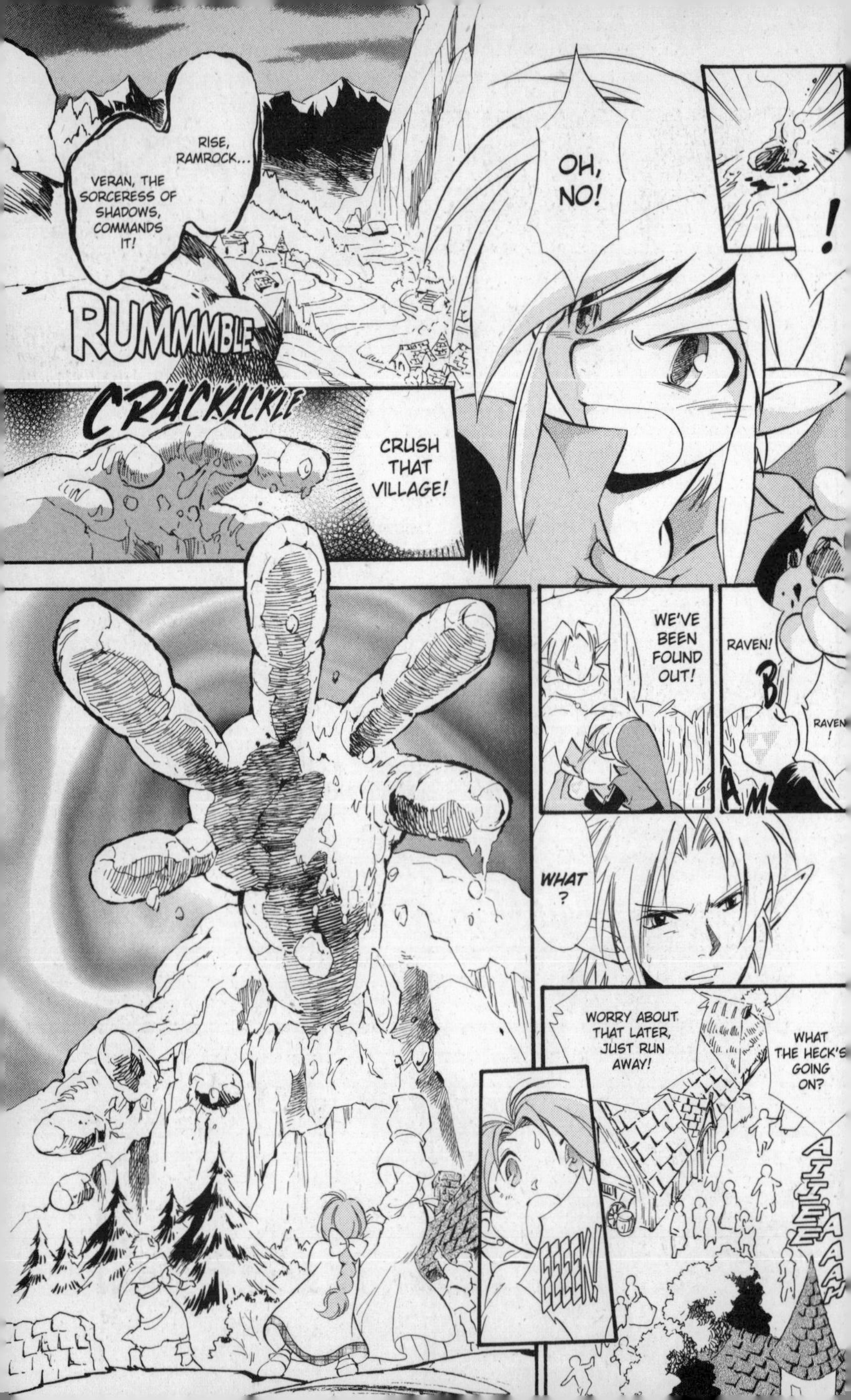
!
OH, NO!
RISE, RAMROCK...
VERAN, THE SORCERESS OF SHADOWS, COMMANDS IT!
RUMMMBLE
CRACKACKLE
CRUSH THAT VILLAGE!
RAVEN!
BAM
RAVEN!
WE'VE BEEN FOUND OUT!
WHAT?
WHAT THE HECK'S GOING ON?
WORRY ABOUT THAT LATER, JUST RUN AWAY!
AIIEEAAAAH
EEEEK!

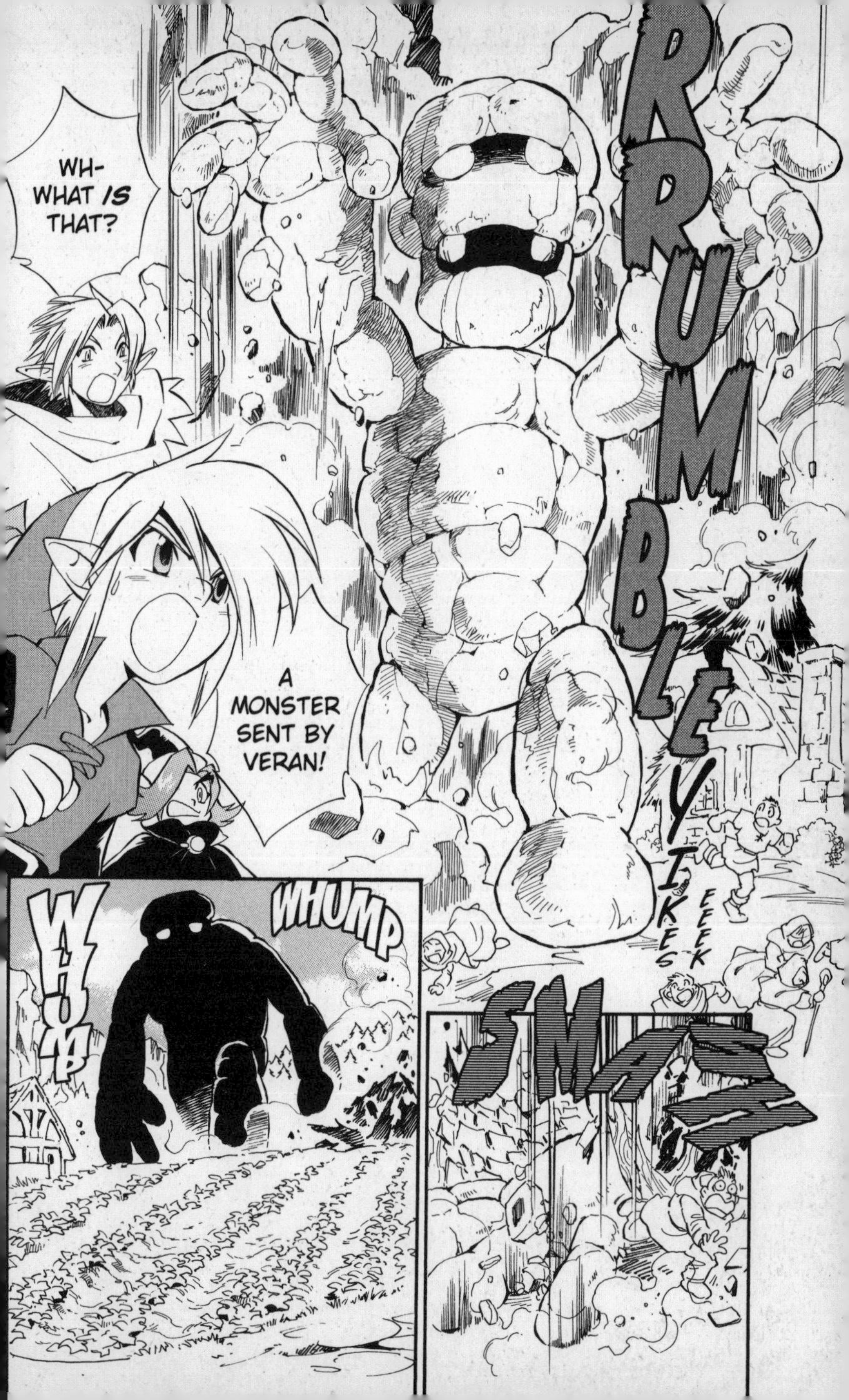
RRUMBLE
WH-WHAT *IS* THAT?
YIKES
EEEK
A MONSTER SENT BY VERAN!
SMASH
WHUMP
WHUMP

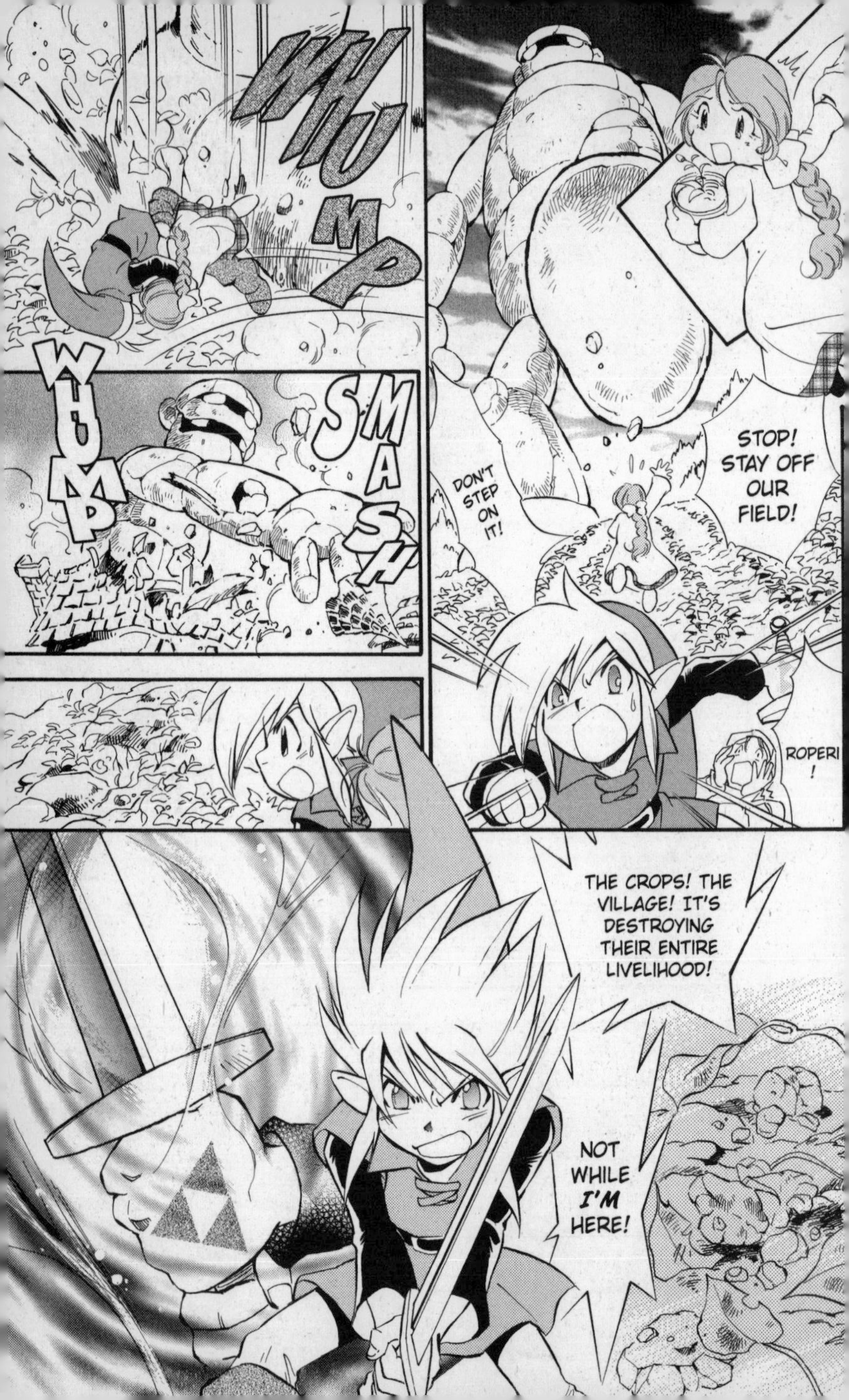
STOP! STAY OFF OUR FIELD!
DON'T STEP ON IT!
ROPERI!
WHUMMP
SMASH
WHUMP
THE CROPS! THE VILLAGE! IT'S DESTROYING THEIR ENTIRE LIVELIHOOD!
NOT WHILE I'M HERE!

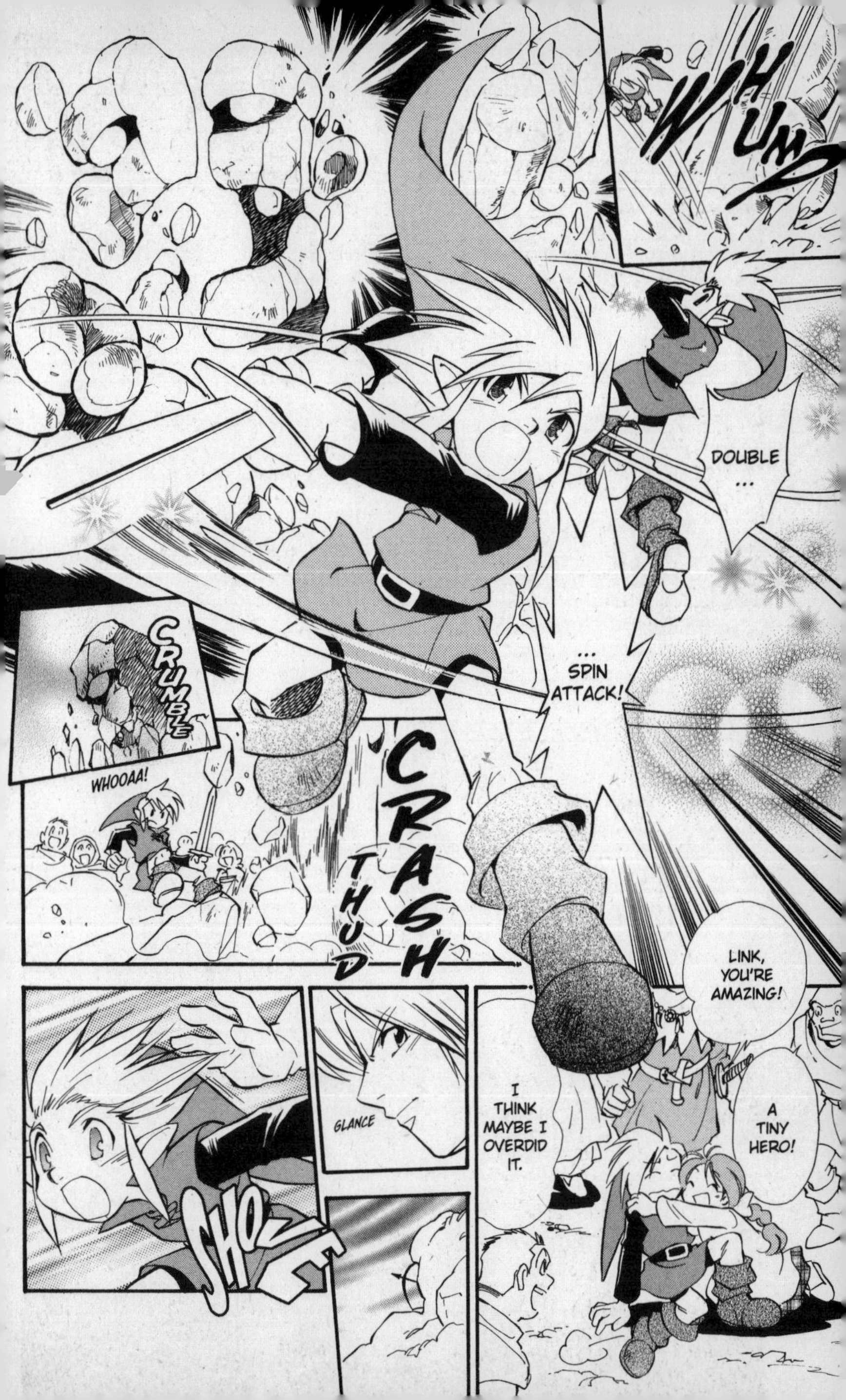
WHUMP
DOUBLE ...
... SPIN ATTACK!
CRUMBLE
WHOOAA!
CRASH
THUD
LINK, YOU'RE AMAZING!
A TINY HERO!
I THINK MAYBE I OVERDID IT.
GLANCE
SHOVE

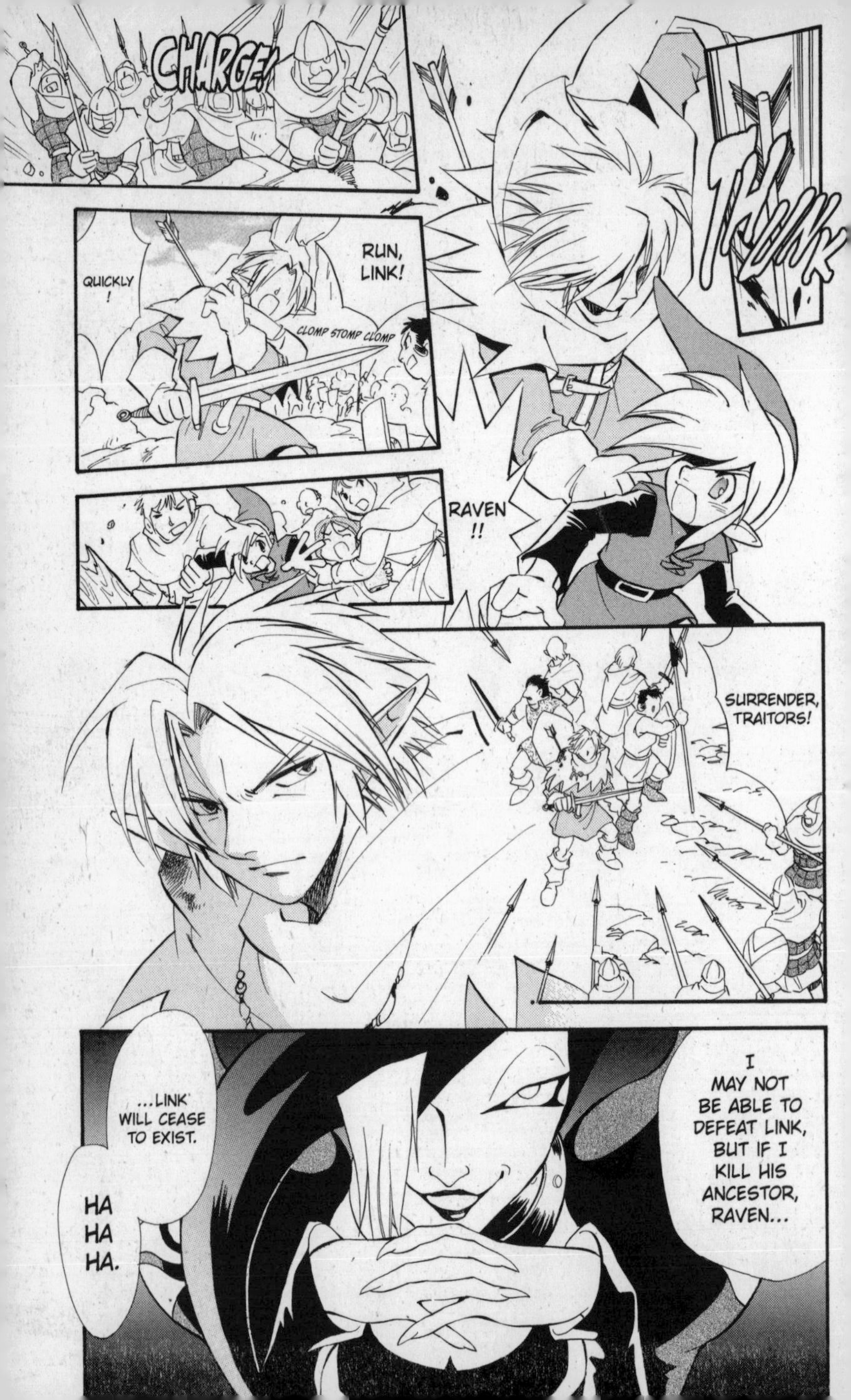
THUNK
CHARGE!
RUN, LINK!
QUICKLY!
CLOMP STOMP CLOMP
RAVEN!!
SURRENDER, TRAITORS!
I MAY NOT BE ABLE TO DEFEAT LINK, BUT IF I KILL HIS ANCESTOR, RAVEN...
...LINK WILL CEASE TO EXIST.
HA HA HA.

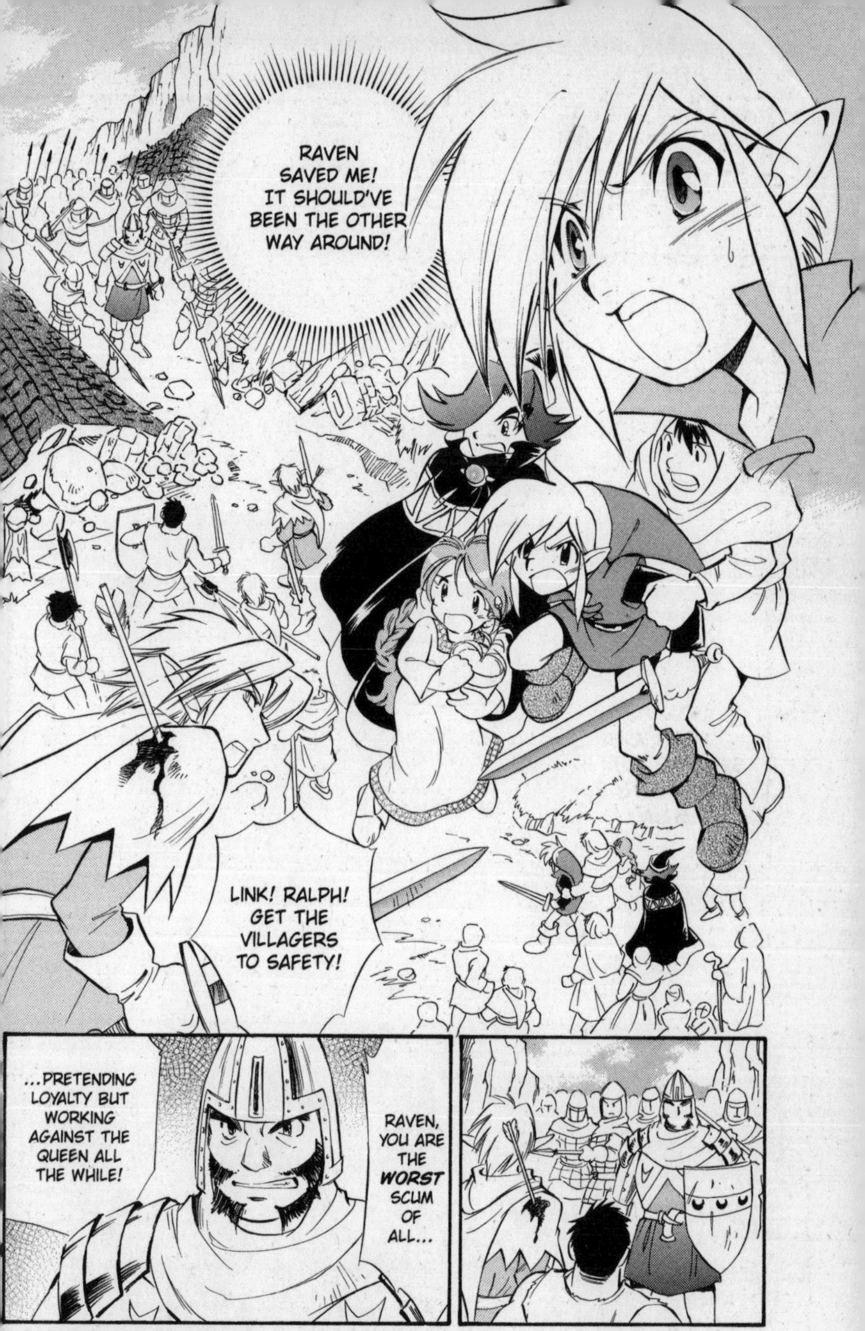
RAVEN SAVED ME! IT SHOULD'VE BEEN THE OTHER WAY AROUND!
LINK! RALPH! GET THE VILLAGERS TO SAFETY!
RAVEN, YOU ARE THE ***WORST*** SCUM OF ALL...
...PRETENDING LOYALTY BUT WORKING AGAINST THE QUEEN ALL THE WHILE!

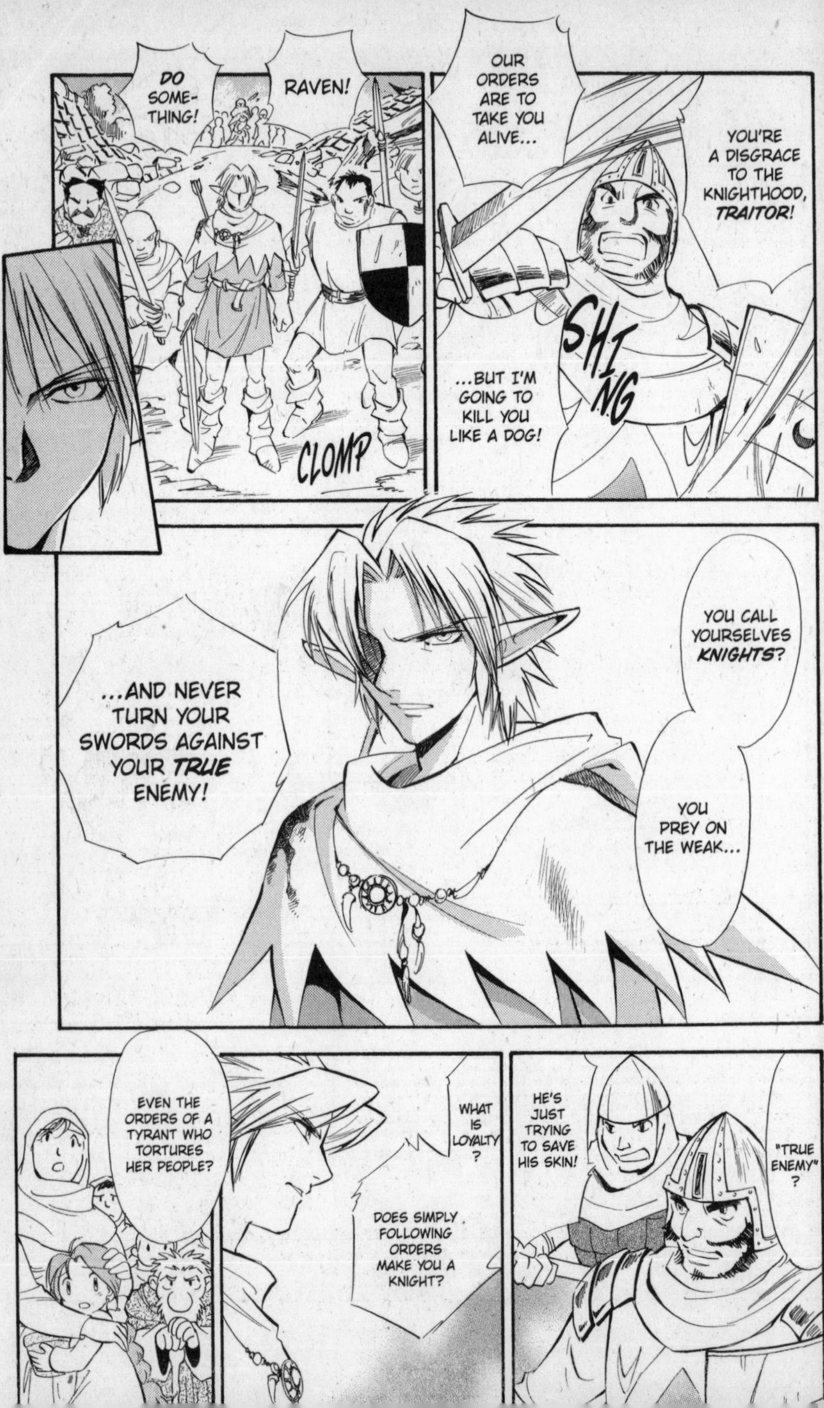
OUR ORDERS ARE TO TAKE YOU ALIVE...
YOU'RE A DISGRACE TO THE KNIGHTHOOD, TRAITOR!
SHING
...BUT I'M GOING TO KILL YOU LIKE A DOG!
RAVEN!
DO SOMETHING!
CLOMP
YOU CALL YOURSELVES KNIGHTS?
YOU PREY ON THE WEAK...
...AND NEVER TURN YOUR SWORDS AGAINST YOUR TRUE ENEMY!
"TRUE ENEMY"?
HE'S JUST TRYING TO SAVE HIS SKIN!
WHAT IS LOYALTY?
DOES SIMPLY FOLLOWING ORDERS MAKE YOU A KNIGHT?
EVEN THE ORDERS OF A TYRANT WHO TORTURES HER PEOPLE?

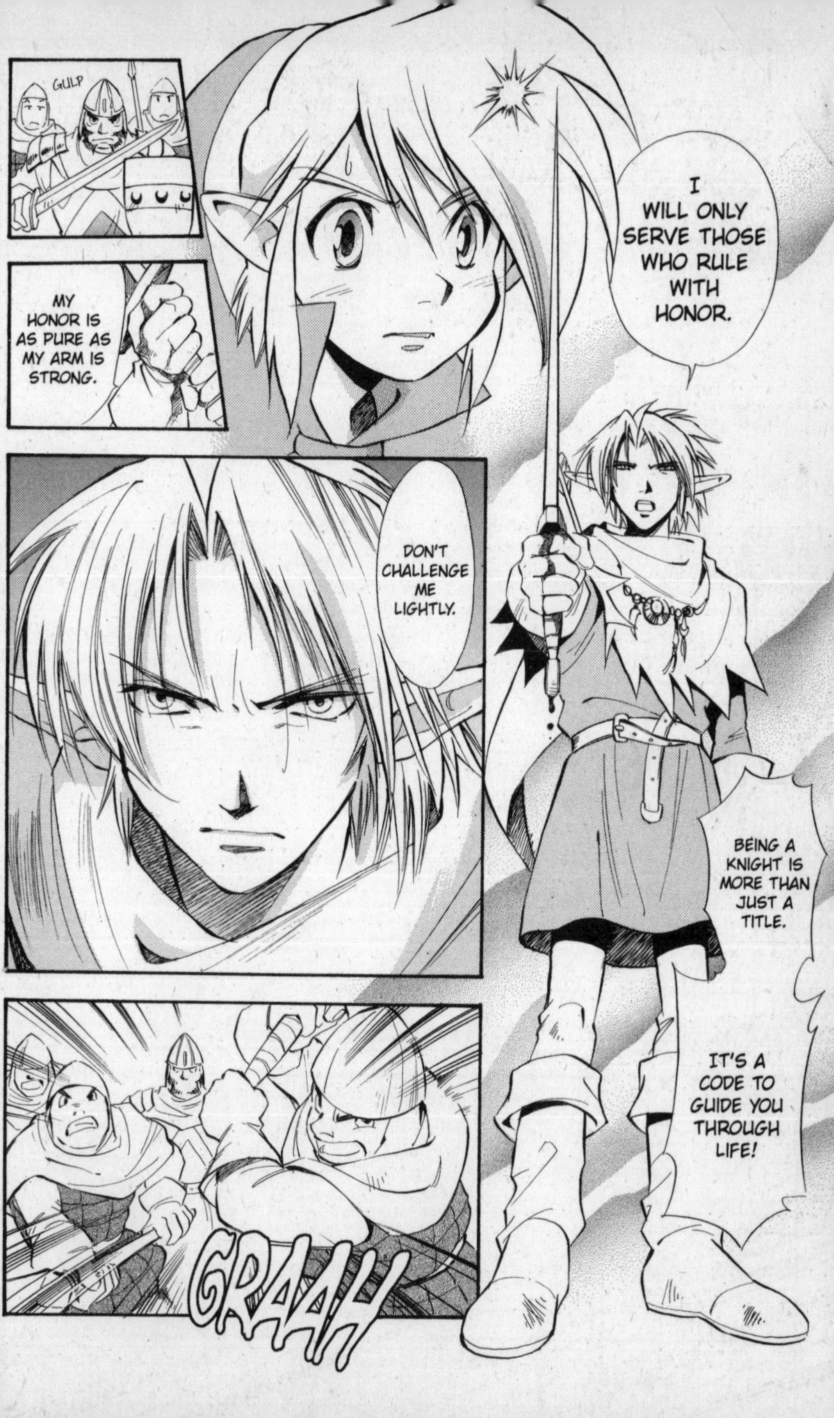
I WILL ONLY SERVE THOSE WHO RULE WITH HONOR.
GULP
MY HONOR IS AS PURE AS MY ARM IS STRONG.
DON'T CHALLENGE ME LIGHTLY.
BEING A KNIGHT IS MORE THAN JUST A TITLE.
IT'S A CODE TO GUIDE YOU THROUGH LIFE!
GRAAH

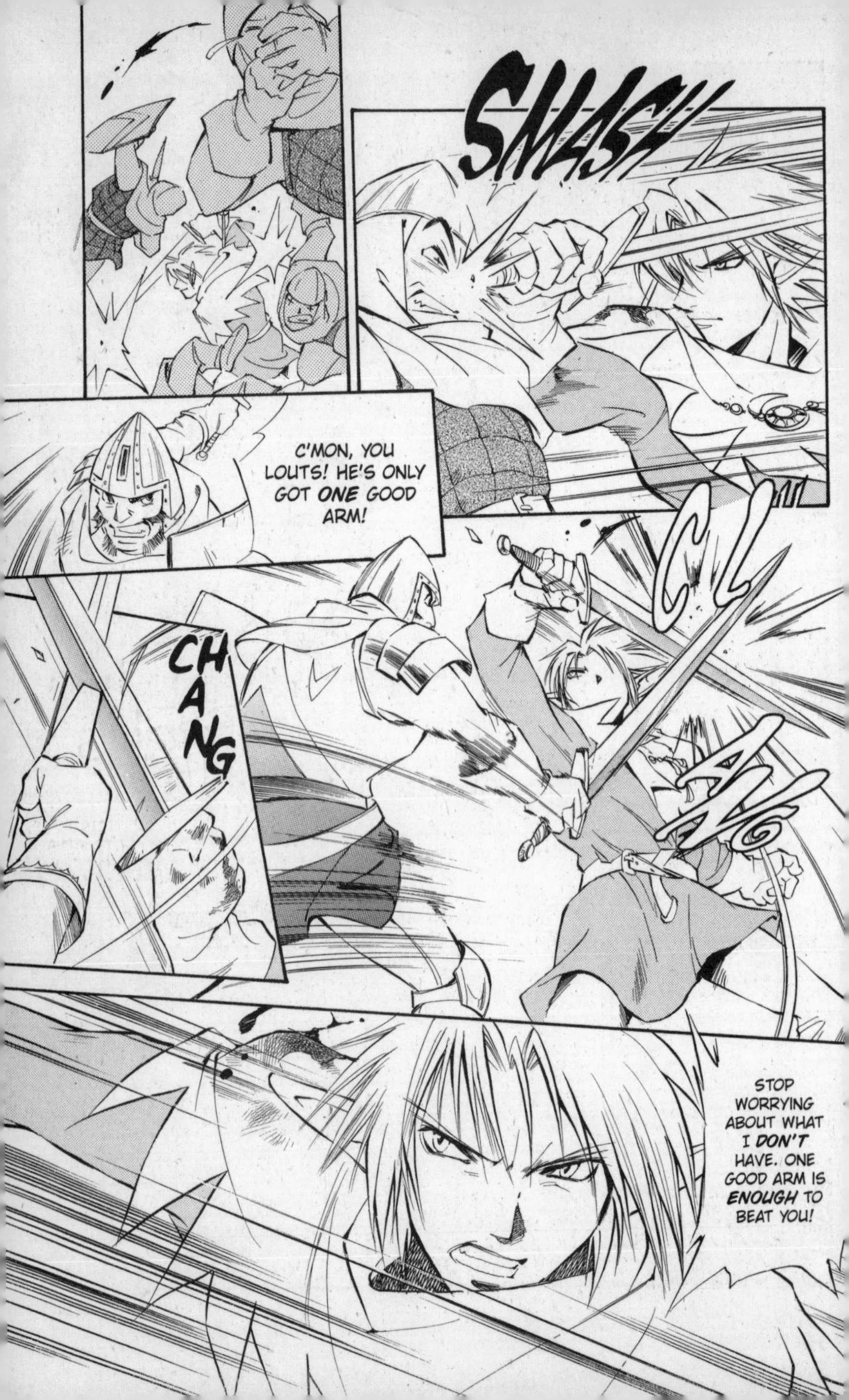
SMASH
C'MON, YOU LOUTS! HE'S ONLY GOT **ONE** GOOD ARM!
CLANG
CHANG
STOP WORRYING ABOUT WHAT I **DON'T** HAVE. ONE GOOD ARM IS **ENOUGH** TO BEAT YOU!

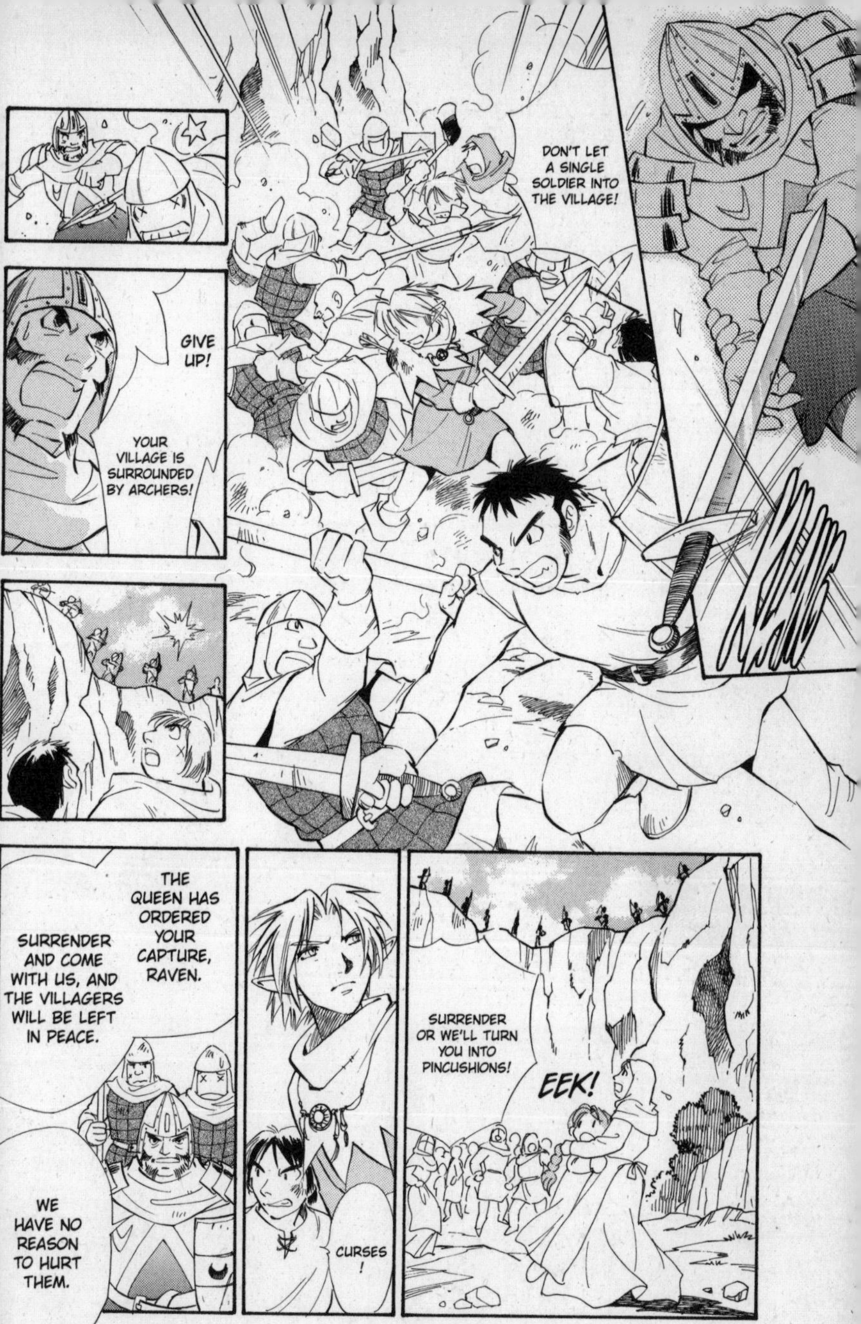
DON'T LET A SINGLE SOLDIER INTO THE VILLAGE!
GIVE UP!
YOUR VILLAGE IS SURROUNDED BY ARCHERS!
SURRENDER OR WE'LL TURN YOU INTO PINCUSHIONS!
EEK!
CURSES!
THE QUEEN HAS ORDERED YOUR CAPTURE, RAVEN.
SURRENDER AND COME WITH US, AND THE VILLAGERS WILL BE LEFT IN PEACE.
WE HAVE NO REASON TO HURT THEM.

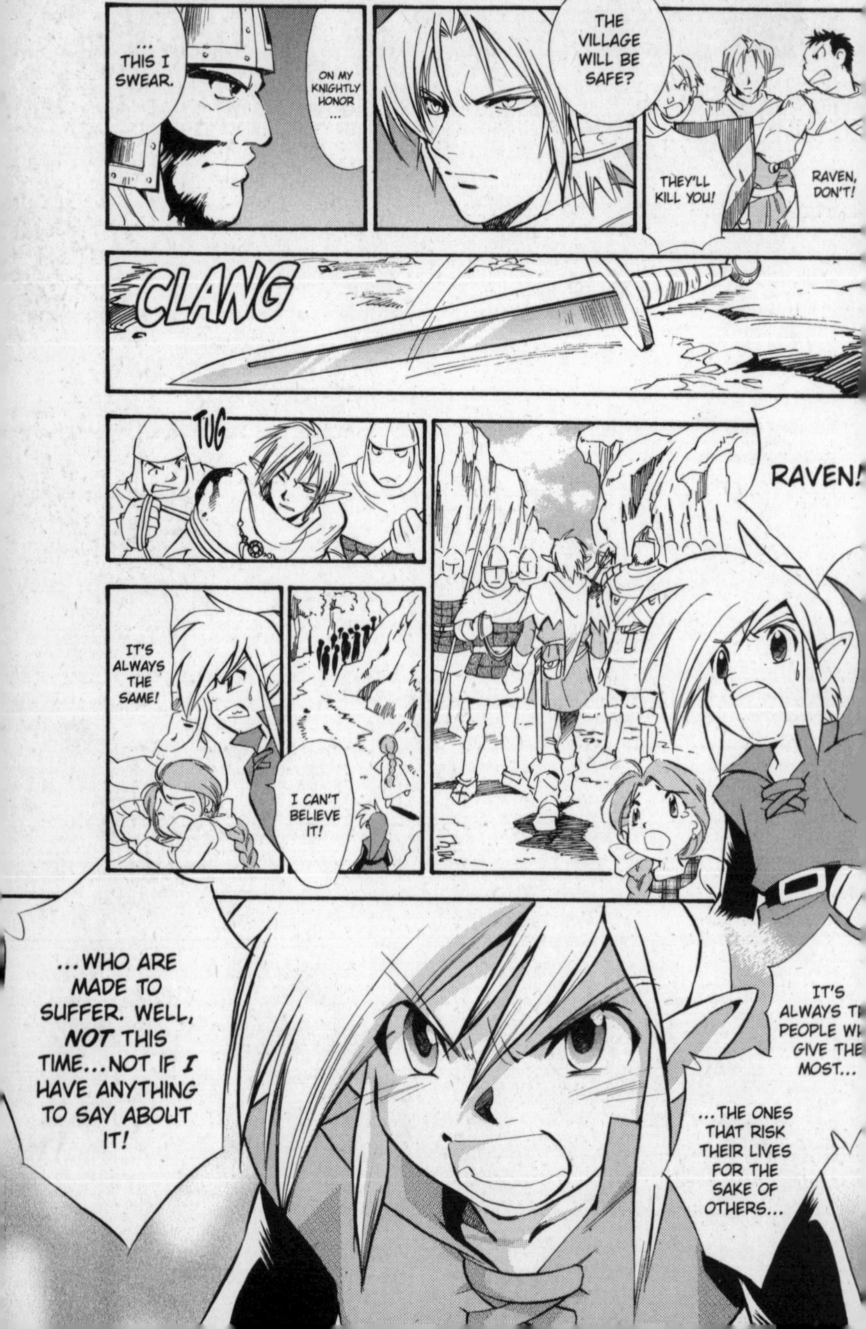
RAVEN, DON'T!
THEY'LL KILL YOU!
THE VILLAGE WILL BE SAFE?
ON MY KNIGHTLY HONOR ...
... THIS I SWEAR.
CLANG
RAVEN!
TUG
I CAN'T BELIEVE IT!
IT'S ALWAYS THE SAME!
IT'S ALWAYS T PEOPLE W GIVE THE MOST...
...THE ONES THAT RISK THEIR LIVES FOR THE SAKE OF OTHERS...
...WHO ARE MADE TO SUFFER. WELL, *NOT* THIS TIME...NOT IF *I* HAVE ANYTHING TO SAY ABOUT IT!

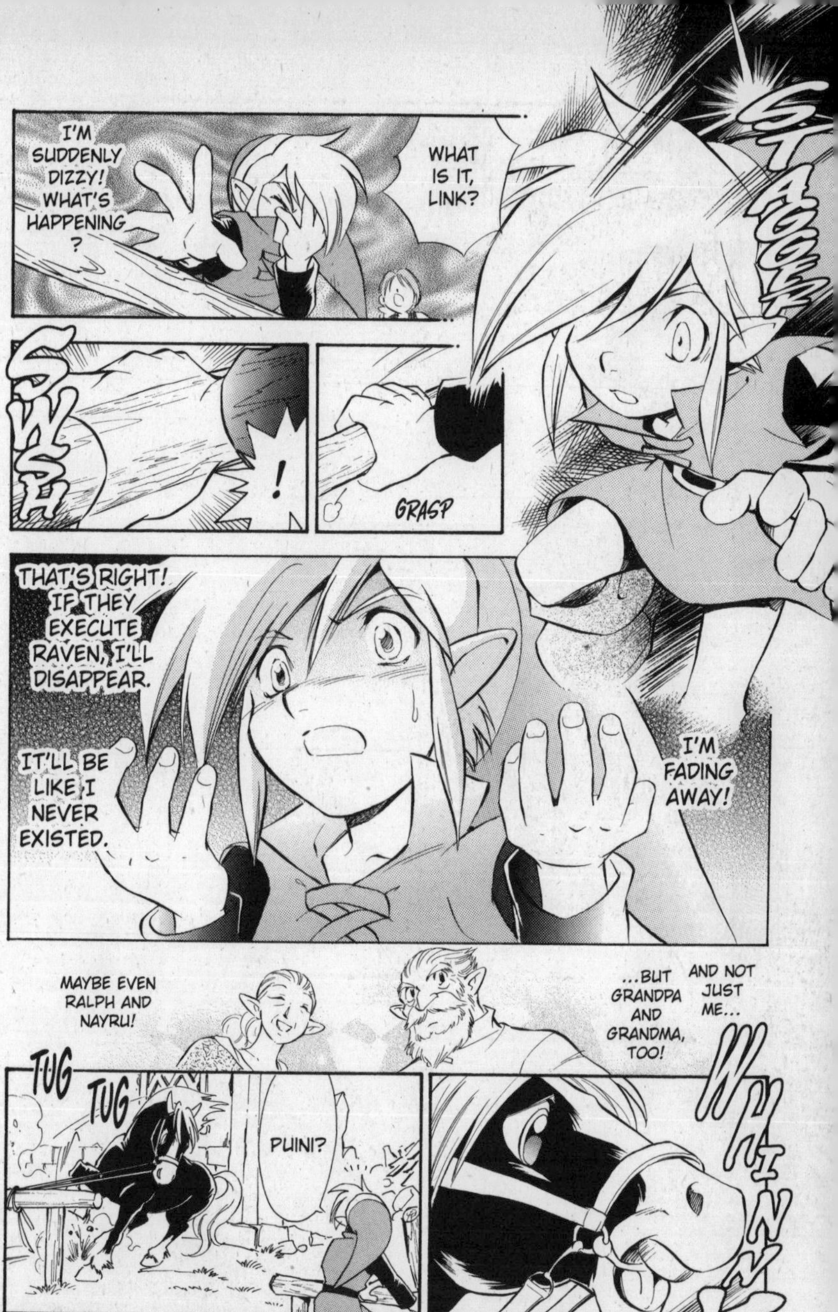
STAGGER
WHAT IS IT, LINK?
I'M SUDDENLY DIZZY! WHAT'S HAPPENING?
GRASP
!
SWISH
THAT'S RIGHT! IF THEY EXECUTE RAVEN, I'LL DISAPPEAR.
IT'LL BE LIKE I NEVER EXISTED.
I'M FADING AWAY!
AND NOT JUST ME...
...BUT GRANDPA AND GRANDMA, TOO!
MAYBE EVEN RALPH AND NAYRU!
NNHINNY
PUINI?
TUG
TUG

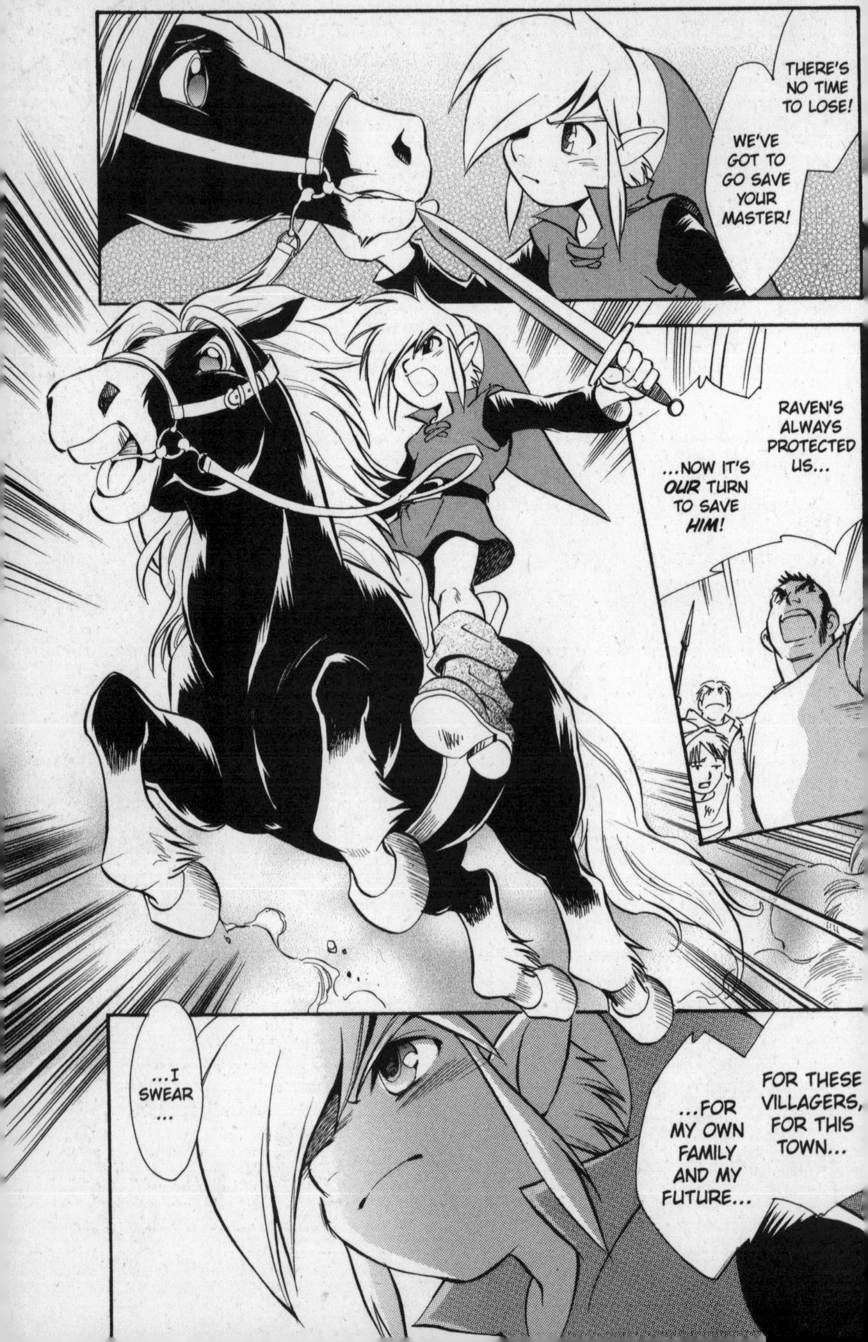
THERE'S NO TIME TO LOSE!
WE'VE GOT TO GO SAVE YOUR MASTER!
RAVEN'S ALWAYS PROTECTED US...
...NOW IT'S *OUR* TURN TO SAVE *HIM*!
FOR THESE VILLAGERS, FOR THIS TOWN...
...FOR MY OWN FAMILY AND MY FUTURE...
...I SWEAR ...

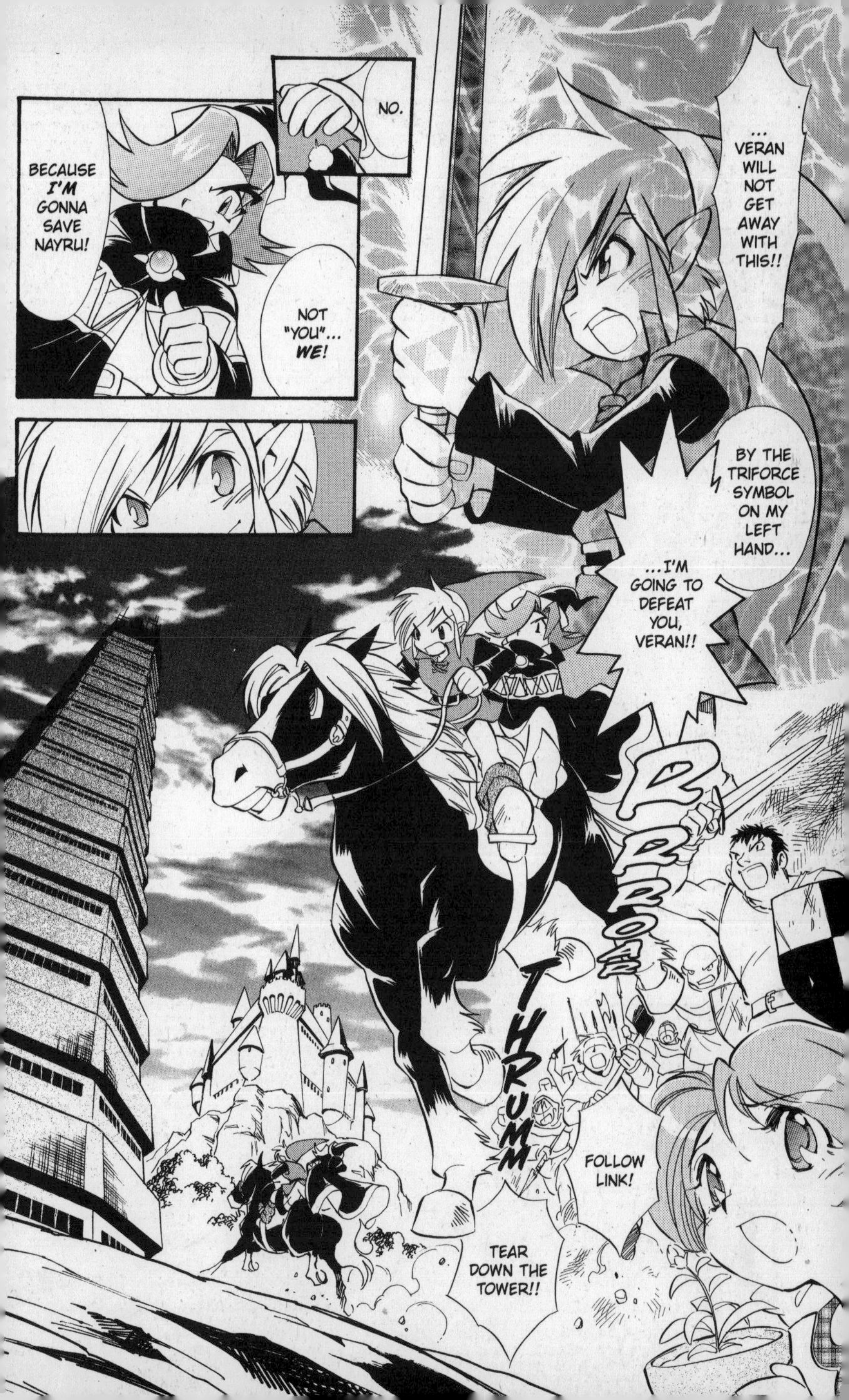
...VERAN WILL NOT GET AWAY WITH THIS!!
BY THE TRIFORCE SYMBOL ON MY LEFT HAND...
...I'M GOING TO DEFEAT YOU, VERAN!!
NO.
BECAUSE I'M GONNA SAVE NAYRU!
NOT "YOU"... WE!
THHRUMM
FOLLOW LINK!
TEAR DOWN THE TOWER!!

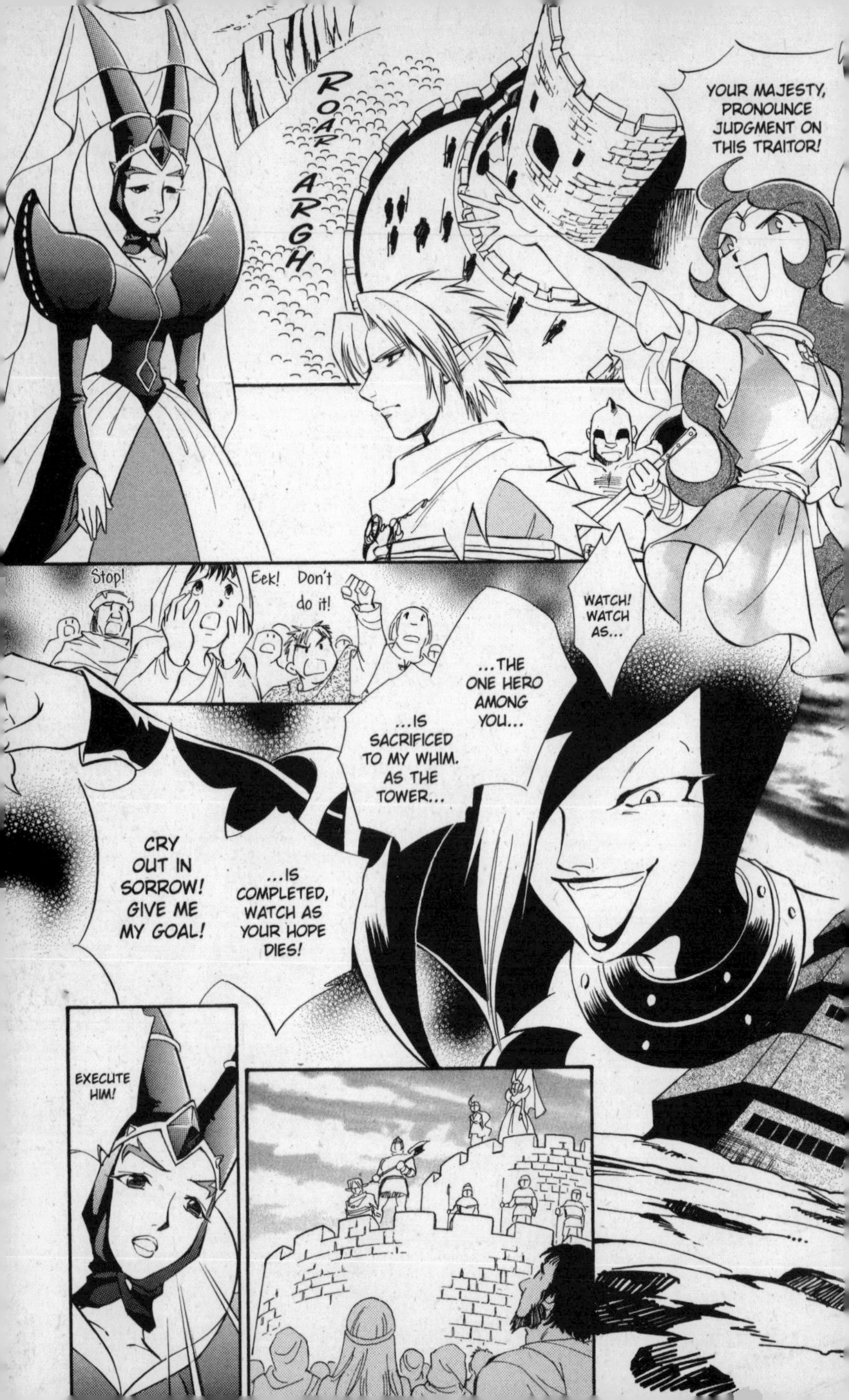
YOUR MAJESTY, PRONOUNCE JUDGMENT ON THIS TRAITOR!
ROAR ARGH
WATCH! WATCH AS...
...THE ONE HERO AMONG YOU...
...IS SACRIFICED TO MY WHIM. AS THE TOWER...
...IS COMPLETED, WATCH AS YOUR HOPE DIES!
CRY OUT IN SORROW! GIVE ME MY GOAL!
Stop!
Eek!
Don't do it!
EXECUTE HIM!

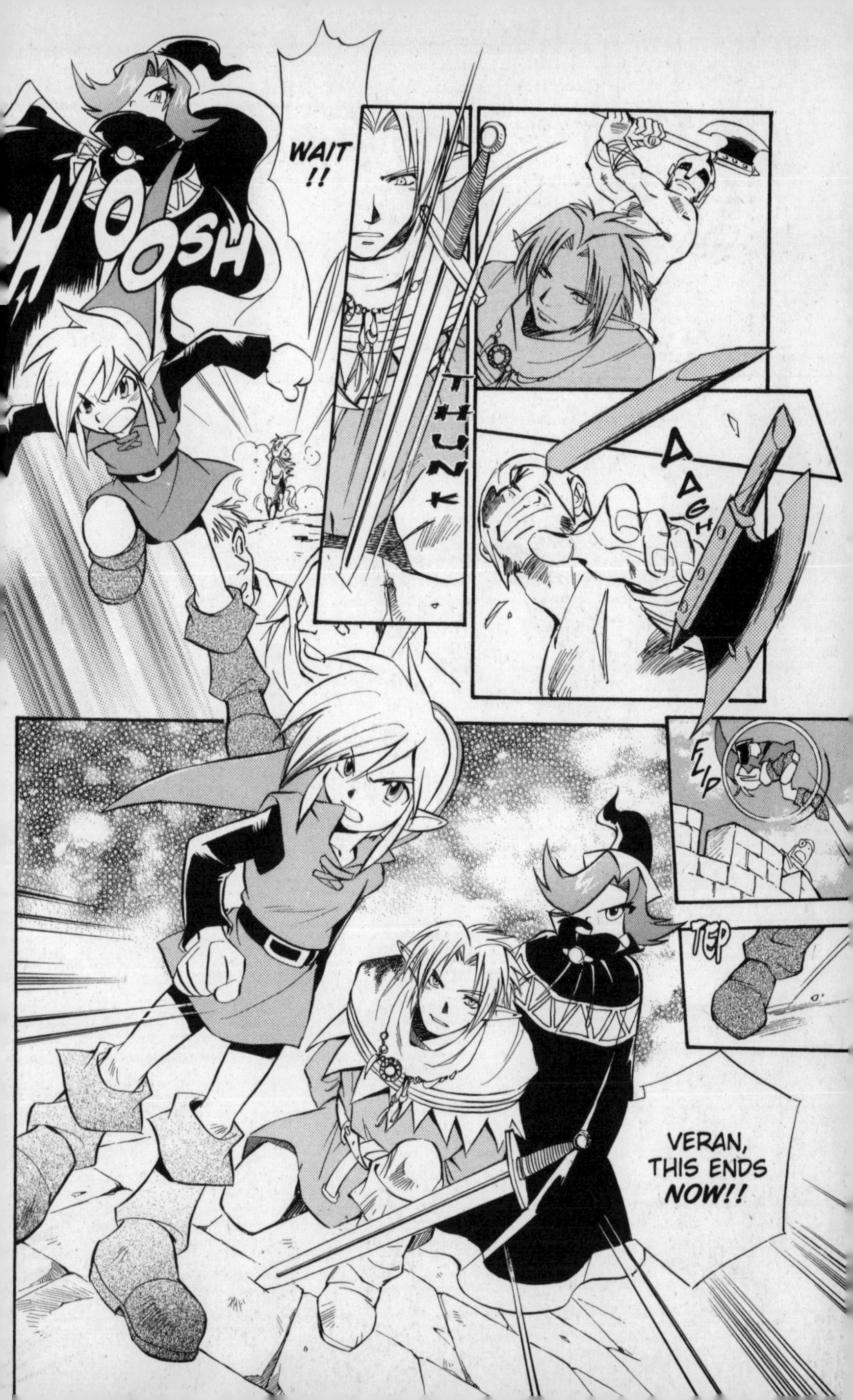
AAGH
WAIT!!
THUNK
WHOOSH
FLIP
TEP
VERAN, THIS ENDS NOW!!

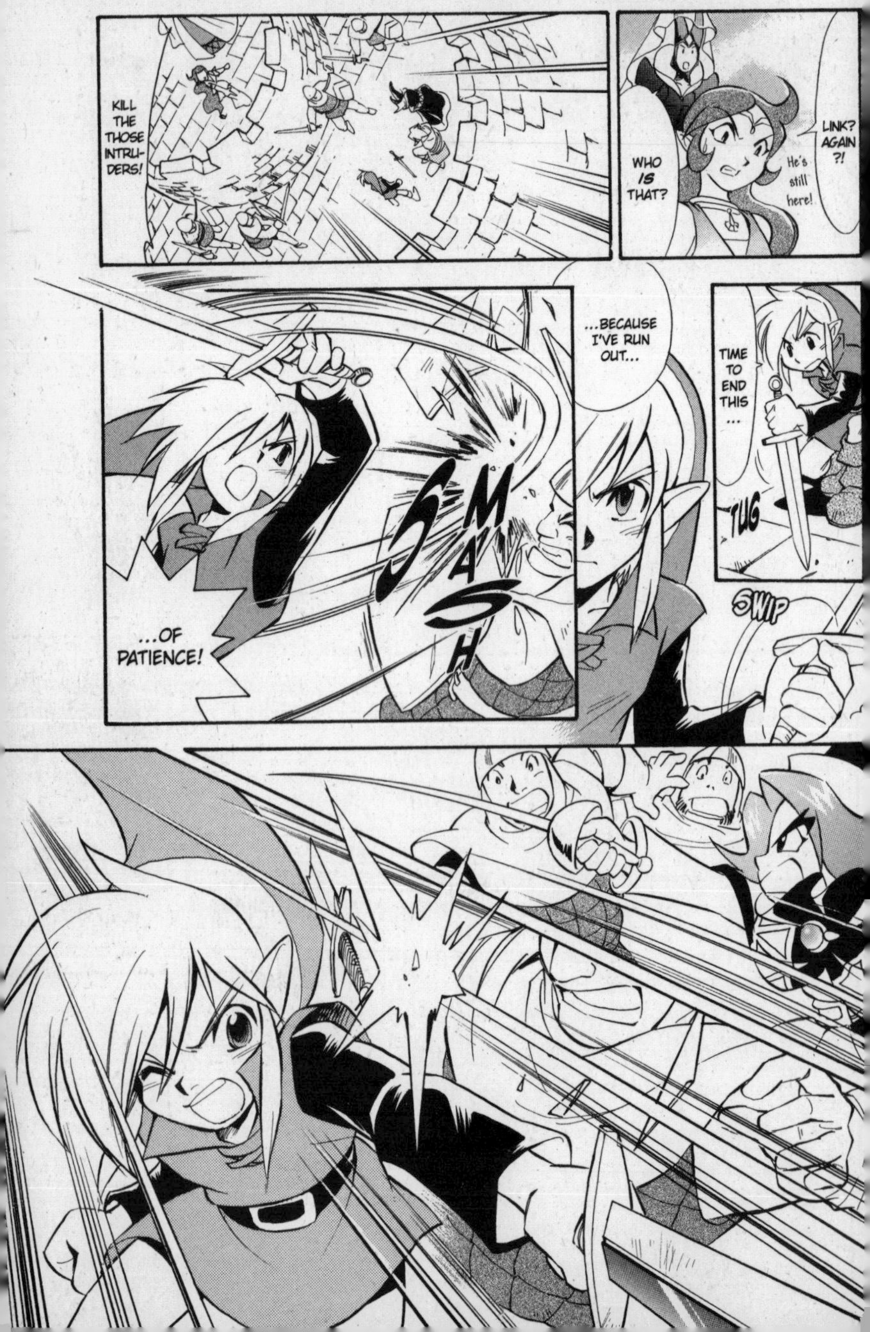
LINK? AGAIN ?!
He's still here!
WHO IS THAT?
KILL THE THOSE INTRUDERS!
TIME TO END THIS ...
TUG
SWIP
...BECAUSE I'VE RUN OUT...
SMASH
...OF PATIENCE!

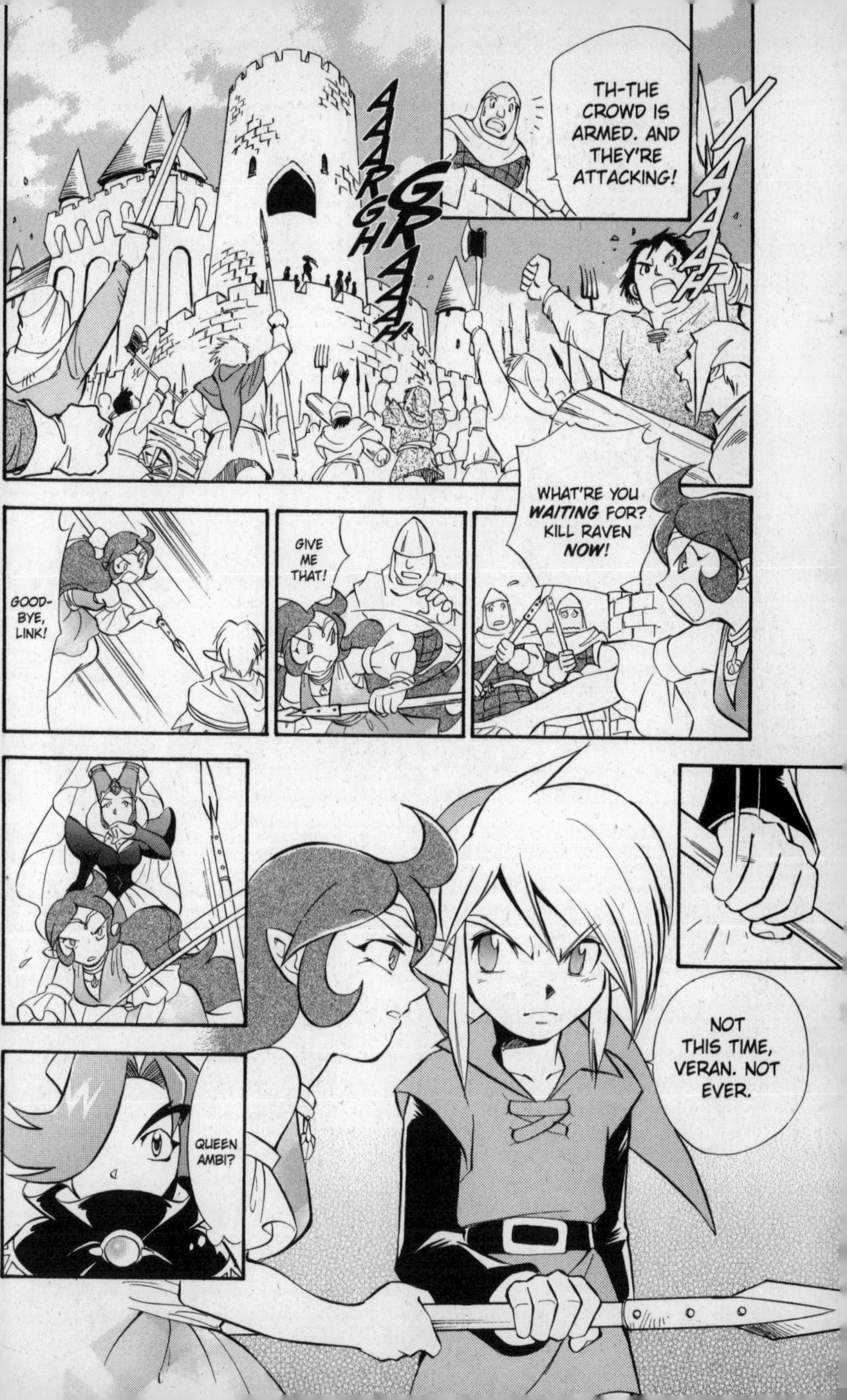
TH-THE CROWD IS ARMED. AND THEY'RE ATTACKING!
YAAAAH
GRAAAAH
AAARGH
WHAT'RE YOU *WAITING* FOR? KILL RAVEN *NOW!*
GIVE ME THAT!
GOOD-BYE, LINK!
NOT THIS TIME, VERAN. NOT EVER.
QUEEN AMBI?

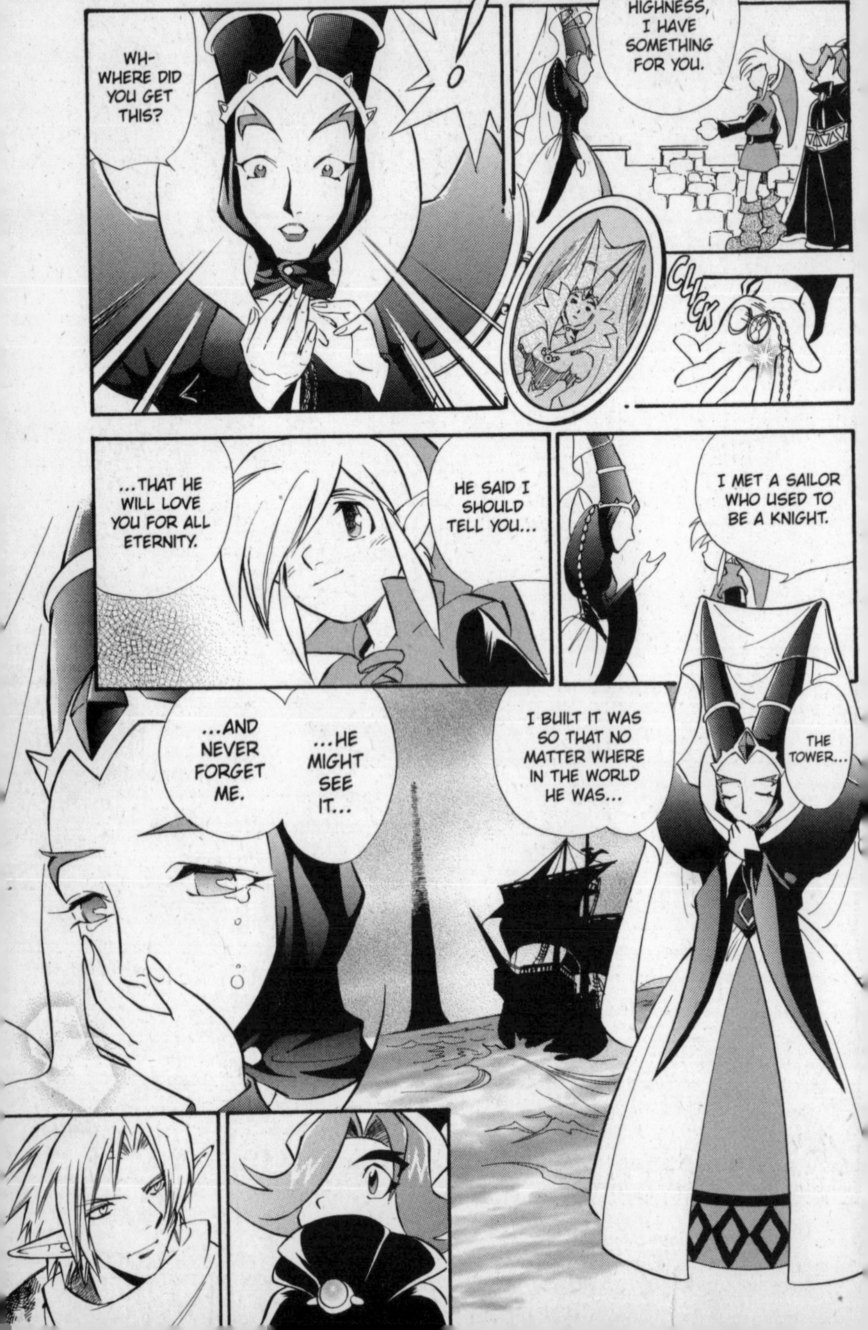
YOUR HIGHNESS, I HAVE SOMETHING FOR YOU.
CLICK
!
WH- WHERE DID YOU GET THIS?
I MET A SAILOR WHO USED TO BE A KNIGHT.
HE SAID I SHOULD TELL YOU...
...THAT HE WILL LOVE YOU FOR ALL ETERNITY.
THE TOWER...
I BUILT IT WAS SO THAT NO MATTER WHERE IN THE WORLD HE WAS...
...HE MIGHT SEE IT...
...AND NEVER FORGET ME.

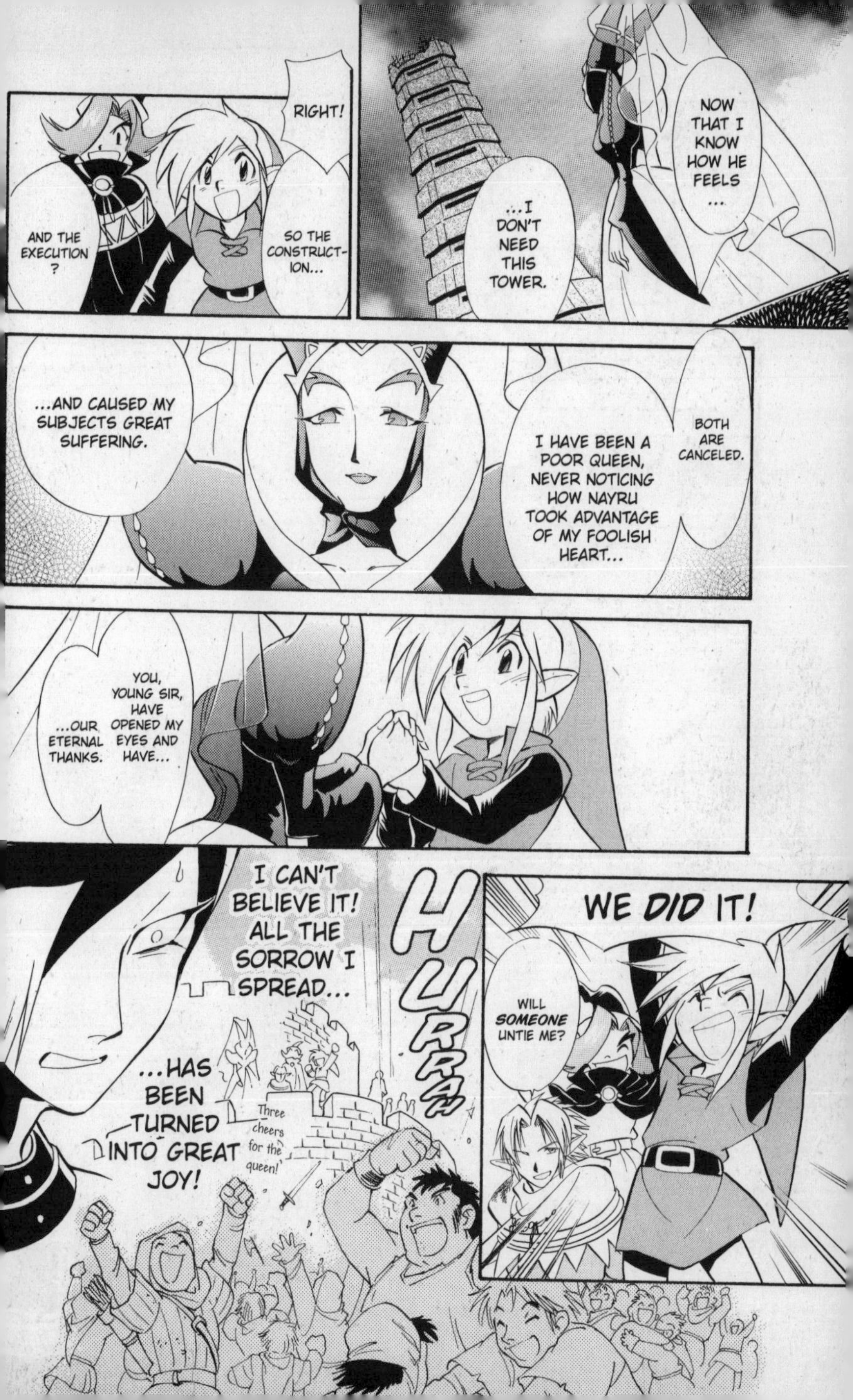
NOW THAT I KNOW HOW HE FEELS ...
...I DON'T NEED THIS TOWER.
RIGHT!
SO THE CONSTRUCTION...
AND THE EXECUTION?
BOTH ARE CANCELED.
I HAVE BEEN A POOR QUEEN, NEVER NOTICING HOW NAYRU TOOK ADVANTAGE OF MY FOOLISH HEART...
...AND CAUSED MY SUBJECTS GREAT SUFFERING.
YOU, YOUNG SIR, HAVE OPENED MY EYES AND HAVE...
...OUR ETERNAL THANKS.
WE DID IT!
WILL SOMEONE UNTIE ME?
HURRAH
I CAN'T BELIEVE IT! ALL THE SORROW I SPREAD...
...HAS BEEN TURNED INTO GREAT JOY!
Three cheers for the queen!

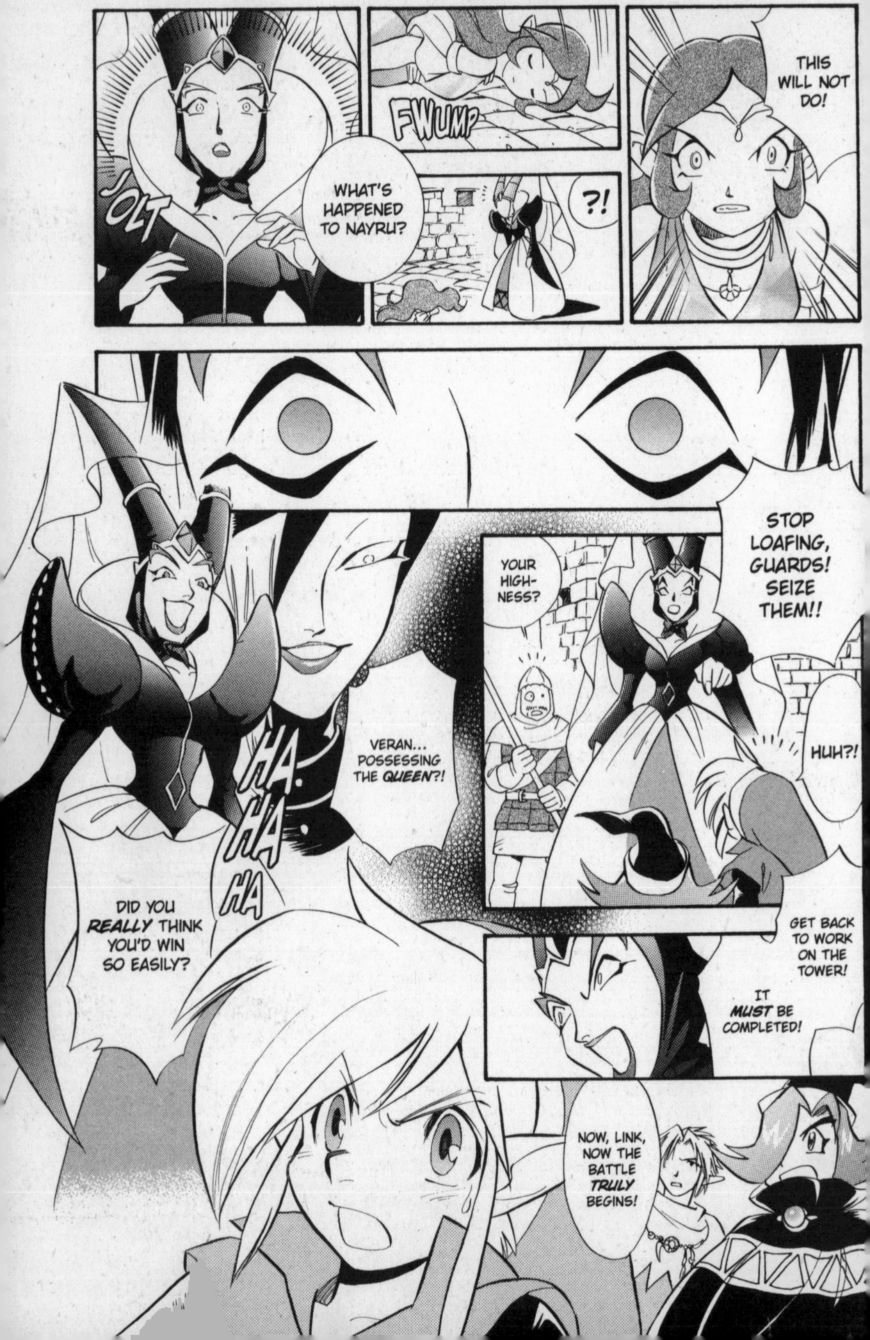
THIS WILL NOT DO!
FWUMP
?!
JOLT
WHAT'S HAPPENED TO NAYRU?
STOP LOAFING, GUARDS! SEIZE THEM!!
YOUR HIGHNESS?
HUH?!
GET BACK TO WORK ON THE TOWER!
IT *MUST* BE COMPLETED!
VERAN... POSSESSING THE *QUEEN*?!
HA HA HA HA
DID YOU *REALLY* THINK YOU'D WIN SO EASILY?
NOW, LINK, NOW THE BATTLE *TRULY* BEGINS!

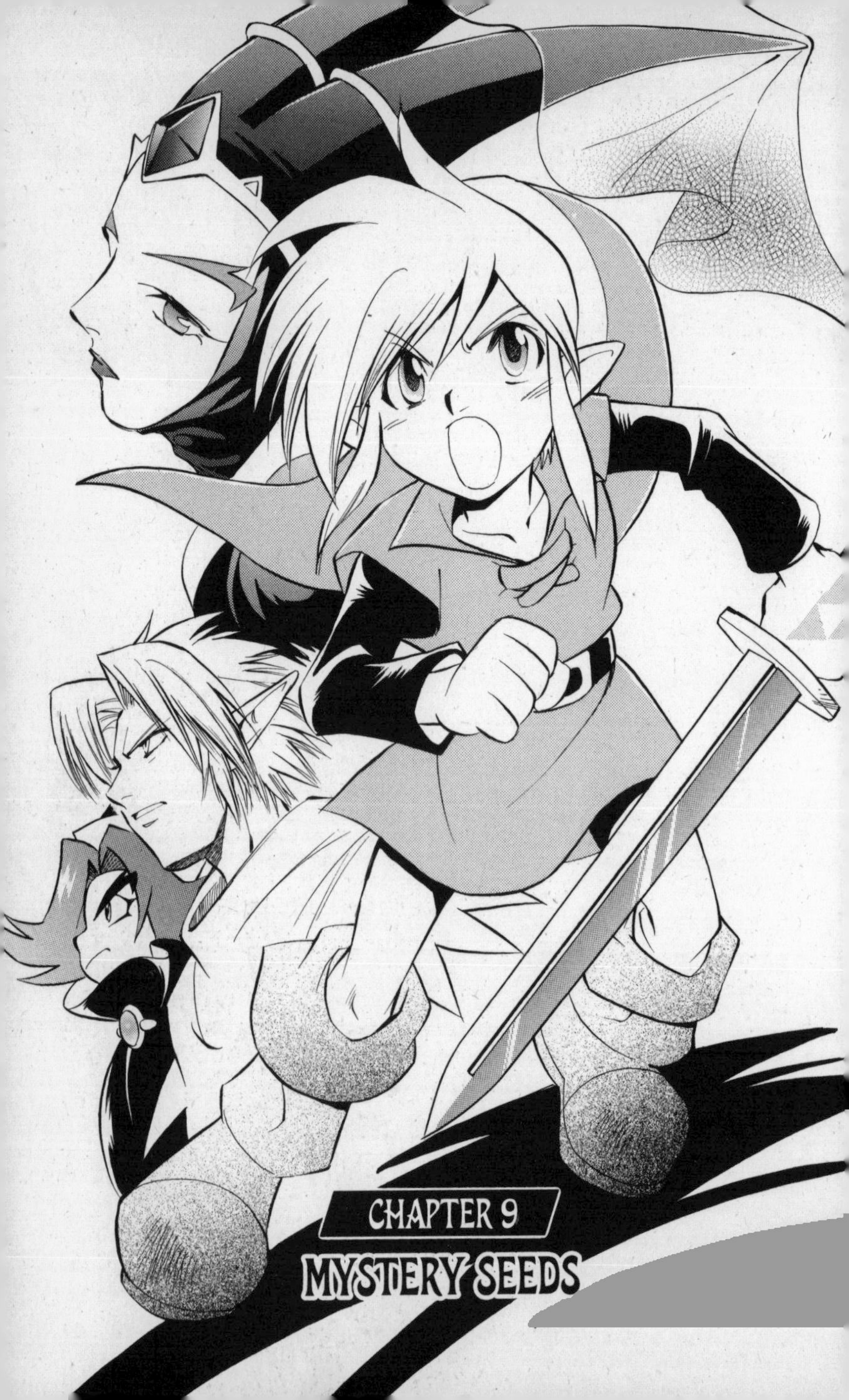
CHAPTER 9
MYSTERY SEEDS

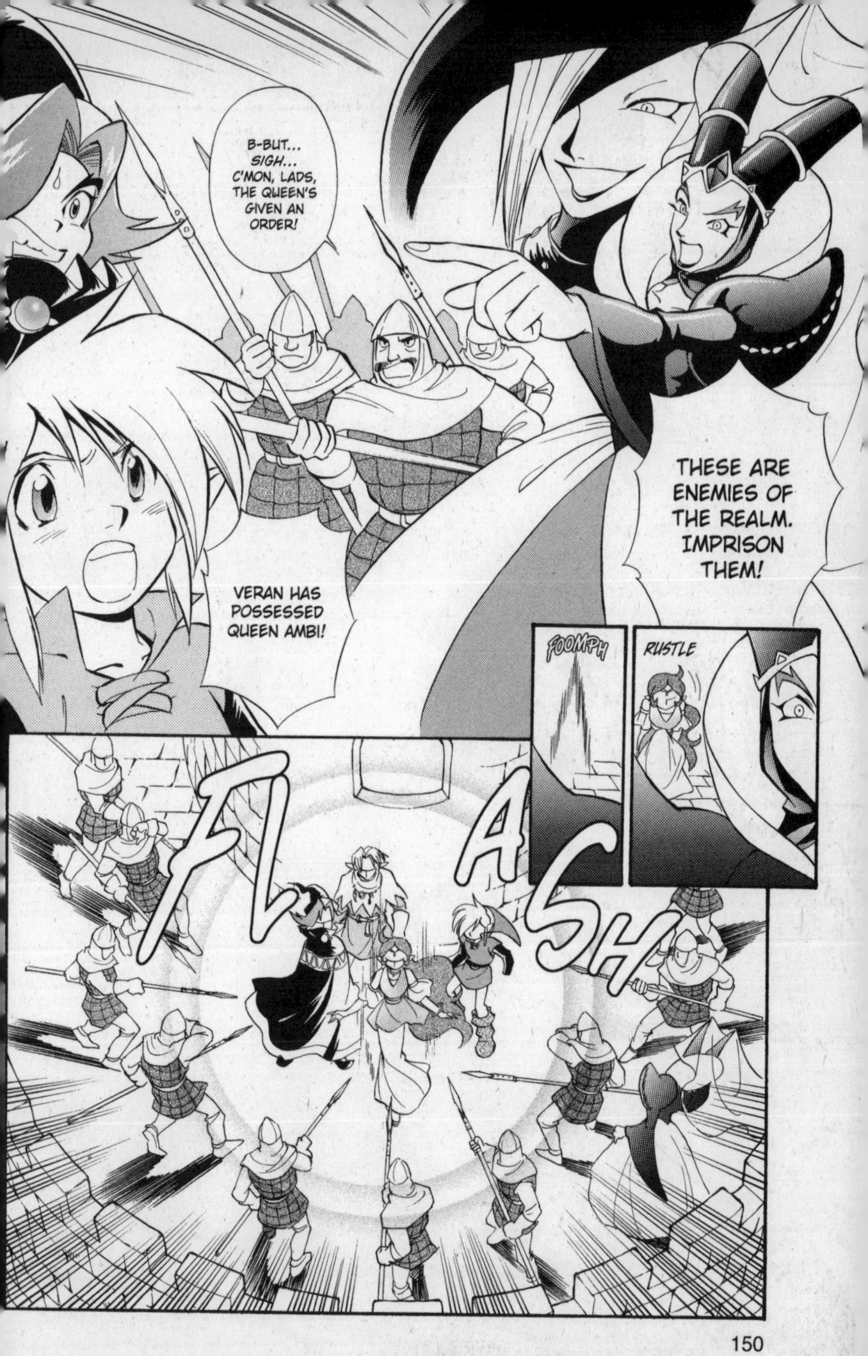
THESE ARE ENEMIES OF THE REALM. IMPRISON THEM!
B-BUT... SIGH... C'MON, LADS, THE QUEEN'S GIVEN AN ORDER!
VERAN HAS POSSESSED QUEEN AMBI!
RUSTLE
FOOMPH
FLASH

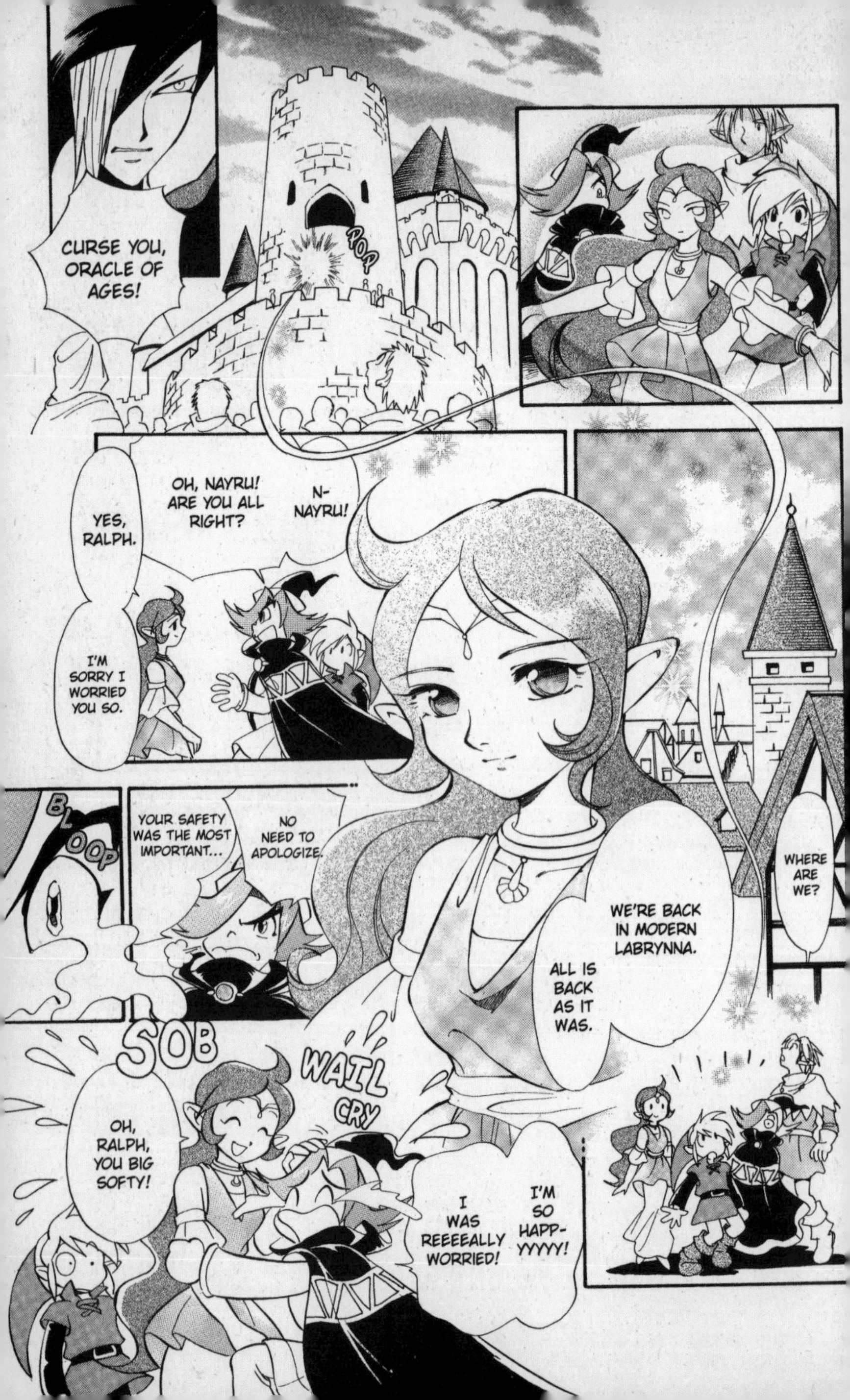
POP
CURSE YOU, ORACLE OF AGES!
WHERE ARE WE?
WE'RE BACK IN MODERN LABRYNNA.
ALL IS BACK AS IT WAS.
N-NAYRU!
OH, NAYRU! ARE YOU ALL RIGHT?
YES, RALPH.
I'M SORRY I WORRIED YOU SO.
NO NEED TO APOLOGIZE.
YOUR SAFETY WAS THE MOST IMPORTANT...
BLOOP
WAIL
CRY
I'M SO HAPP-YYYYY!
I WAS REEEEALLY WORRIED!
SOB
OH, RALPH, YOU BIG SOFTY!

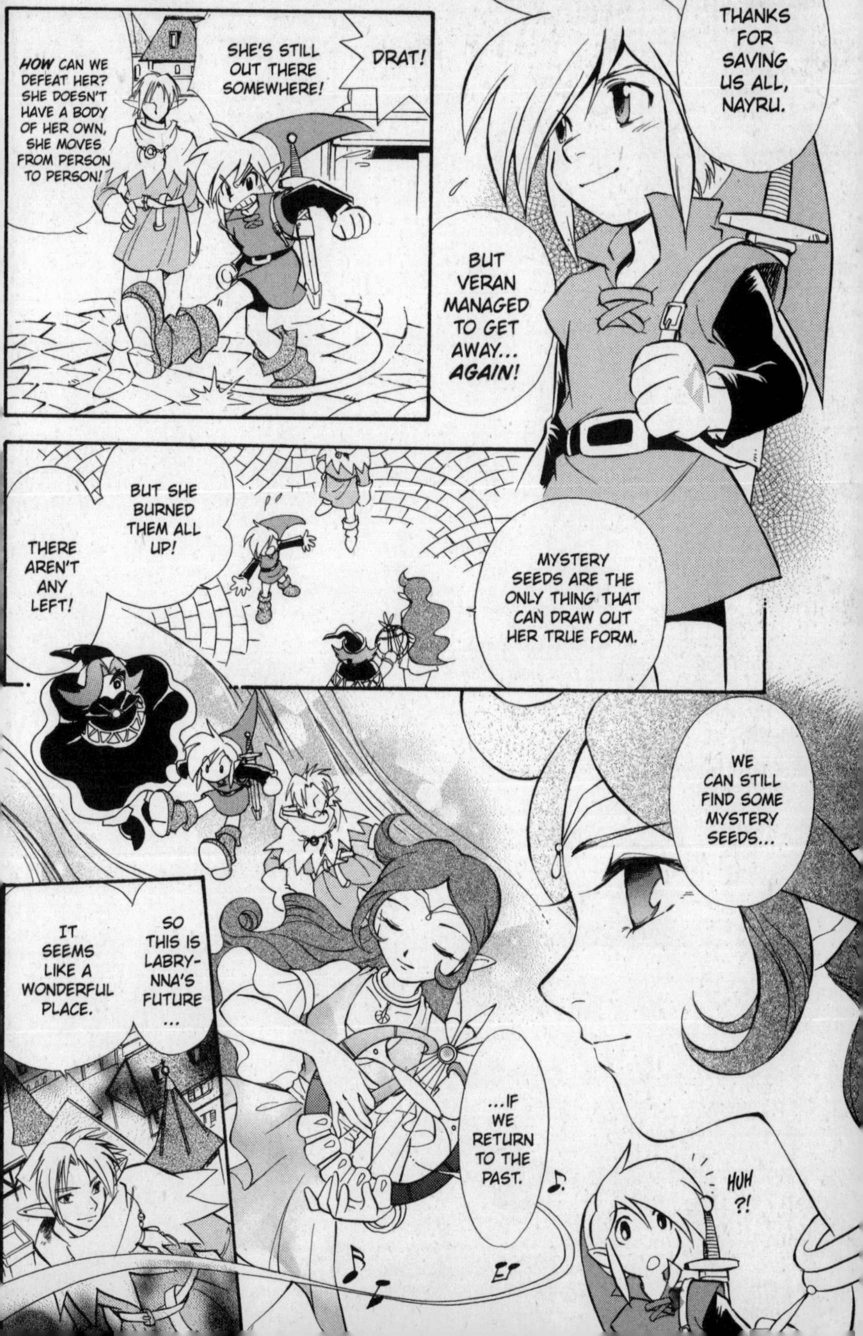
THANKS FOR SAVING US ALL, NAYRU.
BUT VERAN MANAGED TO GET AWAY... *AGAIN!*
MYSTERY SEEDS ARE THE ONLY THING THAT CAN DRAW OUT HER TRUE FORM.
DRAT!
SHE'S STILL OUT THERE SOMEWHERE!
HOW CAN WE DEFEAT HER? SHE DOESN'T HAVE A BODY OF HER OWN, SHE MOVES FROM PERSON TO PERSON!
BUT SHE BURNED THEM ALL UP!
THERE AREN'T ANY LEFT!
WE CAN STILL FIND SOME MYSTERY SEEDS...
...IF WE RETURN TO THE PAST.
HUH ?!
SO THIS IS LABRYNNA'S FUTURE ...
IT SEEMS LIKE A WONDERFUL PLACE.

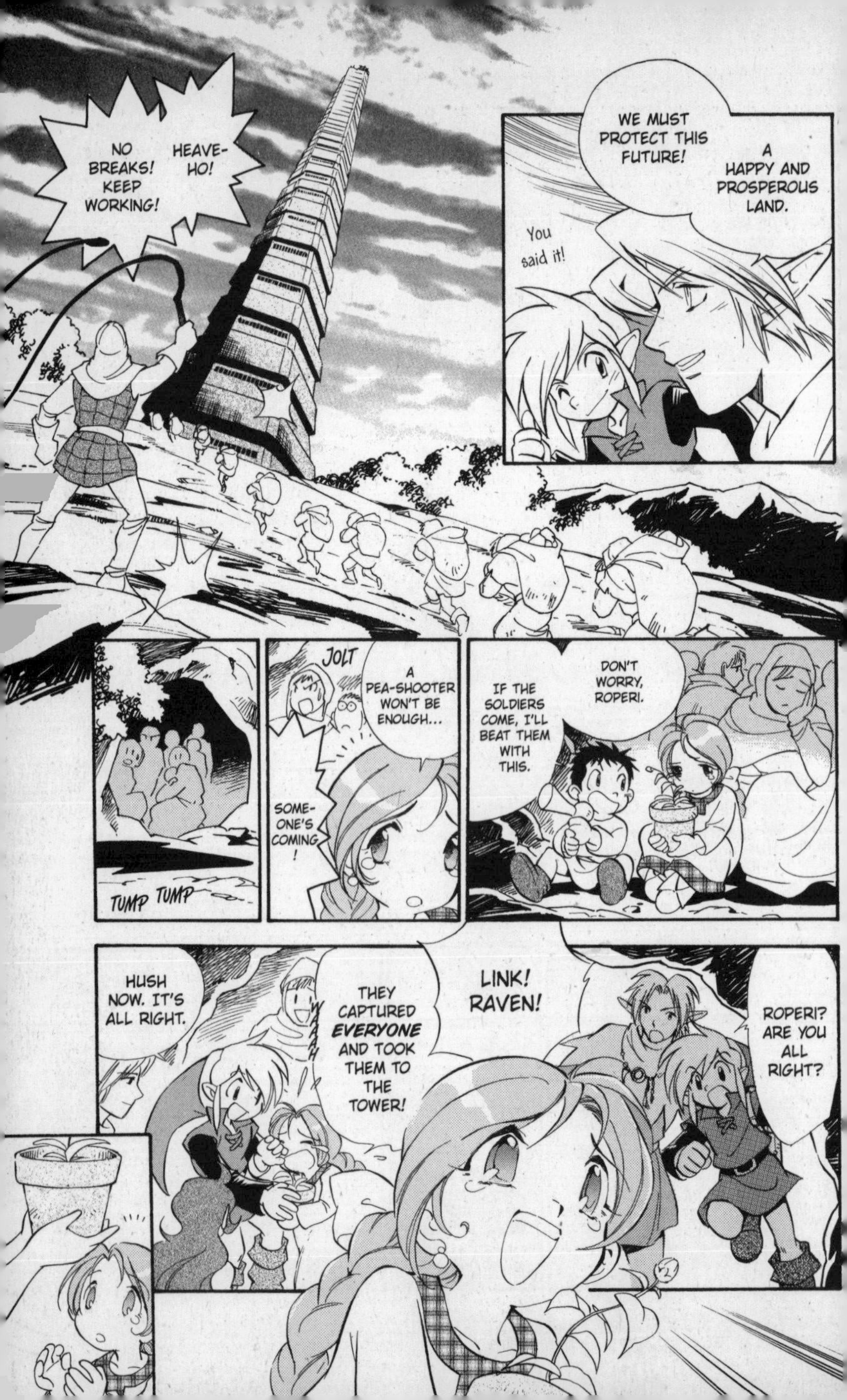
WE MUST PROTECT THIS FUTURE!
A HAPPY AND PROSPEROUS LAND.
You said it!
NO BREAKS! KEEP WORKING! HEAVE-HO!
DON'T WORRY, ROPERI.
IF THE SOLDIERS COME, I'LL BEAT THEM WITH THIS.
JOLT
A PEA-SHOOTER WON'T BE ENOUGH...
SOME-ONE'S COMING!
TUMP TUMP
ROPERI? ARE YOU ALL RIGHT?
LINK! RAVEN!
THEY CAPTURED **EVERYONE** AND TOOK THEM TO THE TOWER!
WAAAH
HUSH NOW. IT'S ALL RIGHT.

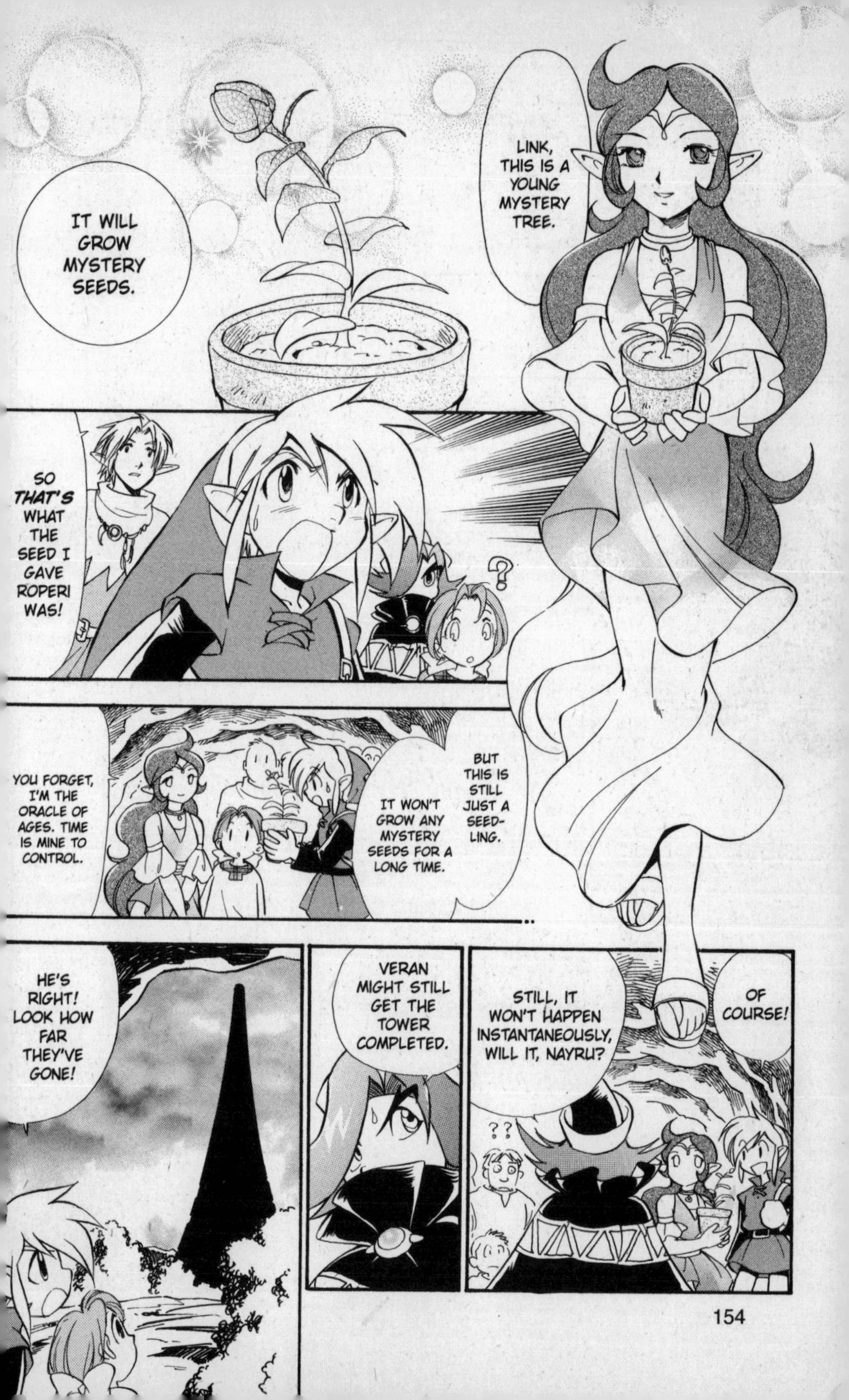
LINK, THIS IS A YOUNG MYSTERY TREE.
IT WILL GROW MYSTERY SEEDS.
SO *THAT'S* WHAT THE SEED I GAVE ROPERI WAS!
BUT THIS IS STILL JUST A SEED-LING.
IT WON'T GROW ANY MYSTERY SEEDS FOR A LONG TIME.
YOU FORGET, I'M THE ORACLE OF AGES. TIME IS MINE TO CONTROL.
STILL, IT WON'T HAPPEN INSTANTANEOUSLY, WILL IT, NAYRU?
OF COURSE!
VERAN MIGHT STILL GET THE TOWER COMPLETED.
HE'S RIGHT! LOOK HOW FAR THEY'VE GONE!

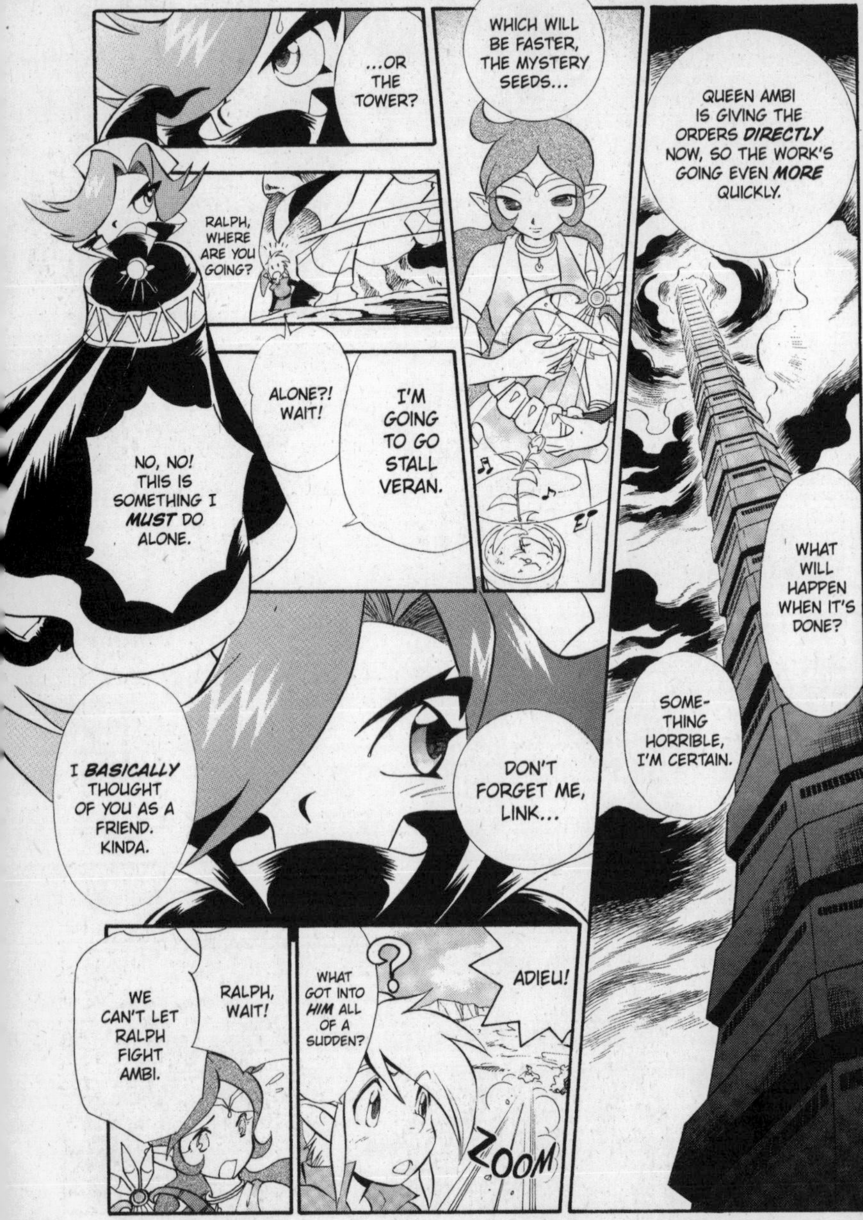
QUEEN AMBI IS GIVING THE ORDERS *DIRECTLY* NOW, SO THE WORK'S GOING EVEN *MORE* QUICKLY.
WHAT WILL HAPPEN WHEN IT'S DONE?
SOME-THING HORRIBLE, I'M CERTAIN.
WHICH WILL BE FASTER, THE MYSTERY SEEDS...
...OR THE TOWER?
RALPH, WHERE ARE YOU GOING?
I'M GOING TO GO STALL VERAN.
ALONE?! WAIT!
NO, NO! THIS IS SOMETHING I *MUST* DO ALONE.
DON'T FORGET ME, LINK...
I *BASICALLY* THOUGHT OF YOU AS A FRIEND. KINDA.
ADIEU!
WHAT GOT INTO *HIM* ALL OF A SUDDEN?
ZOOM
RALPH, WAIT!
WE CAN'T LET RALPH FIGHT AMBI.

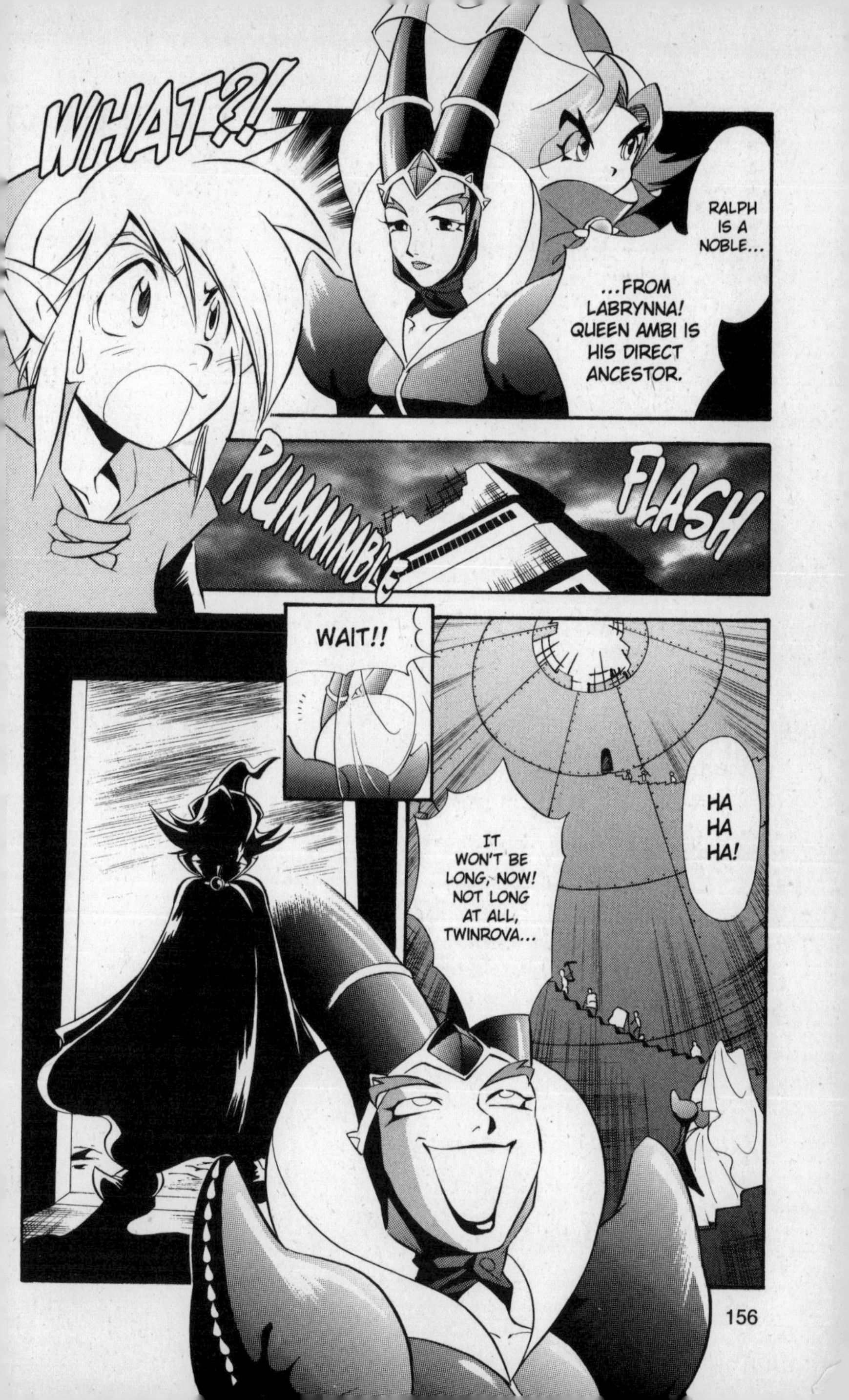
RALPH IS A NOBLE...
...FROM LABRYNNA! QUEEN AMBI IS HIS DIRECT ANCESTOR.
WHAT?!
FLASH
RUMMMBLE
HA HA HA!
IT WON'T BE LONG, NOW! NOT LONG AT ALL, TWINROVA...
WAIT!!

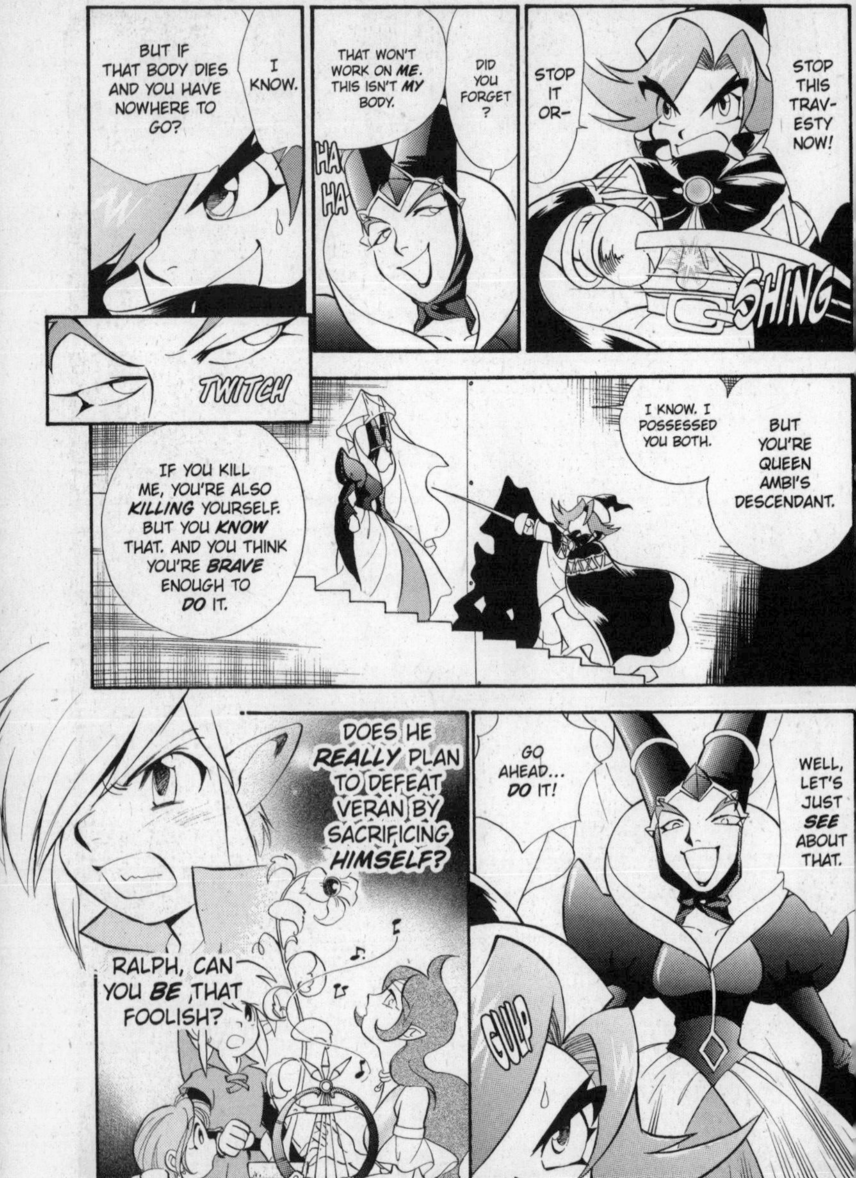
STOP THIS TRAVESTY NOW!
STOP IT OR–
SHING
DID YOU FORGET?
THAT WON'T WORK ON ME. THIS ISN'T MY BODY.
HA HA
I KNOW.
BUT IF THAT BODY DIES AND YOU HAVE NOWHERE TO GO?
TWITCH
BUT YOU'RE QUEEN AMBI'S DESCENDANT.
I KNOW. I POSSESSED YOU BOTH.
IF YOU KILL ME, YOU'RE ALSO KILLING YOURSELF. BUT YOU KNOW THAT. AND YOU THINK YOU'RE BRAVE ENOUGH TO DO IT.
WELL, LET'S JUST SEE ABOUT THAT.
GO AHEAD... DO IT!
GULP
DOES HE REALLY PLAN TO DEFEAT VERAN BY SACRIFICING HIMSELF?
RALPH, CAN YOU BE THAT FOOLISH?

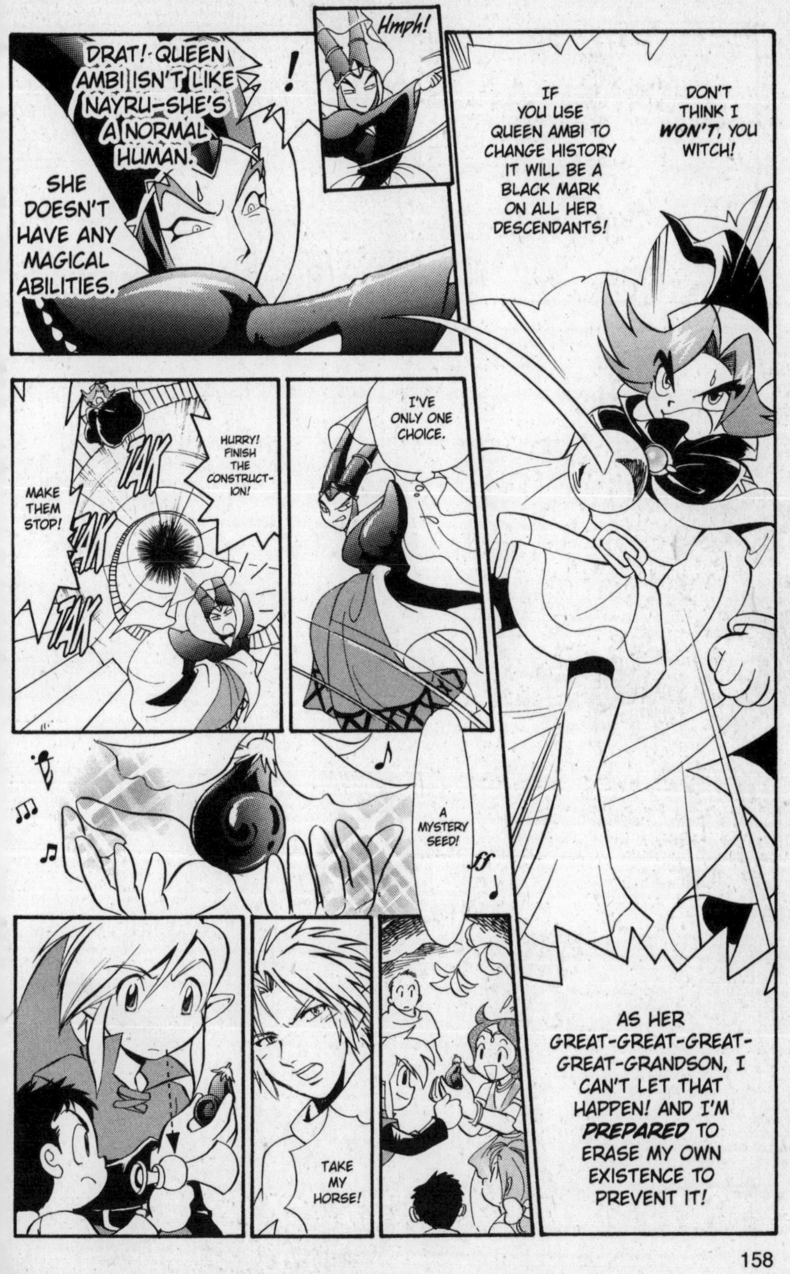
DON'T THINK I WON'T, YOU WITCH!
IF YOU USE QUEEN AMBI TO CHANGE HISTORY IT WILL BE A BLACK MARK ON ALL HER DESCENDANTS!
AS HER GREAT-GREAT-GREAT-GREAT-GRANDSON, I CAN'T LET THAT HAPPEN! AND I'M PREPARED TO ERASE MY OWN EXISTENCE TO PREVENT IT!
Hmph!
!
DRAT! QUEEN AMBI ISN'T LIKE NAYRU—SHE'S A NORMAL HUMAN.
SHE DOESN'T HAVE ANY MAGICAL ABILITIES.
I'VE ONLY ONE CHOICE.
HURRY! FINISH THE CONSTRUCTION!
MAKE THEM STOP!
TAK
TAK
TAK
A MYSTERY SEED!
TAKE MY HORSE!

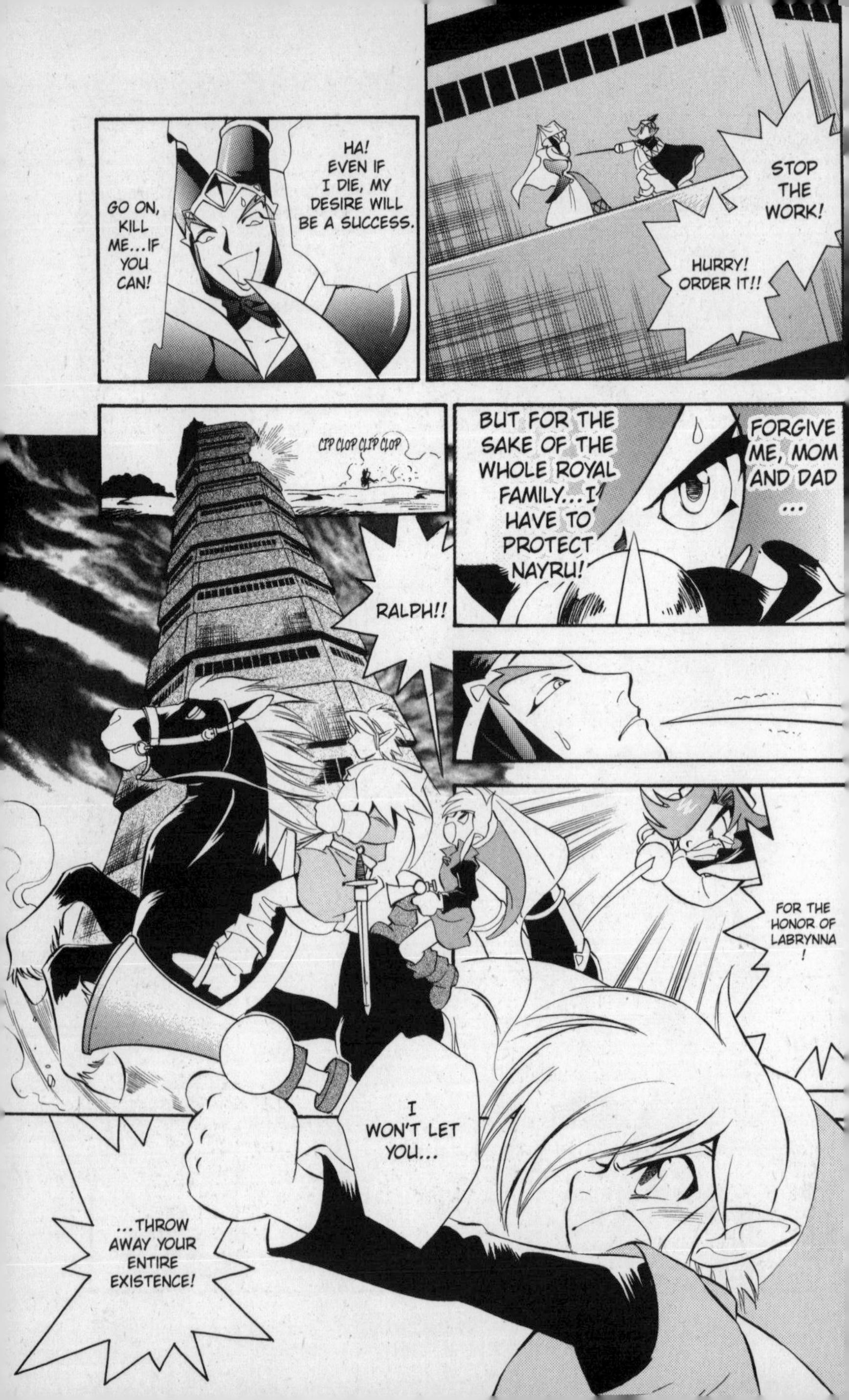
STOP THE WORK!
HURRY! ORDER IT!!
HA! EVEN IF I DIE, MY DESIRE WILL BE A SUCCESS.
GO ON, KILL ME...IF YOU CAN!
FORGIVE ME, MOM AND DAD ...
BUT FOR THE SAKE OF THE WHOLE ROYAL FAMILY...I HAVE TO PROTECT NAYRU!
FOR THE HONOR OF LABRYNNA!
CLIP CLOP CLIP CLOP
RALPH!!
I WON'T LET YOU...
...THROW AWAY YOUR ENTIRE EXISTENCE!

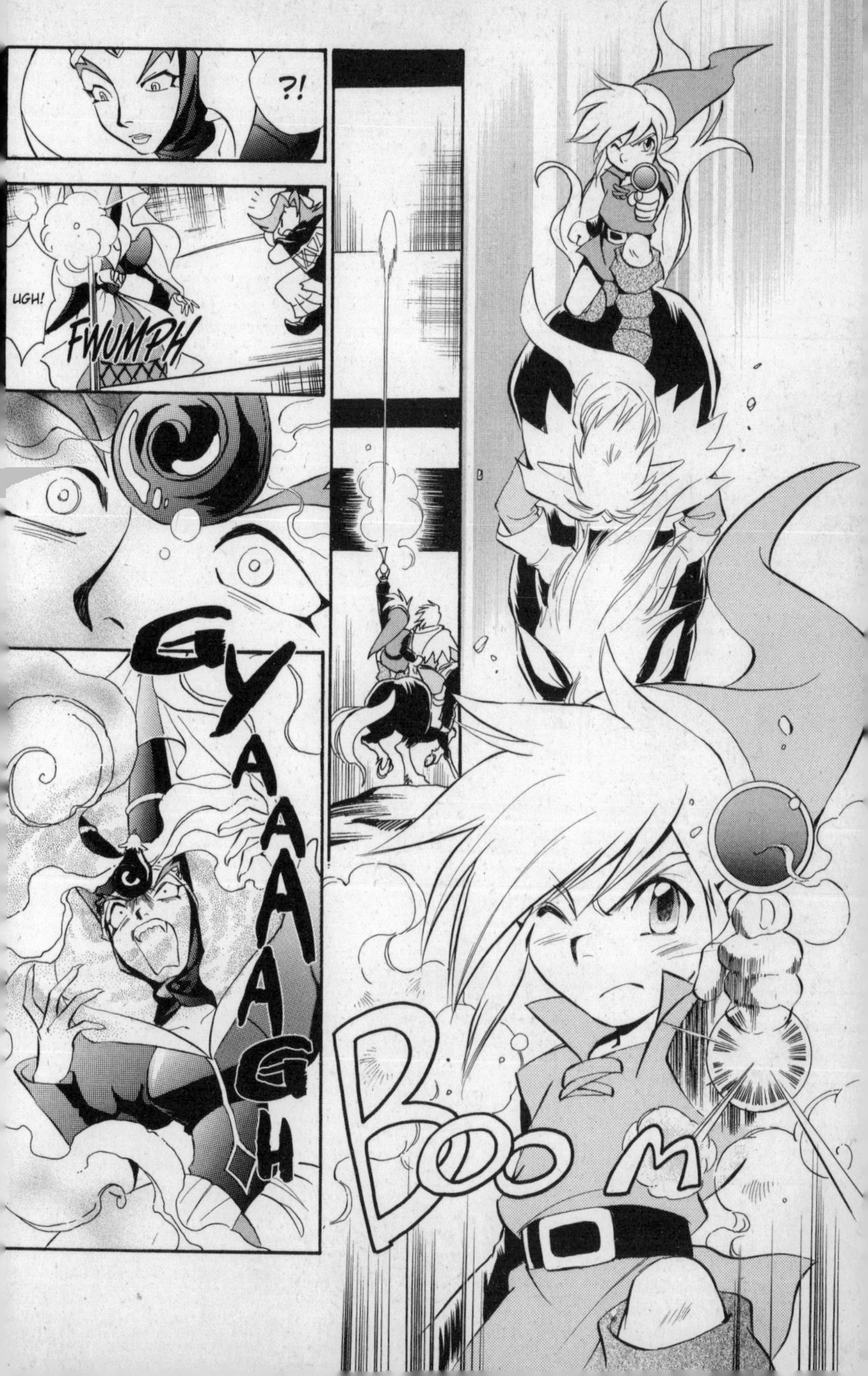
BOOM
?!
UGH!
FWUMPH
GYAAAAGH!

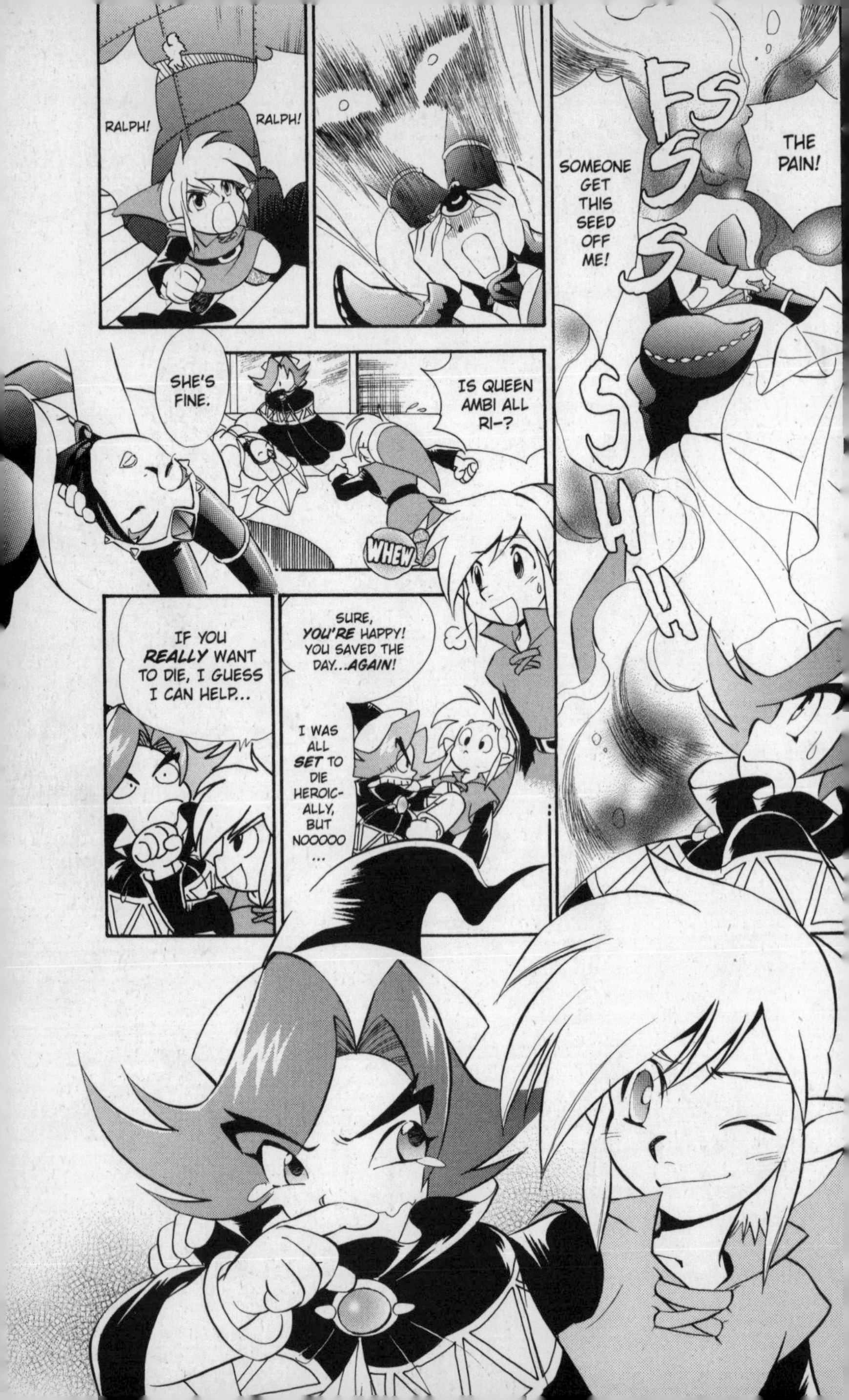
THE PAIN!
SOMEONE GET THIS SEED OFF ME!
FSSSSHHH
RALPH!
RALPH!
IS QUEEN AMBI ALL RI-?
SHE'S FINE.
WHEW
SURE, *YOU'RE* HAPPY! YOU SAVED THE DAY...*AGAIN*!
I WAS ALL *SET* TO DIE HEROIC-ALLY, BUT NOOOOO...
IF YOU *REALLY* WANT TO DIE, I GUESS I CAN HELP...

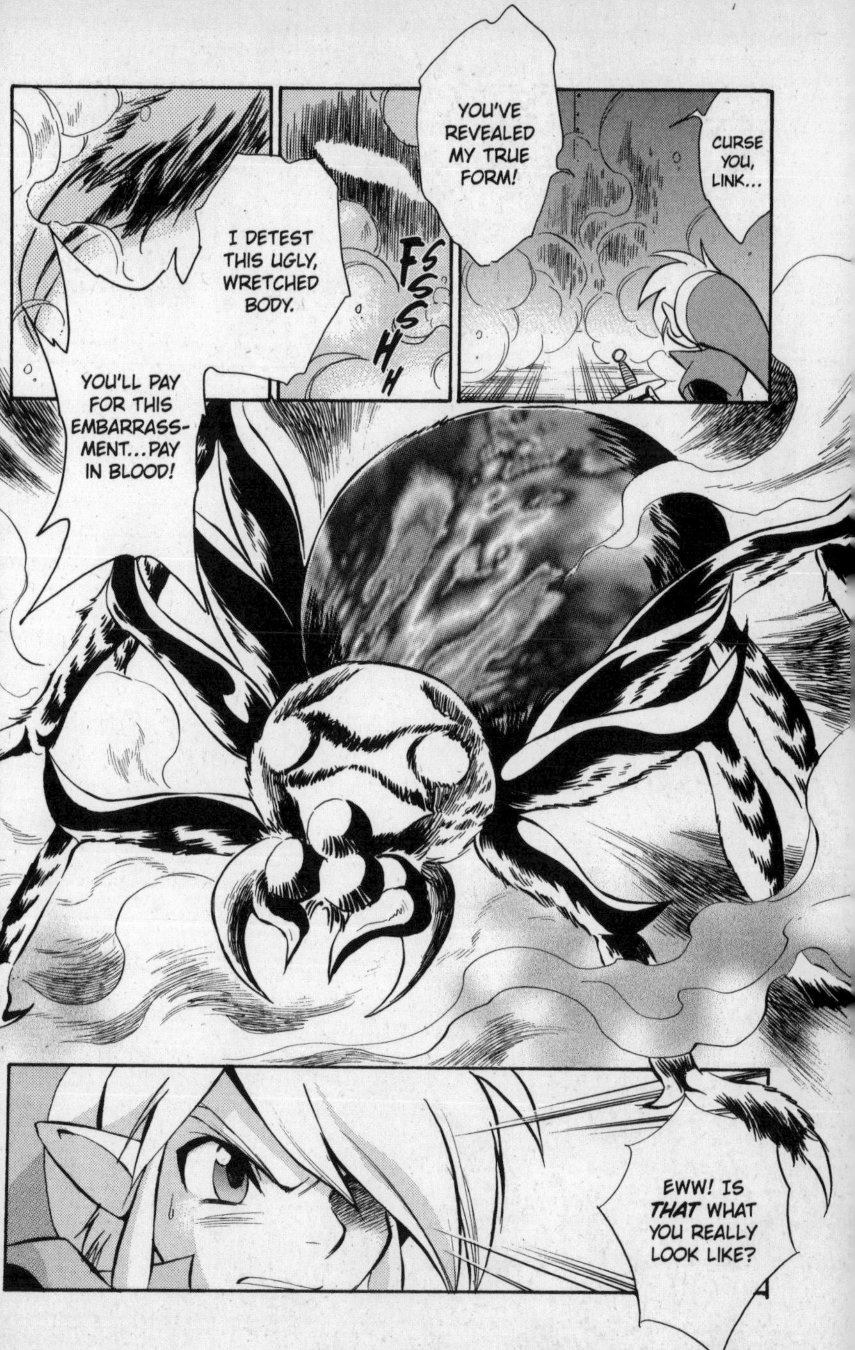
CURSE YOU, LINK...
YOU'VE REVEALED MY TRUE FORM!
I DETEST THIS UGLY, WRETCHED BODY.
FSSSHH
YOU'LL PAY FOR THIS EMBARRASS-MENT...PAY IN BLOOD!
EWW! IS *THAT* WHAT YOU REALLY LOOK LIKE?

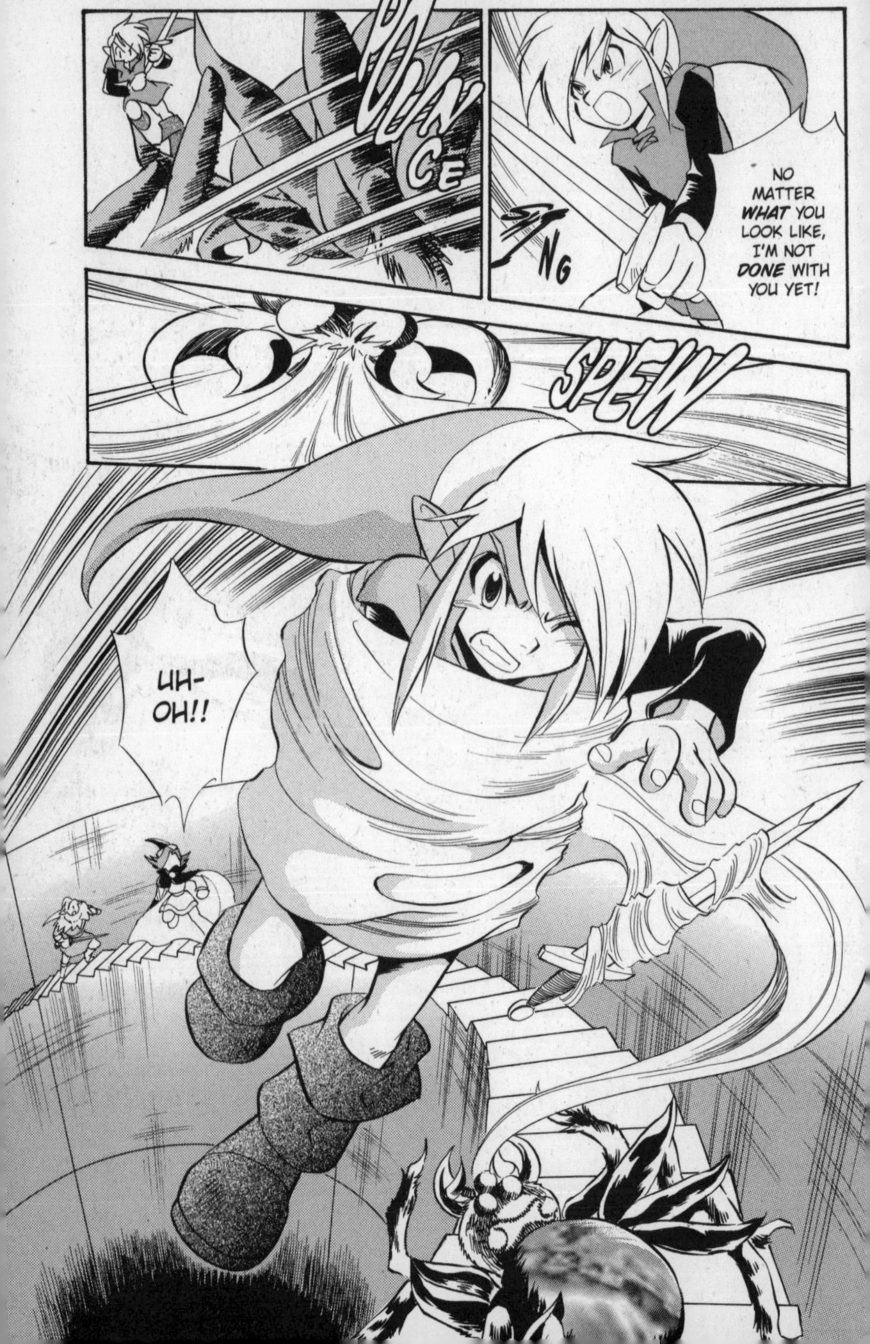
NO MATTER **WHAT** YOU LOOK LIKE, I'M NOT **DONE** WITH YOU YET!
POUNCE
SPEW
UH-OH!!

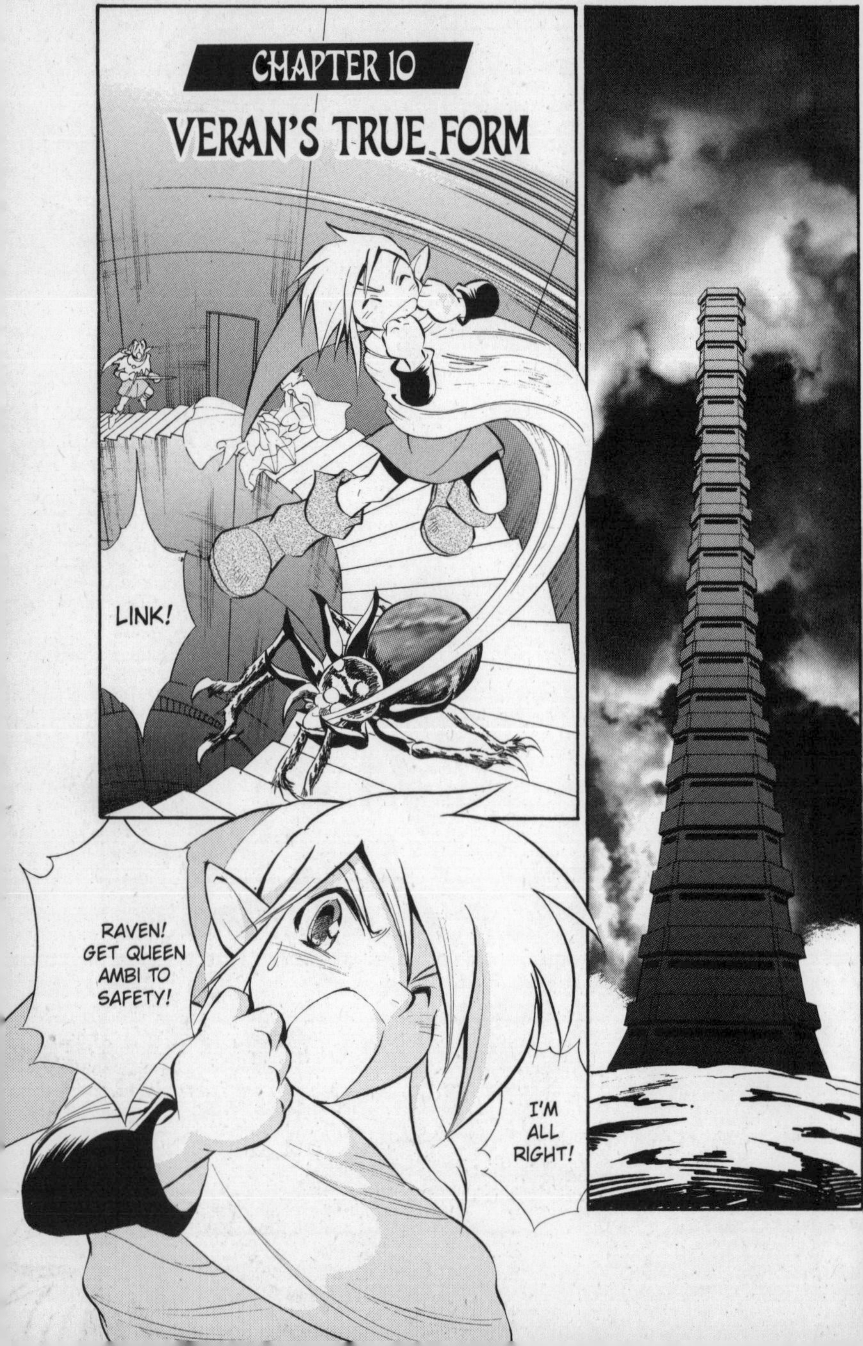
CHAPTER 10
VERAN'S TRUE FORM
LINK!
I'M ALL RIGHT!
RAVEN! GET QUEEN AMBI TO SAFETY!

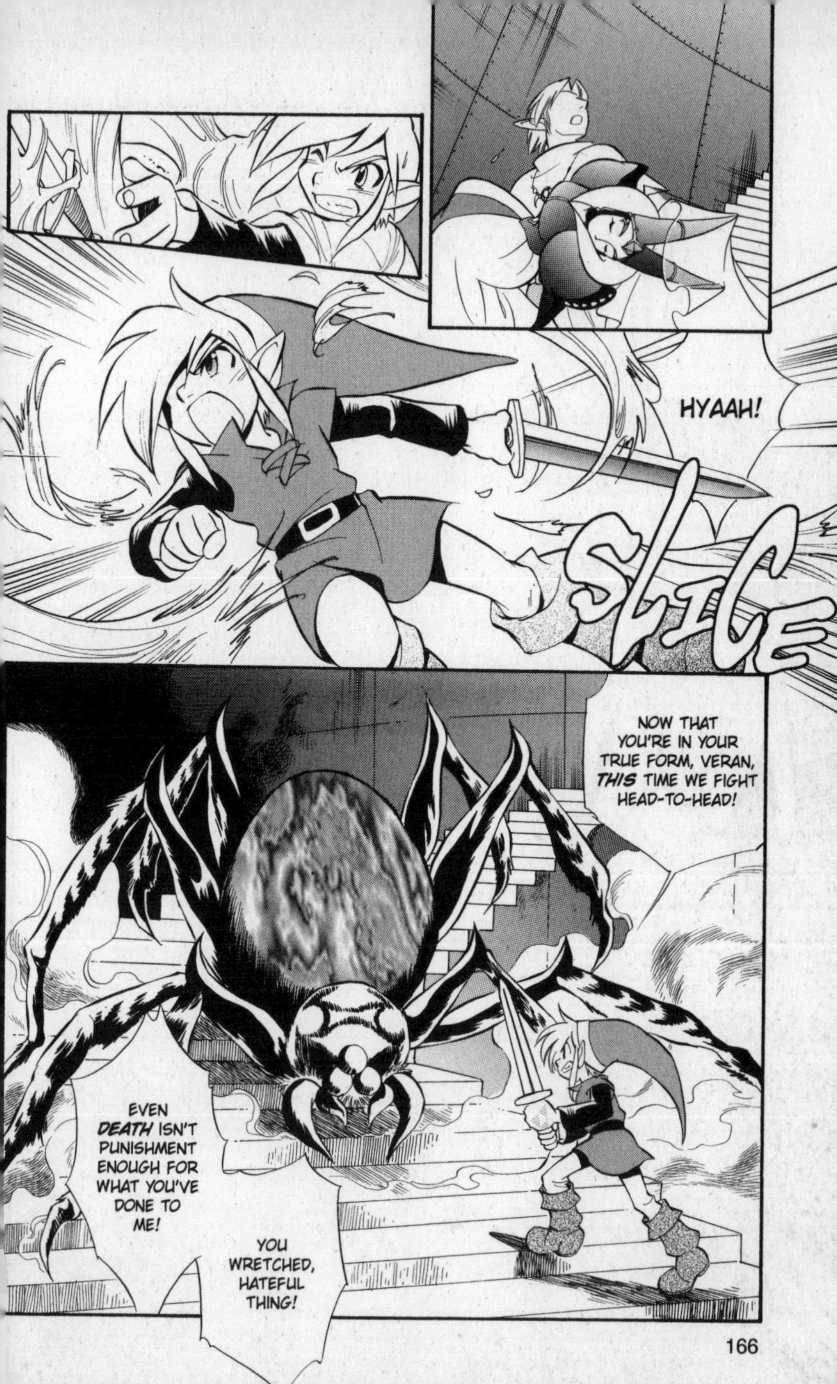
HYAAH!
SLICE
NOW THAT YOU'RE IN YOUR TRUE FORM, VERAN, *THIS* TIME WE FIGHT HEAD-TO-HEAD!
EVEN *DEATH* ISN'T PUNISHMENT ENOUGH FOR WHAT YOU'VE DONE TO ME!
YOU WRETCHED, HATEFUL THING!

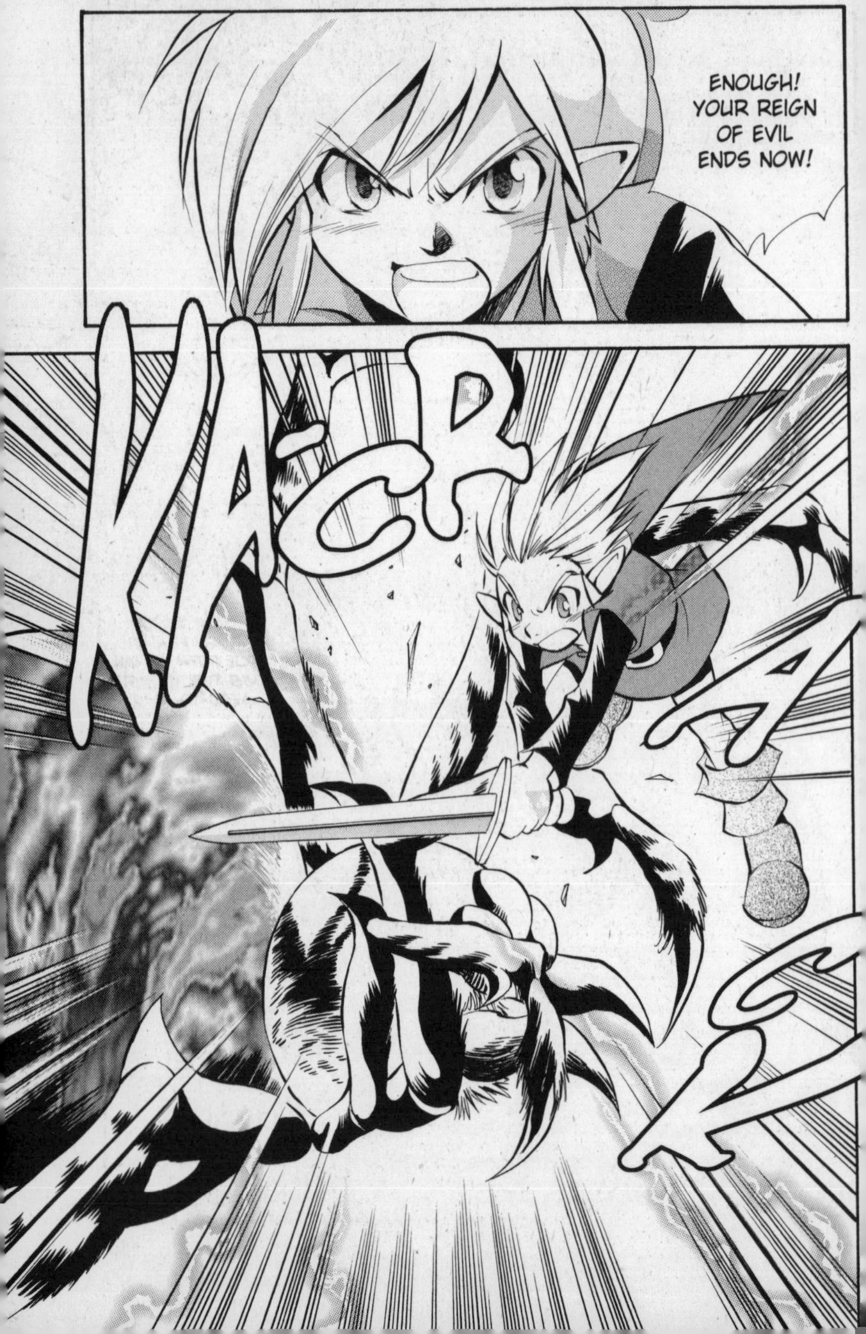
ENOUGH! YOUR REIGN OF EVIL ENDS NOW!
KA-CRACK

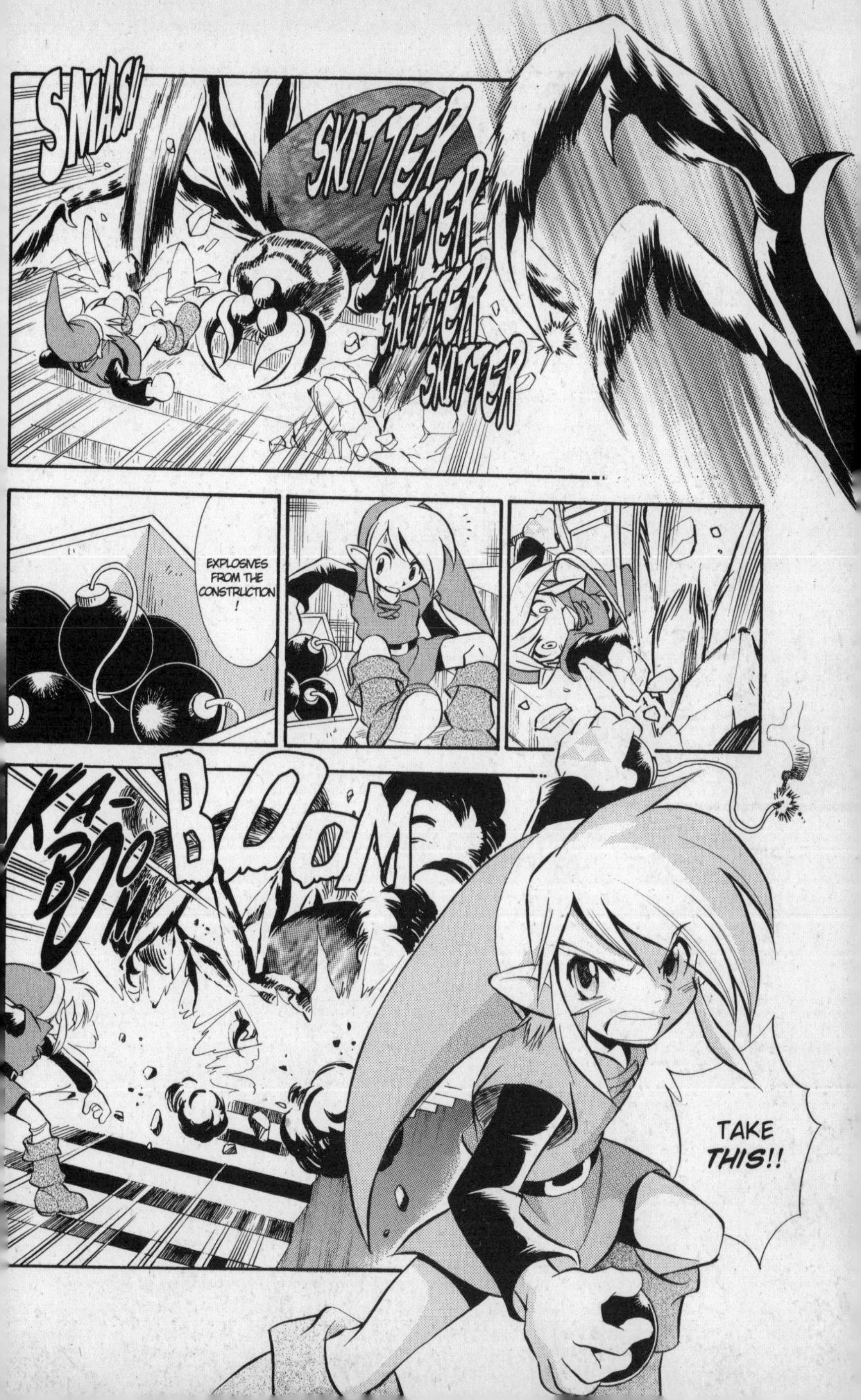
SMASH
SKITTER SKITTER SKITTER SKITTER
EXPLOSIVES FROM THE CONSTRUCTION!
KA-BOOM BOOM
TAKE THIS!!

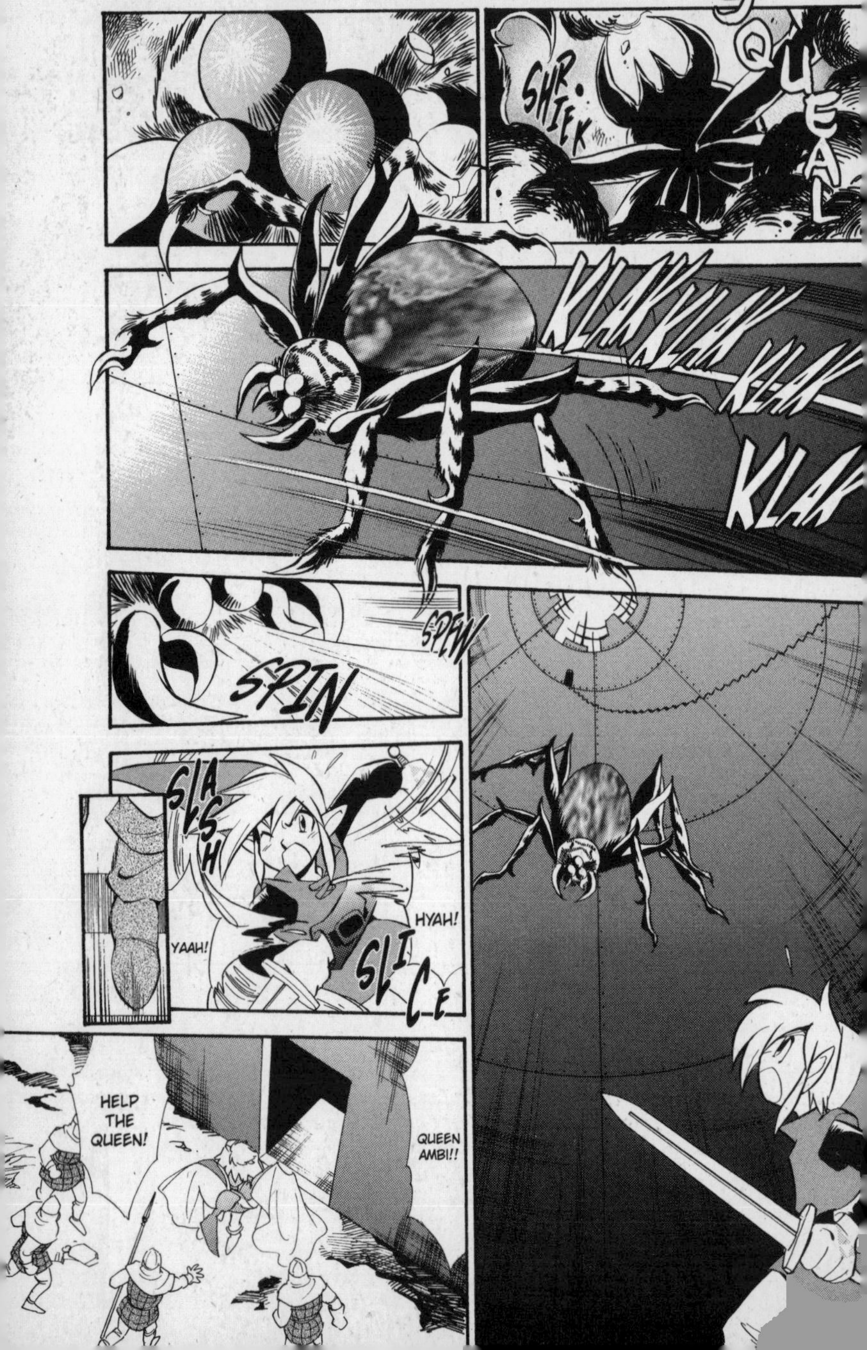
SQUEAL
SHRIEK
KLAK KLAK
KLAK
KLAK
SPEW
SPIN
SLASH
HYAH!
YAAH!
SLICE
QUEEN AMBI!!
HELP THE QUEEN!

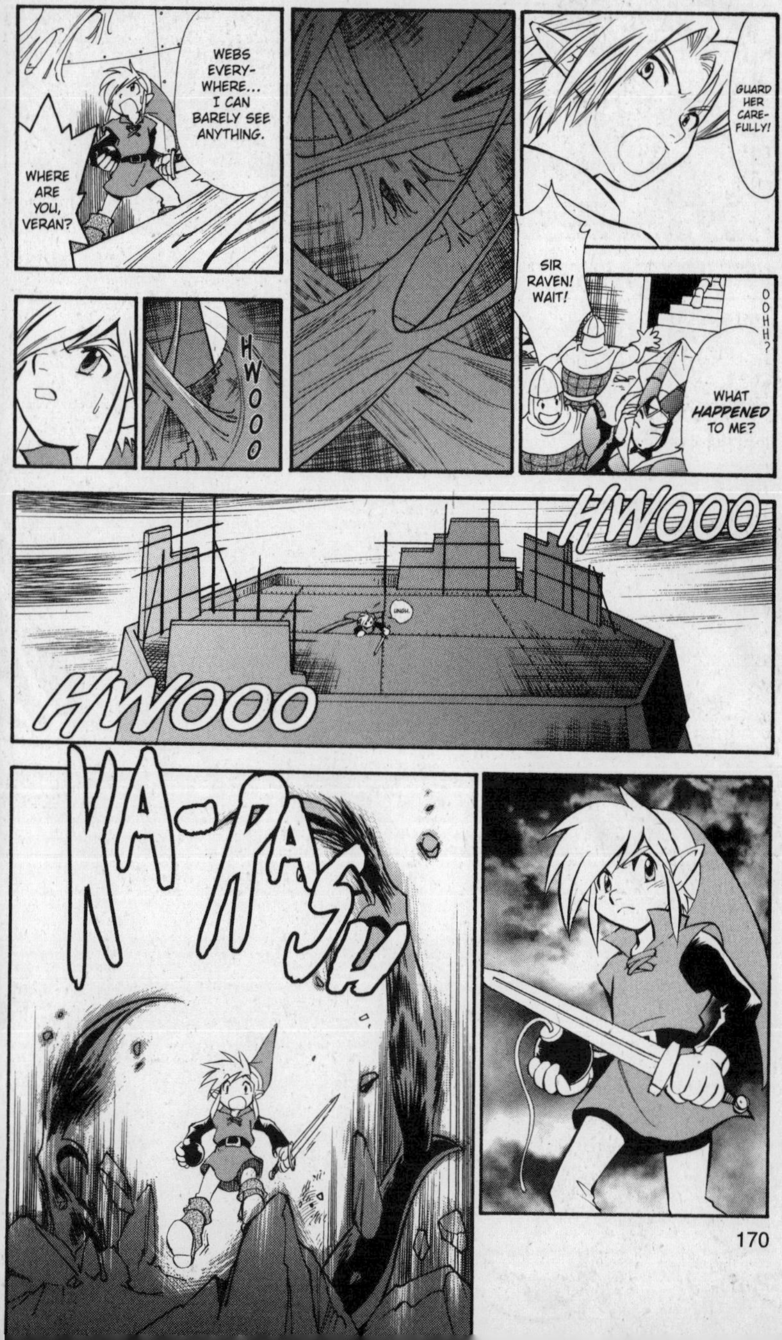
GUARD HER CAREFULLY!
SIR RAVEN! WAIT!
OOHH?
WHAT HAPPENED TO ME?
WEBS EVERYWHERE... I CAN BARELY SEE ANYTHING.
WHERE ARE YOU, VERAN?
HWOOOO
HWOOO
UNGH.
HWOOO
KA-RASH

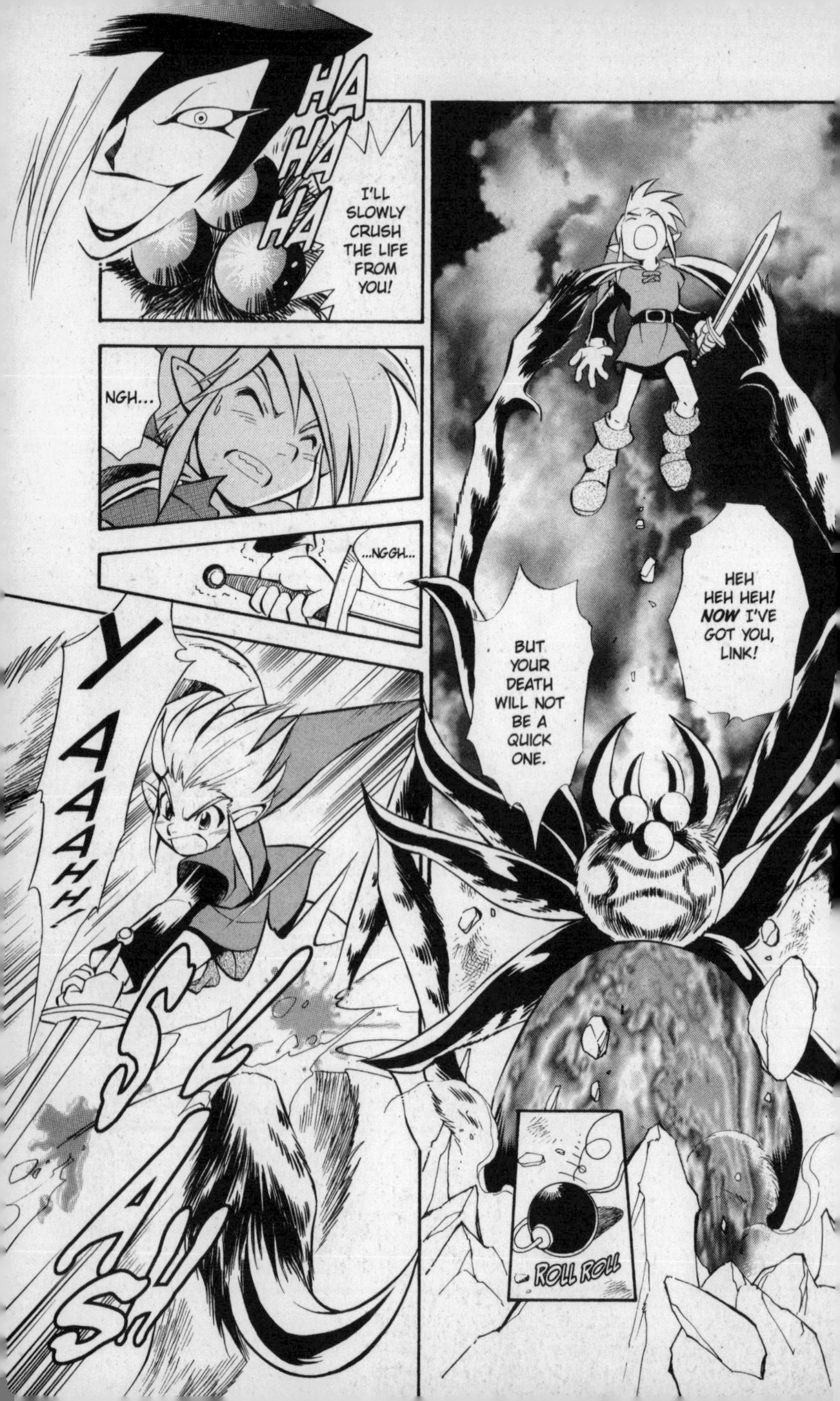

HEH HEH HEH! NOW I'VE GOT YOU, LINK!
BUT YOUR DEATH WILL NOT BE A QUICK ONE.
ROLL ROLL
HA HA HA HA
I'LL SLOWLY CRUSH THE LIFE FROM YOU!
NGH...
...NGGH...
YAAAAHH!

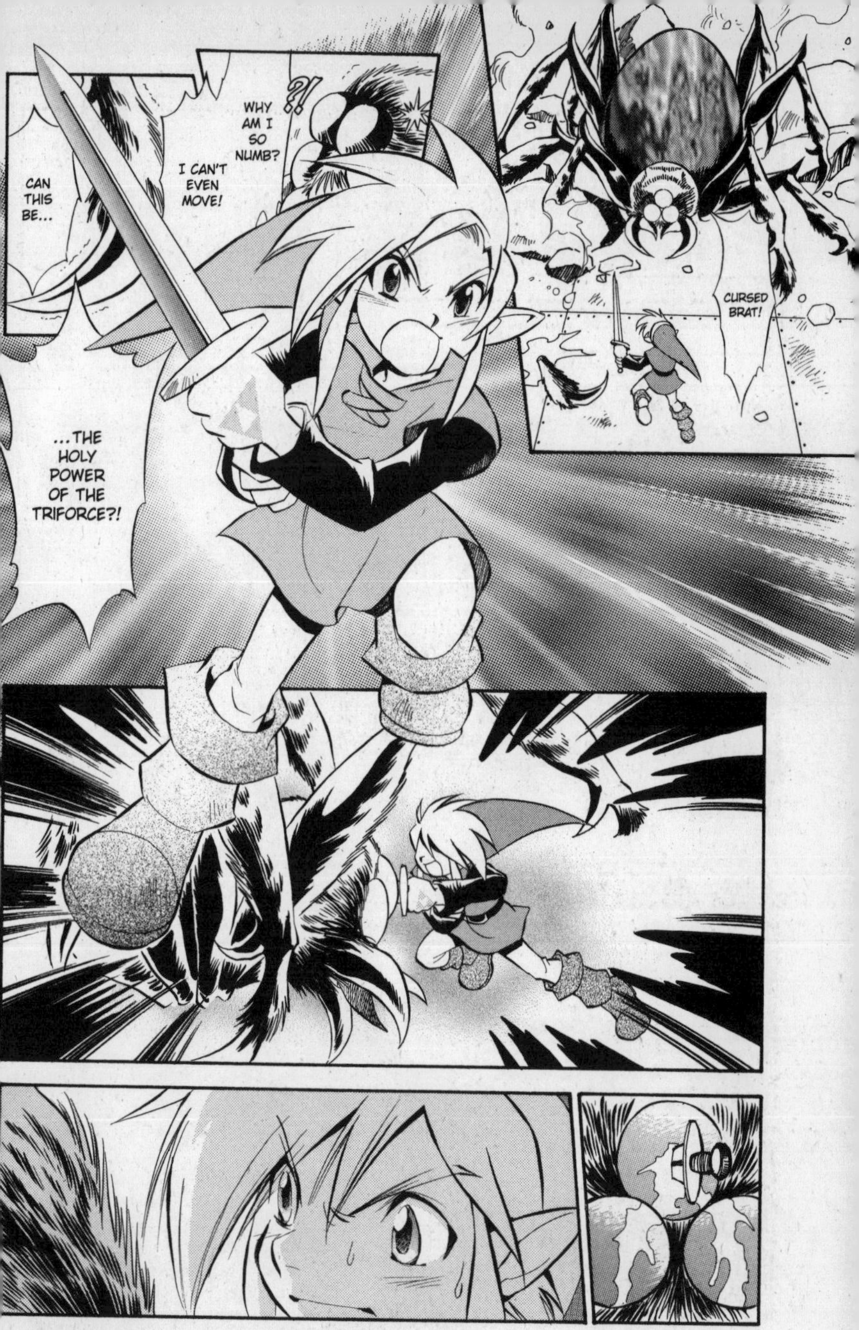
CURSED BRAT!
?!
WHY AM I SO NUMB?
I CAN'T EVEN MOVE!
CAN THIS BE...
...THE HOLY POWER OF THE TRIFORCE?!

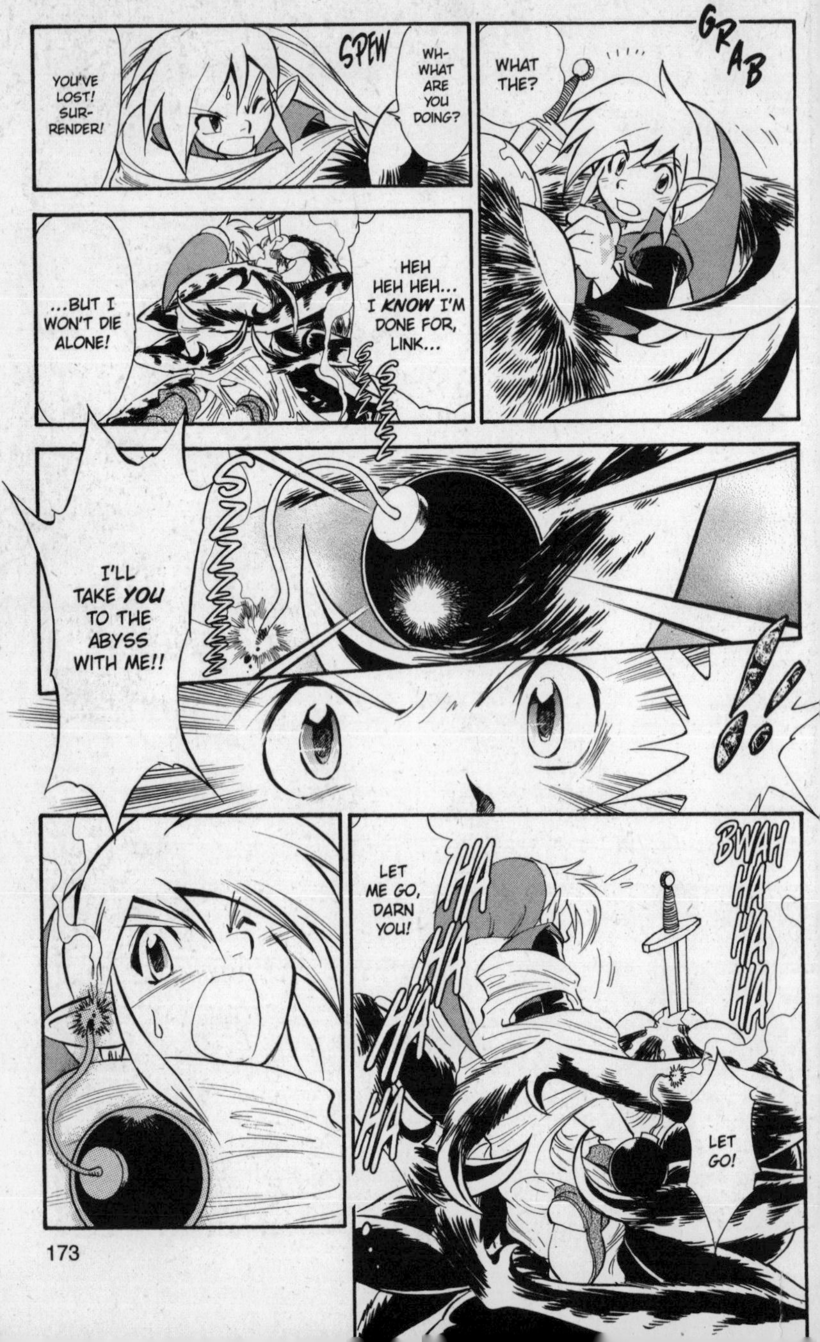
GRAB
WHAT THE?
YOU'VE LOST! SUR-RENDER!
SPEW
WH- WHAT ARE YOU DOING?
HEH HEH HEH... I *KNOW* I'M DONE FOR, LINK...
...BUT I WON'T DIE ALONE!
SZZZZ
SZZZZZZZZ
I'LL TAKE *YOU* TO THE ABYSS WITH ME!!
!!
BWAH HA HA HA HA
LET ME GO, DARN YOU!
HA HA HA HA HA
LET GO!

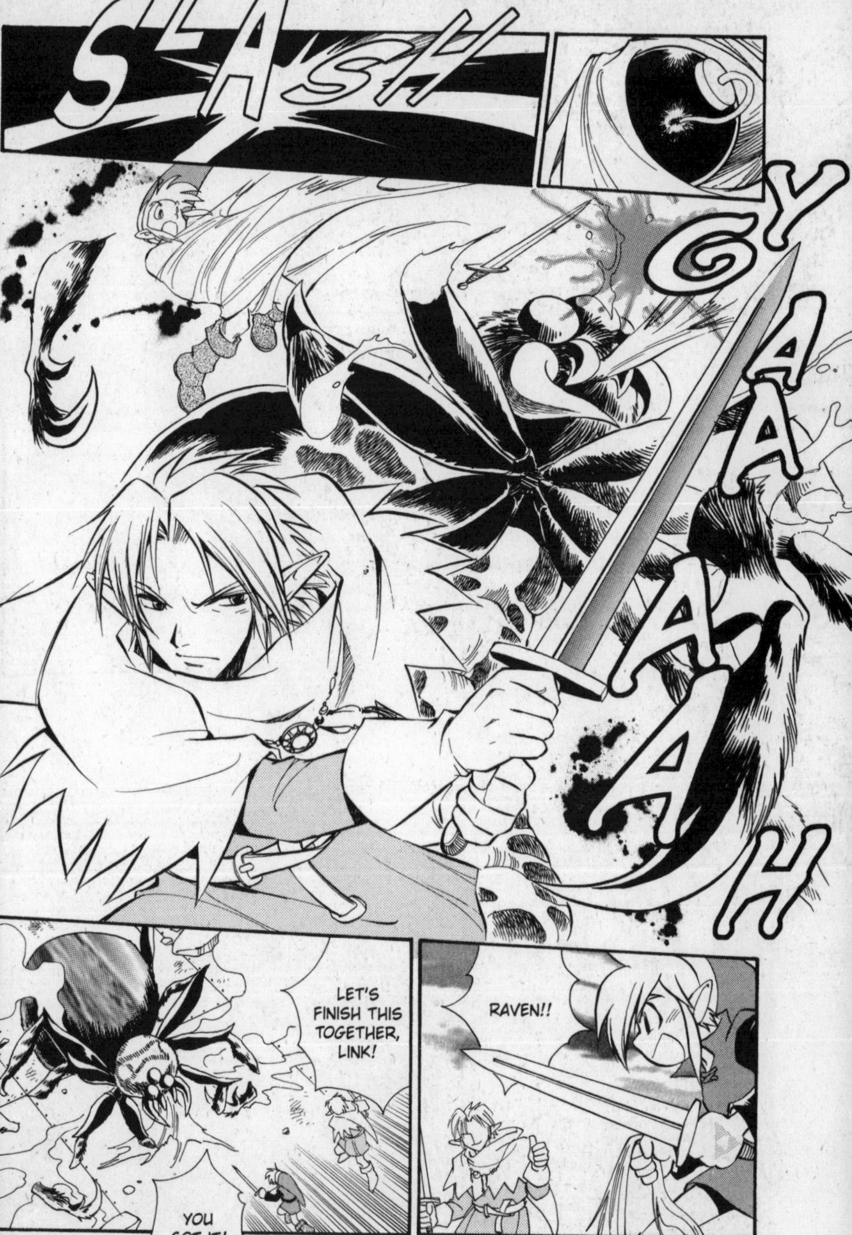
SLASH
GYAAAAAH
RAVEN!!
LET'S FINISH THIS TOGETHER, LINK!
YOU GOT IT!

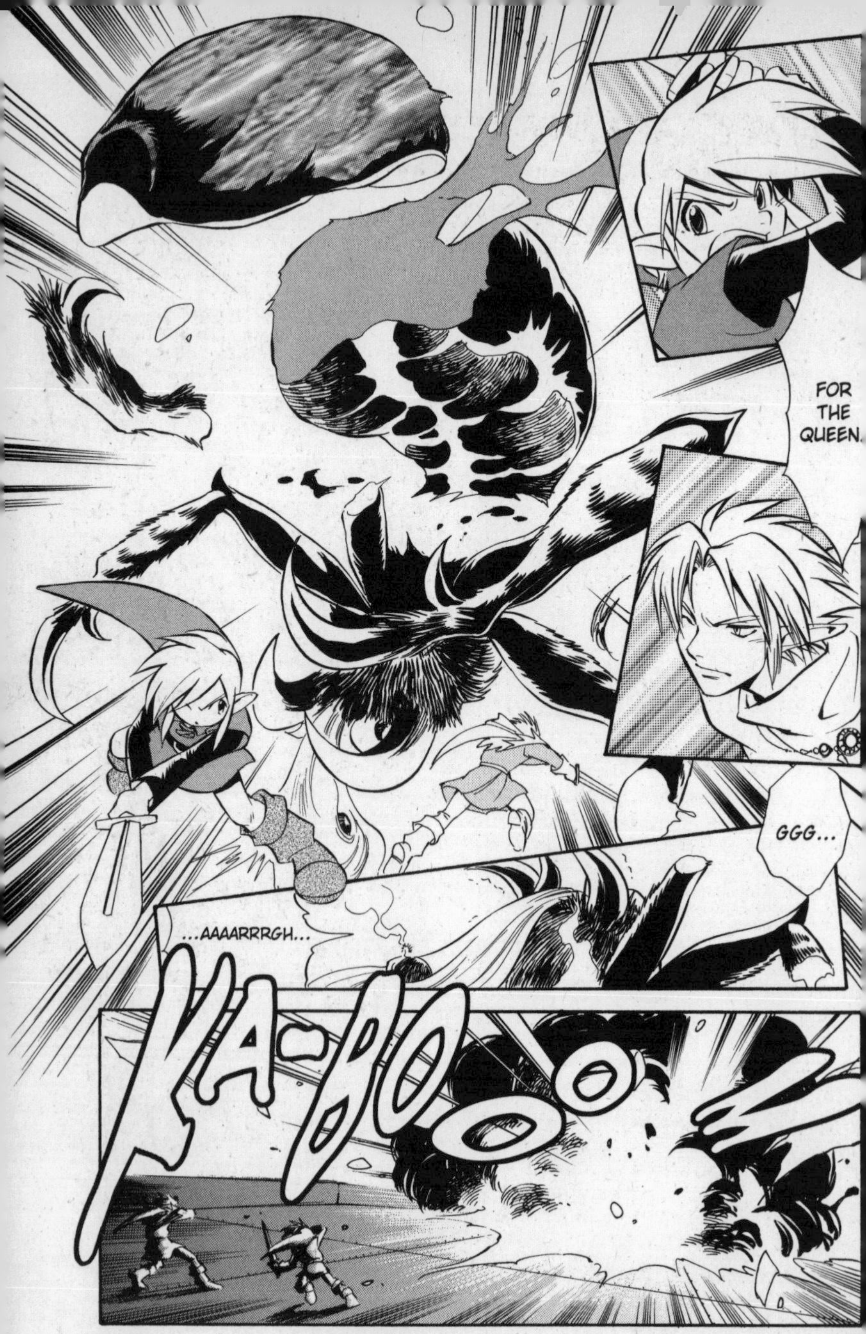
FOR THE QUEEN.
GGG...
...AAAARRRGH...
KA-BOOOOM

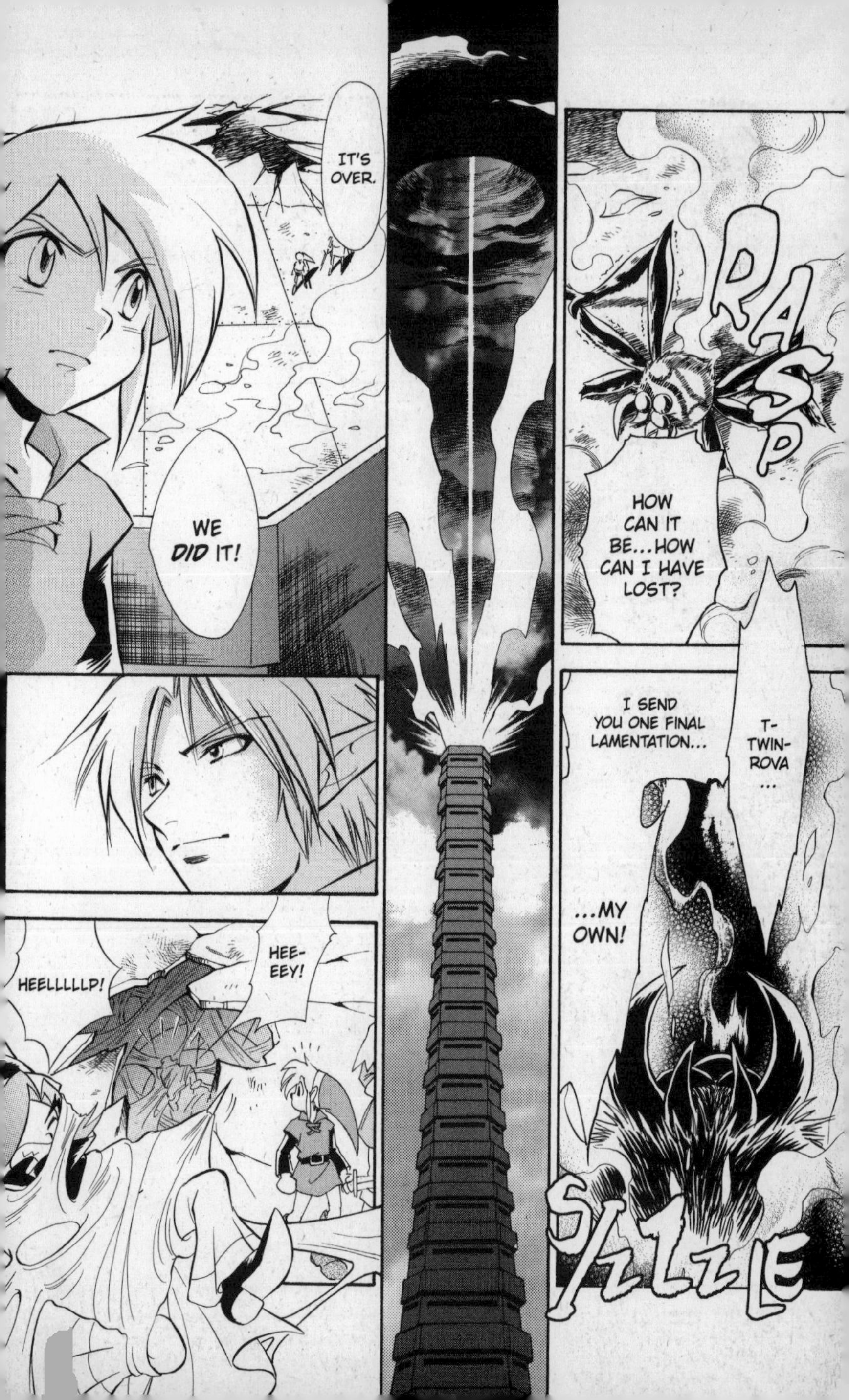
RASP
HOW CAN IT BE...HOW CAN I HAVE LOST?
T-TWIN-ROVA...
I SEND YOU ONE FINAL LAMENTATION...
...MY OWN!
SIZZLE
IT'S OVER.
WE DID IT!
HEE-EEY!
HEELLLLLLP!

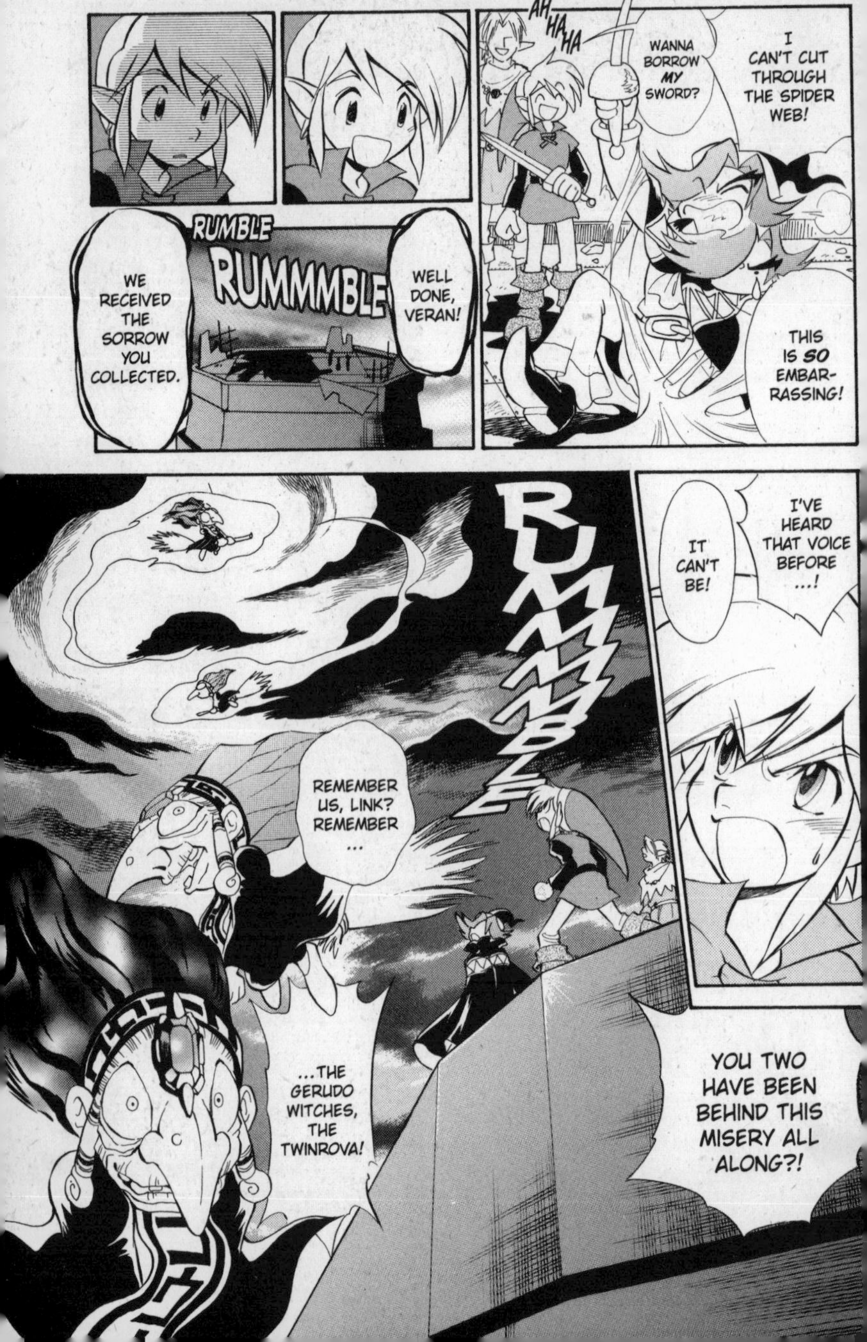
I CAN'T CUT THROUGH THE SPIDER WEB!
WANNA BORROW MY SWORD?
AH HA HA
THIS IS SO EMBARRASSING!
WELL DONE, VERAN!
RUMBLE RUMMMBLE
WE RECEIVED THE SORROW YOU COLLECTED.
I'VE HEARD THAT VOICE BEFORE ...!
IT CAN'T BE!
RUMMMMBLE
REMEMBER US, LINK? REMEMBER ...
YOU TWO HAVE BEEN BEHIND THIS MISERY ALL ALONG?!
...THE GERUDO WITCHES, THE TWINROVA!

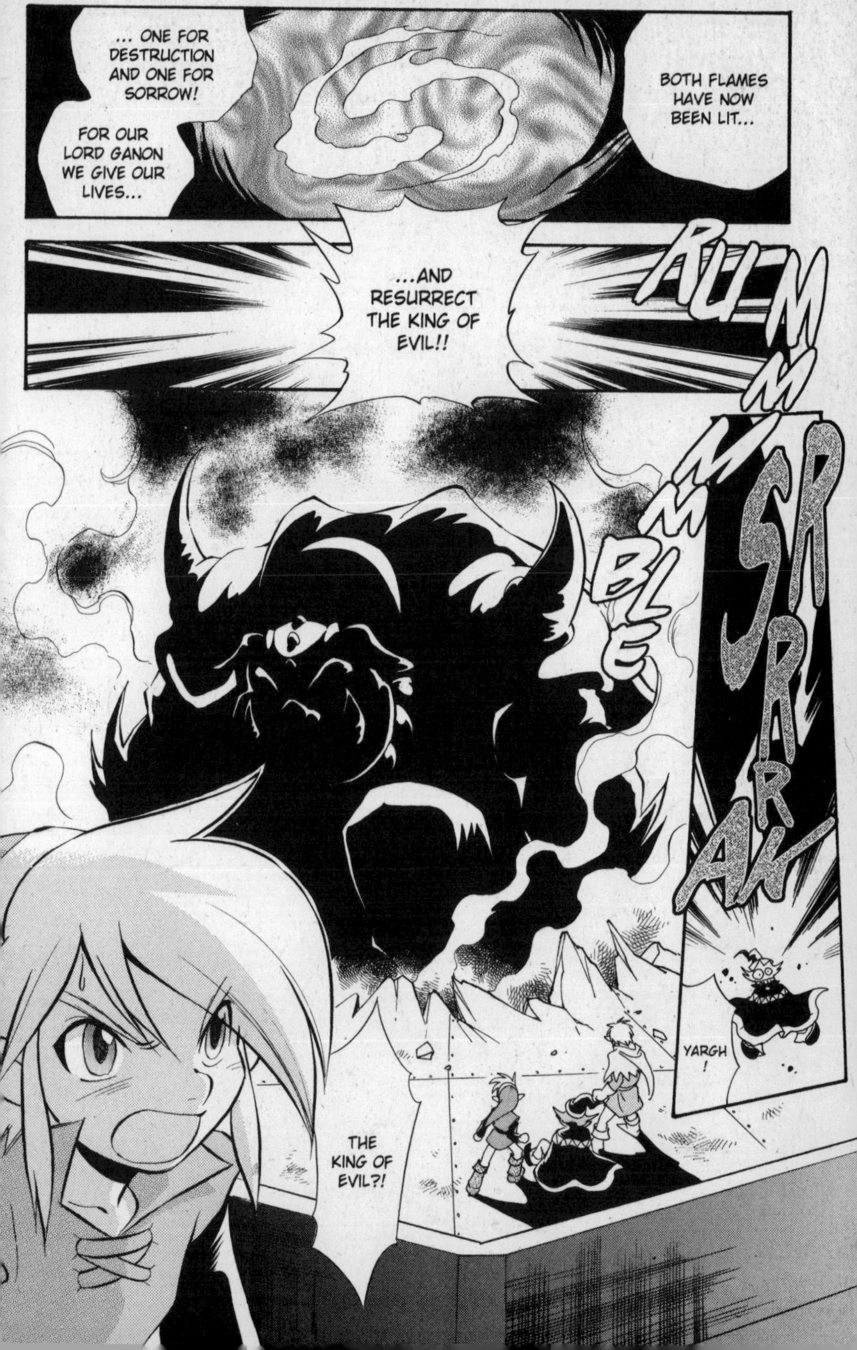
BOTH FLAMES HAVE NOW BEEN LIT...
... ONE FOR DESTRUCTION AND ONE FOR SORROW!
FOR OUR LORD GANON WE GIVE OUR LIVES...
...AND RESURRECT THE KING OF EVIL!!
RUMMMMMBLE
SRRRAK
YARGH!
THE KING OF EVIL?!

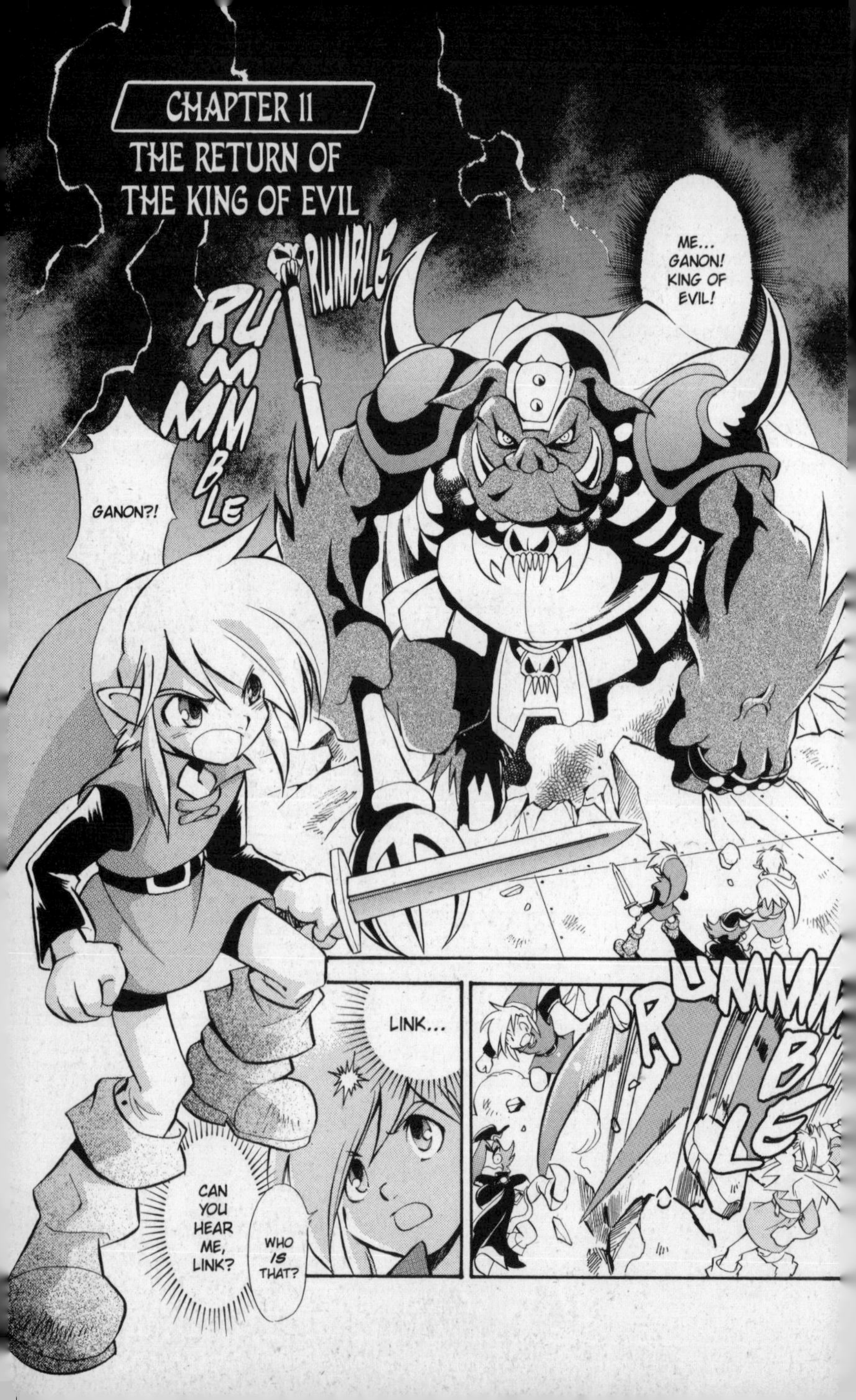
CHAPTER 11
THE RETURN OF THE KING OF EVIL
RUMBLE
RUMMMBLE
ME... GANON! KING OF EVIL!
GANON?!
RUMMMBLE
LINK...
CAN YOU HEAR ME, LINK?
WHO IS THAT?

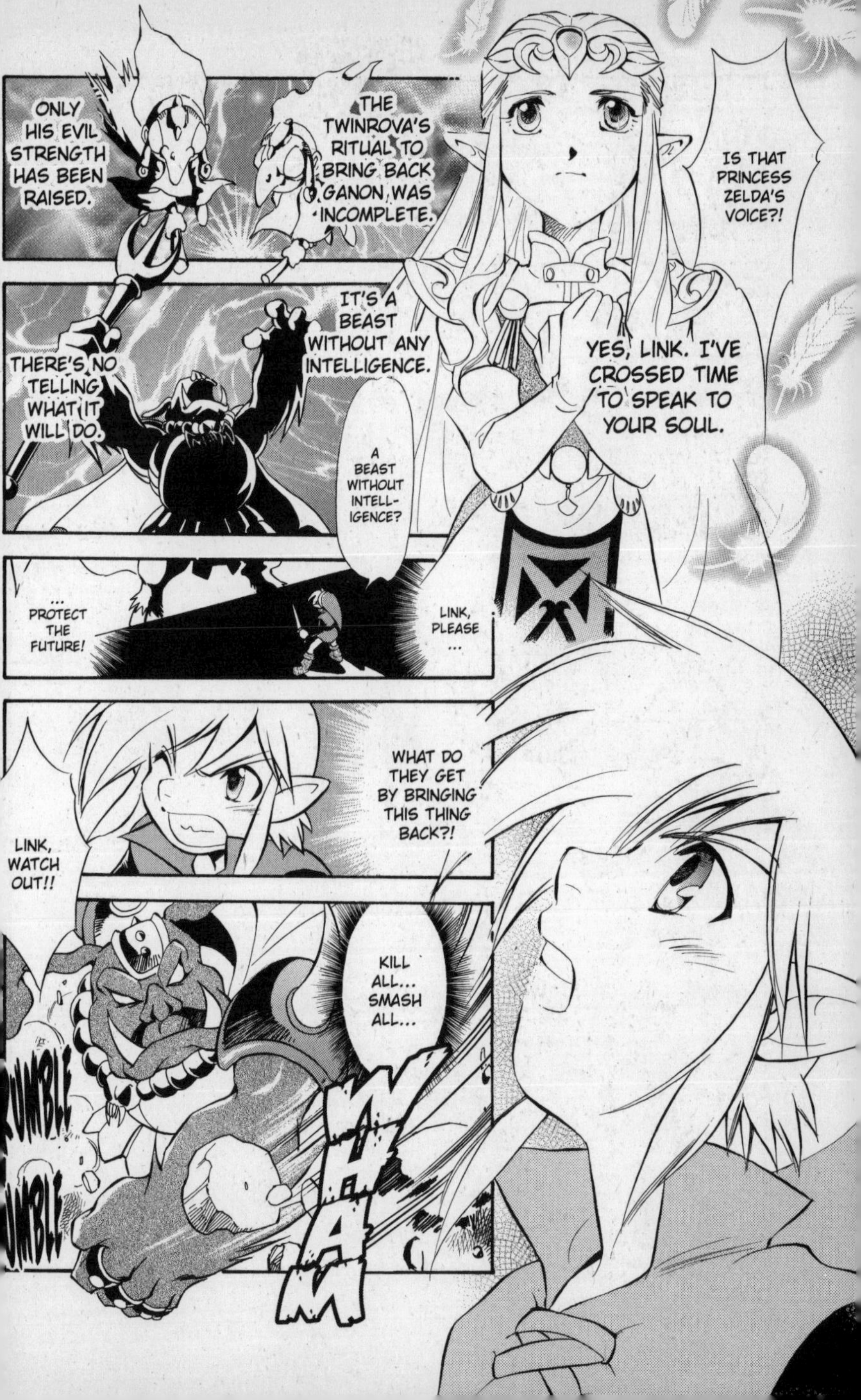
IS THAT PRINCESS ZELDA'S VOICE?!
YES, LINK. I'VE CROSSED TIME TO SPEAK TO YOUR SOUL.
THE TWINROVA'S RITUAL TO BRING BACK GANON WAS INCOMPLETE.
ONLY HIS EVIL STRENGTH HAS BEEN RAISED.
IT'S A BEAST WITHOUT ANY INTELLIGENCE.
THERE'S NO TELLING WHAT IT WILL DO.
A BEAST WITHOUT INTELL-IGENCE?
LINK, PLEASE ...
... PROTECT THE FUTURE!
WHAT DO THEY GET BY BRINGING THIS THING BACK?!
LINK, WATCH OUT!!
KILL ALL... SMASH ALL...
WHAM
RUMBLE!
UMBLE!

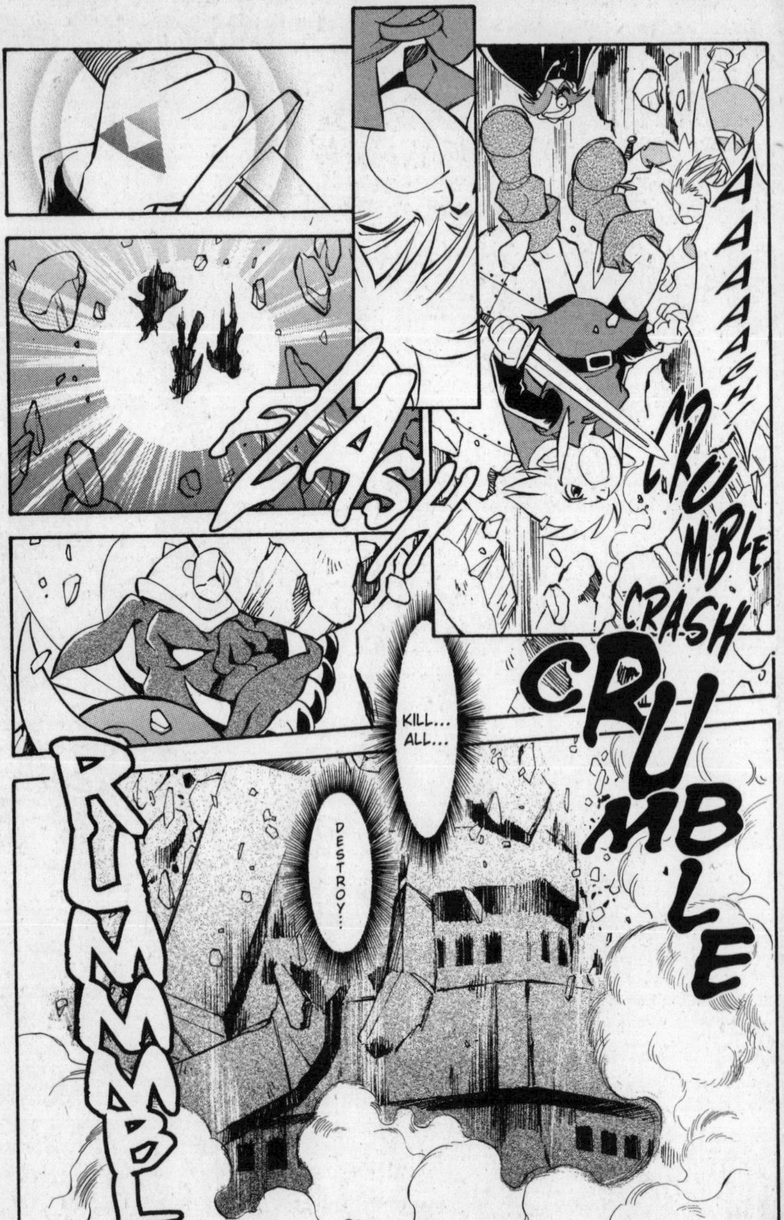
AAAAAAGH!
CRUMBLE
CRASH
FLASH
KILL... ALL...
DESTROY...
CRUMBLE
RUMMBLE

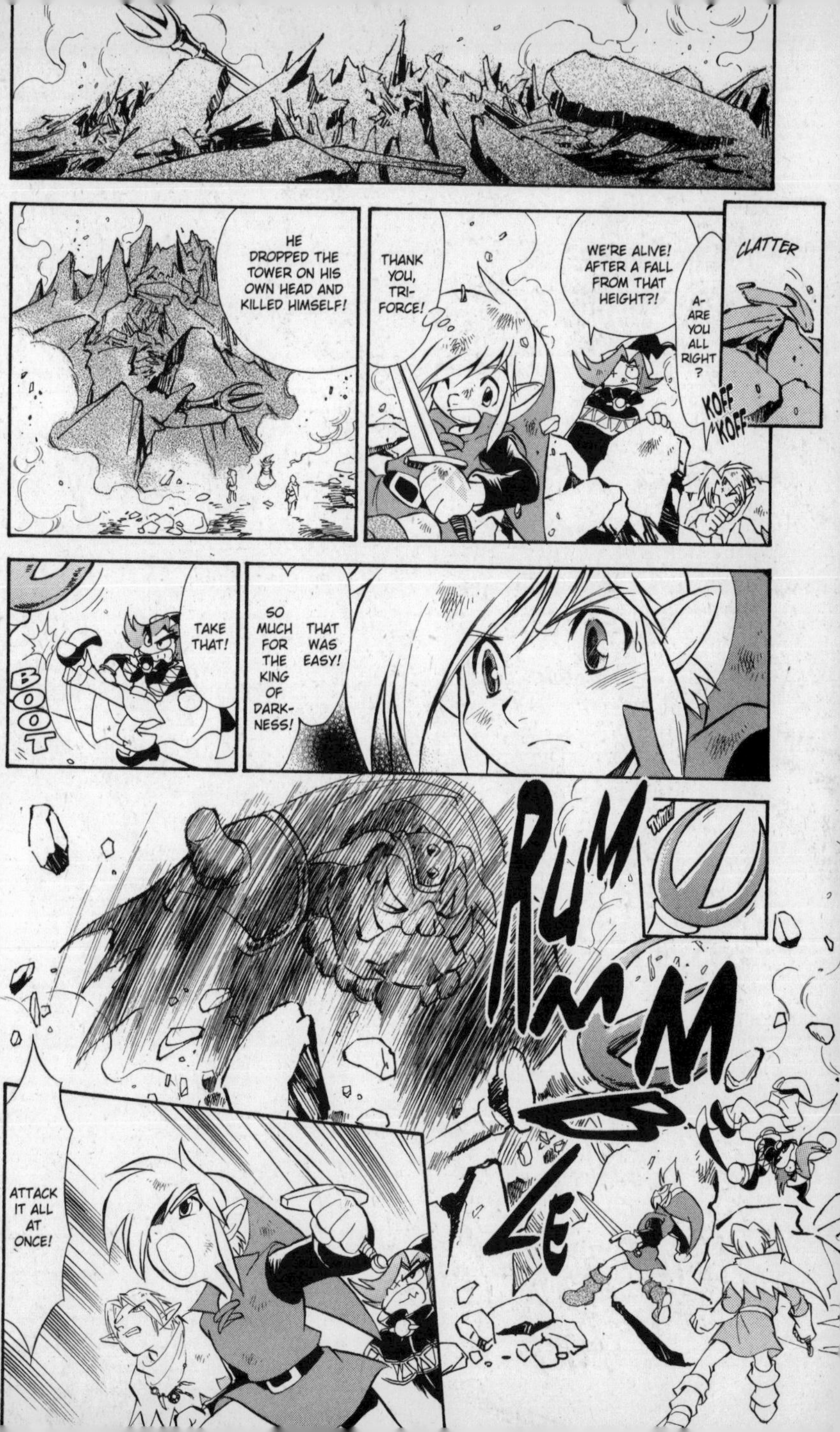
CLATTER
A-
ARE YOU ALL RIGHT?
KOFF KOFF
WE'RE ALIVE! AFTER A FALL FROM THAT HEIGHT?!
THANK YOU, TRI-FORCE!
HE DROPPED THE TOWER ON HIS OWN HEAD AND KILLED HIMSELF!
THAT WAS EASY!
SO MUCH FOR THE KING OF DARKNESS!
TAKE THAT!
BOOT
TWITCH
RUMMMBLE
ATTACK IT ALL AT ONCE!

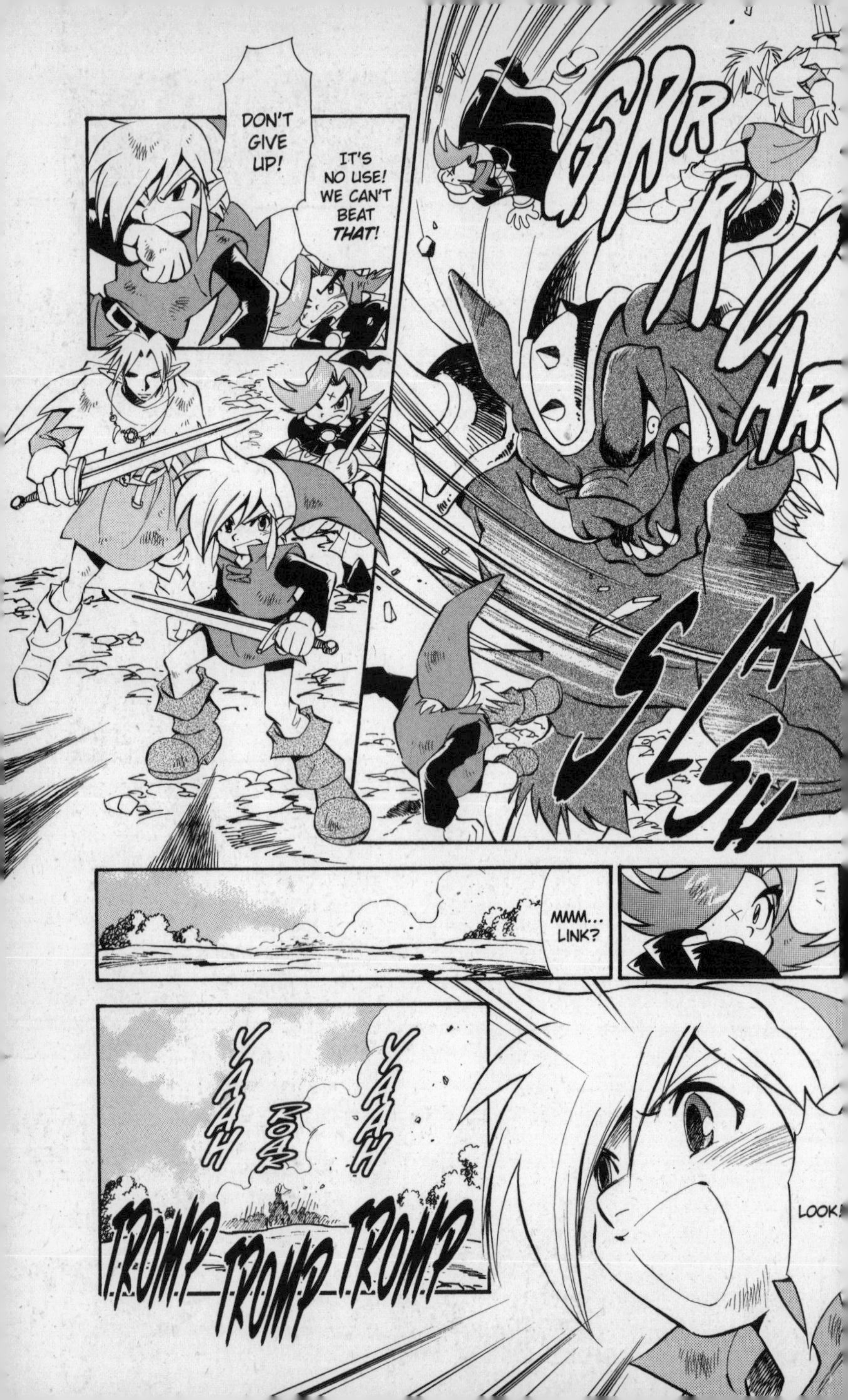
GRRRAAAR
SLASH
DON'T GIVE UP!
IT'S NO USE! WE CAN'T BEAT *THAT!*
MMM... LINK?
LOOK!
YAAAH
ROAR
YAAAH
TROMP TROMP TROMP

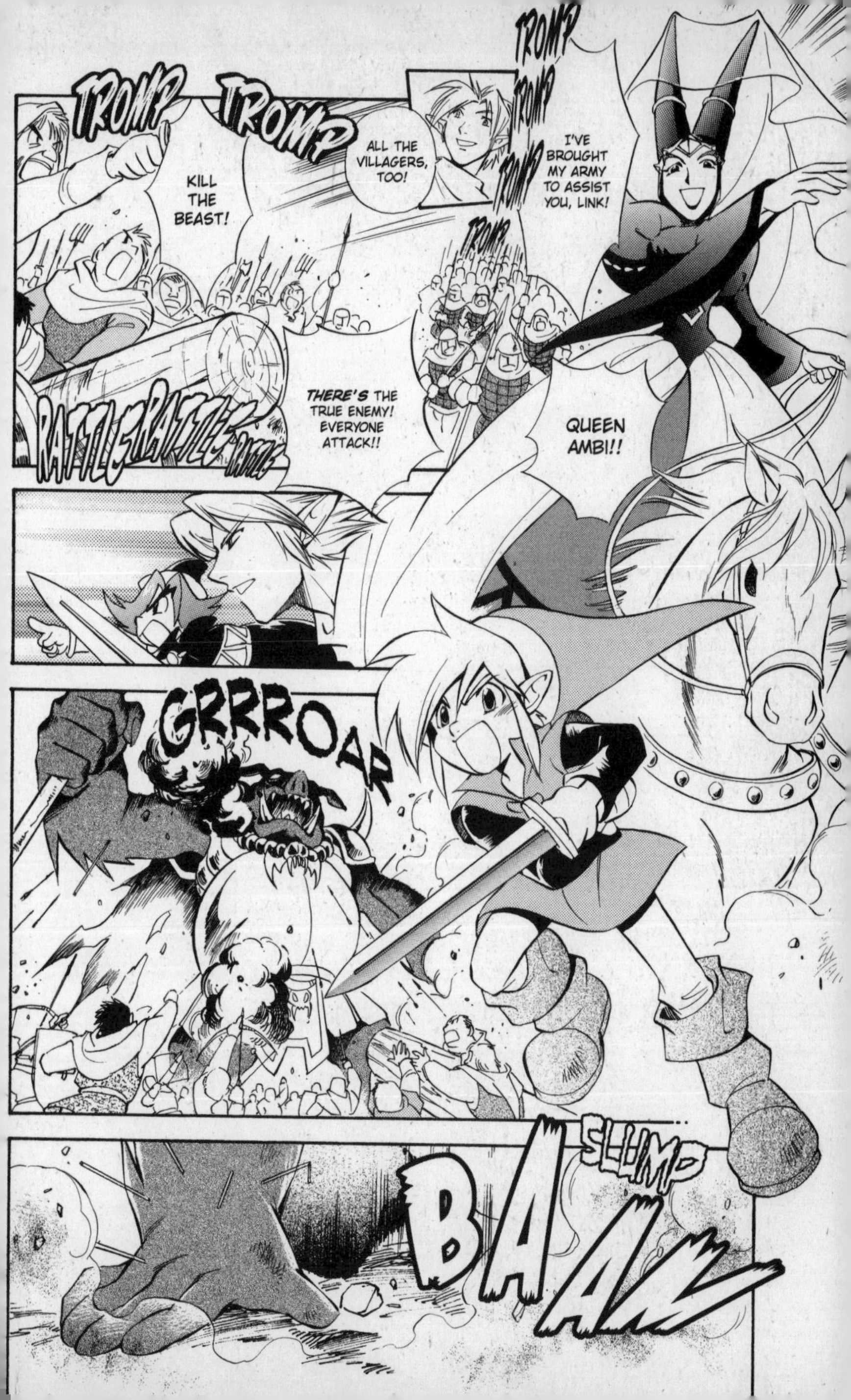
TROMP TROMP TROMP TROMP
I'VE BROUGHT MY ARMY TO ASSIST YOU, LINK!
QUEEN AMBI!!
ALL THE VILLAGERS, TOO!
TROMP
TROMP TROMP
KILL THE BEAST!
RATTLE RATTLE RATTLE
THERE'S THE TRUE ENEMY! EVERYONE ATTACK!!
GRRROAR
SLUMP
BAAM

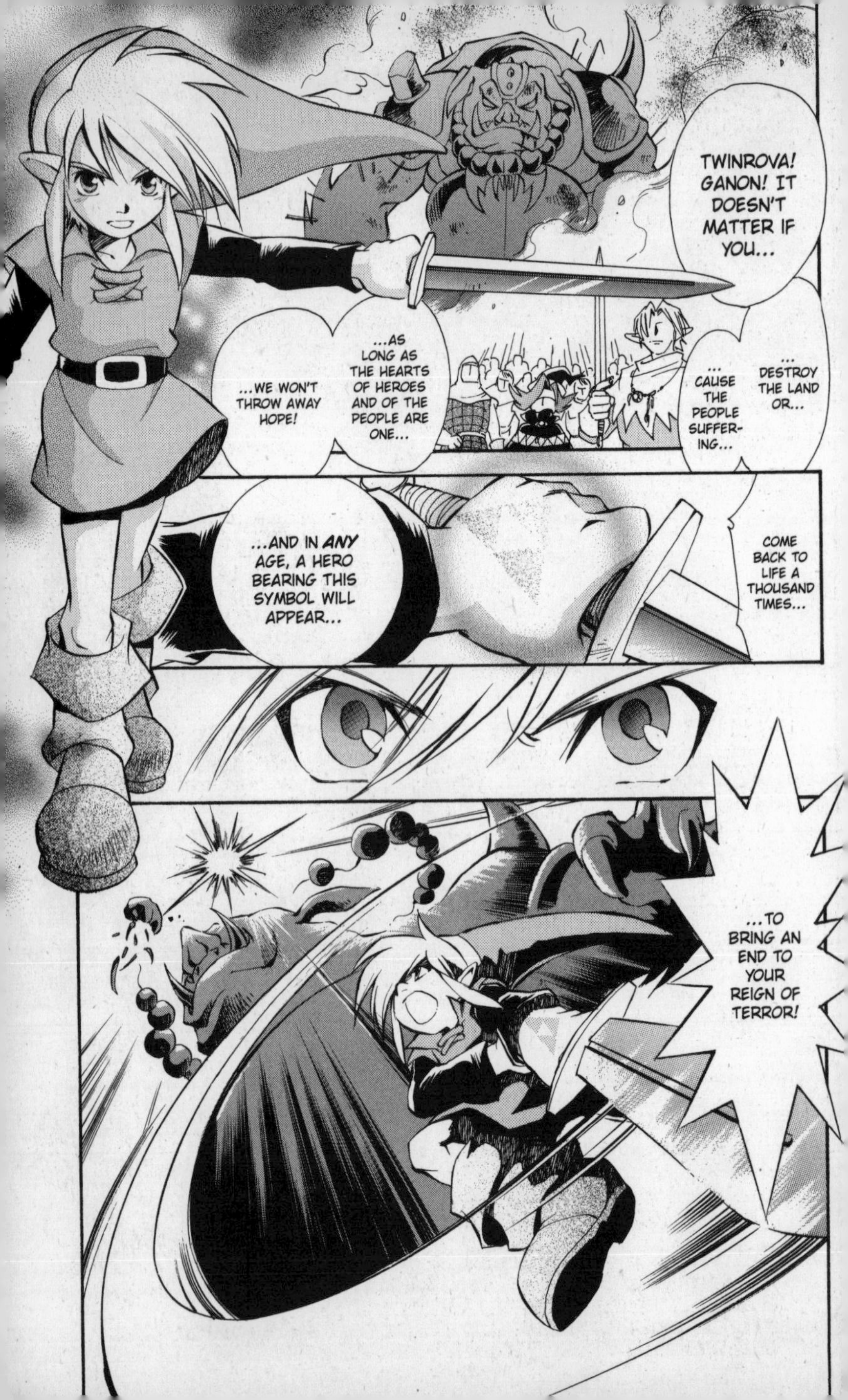
TWINROVA! GANON! IT DOESN'T MATTER IF YOU...
...DESTROY THE LAND OR...
...CAUSE THE PEOPLE SUFFERING...
COME BACK TO LIFE A THOUSAND TIMES...
...AS LONG AS THE HEARTS OF HEROES AND OF THE PEOPLE ARE ONE...
...WE WON'T THROW AWAY HOPE!
...AND IN *ANY* AGE, A HERO BEARING THIS SYMBOL WILL APPEAR...
...TO BRING AN END TO YOUR REIGN OF TERROR!

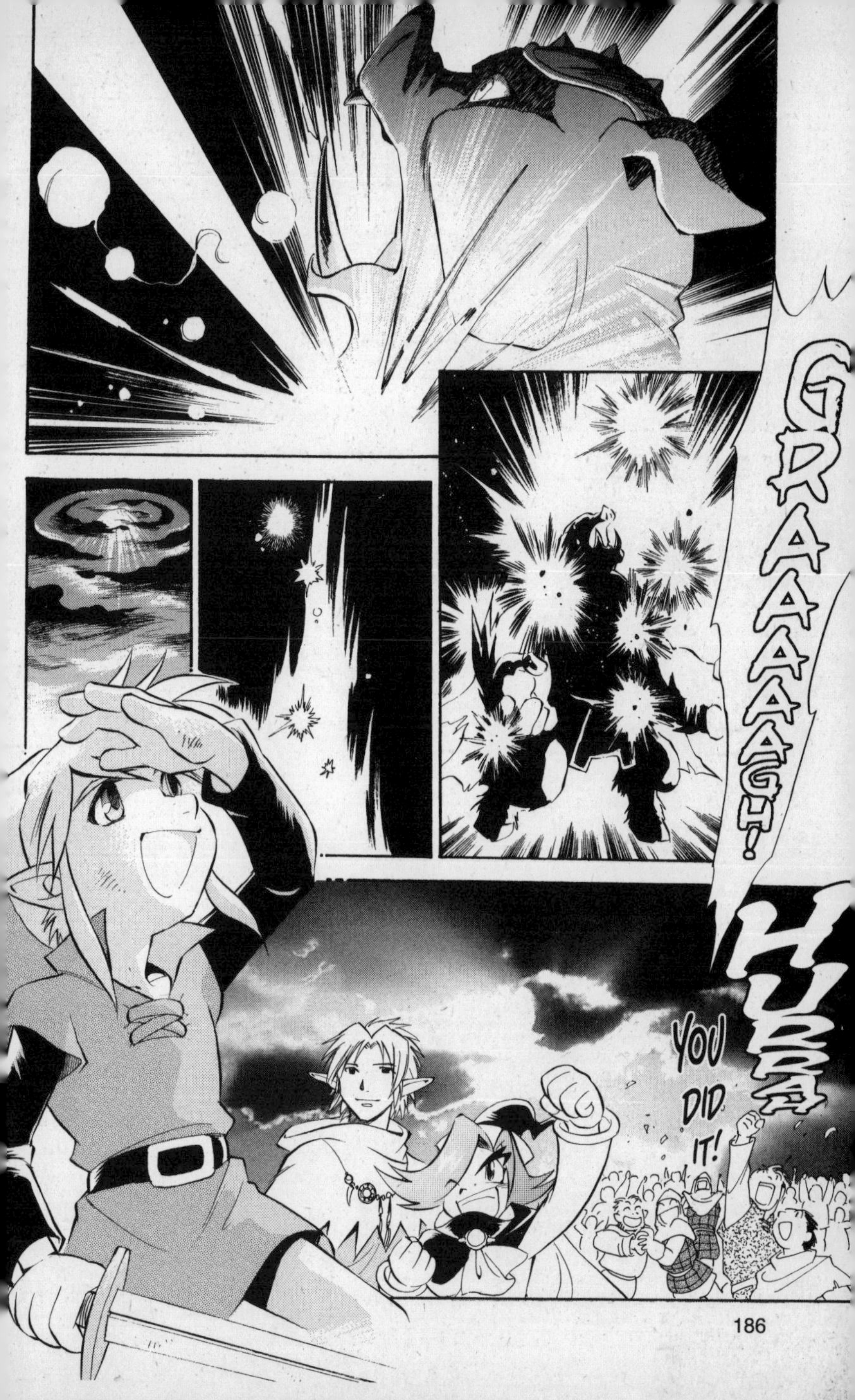
GRAAAAAGH!
HUZZA
YOU DID IT!

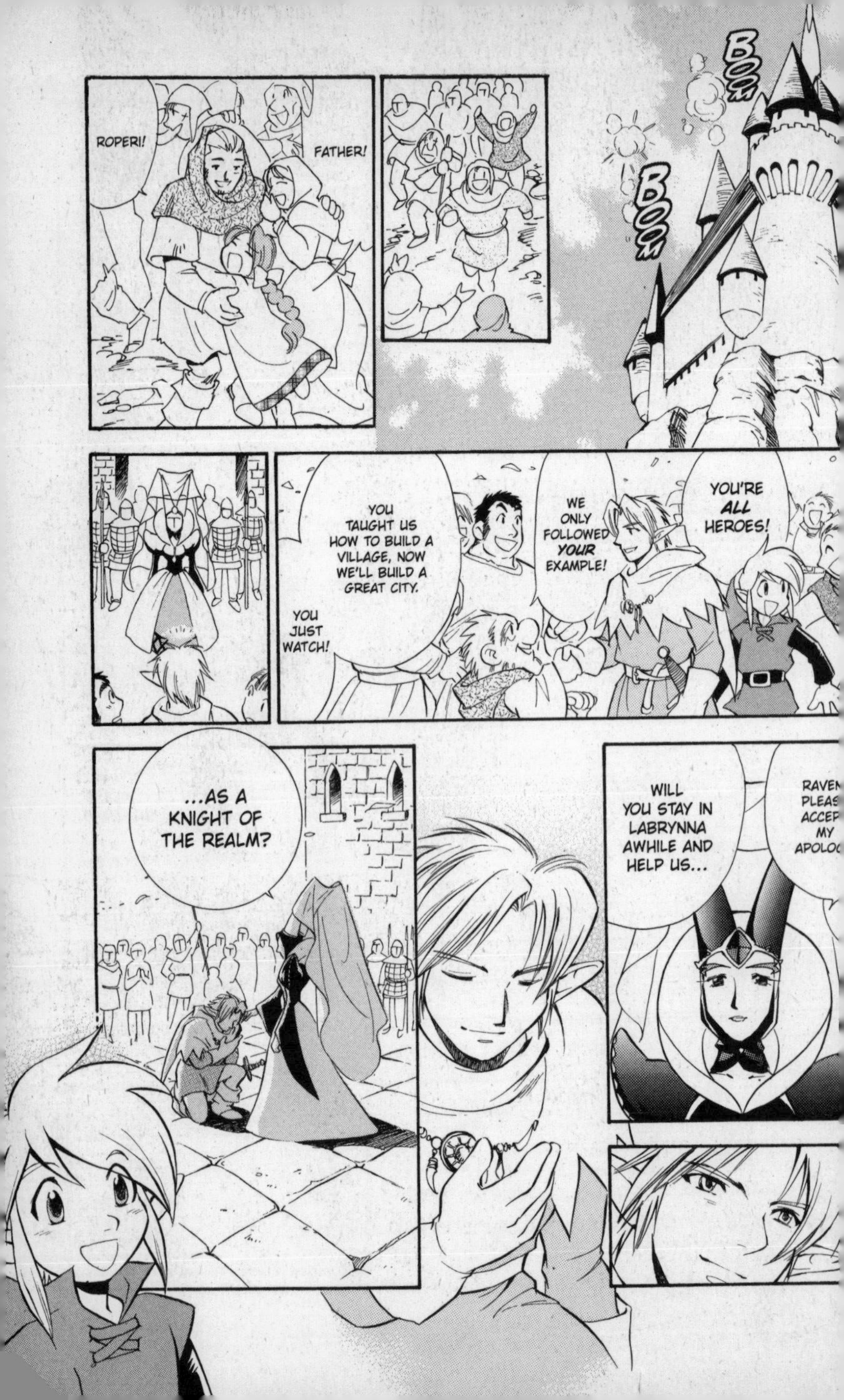
BOOM
BOOM
FATHER!
ROPERI!
YOU'RE ALL HEROES!
WE ONLY FOLLOWED YOUR EXAMPLE!
YOU TAUGHT US HOW TO BUILD A VILLAGE, NOW WE'LL BUILD A GREAT CITY.
YOU JUST WATCH!
RAVEN PLEAS ACCEP MY APOLOG
WILL YOU STAY IN LABRYNNA AWHILE AND HELP US...
...AS A KNIGHT OF THE REALM?

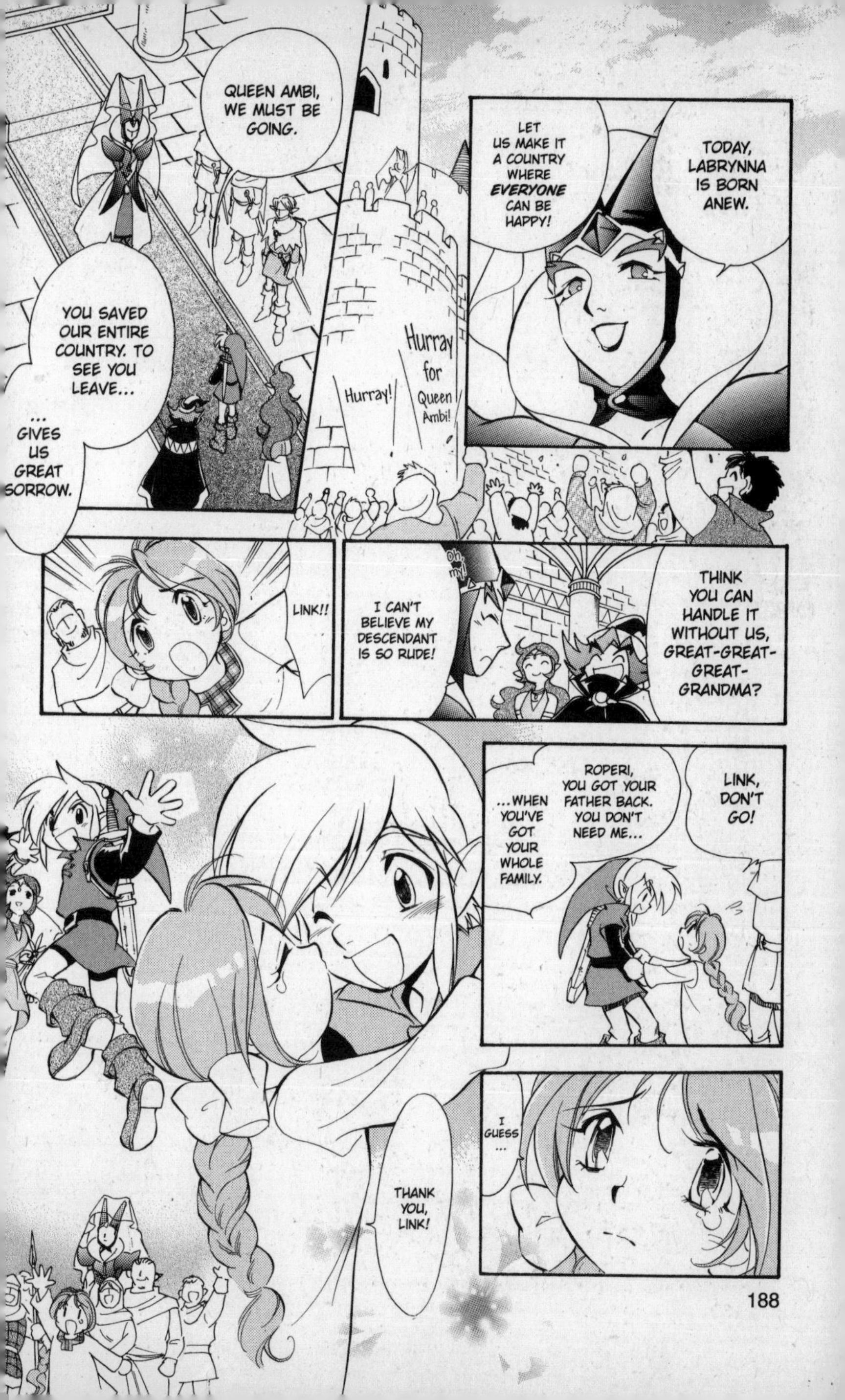
TODAY, LABRYNNA IS BORN ANEW.
LET US MAKE IT A COUNTRY WHERE **EVERYONE** CAN BE HAPPY!
Hurray for Queen Ambi!
Hurray!
QUEEN AMBI, WE MUST BE GOING.
YOU SAVED OUR ENTIRE COUNTRY. TO SEE YOU LEAVE...
... GIVES US GREAT SORROW.
THINK YOU CAN HANDLE IT WITHOUT US, GREAT-GREAT-GREAT-GRANDMA?
Oh, my!
I CAN'T BELIEVE MY DESCENDANT IS SO RUDE!
LINK!!
LINK, DON'T GO!
ROPERI, YOU GOT YOUR FATHER BACK. YOU DON'T NEED ME...
...WHEN YOU'VE GOT YOUR WHOLE FAMILY.
I GUESS...
THANK YOU, LINK!

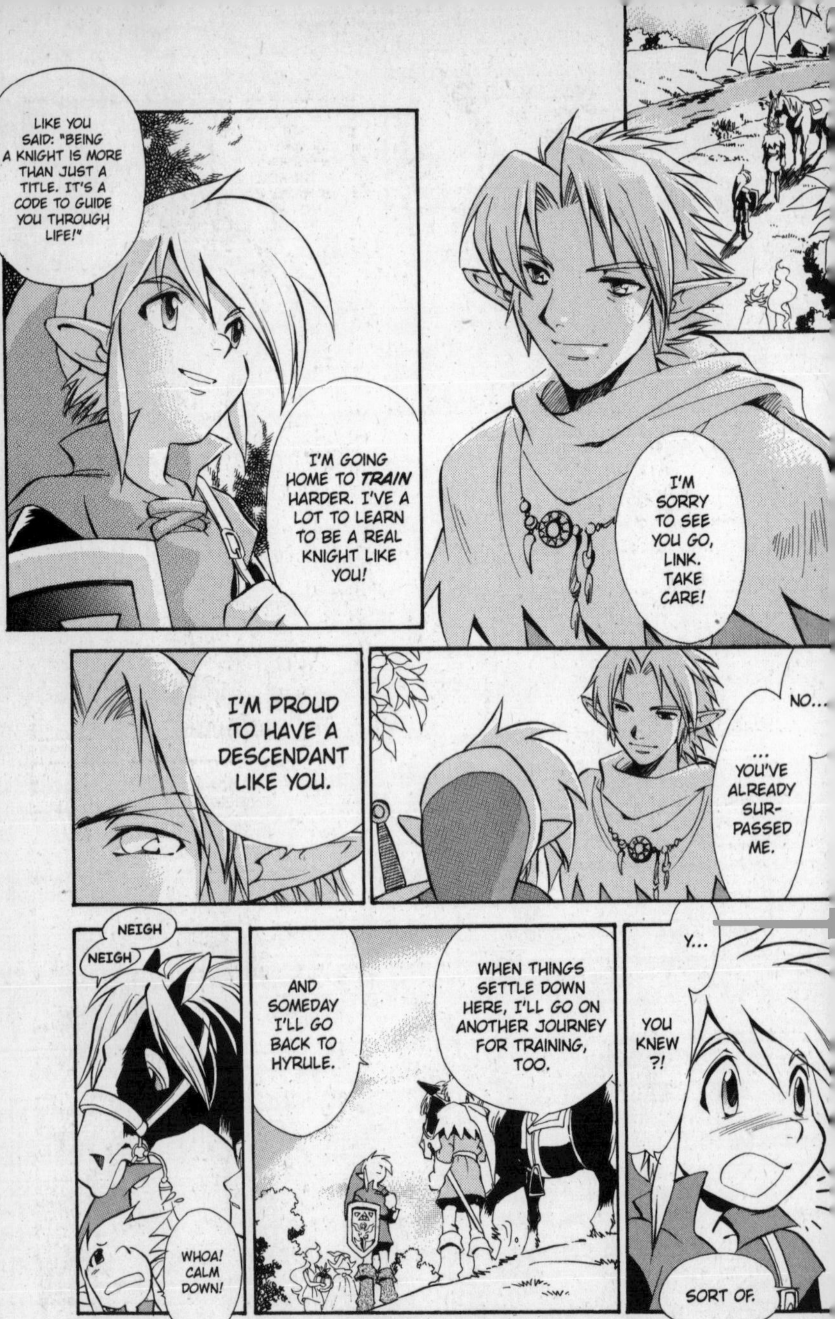
I'M SORRY TO SEE YOU GO, LINK. TAKE CARE!
LIKE YOU SAID: "BEING A KNIGHT IS MORE THAN JUST A TITLE. IT'S A CODE TO GUIDE YOU THROUGH LIFE!"
I'M GOING HOME TO ***TRAIN*** HARDER. I'VE A LOT TO LEARN TO BE A REAL KNIGHT LIKE YOU!
NO...
...YOU'VE ALREADY SUR-PASSED ME.
I'M PROUD TO HAVE A DESCENDANT LIKE YOU.
Y...
YOU KNEW ?!
SORT OF.
WHEN THINGS SETTLE DOWN HERE, I'LL GO ON ANOTHER JOURNEY FOR TRAINING, TOO.
AND SOMEDAY I'LL GO BACK TO HYRULE.
NEIGH
NEIGH
WHOA! CALM DOWN!

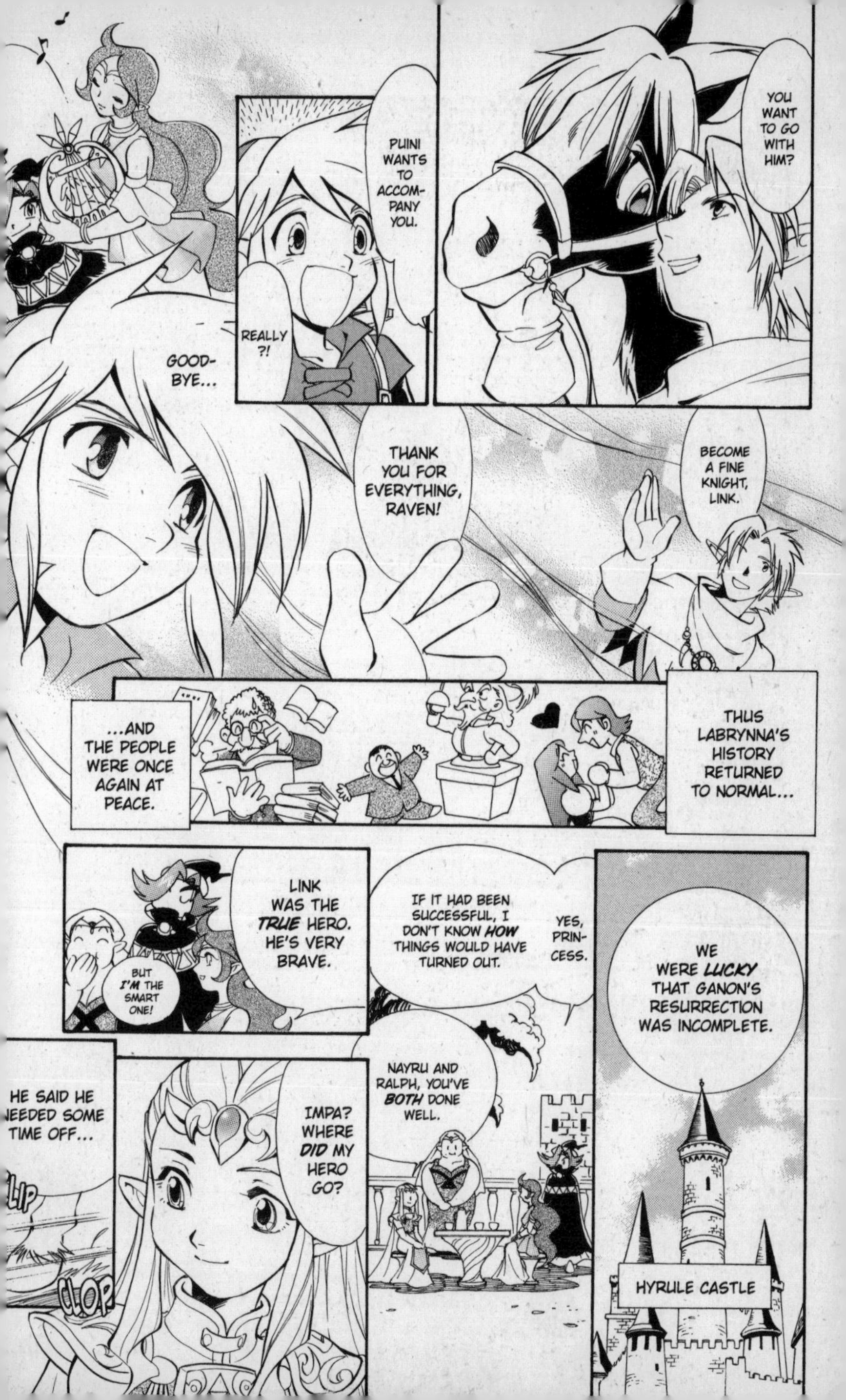
YOU WANT TO GO WITH HIM?
PUINI WANTS TO ACCOMPANY YOU.
REALLY ?!
GOOD-BYE...
BECOME A FINE KNIGHT, LINK.
THANK YOU FOR EVERYTHING, RAVEN!
THUS LABRYNNA'S HISTORY RETURNED TO NORMAL...
...AND THE PEOPLE WERE ONCE AGAIN AT PEACE.
WE WERE LUCKY THAT GANON'S RESURRECTION WAS INCOMPLETE.
HYRULE CASTLE
YES, PRINCESS.
IF IT HAD BEEN SUCCESSFUL, I DON'T KNOW HOW THINGS WOULD HAVE TURNED OUT.
LINK WAS THE TRUE HERO. HE'S VERY BRAVE.
BUT I'M THE SMART ONE!
NAYRU AND RALPH, YOU'VE BOTH DONE WELL.
IMPA? WHERE DID MY HERO GO?
HE SAID HE NEEDED SOME TIME OFF...
LIP
CLOP

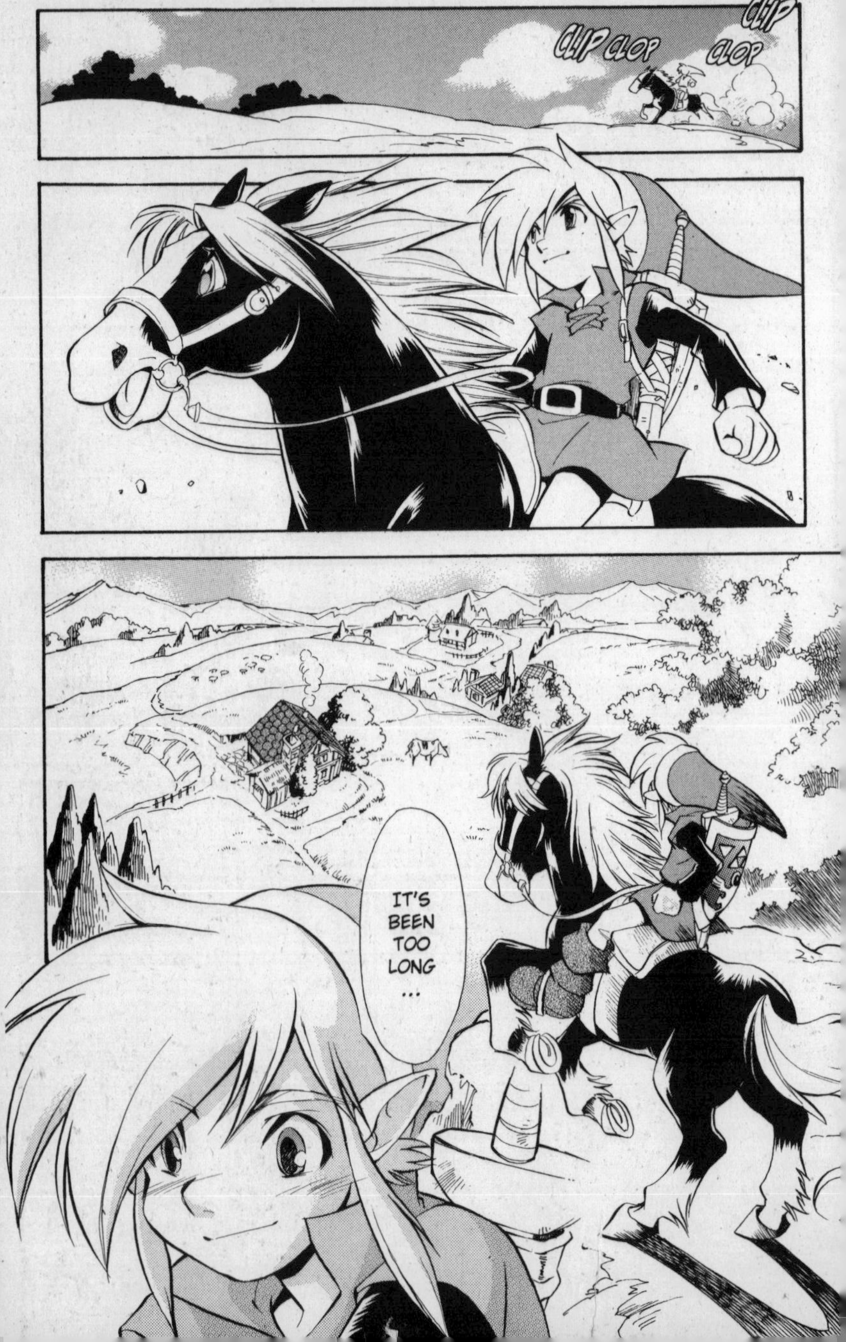
CLIP CLOP
CLIP CLOP
IT'S BEEN TOO LONG ...

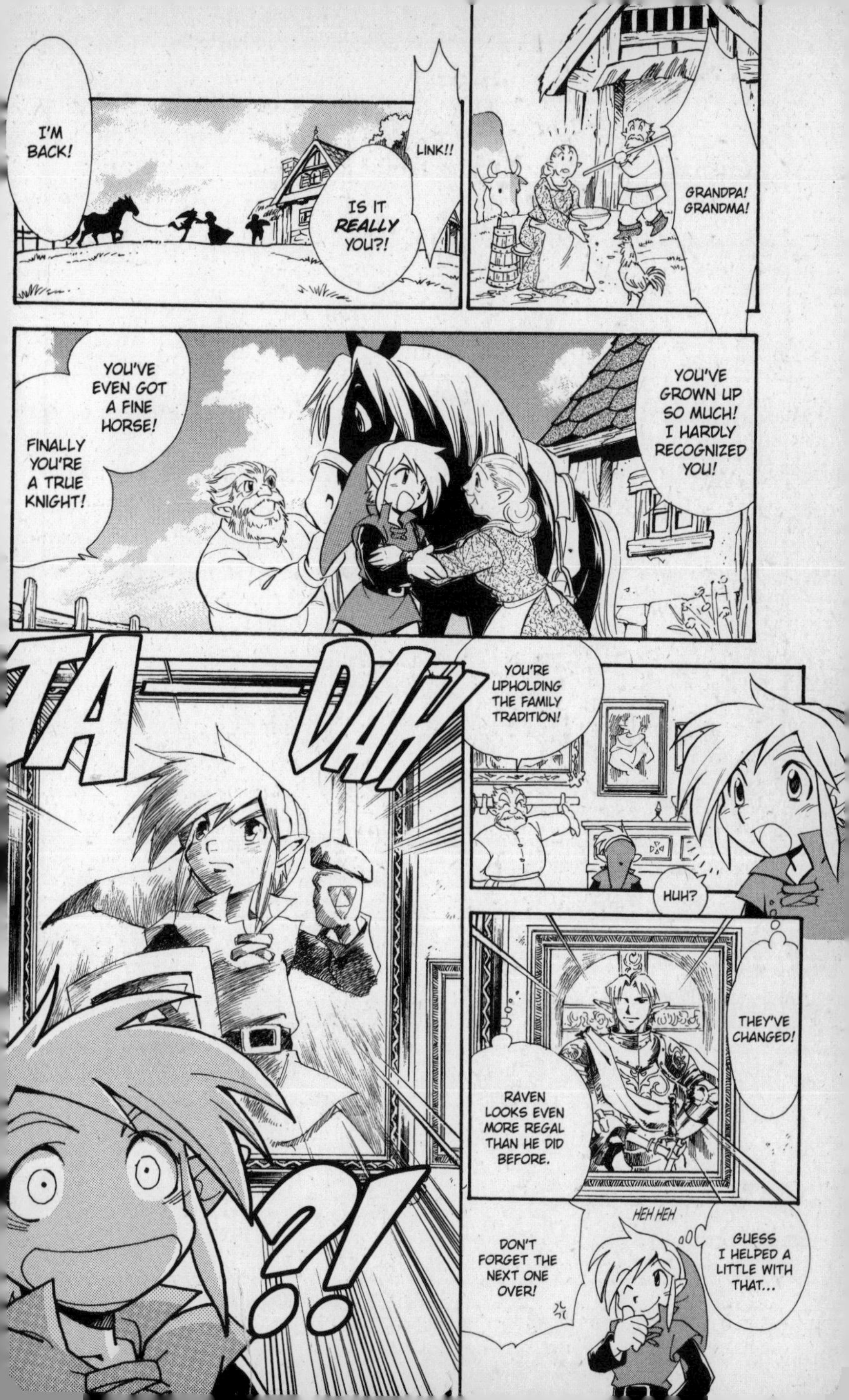
GRANDPA! GRANDMA!
I'M BACK!
LINK!!
IS IT REALLY YOU?!
YOU'VE GROWN UP SO MUCH! I HARDLY RECOGNIZED YOU!
YOU'VE EVEN GOT A FINE HORSE!
FINALLY YOU'RE A TRUE KNIGHT!
YOU'RE UPHOLDING THE FAMILY TRADITION!
HUH?
THEY'VE CHANGED!
RAVEN LOOKS EVEN MORE REGAL THAN HE DID BEFORE.
GUESS I HELPED A LITTLE WITH THAT...
HEH HEH
DON'T FORGET THE NEXT ONE OVER!
TA-DAH
?!

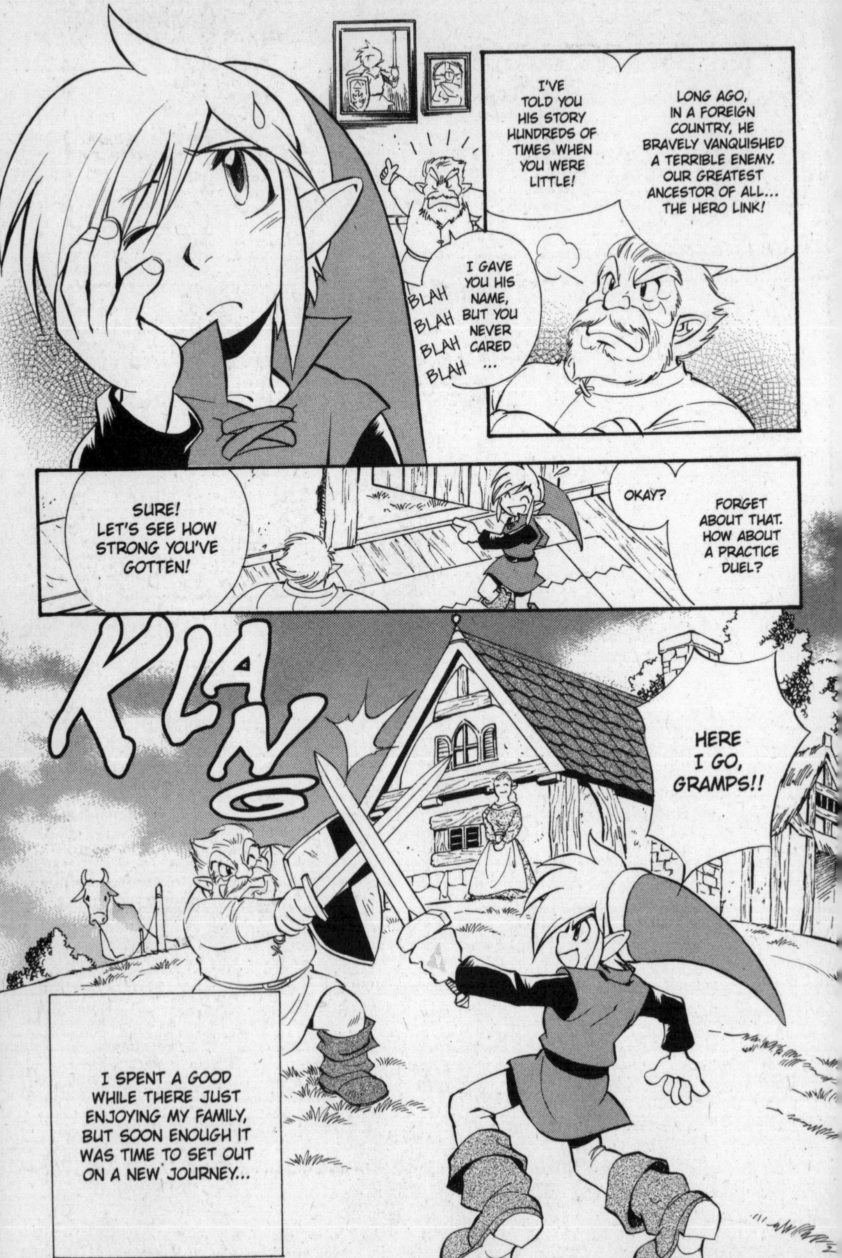
LONG AGO, IN A FOREIGN COUNTRY, HE BRAVELY VANQUISHED A TERRIBLE ENEMY. OUR GREATEST ANCESTOR OF ALL... THE HERO LINK!
I'VE TOLD YOU HIS STORY HUNDREDS OF TIMES WHEN YOU WERE LITTLE!
I GAVE YOU HIS NAME, BUT YOU NEVER CARED ...
BLAH BLAH BLAH BLAH
FORGET ABOUT THAT. HOW ABOUT A PRACTICE DUEL?
OKAY?
SURE! LET'S SEE HOW STRONG YOU'VE GOTTEN!
HERE I GO, GRAMPS!!
KLANG
I SPENT A GOOD WHILE THERE JUST ENJOYING MY FAMILY, BUT SOON ENOUGH IT WAS TIME TO SET OUT ON A NEW JOURNEY...

THE END

Coming Next Volume

When Shadow Link kidnaps Princess Zelda, Link once again must prepare himself to defeat the forces of evil. To do so, he needs the legendary Four Sword, but getting it means battling the ancient evil power Vaati. The Four Sword also splits Link into four different versions of himself, and these new Links aren't team players! Rescuing Zelda, beating Vaati, and getting all his rambunctious alter-egos under control isn't going to be easy!

Available Now!

THE LEGEND OF ZELDA™
Manga Series

Don't miss any of Link's exciting adventures!

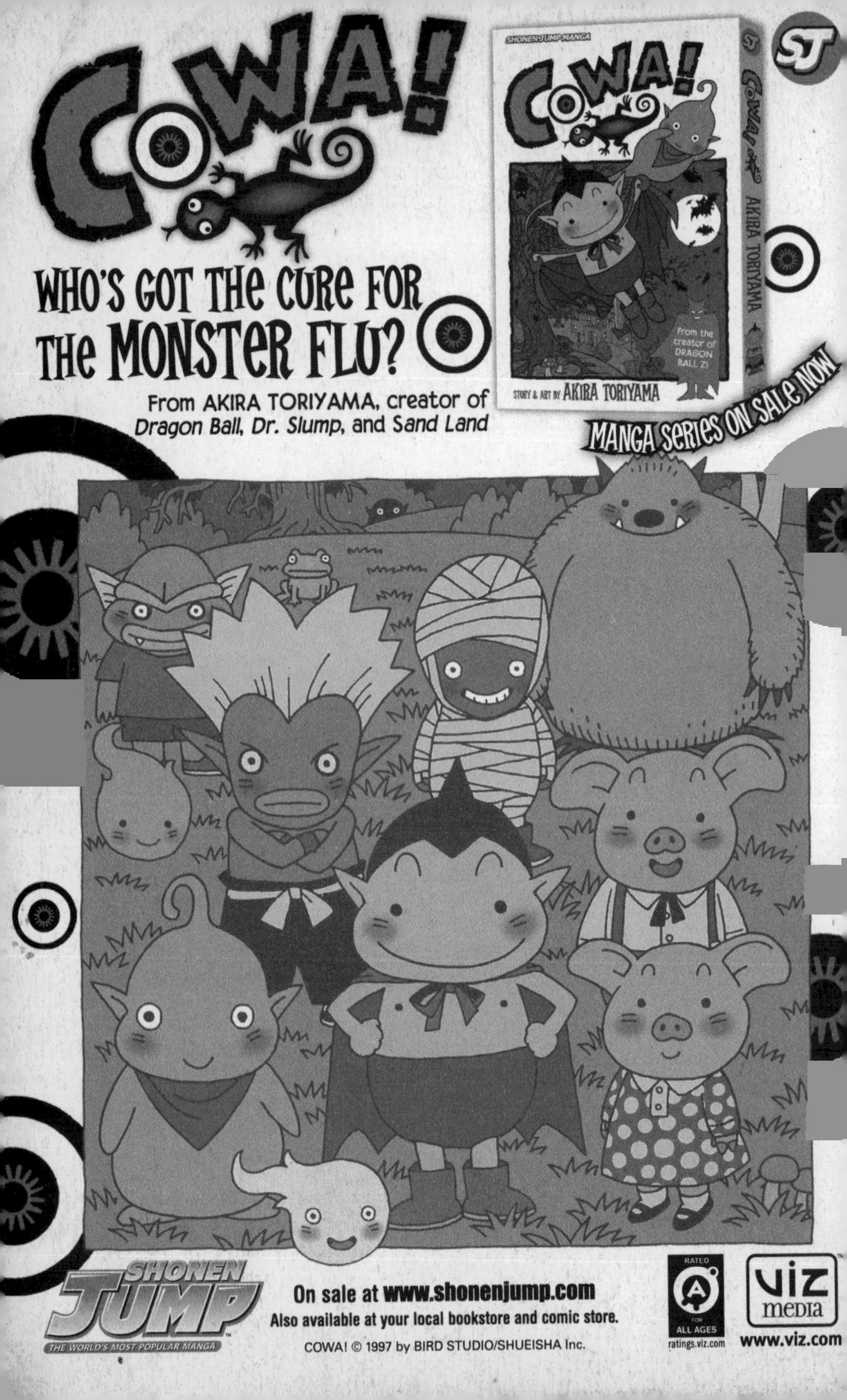
COWA!
WHO'S GOT THE CURE FOR THE MONSTER FLU?
From AKIRA TORIYAMA, creator of Dragon Ball, Dr. Slump, and Sand Land
SHONEN JUMP MANGA
COWA!
From the creator of DRAGON BALL Z!
STORY & ART BY AKIRA TORIYAMA
SJ
MANGA SERIES ON SALE NOW
SHONEN JUMP
THE WORLD'S MOST POPULAR MANGA
On sale at www.shonenjump.com
Also available at your local bookstore and comic store.
COWA! © 1997 by BIRD STUDIO/SHUEISHA Inc.
RATED A FOR ALL AGES
ratings.viz.com
VIZ media
www.viz.com

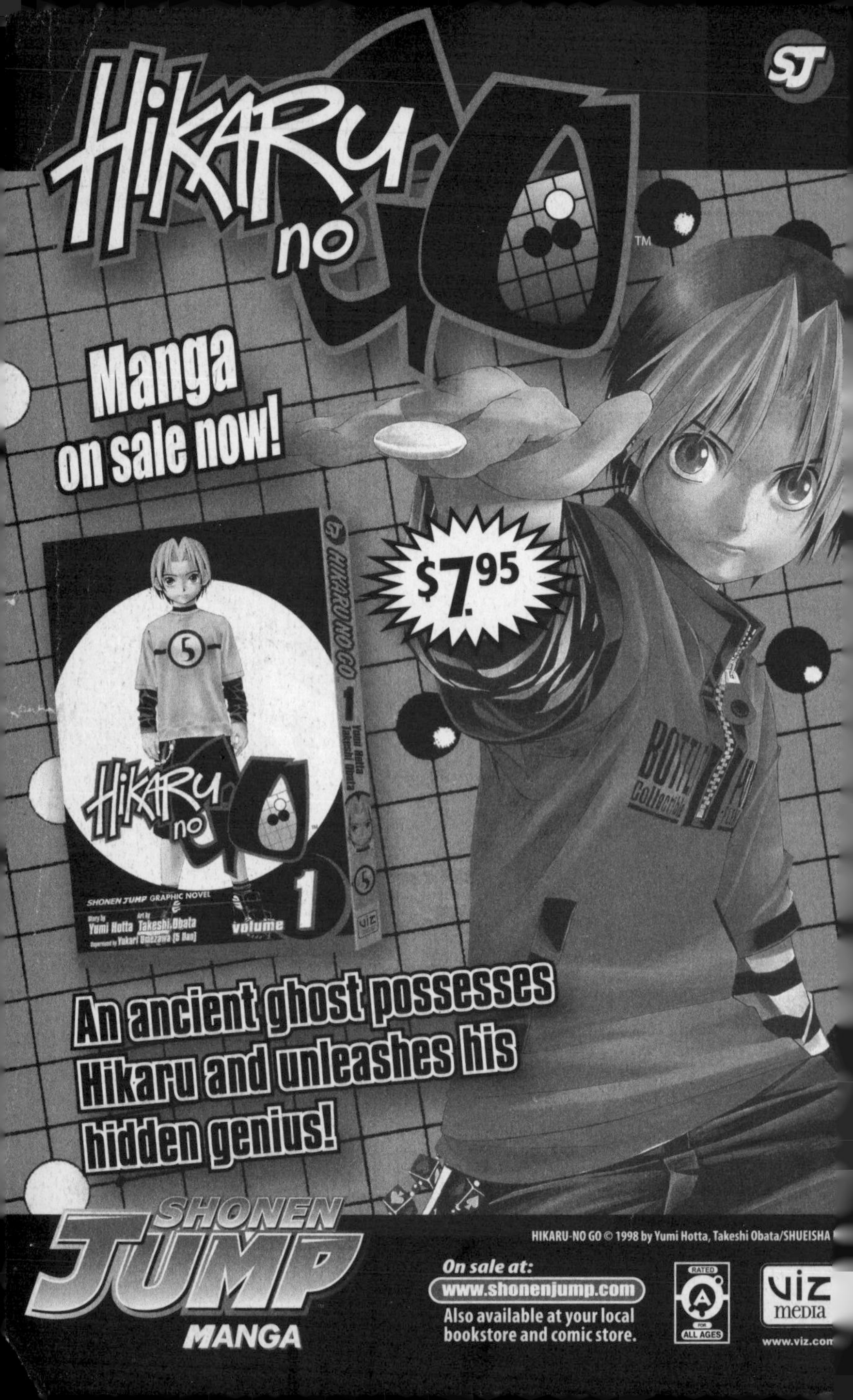
SJ
HIKARU no GO™
Manga on sale now!
$7.95
SJ HIKARU NO GO 1 Yumi Hotta Takeshi Obata
HIKARU no GO™
SHONEN JUMP GRAPHIC NOVEL
Story by Yumi Hotta Art by Takeshi Obata
Supervised by Yukari Umezawa (5 Dan)
volume 1
An ancient ghost possesses Hikaru and unleashes his hidden genius!
SHONEN JUMP MANGA
HIKARU-NO GO © 1998 by Yumi Hotta, Takeshi Obata/SHUEISHA
On sale at:
www.shonenjump.com
Also available at your local bookstore and comic store.
RATED A FOR ALL AGES
VIZ media
www.viz.com